T0329796

PIRATES AND PUBLISHERS

HISTORIES OF ECONOMIC LIFE

Jeremy Adelman, Sunil Amrith,
and Emma Rothschild, Series Editors

Pirates and Publishers: A Social History of Copyright in Modern China by
Fei-Hsien Wang

*Sorting Out the Mixed Economy: The Rise and Fall of Welfare and Developmental
States in the Americas* by Amy C. Offner

Red Meat Republic: A Hoof-to-Table History of How Beef Changed America by
Joshua Specht

*The Promise and Peril of Credit: What a Forgotten Legend about Jews and Finance
Tells Us about the Making of European Commercial Society* by Francesca
Trivellato

A People's Constitution: The Everyday Life of Law in the Indian Republic by Rohit De

A Local History of Global Capital: Jute and Peasant Life in the Bengal Delta by
Tariq Omar Ali

STUDIES OF THE WEATHERHEAD EAST
ASIAN INSTITUTE, COLUMBIA UNIVERSITY

The Studies of the Weatherhead East Asian Institute of Columbia University
were inaugurated in 1962 to bring to a wider public the results of significant
new research on modern and contemporary East Asia.

Pirates and Publishers

A SOCIAL HISTORY OF
COPYRIGHT IN MODERN CHINA

FEI-HSIEN WANG

PRINCETON UNIVERSITY PRESS
PRINCETON & OXFORD

Published by Princeton University Press
41 William Street, Princeton, New Jersey 08540
6 Oxford Street, Woodstock, Oxfordshire OX20 1TR

press.princeton.edu

Library of Congress Control Number: 2019936016
ISBN 978-0-691-17182-1

British Library Cataloging-in-Publication Data is available

Editorial: Eric Crahan and Thalia Leaf
Production Editorial: Lauren Lepow
Jacket Design: Chris Ferrante
Jacket Credit: Decorative frame for copyright seal from the copyright page of
Zhina shiyao [Essentials of Chinese history] (Shanghai: Guangzhi Shuju, 1905).
The frame reads, "banquan suoyou [copyright retained]."
Production: Merli Guerra
Publicity: Alyssa Sanford and Julia Hall

This book has been composed in Arno Pro

Printed on acid-free paper. ∞

Printed in the United States of America

10 9 8 7 6 5 4 3 2 1

To the Wild Geese

CONTENTS

Acknowledgments   ix

List of Abbreviations   xiii

Introduction   1

1   The Curious Journey of "Copyright" in East Asia   21

2   The Business of "New Learning"   62

3   "The Everlasting Reward for My Labor of Mind"   93

4   Between Privilege and Property   118

5   The "Copyright" Regime of Chessboard Street   158

6   Hunting Pirates in Beiping   211

7   A World without Piracy?   252

Conclusion   298

Glossary of Chinese and Japanese Terms, Titles, and Names   311

Selected Bibliography   317

Index   337

ACKNOWLEDGMENTS

GROWING UP in a small family-run publishing house, I had books as my earliest playmates. For a long time, I was determined to become a writer, an editor, or a publisher, so that I could play a part in the magic of book production. Instead, I ended up becoming a historian studying the sociocultural making of publishing industry, as the reality behind my childhood fantasy of a magical book world is more enchanting.

One thing I've learned since my childhood by watching my parents writing and publishing their works is that no author can make his or her book alone. This book would not have been completed without the unstinting help and encouragements I have received since I began to work on this project as a graduate student. At the University of Chicago, I owe a deep debt of gratitude to my dissertation adviser Guy Alitto, for his endless support and mentorship over the years. Adrian Johns inspired me to work on piracy and copyright. Without his thought-provoking feedback, the project would not have been able to take its shape. Prasenjit Duara and Susan Burns taught me how to situate my project in a more comparative and transregional framework. A Mellon postdoctoral fellow at the Centre for History of Economics at the University of Cambridge offered me a unique opportunity to expand my intellectual horizon beyond Chinese history and book history. I am deeply grateful to Emma Rothschild for her generous support, warm guidance, and insightful comments about the history of law and economic life; she inspires me to become a better historian.

I benefited immensely from many scholars, colleagues, and friends around the world who lent their hands during my research and took time to discuss parts of the manuscripts with me. They include Lü Fangshang, Wang Fansen, Li Hsiao-ti, Wang Taisheng, Yamamoto Eishi, Hisatsugu Kusabu, Xiong Yuezhi, Wu Zhou, Hans van de Ven, Adam Chau, James Raven, Bill Cornish, Gareth Stedman Jones, Tim Harper, Cynthia Brokaw, Yuming He, Judith Zeitlin, William Alford, and Billy So, among others. I am grateful to Noto Hiroyoshi for helping me read Fukuzawa Yukichi's petitions in our premodern Japanese tutorial class. I learned a lot from the long conversations Joseph McDermott and I had at St. Johns about the social and economic aspects of Chinese books. Joshua A. Fogel kindly read the first chapter and made constructive suggestions. Special thinks to Rob Culp and Jennifer Altehenger for letting me read their unpublished manuscripts when I extended my research to the post-1949 period. I was also privileged to discuss my project with the late T. H. Tsien (1910–2015) and Zhu Weizheng (1936–2012). Their incisive advice was invaluable, and I hope this book lives up to their expectations.

Thank you to the staff of Shanghai Municipal Archives; Shanghai Library; China No. 1 Archives; Diplomatic Records Office of the Ministry of Foreign Affairs of Japan; Archives in the Institute of Modern History, Academia Sinica; Academia Historica; National Archives and Records Administration College Park; National Taiwan University Library; Yale University Library; Harvard-Yenching Library; National Diet Library in Tokyo; Waseda University Library; Keio University Library; Fukuzawa Yukichi Research Center; Guo Tingyi Library; Fu Ssu-nien Library; Cambridge University Library; and the Baker Library at Harvard Business School. I am particularly grateful to Yuan Zhou and the staff of the East Asian Library at the University of Chicago for allowing me to work as a student clerk while exploring the wonderful Chinese collection in the Regenstein at the same time.

The extensive research would not have been possible without the support of the American Bibliographical Society, the Department of History and the Center for East Asian Studies at the University of Chicago, the Michael and Ling Markovitz Dissertation Fellowship, the Centre for History and Economics at the University of Cambridge, and the Department of History at Indiana University. The Scholarly Writing Program at Indiana University held me accountable when I revised the manuscript. Without the encouragement and emotional support of Laura Plummer and my fellow writers in the faculty writing groups, I might never have been able to finish the manuscript.

The editors of the Histories of Economic Life series encouraged me to think critically about the interplay of knowledge production, intellectual property rights, and the cultural economy. I benefited enormously from the thoughtful and extensive comments of the two readers for Princeton University Press. It was a great pleasure to work with Quinn Fusting, Amanda Peery, and Eric Crahan, and I am thankful for the great care they gave to this manuscript. I am grateful to Thalia Leaf, Pamela Weidman, and Lauren Lepow for their editorial assistance and to Cynthia Col for producing its index. Thank you, Eugenia Lean, for introducing me to the Studies of the Weatherhead East Asian Institute series, and Kenneth Ross Yelsey for making it possible for this book to be in two different book series.

I've learned tremendously from the knowledgeable audiences when I presented parts of this book at the following venues: East Asian Legal Studies at Harvard Law School; the Joint Center for History and Economics at Harvard University; the History and Economics seminar at the University of Cambridge; the China Research Seminar at the University of Cambridge; the Department of History at Indiana University; the Department of History at Duke University; the China studies lecture series at Ohio State University; the Tidings Lecture Series; the Center for Law, Society, and Culture, Mauser School of Law at Indiana University; the Modern East Asian Law workshop at Columbia University; the Academia Historica in Taiwan; the Institute of History and Philology, Academia Sinica in Taipei; the Department of History and the College of Law at National Taiwan University in Taipei; the Institute of History at Shanghai Academy of Social Sciences; the annual meeting of the Association for Asian Studies; the annual meeting of the American Society for Legal History; the World Congress of Economic History; and the Business History Conference.

Portions of chapter 7 were published in *Twentieth-Century China*. I thank *Twentieth-Century China* for permission to reprint here.

I am lucky enough to have the wonderful company of friends and colleagues across three continents: Stephen Halsey, Paul Mariani, Jun-Hyung Chae, Suyoung Son, Cheng-Yi Huang, Chia-Ming Chen, Sinying Sung, Hai Zhao, Susan Karr, Guo Quan Seng, John Deak, Jason Dawsey, Elizabeth Heath, Andrew Sloin, Fumiko Joo, Tadashi Ishikawa, Tomoko Seto, Noriko Yamakuchi, Clinton Godart, Yuko Murata Godart, Limin Teh, Wei-ti Chen, Hao-yuan Lo, Ren-Yuan Li, Yun-Ru Chen, Shaw-Yu Pan, Tan Uiti, Bill O'Connor, John Feng, Lily Chang, Rohit De, Inga Huld Markan, Mary-Rose Cheadle, Fu Yang, Ghassan Moazzin, He Bian, Margaret Tillman, Yan Long, Yea-fen Chen, Jonathan Schlesinger, and Yin Chung Au. Thank you for believing in me when others (even myself) might not, and for sharing your insightful ideas about life, knowledge, and happiness.

Ke-chin Hsia has been my best friend, my most critical reader, and my dearest companion all these years. He endured my endless gabbling about nasty Chinese pirates and calmed me down when I got lost in my project, while working on his own dissertation and then book manuscript. Our journey together has brought us from Taipei to Chicago, Vienna, Cambridge, and

Bloomington, and his company made it a joyful and exciting adventure, even when we faced great uncertainty.

Without the unconditional love and support of my parents, Yi-Chia Wang and Man-Li Yen, it would have been impossible for me to finish this book. They immersed me in the world of books and gave me "insider's knowledge" long before I realized I wanted to become a book historian. Thanks to Mom for consistently reminding me that Papa had published yet another new book and I was still working on the same one. There is no way that I can match my father's intellectual productivity; he is and will always be my inspiration to become an original human being. My parents established their two-person publishing house when I was two and named it *Ye'e* 野鵝 (wild goose) after a short story by Søren Kierkegaard. It closed down as I was finishing up this book. I thus dedicate this book to them, their beloved *Ye'e Chubanshe*, and all the wild geese in the world that want to have a freer soul.

LIST OF ABBREVIATIONS

DGB   *Dagong bao* (L'impartial)
FYZ   *Fukuzawa Yukichi zenshu*
(Complete collection of Fukuzawa Yukichi's writings)
GPA   General Publishing Administration (*Chuban zongshu*)
NCA   National Copyright Administration of the People's
Republic of China (*Guojia banquan ju*)
RMRB   *Renmin ribao* (People's daily)
SB   *Shen bao/Shun pao* (Shanghai news)
SBG   Shanghai Booksellers' Guild (*Shanghai shuye gongsuo/
Shanghai shuye tongye gonghui*)
SBTA   Shanghai Booksellers' Trade Association
(*Shanghai shuye shanghui*)
SDCK   Society for the Diffusion of Christian and General
Knowledge among the Chinese (*Guangxue*)
SMA   Shanghai Municipal Archive
XBGB   *Xuebu guanbao* (The official newsletter of the
Ministry of Education)
ZGXSYB   *Zhongguo xinshu yuebo* (China new books monthly)
ZRGCS   *Zhonghua Renmin Gongheguo chuban shiliao*
(Primary sources for People's Republic of China
publishing history)
ZWRB   *Zhongwai ribao* (The universal gazette)

PIRATES AND PUBLISHERS

Introduction

JULY 2007, Beijing. Just a few days after the long-anticipated finale of J. K. Rowling's *Harry Potter* series was officially released, bootleg softcover English-language copies of *Harry Potter and the Deathly Hallows* were appearing on street vendors' bookstalls; they were sold at only one-fifth the price of authentic ones.[1] By early August, while People's Literature Publishing House, which owns the mainland rights to this book, was still preparing for its Chinese version, cheap Chinese-language copies—put together by pirates, based on amateur translations from fan websites—had hit the marketplace.[2] Not to mention the series of "fake" Harry Potter books, such as *Hali Bote yu baozou long* (Harry Potter and the leopard walk-up-to dragon), that have been bootlegged in China by publishers who hoped to seize upon the young wizard's popularity to make a quick fortune.[3] These knockoff Harry Potter novels, along with the unlicensed Windows software found on the computers of China's universities and companies,[4] and the Chinese seed thieves caught stealing genetically modified

---

1. "Harry Potter's Magic Can't Beat Chinese Pirates," Reuters, July 27, 2007, https://www .reuters.com/article/industry-arts-potter-china-dc-idUSPEK29273520070727.

2. "Cuzhi lanzao buhui maizhang Ha 7 jingxian zhongwen daoban" [Don't purchase poorly made copies; pirated editions of Harry Potter 7 in the Chinese language appeared in the market with surprise], *Renmin wang* [People's news online], August 13, 2007, http://culture.people.com .cn/GB/22219/6103568.html.

3. For the phenomena of China's "fake" Harry Potter novels, see Henningsen, "Harry Potter with Chinese Characteristics." Other notable "fake" books compiled by Chinese pirates include Bill Clinton's autobiography, *My Life*; see "Bill Clinton's Fake Chinese Life," *New York Times*, October 24, 2004, https://www.nytimes.com/2004/10/24/opinion/bill-clintons-fake-chinese -life.html.

4. For example, in 2017, about forty thousand institutions in China were hit by the Wanna-Cry ransomware attack because the Windows systems installed on their computers were pirated

corn from the United States,[5] are just a few examples of China's current state of intellectual property piracy. Jurists, journalists, and policymakers outside China are convinced that the Chinese, even though they are now fully participating in the global economy, have not yet learned to appreciate the universally recognized intellectual property rights (IPR) doctrine.

While the Chinese government's lax enforcement against IPR piracy is often attributed to its administrative impediments and fragmentation, many further point the finger at the Chinese society's general lack of IPR awareness as the fundamental reason for its long-standing "addiction to counterfeiting."[6] This widely shared impression, if not myth, has shaped the general discussion on the past and the future of IPR in China: China has become the piracy haven it is today because, despite various attempts to transplant it, modern IPR doctrine did not strike root in China, but one day this will change when the Chinese are enlightened as to the true value of copyright. Or, in an alternative future, as one novelist imagines, the current IPR regime will eventually be ruined by the Chinese, since they "never liked 'intellectual property.'"[7]

Do the Chinese pirate because they don't *have* a sense of copyright? In spring 1911, when the first Sino-American copyright infringement lawsuit was brought to the International Mixed Court at Shanghai, an American lawyer tried to argue otherwise. To win the case for his client Ginn & Co., T. R. Jernigan (1847–1920), a renowned commercial lawyer and a former American consul general in Shanghai, wanted to prove that the Chinese pirates were also earnest practitioners of copyright in their own terms. He cited a petition that the defendants had submitted years earlier asking local officials to prohibit unauthorized reprinting of their publications, along with several similar prohibitions he had

ones. "China, Addicted to Bootleg Software, Reels from Ransomware Attack," *New York Times*, May 15, 2017, https://www.nytimes.com/2017/05/15/business/china-ransomware-wannacry-hacking.html.

5. Ted Genoways, "Corn Wars," *New Republic*, August 16, 2015, https://newrepublic.com/article/122441/corn-wars.

6. For discussions of China's inability to enforce IPR protection, see Mertha, *The Politics of Piracy*; Massey, "The Emperor Is Far Away"; Chow, "Why China Does Not Take Commercial Piracy Seriously." For examples of more recent media discussion, see David Volodzko, "China's Addiction to Counterfeiting," *Diplomat*, October 17, 2015, https://thediplomat.com/2015/10/chinas-addiction-to-counterfeiting/. For a more recent US government take on China's current IPR environment, see "Protecting Your Intellectual Property Rights (IPR) in China," https://2016.export.gov/china/doingbizinchina/riskmanagement/ipr/index.asp.

7. Sterling, *Distraction*, 104.

handled as consul general in the 1890s,[8] as support for his argument that the defendants could and should be punished according to the local rules they themselves invoked.[9] When the defendants—Commercial Press (*Shangwu yinshuguan*), a leading Chinese publisher in town—reprinted his client's history textbook, Jernigan stated, they were not only fully aware that the "literary piracy and theft" they committed was "universally condemned as wrong," but they subscribed to this very idea.[10]

Jernigan made this paradoxical argument chiefly to overcome the legal obstacles he faced. As China's recently promulgated copyright law did not apply to foreigners and the only applicable treaty clause was flawed, he resorted to local customs and practices as a sort of common law.[11] Although Jernigan's bold statement didn't persuade the Mixed Court judges to rule the case based on what he identified as a "general norm" of copyright, his intriguing remarks provide a revealing insight into the history of copyright in China. It provokes a rethinking of our conventional wisdom as to why the Chinese pirate.

Retrospectively analyzing the current piracy problem in China, scholars and commentators have comfortably declared that the development of IPR law, particularly copyright, in modern China has been a failure, if not a nonstarter, because Chinese tradition and political culture privilege imitation over innovation, community over the individual. The subsequent attempts to transplant Western IPR law in China throughout the long twentieth century were mostly made under foreign pressure and with minimal local resonance.[12] In the *Ginn & Co. v. Commercial Press* case, however, the alleged Chinese "pirates" freely admitted reprinting the American textbooks, but not because the Chinese cultural tradition or economic norms prevented them from comprehending

---

8. For the petitions and prohibitions he handled in the 1890s, see chapters 2 and 4 of this book.

9. "The Copyright Case," newspaper clipping from *North China Daily News*; April 3, 1911; 893.544-G43; Box 10237; DF 1910–1929; RG 59; NACP.

10. "The Mixed Court Shanghai, March 29. Before Magistrate Pao and Mr. Jameson, American Assessor. Alleged Infringement of Copyright," newspaper clipping from *North China Daily News*; March 30, 1911; 893.544-G43; Box 10237; DF 1910–1929; RG 59; NACP.

11. For further discussion on this case, see Fei-Hsien Wang, "Partnering with Your Pirate," *Modern Asian Studies* (forthcoming 2020).

12. This cultural determinist argument is best articulated in Alford's *To Steal a Book Is an Elegant Offense*. For examples of more recent variations of this argument, see Shi, "The Paradox of Confucian Determinism," and Lehman, "Intellectual Property Rights and Chinese Tradition Section: Philosophical Foundations."

modern copyright doctrine. In 1903, Commercial Press had published a pamphlet on European copyright law as part of their effort to urge the Chinese government to institutionalize domestic copyright.[13] The statements made by its general manager and attorneys during the 1911 trial indicated that the firm was well-informed about the relevant laws and their limitations before they reprinted Ginn & Co.'s textbooks.[14] The alleged Chinese pirates were not IPR savages but copyright-savvy economic actors. For them, pirating others' intellectual property and embracing copyright in their own interest were not mutually exclusive. This seemingly self-contradictory and bipolar disposition is the real face of Chinese copyright pirates.

This book uses a new conceptual framework to unveil this intertwined history of copyright and piracy in modern China that most scholars and commentators have so far neglected to see. While we may quickly take for granted that the law defines what constitutes copyright and piracy, they are never merely legal matters, but practices and concepts formed and evolved in the specific local nexus of cultural production and consumption. To uncover these practices, as well as the local nexus upholding them, I shift attention from the copyright legislations to their potential users. Authors, translators, publishers, and booksellers may not have the authority to make copyright law, but they hold dear the ownership of books and are more deeply concerned than the rest of society with the issues of piracy. This book explores how they received, appropriated, practiced, and contested the very concept of copyright—or *banquan* 版權 in Chinese, literally "right to printing blocks"—from the 1890s, when this term was first introduced in the Chinese cultural community, to the 1950s, when it gradually faded from public discussion.

Given the political circumstances of the long twentieth century in China, if we are to comprehend that country's history of intellectual property, it is particularly crucial, I believe, that we grasp this shifting of focus from "how copyright law was made" to "how the concept of copyright was practiced." It is certainly true that China's track record on instituting copyright law was far from impressive. Most clauses of *Da Qing zhuzuoquan lü* (Copyright Law of the Great Qing) were borrowed indiscriminately from the 1899 Copyright Law of Japan. As the Qing government was overthrown by the revolutionaries a few months after it took effect, it is doubtful whether this first Chinese

13. Sikeluodun, *Banquan kao*.
14. "The Mixed Court Shanghai, March 29," 893.544-G43; Box 10237; DF 1910–1929; RG 59; NACP.

copyright law was ever seriously enforced. In 1915, *Zhonghua Minguo zhuzuo-quan fa* (Copyright Law of the Republic of China), almost identical to its predecessor, was passed by the ROC National Assembly. When it was to become effective, the then president, Yuan Shikai (1859–1916), installed himself as the emperor of the Chinese Empire. The decade of civil wars between regional military leaders following Yuan's short-lived Chinese Empire further obstructed law and order in China. New copyright legislation was promulgated in 1928 by the Nationalist government of Chiang Kai-shek (1887–1975) after he nominally reunified the nation, but the escalating conflicts with the Communists and the intensified aggressions from Japan constrained the Nationalist government's capacity and determination to attend to this less urgent matter of copyright. As the continuous political upheavals throughout the first half of the twentieth century hindered these legislations from realizing their potential, the new communist regime established in 1949 further removed the doctrine of copyright from its legal landscape. As a matter of fact, the People's Republic did not issue its copyright law until 1990, when it was working toward joining the Berne Convention and the World Trade Organization (WTO). Given these twists and turns, it is understandable that the transplantation of copyright law in China has been so easily regarded as a failure. However, we must keep in mind what Jernigan stated in his intriguing defense: Chinese authors and publishers might not have relied solely on the state's formal laws and courts to protect their literary creations and settle ownership disputes. They had many other means to regulate and protect what they believed to be "copyright."

The most powerful testimony that the actual practices of copyright in China might be a more vibrant and more compelling subject to excavate than the copyright legislation resides in the language itself. There are two Chinese terms/translations for "copyright," one more popular than the other.[15] *Zhuzuoquan* 著作權, literally "author's right,"[16] which has been used to denote "copyright" in all the copyright laws in China since 1910, is less commonly used, except in legal documents, than the other term for copyright: *banquan*. Every proper book published in China is expected to have a *banquan ye* (copyright page) that provides basic identification information for the book. In it, readers will likely find the following convention: *banquan suoyou fanin bijiu* (copyright is reserved, and

---

15. I would like to thank Wang Taisheng and Chen Yunru for bringing up the issue of the different legal validity of the two Chinese terms for copyright.

16. This term is a loanword from the Japanese term *chosakuken*, which is a translation of the French term *droit d'auteur* (or *Urheberrecht* in German).

reprinting will be pursued and punished).[17] The same statement also appears on DVD covers, food wrappings, and other commercial products as a Chinese equivalent of "all rights reserved." Artists and authors sign a *banquan qiyue* (copyright contract) with their publishers and are entitled to receive a *banquan fei* (copyright fee) or *banshui* (copyright royalty) for every reproduction or broadcast of their works. The state's copyright law does not necessarily validate these practices that people employ to declare, protect, or trade *banquan*, because the subject of protection in the law is *zhuzuoquan*, not *banquan*. But that has not lessened their popularity in China's cultural industry.[18]

Examining merely the state's law and legal records is thus not adequate to unveil the whole picture. The understanding of copyright and the controversies that continue to surround the notion of IPR today in China requires study of the *social* history of *banquan*/copyright. To reconstruct and analyze the day-to-day, on-the-ground debates, conflicts, and negotiations between authors and publishers, publishers and publishers, and publishers, authors, and state agents, in the name of *banquan*/copyright, I consult a wide range of sources that have previously been underutilized by legal historians. The rich and complex everyday practices of *banquan*/copyright attested in company records, individual petitions, guild archives, diaries, correspondence, advertisements, bibliographies, book lists, and the actual books produced at the time allow me extend my inquiry into the history of copyright and piracy in China beyond the state's legislation. Such an approach also offers the possibility of examining legal transplantation in a legally pluralistic setting, as merchants and civic organizations were leading agents in disseminating and practicing *banquan*/copyright in modern China through customs and community regulations. The booksellers' and authors' illuminating everyday struggle with piracy and enforcement of copyright reveals how business and culture converged, law and economic life intertwined, as the country underwent profound sociopolitical changes and transitioned from late imperial China to modern China.

By conceptualizing Chinese booksellers' and authors' nitty-gritty and sometimes nasty efforts to claim, regulate, and protect what they believed to be copyright, this book also tries to connect the everyday enforcement and practices they used to manage their economic life with the economic, political, and legal ideas upon which they depended. The statements on copyright pages, ownership registrations, publication contracts, and actions against pirates

17. For a discussion of the making of this convention, see chapter 1.
18. The PRC Copyright Law now recognizes *banquan* as a synonym for *zhuzuoquan*.

provide us a bottom-up view of how different commercial interests and prac- tices, legal concepts, and cultural understandings of human intellectual cre- ation converged in China, a society that had just been sucked into the vortex of globalization.

Copyright/*Banquan*: Alien Doctrine and Local Practices

"Why couldn't copyright law have a strong foothold in China?" This has been *the* focus of inquiry for scholars who look into the past of IP law in China since the 1990s. In his pioneering study, William Alford argues that the character of Chinese political culture and Confucian traditions prevented imperial China from developing an indigenous counterpart to Western copyright law. With- out the pressures exerted by Western gunboats, he declares, China would never have adopted IPR doctrines. However, the lack of awareness and institutional support of private property rights and a market economy have hindered sub- sequent efforts to transplant modern IP law in China since the turn of the twen- tieth century. As a result, China has continued to be a piracy haven even after joining the WTO. This sort of cultural determinist explanation still dominates public discussion in the West regarding Chinese piracy.

On the other hand, we see waves of Chinese scholars, driven by both nation- alist pride and state policies, contesting Alford's contention.[19] In general, they present an alternative history of copyright in China that fits the reform era's political agenda: the precondition of copyright is not the recognition of indi- vidual property rights or a free market economy, as Alford hints, but the tech- nology of printing. It would thus be only natural that China, the "first inventor of printing," developed "a concept of copyright" earlier than the rest of the world. Tender sprout though it might be, they state, there was undoubtedly a home- grown "copyright with Chinese characteristics" emerging as early as the tenth century, long before the Statute of Anne, the accredited first copyright law in Europe, was promulgated. For them, even though the initial attempts to intro- duce European and American IP law since the late Qing did "enrich" indige- nous copyright protection, those efforts should still be seen as part of the

---

19. A few examples of Chinese scholars' pushback: Zheng, "Zhongwai yinshua chuban wu banquan gainian de yenge"; Shao, "An Shoulian yu qu jie de zhong guo zhi shi chan quan shi"; Li, "Guanyu Zhongguo gudai yinhe wu banquan yanjiu de jidian fansi"; Li, *Qiangkou xia de falü*; Liu and Kong, "Zhongguo shi shijie shang zuizao shixing banquan baohu de guojia."

Western imperialist aggression that interrupted the unique "developmental path" of Chinese law and economy.[20]

Despite the apparent contrasts in their arguments and the political economy agendas behind them, Alford and his Chinese counterparts share more conceptual presuppositions than they might realize. Taking "having the law" as a maker of modernity to assess the "progress" of a society, they both retroject modern IP doctrine into the past to determine *whether* China "had" something equivalent or similar to present-day IPR law. Borrowing concepts and categories from the modern Western legal system as analytic vocabularies and tools is not uncommon in the field of Chinese legal history. Such practices, however, might bring along the normative assumptions that reinforce the discourse of Western legal doctrines as universal, timeless, and civilized, and orientalize China as standing at odds with the liberal legal order and Enlightenment values.[21]

Furthermore, the modern conceptions of IPR, which Alford and his counterparts use as a priori criteria, are historical constructs themselves. As demonstrated in the works of Adrian Johns, Brad Sherman, Lionel Bently, and others, modern IPR doctrines were not invented according to certain abstract philosophical principles of innovation and property rights. They emerged from the complex dynamics of publishing business, lawmaking, and knowledge production in eighteenth- and nineteenth-century Western Europe.[22] The timeless, modern, and universal appearances of copyright, as well as the myth that the rise of IPR would lead to the elimination of piracy, are part of this historical construct, especially since the internationalization of IPR in the second half of the nineteenth century. Even within the "Western" world, the fundamental differences and tensions between the Continental and Anglo-American approaches to the nature of copyright have never been settled.[23]

20. In 1995, the PRC government sponsored a five-year research project on the history of copyright in China and based the research on Zhang's vision. A series of monographs and articles, by the PIs Li Mingshan and Zhou Lin, resulted. For example, Li, ed., *Zhongguo jindai banquan shi* and *Zhongguo gudai banquan shi*; Li and Chang, *Zhongguo dangdai banquan shi*. This three-part series, though introducing several interesting new sources, often interpreted them in a casual and arbitrary fashion and made self-contradictory claims.

21. For a discussion of legal orientalism and the methodological problem of using modern, Western legal language to discuss Chinese legal history, see Riskola, *Legal Orientalism*, and Chen, *Chinese Law in Imperial Eyes*.

22. See Johns, *Piracy*; Sherman and Bently, *The Making of Modern Intellectual Property Law*; Seville, *The Internationalisation of Copyright Law*.

23. Baldwin, *The Copyright Wars*.

Building on this emerging scholarship that historicizes the development of piracy and IPR in Europe and North America, this study situates the equally rich and contingent case of modern China in this larger story of the internationalization of copyright doctrine. I will suspend judgment as to whether imperial China had its indigenous "copyright," and attend instead to the practices and instruments the Chinese developed and employed in the name of *banquan*. Like many other Western locutions introduced into the Chinese language at the turn of the twentieth century, *banquan*/copyright was presented by its early advocates as a foreign, new, and thus progressive concept that the struggling empire needed to embrace so it could become modern. Indeed, such rhetoric might help copyright to gain legitimacy, but it could operate and be realized only within the local book-trade structure and the existing legal orders. While the attempts to establish new copyright procedures might pose challenges to the existing norms of literary ownership and their legality, native commercial customs and practices provided early Chinese advocates of *banquan*/copyright with the inspiration and apparatus to make it work on the ground. By starting the story from the moment of encounter and exchange, the book aims to tell a twofold tale of the transplantation of an alien legal concept in a society that has a long and sophisticated book culture and legal tradition.

Printed books played an essential role in shaping and sustaining culture and knowledge production in late imperial China. Woodblock printing, the dominant printing method in China before the early twentieth century, allowed a mobile, decentralized, less-capital-intensive book production to flourish. The standardized written language and the core textbooks for the civil service examination system also contributed to a surprisingly homogenous reading and textual reproduction tradition across times and spaces. Book learning was treasured, and the tastes of the literati were admired and mimicked by members of other social classes, who were inspired to join the educated elites' club.[24] If the modern doctrine of copyright was emerging from and shaped by the early modern European publishing business, which required more substantial initial capital to set up and maintain the movable-type printing operation, in theory the xylographic print cultures in China might be likely to have yielded a different conception of literary and book ownership. Indeed, since Ye Dehui,

---

24. For an overview of the history of books and printing in China, see Brokaw, "On the History of the Book in China," 3–54. For a comparison between the East Asian woodblock printing method and European movable-type printing, and how different printing methods might affect the structure of book trade, see McDermott and Burke, "Introduction."

bibliographers of Chinese books have noticed random statements, seals, and colophons in late imperial imprints that warned against unauthorized reprinting.[25] The nature and effectiveness of such scattered proprietary declarations have been debated by scholars ever since. Quick to deny them as any equivalent of copyright, Alford considers them to be merely the by-product of the imperial state's press control;[26] on the other hand, his Chinese counterparts insist that these are firm evidence of Chinese local-grown copyright, because, in the modern IPR regime, unauthorized reproduction is also strictly banned.[27] Other bibliographers and cultural historians, such as Sören Edgren and Inoue Susmu, settle on the halfway term "pseudo-copyright."[28] As discussed earlier, using copyright or modern IPR terminology to label and discuss these proprietary declarations in traditional China might run the risk of ahistoricization and couldn't really yield productive discussions. That said, these anecdotal accounts and examples of proprietary declarations found in Chinese books clearly indicate that there were certain norms of literary ownership extant in China before the late Qing.

The introduction of copyright doctrine to China at the turn of the twentieth century, thus, should not be seen merely as another case of legal transplantation or legal modernization; it is also a point of encounter and exchange between two systems of textual reproduction and knowledge economy. Beginning in the second half of the nineteenth century, mechanical letterpress, lithography, and other Western printing technologies, along with new print media, such as newspapers, were brought by European missionaries and businessmen to China's treaty ports. The arrival of these new printing technologies has conventionally been treated as a sharp departure from the late imperial woodblock printing tradition, but the transition from woodblock printing to Western-style letterpress did not happen overnight. In the first half of the twentieth century, different modes of communication and printing technologies coexisted in China. This created a unique environment in which even

25. For example, Ye, *Ye Dehui shu hua*, 52–57; Tsien, *Paper and Print*; Poon, "The Printer's Colophon in Sung China, 960–1279."

26. Alford, *To Steal a Book Is an Elegant Offense*, 14.

27. For example, Zheng, "Zhongwai yinshua chuban wu banquan gainian de yenge," and Li, ed., *Zhongguo gudai banquan shi*. In *Zhongguo gudai banquan shi*, Li even traced the "origin of copyright" in China to the Warring States period.

28. Edgren, "The Fengmianye (Cover Page) as a Source for Chinese Publishing History"; Inoue, *Chūgoku shuppan bunkashi* and *Shorin no chōbō*. Also see chapter 1 in this book for further discussion.

publishers and printers themselves were unable to provide a consensual answer as to what constitutes "copying," how a printed "book" should look, and
who gets to declare "ownership" of particular imprints, as answers to these questions may vary depending on what kind of textual reproduction process is involved. Such uncertainty prompted publishers, printers, and booksellers in
China to articulate the "old" norms in the late imperial book trade, as well as to
work out "new" conventions and customs in the name of *banquan*/copyright,
to accommodate this changing environment. As the first two chapters of this
book will show, the early *banquan*/copyright advocates and practitioners in
China neither imported European or American copyright practices nor invented
something brand-new for this alien doctrine. They drew inspiration from earlier
conventions and customs in the Ming-Qing book trade to develop a workable
and sustainable *banquan*/copyright of their own. These local commercial practices, as well as norms and ideas of book ownership, conditioned copyright's
reception in China and profoundly reshaped the definition of owning the "right
to copy."

This book also situates the various practices and mechanisms that Chinese
booksellers and authors developed to enforce what they believed to be *banquan*/
copyright in China's plural legal orders. It moves the focus away from the
state's legislative and formal apparatus and toward customary regulations and
practices to grasp the substance of transcultural exchanges and negotiations of
legal ideas.[29] As revisionist scholars of Chinese legal practice have pointed out,
while serious cases, such as murder or robbery, were ruled according to formal
codes at the state's courts, guilds, lineage groups, and other communal organizations played an important role in regulating daily transactions and settling
minor disputes.[30] And the various instruments and practices the ordinary
Chinese employed to protect their interests in these nongovernmental institutions also acquired legality. Though the presence and popularity of these extralegal mechanisms are well acknowledged and analyzed by legal historians

29. For a discussion of the methodological benefits of employing legal pluralism in the field
of Chinese legal history, see the introduction to Cassel, *Grounds of Judgment*. Another good example of discussion of how seemingly foreign legal concepts and systems were received and
realized in China by focusing on practices is Ng, *Legal Transplantation in Early Twentieth-
Century China*.

30. For disputes related to family and gender relations, see, for instance, Sommer, *Polyandry
and Wife-Selling in Qing Dynasty China*; on contract and debt, see Zelin, Ocko, and Gardella,
eds., *Contract and Property in Early Modern China*; on commercial dispute resolutions, see Qiu,
Dang falü yushang jingji, and Dykstra, "Complicated Matters."

of Ming-Qing China, their discussions generally do not extend into the Republican period, as if such mechanisms faded away at the dawn of the legal reform in the last decade of the Qing. These vibrant community regulations, however, did not disappear after the new Chinese nation-state declared itself as the supreme and exclusive legal authority. For instance, studies of civil justice from the late Qing to the Republic reveal that the courts had to consistently mediate between the code and the customs, and often departed from the letter of the law to accommodate the popularity of local customs.[31] When set in comparison with the formal codes, especially the modern civil and criminal laws, these customs are often presented as some sort of native and timeless entity ("Chinese tradition"). If they emerged organically from local settings to uphold certain community or market orders, as China engaged more and more intensively in global competition beginning in the second half of the nineteenth century, new customs and communal regulation were likely to evolve to deal with new issues arising from the changing economy and society.

In the name of *banquan*/copyright, Chinese booksellers and authors seem to have developed multiple mechanisms and remedies to declare and justify their exclusive ownership of their books, and managed to create a sense of order and legality in the absence of an adequate formal justice system. The archive of the Shanghai Booksellers' Guild (*Shanghai shuye tongye gonghui*), held in the Shanghai Municipal Archives, is essential to my reconstruction of how Chinese booksellers in Shanghai, China's new publishing center, utilized the tradition of the trade guild to form a customary *banquan*/copyright regime. Dating from 1895 to 1958, this rich archive includes the guild administration records, its financial statements, ownership register, meeting minutes, and, most importantly, the detailed records of private prosecutions and member-to-member negotiations relative to piracy matters. These previously underused materials shed light on these booksellers' daily operations to establish and maintain a *banquan*/copyright order in the marketplace of knowledge.

The illuminating case of Chinese booksellers' and authors' practices of *banquan*/copyright beyond or parallel to the state's formal legal system is also part of a larger story of the internationalization of modern IPR. This nuanced picture of the encounter and cross-fertilization of Chinese and foreign ideas and institutions demonstrates how the internationalization of legal doctrine was always realized locally when transregional commercial and intellectual exchanges intensified during the past two centuries. By providing an extensive

---

31. For example, Huang, *Code, Custom, and Legal Practice in China.*

study of how a non-Western society with its own printing and legal cultures encountered and made use of copyright doctrine, this book also aims to enrich, if not complicate, the current Euro-American-centered discussion of "global copyright."[32]

Economic Life of the Culture

The popularization of *banquan*/copyright and the criminalization of unauthorized reprinting in the late Qing and early Republican period, I argue, are inseparable from the changing landscape of the Chinese knowledge economy. As new printing technologies and new intellectual trends from the West challenged the existing structures of the Chinese book trade, the interrelationship of creativity, commerce, and communication was unsettled and reconfigured. This further created uncertainty, anxiety, and conflicts regarding the ownership and value of printed books and the information they contained. By promoting *banquan*/copyright and discrediting *fanyin*/reprinting,[33] many early advocates of this position in China openly stated that they were searching for a sense of order in answer to the rapid and profound changes they experienced in the field of knowledge at the time.

The paradigm shift from traditional Chinese learning to a new system of Western knowledge in the late Qing and early Republican period may be the most extensively studied subject regarding the formation of Chinese modernity.[34] The intensified military and commercial aggressions from the Western imperialist powers, the demise of the imperial state as the absolute political and

32. For instance, Lionel Bently, Uma Suthersanen, and Paul Terremans edited a volume in 2010 to address the global history of copyright, but the cases included are all European and North American ones. See Bently, Suthersanen and Terremans, eds., *Global Copyright*.

33. In China's late imperial book culture, *fanyin*, literally "reprinting," was considered a neutral practice. In the late Qing and early Republican period, it gradually came to refer to literary piracy. Interestingly, the Chinese did not coin a specific term for literary piracy until probably the 1940s. *Daoban* 盜版 (literally "stealing printing blocks"), the contemporary Chinese term denoting copyright and other IPR piracy, was not available to the Chinese booksellers and authors I study in this book. The metaphorical connection between high-seas piracy and literary piracy that appears in the European context did not exist in the Chinese context. I would like to thank Susan Burns, Fahad Ahmad Bishara, and Johan Mathew for raising the question about the term the Chinese used for piracy.

34. Here I use Yü Yingshi's borrowing of Thomas Kuhn's "paradigm shift" to discuss this radical transition from Chinese learning to Western knowledge. See Yü, *Zhongguo jindai sixiang shi shang di Hu Shi*.

knowledge authority, the abolishment of the centuries-old civil service examination system, and the sudden influx of new knowledge and technology from Europe, North America, and Japan triggered a fundamental crisis in China's world of learning. In the name of national survival, "Civilization," and "Enlightenment," learned Chinese avidly consumed, if not worshipped, anything "Western" and "new," as a way to respond to the challenges from the advancing Western powers. This shift in intellectual discourse led not only to the decline and eventual discredit of Chinese learning and its canons, but also to the withering away of the cultural institutions, the value systems, and the educated elites' identities that were deeply rooted in it. When the default path to officialdom though studying the classics was terminated at the turn of the century, the existential questions literate Chinese confronted were intellectual (Is the knowledge system I subscribe to wrong?), sociocultural (Will I lose my prestige?), and economic (How will I make a living from now on?).[35]

While some Chinese literati retooled themselves to avoid being marginalized in the changing knowledge landscape,[36] new types of men of letters emerged from this paradigm shift. Treaty-port literati, translators, journalists, political novelists, print capitalists, college academics, technical professionals, and other types of entrepreneurial figures who claimed to have access to the "new" knowledge were able to carve out alternative careers outside the old scholar-official route by producing, disseminating, and practicing the rising new paradigm of knowledge.[37] This redistribution of cultural and symbolic capital brought them concrete economic benefits, too. They would eventually become the first generation of modern intellectuals in China who did not need to rely on the state for employment or credentials. These cultural producers' economic independence came at a price: they would now be subject to market forces.

35. Levenson, *Liang Ch'i-ch'ao and the Mind in Modern China* and *Confucian China and Its Modern Fate*; Chang, *Chinese Intellectuals in Crisis*; Lin, *The Crisis of Chinese Consciousness*; Schwartz, *In Search of Wealth and Power*; Yü, *Zhongguo wenhua yu xiandai bianqian*.

36. For the marginalization of the Chinese intelligentsia after the abolishment of the civil service examination, see Yü, "Zhongguo zhishi fenzi de bianyuanhua." Also see Luo, *Quanshi Zhuanyi*. For the Chinese literati's effort to retool themselves, see Culp, "Mass Production of Knowledge and the Industrialization of Mental Labor."

37. A few examples of these new types of men of letters: Cohen, *Between Tradition and Modernity*; C. Yeh, *Shanghai Love*; W. Yeh, *The Alienated Academy*; Culp, U, and W. Yeh, eds., *Knowledge Acts in Modern China*; Hill, *Lin Shu, Inc.*; Rea and Volland, eds., *The Business of Culture*. Also see Li, *Wan Qing de xinshi chuanbo meiti yu zhishi fenzi*.

Reconstructing the Chinese authors' and publishers' daily dealings with copyright and piracy, this book is also an attempt to explore the impact of this paradigm shift on its participants' economic life.[38] As illustrated in chapters 2 and 3, the changing intellectual trends, together with the political and educational reforms between 1895 and 1905, turned "Western" knowledge into a desirable and valuable cultural commodity. At the same time, as the traditional classics, their annotations, and examination preps lost their commercial value, their publishers faced business crises. The sudden information boom brought about by learned Chinese's pursuit of "new" knowledge, together with the decline of "Chinese learning" publishing, profoundly reshaped the Chinese book world and turned it into an exciting, expanding, yet chaotic mess. As no one was able to keep track of all the new information, and the old bibliographical knowledge with which a learned Chinese reader was equipped would fall short when it came to evaluating new publications in strange subjects, the authenticity and credibility of any given new title became ever more ambiguous and questionable. It was in this context that unauthorized reprinting was increasingly regarded as a threat to both the stability of the book trade and the order of knowledge. The general uncertainty and commercial potential in this new cultural market prompted these cultural figures to utilize *banquan*/copyright to justify their exclusive ownership of their works, request payment or royalty, and settle disputes over profit, as now producing and selling "new" books and knowledge were becoming their livelihood.

Many individuals who appear in this book are the leading public intellectuals and literary figures contributing to this paradigm shift or making their careers during this intellectual watershed and its aftermath, such as Liang Qichao (1873–1929), Lin Shu (1852–1924), Yan Fu (1854–1921), and Lu Xun (1881–1936). Because of their importance in modern Chinese history and literature, their writings, even the most minor and obscure ones, have been diligently collected, published, and thoroughly studied by intellectual historians and literary scholars. Seeing these well-known cultural figures as economic actors, I take advantage of the trivial details recorded in their diaries, correspondence, and personal writings to reconstruct their everyday practice of *banquan*/copyright. Such details might not excite scholars interested in these cultural figures' intellectual development, but they are vital resources for understanding how the modern

---

38. In this book I use William Swell's definition of "economic life." According to Swell, "economic life" is "human participation in production, exchange, and consumption of goods." Swell, "A Strange Career," 146.

Chinese knowledge economy *actually* worked: how translations and novels were produced, how books were printed and consumed, how authors negotiated and received payments, how publishers dealt with demanding authors and devious pirates, how cultural figures, now under the spell of the market, justified and maintained a stable living when the intellectual and literary orders had been turned upside down.

Along the same lines, books are examined and discussed in this study primarily as goods that these cultural figures/economic actors participated in producing, circulating, and consuming. They are treated as tangible containers of information. Actual copies of books (both the authentic and the pirated ones) published in China between the 1890s and the 1950s constitute another body of primary sources I consult to reconstruct the everyday enforcement and declaration of *banquan*/copyright.[39] The title page, copyright page, appendixes, advertisements, and petitions that are inserted before or after the main text have been used by bibliographers to identify a book's publication information, edition, previous owners, and the like. The information provided and displayed on the physical copies of books, as well as how it was presented, also offers hints about the production process, marketing strategies, and bookmen's self-identification; these hints are particularly valuable for us in studying Chinese publishing culture, as most publishers did not leave personal records or archives.[40] Borrowing some traditional Chinese bibliographical techniques, I analyze the changing appearance of the title page and the copyright page (as a default part of the Chinese book since the turn of the twentieth century) to reconstruct how booksellers and authors used seals, stamps, and fixed conventions to declare and certify their ownership and the authenticity of particular copies.

These Chinese cultural figures' daily dealings with *banquan*/copyright and piracy, together with the Shanghai Booksellers' Guild's rich records of their customary "copyright" regime, and the actual copies of books published in the first half of the twentieth century, further offer unique insights into the ideas

39. For this book, I consulted the collections of Shanghai Library, Regenstein Library at the University of Chicago, National Taiwan University Library, Fu Sinian Library and Guo Tingyi Library at Academia Sinica (Taiwan), Tōyō Bunko Library (Tokyo, Japan), Keio University Library, Waseda University Library, Yale University Library, Harvard Yanjing Library, Cambridge University Library, and Indiana University Wells Library.

40. For a discussion of the title pages of Chinese books as primary sources, see Edgren, "The Fengmianye (Cover Page) as a Source for Chinese Publishing History."

of these cultural figures/economic actors regarding labor, property, ownership, value, authenticity, and counterfeiting. What is *banquan*/copyright? Is it a kind of property or a privilege? On what basis could one claim a manuscript he wrote or a book he published as his property? Is it the content or the physical imprint that makes a book a book? How can one know whether a book is original and authentic? These cultural figures might not be political economists developing their original or sophisticated economic theories, but when they employed the doctrine of *banquan*/copyright and tried to make it work, they were forced to engage with these questions. At the core of the frequent disputes and contestations revolving around *banquan*/copyright throughout the first half of the twentieth century, what Chinese publishers, authors, and state agents were consistently wrestling over was the relationship between the good (book) and its producers (author or publisher).

However, articulating the correlation between human creative activities and the creator's exclusive rights—the fundamental principle of modern copyright—was particularly a challenge for these practitioners of *banquan*/copyright in China. The paradigm shift to Western learning resulted in the Chinese increasingly engaging in a globalizing field of knowledge as consumers rather than producers. Many of the early champions of *banquan*/copyright were essentially cultural brokers who translated and appropriated others' (mostly European and Japanese) works without proper authorization. They would technically all be pirates and plagiarists according to our contemporary IPR standard.[41] They thus emphasized their mental labor as translators, their capital investment in publishing, or their commitment to the enlightenment mission as the primary justification for *banquan*/copyright. As the second half of this book illustrates, such deviation from the conventional creativity-ownership argument made booksellers and publishers the more powerful advocates for *banquan*/copyright and left authors subordinated to the booksellers' customary *banquan*/copyright regime. The emphasis on mental labor in their *banquan*/copyright discourse further became a major setback for authors after 1949 when the new communist government introduced its system to reward authors according to their "labor output."

41. For example, Liang Qichao had a habit of appropriating his Japanese contemporaries' works as his own. See Bastid-Bruguière, "The Japanese-Induced German Connection on Modern Chinese Ideas of the State."

Under the Shadow of the State

Throughout this book, I trace the same group of Chinese cultural actors, mostly Shanghai- and Beijing-based booksellers and authors, who employed various tactics and practices of *banquan*/copyright to tackle the same issue of piracy from the late Qing to the early People's Republic. Regarding the state-society dynamic in modern China, this book, breaking the conventional periodization, illustrates how these rule-savvy individuals negotiated with the changing shape and forms of state power and its law to secure and advance their economic interests.

Since the late Qing's legal reform, the Chinese state(s) presented itself as having a monopoly on law, but in reality continual wars and revolutions limited its capacity to enforce its laws effectively and impeded its becoming the exclusive legal authority. While civil law and criminal law did have a noticeable impact on cities in this period,[42] the development of less urgent (or secondary) legislation, like copyright law, was lax and unimpressive. However, as discussed earlier, vibrant customary *banquan*/copyright mechanisms were also available to Chinese authors, publishers, and booksellers. In this pluralist legal environment, they got to choose and navigate between the two legal regimes (the state's law and the cultural circle's customs). The second half of the book focuses on the extralegal *banquan*/copyright regime Chinese booksellers in Shanghai established through their guild between 1905 and 1958. Drawing from the rich but underused guild archives, chapters 5 through 7 reveal how the Shanghai booksellers established and enforced their own private *banquan*/copyright regulations when the Chinese central state and its law were unable or unwilling to do so. From the 1900s to the 1920s, in China's new publishing center, Shanghai, the guild operated its *banquan*/copyright regime efficiently in parallel to the state's law to accommodate the weak state's limited legal capacity. The limitations of this local community self-regulation became apparent when the guild attempted to extend it nationwide in the 1930s by setting up China's first private antipiracy policing force. Though Shanghai booksellers dominated the domestic book industry, their customs were deemed by the state to be not legally grounded, and their territorial peer pressure could not really be applied to

---

42. On the establishment and enforcement of civil law and criminal law in the early Republic, see Bernhardt and Huang, eds., *Civil Law in Qing and Republican China*; Mühlhahn, *Criminal Justice in China*; Ma, *Runaway Wives, Urban Crimes, and Survival Tactics in Wartime Beijing*; Ransmeier, *Sold People*.

booksellers outside Shanghai. Shanghai booksellers had to resort to the state's power to crack down on pirates in northern China. When the ROC Copyright Law failed to help them attain the desirable outcome, they cleverly manipulated the Nationalist government's symbolic authority and its obsession with controlling/censoring the press to further the guild's specific interests in protecting its members' copyright.

How the guild "used" the Nationalist state's obsession with information control, at the same time, is one of the many cases in this book that illuminate the continuous and intensified efforts of the Chinese state to maintain its status as the ultimate cultural authority in the aftermath of the intellectual paradigm shift. Compared to their European counterparts, the Chinese imperial governments between the sixteenth and nineteenth centuries had played a more active role in publishing. They printed the government-approved standardized editions of essential texts, legal codes, and calendars to maintain a certain level of educational orthodoxy; they established an official order of knowledge via their ambitious encyclopedia, dictionary, and literary collections projects; and they removed the "scandalous," "licentious," and potentially "treasonous" texts via censorship and literary inquisitions.[43] At the turn of the twentieth century, the Qing state's supreme intellectual authority was undermined as the Confucian learning and the meritocratic civil service examination that upheld it lost their currency. For a while, as shown in chapter 4, Chinese authors and publishers counted on the state, as China's supreme intellectual authority, to create a new knowledge order via *banquan*/copyright regulation. Copyright and censorship were bundled together as a result, but late Qing cultural producers and readers did not oppose this arrangement. The Qing state's inability to produce higher-quality books on Western knowledge, as it turned a blind eye to the pirating of private publishers' textbooks, and its delayed promulgation of a domestic copyright law, however, quickly sabotaged its credibility as an authority suitable to issue the seal of approval to books and other publications.

Self-identification as *the* intellectual and cultural authority, as well as consistent anxiety about information control, was inherited by the Republican governments and later the communist regime.[44] As the expansion of print media made possible text-centered political mobilizations, both the Guomindang (Nationalist party, GMD) and the Chinese Communist Party (CCP), who

43. For a discussion of the late imperial Chinese state's censorship and literary inquisitions, see Guy, *The Emperor's Four Treasuries*, and Spence, *Treason by the Book*.

44. See Volland, "The Control of the Media in the People's Republic of China."

benefited directly from the power of the printed texts in their revolution, saw the necessity to establish firm control over the publishing sector.[45] From the late 1920s to the late 1950s, as the last two chapters of this book illustrate, the state devoted increasing resources to censoring unwanted texts in the name of rectifying cultural production. Such policies offered the possibility for the Shanghai Booksellers' Guild to manipulate the state's obsession with information control to assist its customary copyright regime in the 1930s. But these same policies would eventually suffocate the guild's entrepreneurial autonomy in the 1940s and 1950s, when the cultural market was under the state's intensified control. Spaces left for them to negotiate with the state and its law shrank over time as now the production and distribution of books were subsumed into the state's machine. Hu Yuzhi (1896–1986), Mao Dun (1896–1981), and Ye Sheng-tao (1894–1988), who suffered from piracy in the Republican era as authors and publishers, were the top cultural officials of the People's Republic now. These veterans of the Shanghai publishing world proposed a bold solution to their former colleagues and bosses to square away the issue of piracy for good: When the market was entirely under the shadow of the state, the knowledge economy would be reconfigured. When authors were no longer creators, but laborers, and books were "intellectual foods" rather than commodities, *banquan*/copyright would become irrelevant, and literary piracy would eventually vanish on its own.

45. For a discussion of the CCP (and, to a certain extent, the GMD as well) as the text-centered party, see van de Ven, "The Emergence of the Text-Centered Party." Also see Reed, "Advancing the (Gutenberg) Revolution."

1

The Curious Journey of "Copyright" in East Asia

IN THE SPRING OF 1899, a provincial teacher in Fujian named Lin Shu received a strange request from Wang Kangnian (1860–1911), proprietor of a progressive journal in Shanghai, regarding *Bali chahua nü yishi* (The story of the lady of the camellias in Paris), his Chinese translation of Alexandre Dumas's *La Dame aux camélias*, which Lin and his friend Wang Shouchang (1864–1926) had completed not long before, initially as a winter pastime project.[1] It became an instant best seller after their friend Wei Han (1850–1929) published the first edition in Fuzhou with woodblock printing.[2] Sensing the potential commercial value of this work, Wang expressed a keen interest in paying a lump sum for Lin's permission to republish it in Shanghai. This is probably one of China's earliest copyright deals in a modern sense.

Lin Shu would later become China's highest-paid translator of Western fiction in the early twentieth century.[3] In 1899, however, he declined the deal proposed to him. Lin told Wang via a mutual friend that he had no interest in receiving payment because they had translated the work for their amusement, not for profit. The one really entitled to "sell" the rights to publish *Bali chahua nü yishi*, he also believed, was not him, but Wei Han, who had invested money

1. Shanghai tushuguan, ed., *Wang Kangnian shiyou shuzha*, 2:1652–1654.

2. Ah Ying, "Guanyu *Chahua nü yishi*." Scholars estimate that there were at least seven different editions of *Chahua nü yishi* circulating in China at the turn of the century.

3. Lin Shu would go on to "translate" more than two hundred foreign novels by collaborating with people who knew foreign languages. For Lin Shu's literary career and his "factory of writing," see Hill's *Lin Shu, Inc.*

in having the woodblocks carved and copies printed.[4] When Wang reached out to Wei, Wei did agree to "sell" the book, but, sharing Lin's disinterest in financial gain, he asked only for the cost of the woodblocks. To complete the deal, Wei insisted on sending the whole set of printing blocks to Shanghai, despite his awareness that Wang planned to republish the book using Western movable-type printing.[5]

Occurring at a turning point in the development of China's cultural economy, this incident offers us a unique window onto how copyright, as a newly introduced "Western" concept, shaped (and was shaped by) the changing conceptions of book ownership in China. At the turn of the twentieth century, foreign knowledge and literary works were suddenly in high demand in the marketplace, owing to a decisive intellectual turn among educated Chinese and the Qing government's Westernization initiatives. As an unprecedented number of foreign works were being translated into Chinese, hundreds, if not thousands, of new terms were created to translate and introduce foreign ideas, practices, institutions, and things that were deemed "new," "civilized," "progressive," and therefore worth the Chinese effort to learn and adapt. Among them was the concept of "copyright," or *banquan* in Chinese.

The somewhat amusing negotiations over *Bali chahua nü yishi*, to a certain extent, can be seen as a not-so-effective conversation between those who spoke the language of copyright and those who did not. What Wang intended to acquire was an authorization from Lin, the translator, likely with the belief that whoever creates the literary work owns it and should exclusively control the use and distribution of the work, an understanding that is close to the contemporary meaning of intellectual property rights. What he eventually received, however, was a set of tangible printing blocks that were useless to him. This incident provides a snapshot of the time lag in the transmission of Western ideas to China between the country's center and its periphery. Wang, who had been running several progressive, pro-Westernization political journals in the treaty port of Shanghai, was better equipped with Western ideas and "enlightened" earlier than those in Fujian.

Lin's and Wei's response, however, suggests that, when the idea of copyright was introduced in China, it was not "spreading" onto a tabula rasa. They might not comprehend the notion of copyright, but they had a clear idea of book ownership as a kind of proprietary claim of transmittable private property. They

4. *Wang Kangnian shiyou shuzha*, 2:1159, 1653–1654.
5. Ibid., 1653–1655.

considered that the exclusive right and ability to produce copies of *Bali chahua nü yishi* belonged to whoever paid for and retained the woodblocks used to print it. For them, it was the printing blocks, not the writing or translation, that made the book come into being. Therefore, the proper ownership transaction would not be complete unless the block set was transferred from Fujian to Shanghai, even if Wang had chosen a different printing method. Only by sending the blocks to him, they argued, could the capacity to produce (and sell) more copies of the book be transferred to Wang, the new owner of *Bali chahua nü yishi*.

Therefore, this was not merely a conversation between those who spoke the language of copyright and those who did not, but a negotiation between two different understandings of what embodies "the right to copy." In this chapter, tracing how the English word "copyright" became the Chinese term *banquan*, which literally means "the right to printing blocks," I will examine the negotiations and struggles of the early East Asian promoters and practitioners of copyright between these two understandings of ownership of the book. While this chapter looks at the use of words the early promoters associated with the notion of copyright, the *practices* they and their contemporaries undertook in the name of "the right to printing blocks" would be an even more crucial subject of inquiry. The early promoters of copyright in East Asia portrayed copyright as a progressive universal doctrine completely alien to the local culture, one that, for the sake of national survival, needed to be transplanted artificially. This chapter argues, however, that their contemporaries' actual practices of "copyright" tell a different story—the "new" means used to declare *banquan* ownership were derived from some early modern practices whereby profits were secured from printed books.

Making Copyright the "Public Law under Heaven"

To trace the journey of the very concept of "copyright" to China, one has to start in Japan. The Chinese term for copyright, *banquan*, was, after all, not coined in China. The person responsible for combining *han/ban* (printing block(s)) and *ken/quan* (right) to translate "copyright" was Fukuzawa Yukichi (1835–1901), one of the most influential public intellectuals of the Meiji era. In most standard narratives of modern Japanese history, he appears as a major champion of *bunmeikaika* (enlightenment and civilization), and the Benjamin Franklin of Japan. In the 1860s and 1870s, he introduced a wide range of Western ideas and practices in Japan, from civil rights to eating beef, to transform his country into a strong and independent modern nation. Looking back from the 1890s,

Fukuzawa proudly credited his translations of foreign ideas with the birth of a "new Japan." In his autobiography, he highlighted the significance of his coining of *hanken* 版権: "At the time there was no term [in Japanese] to convey the meaning of copyright," he stated. "No one truly understood that the exclusive right of publishing work belongs to its author; this is a form of private property."[6] By inventing *hanken* to capture the essence of copyright, he proclaimed, he did not merely translate a term from English to Japanese, but enlightened his fellow countrymen on an advanced type of property rights that had not existed in Japan before.

What Fukuzawa did not mention in this self-aggrandizing account is that his introduction of copyright to early Meiji Japan did not proceed without a hitch. He actually translated "copyright" into Japanese twice, first as *zōhan no menkyo* (license for possessing the printing blocks) around 1868, and then as *hanken* in 1873, to convince his contemporaries to respect this new doctrine. He also failed to mention that his enthusiastic promotion of copyright was driven not entirely by certain noble Enlightenment ideals, but by his struggle to protect his livelihood against unauthorized reprinting at the time. The period between Fukuzawa's two translations of "copyright" coincided with the peak of his publishing business, as well as the most active period of his legal actions against unauthorized reprints. His translations and practices of copyright must thus be understood in conjunction with his economic life, especially his "business of Enlightenment."

Fukuzawa started his "business of Enlightenment" on the eve of the Meiji Restoration. Born into a low-ranking samurai family, he was first a student of traditional Confucian learning and then a devotee of Dutch studies (*rangaku*), a body of Western knowledge, especially technology and medicine, developed in early modern Japan via its contact with the Dutch. Although his command of Dutch studies earned him a position as the official Dutch teacher of his home domain, he quickly moved on to study English, after discovering that the international language of the time was English rather than Dutch. To improve his English, he served voluntarily in the Tokugawa government's first official delegation to the United States in 1860 and in another delegation to Europe in 1862. Being one of the exceptional few Japanese with firsthand experiences in the West, he started writing about the "civilized nations" he saw overseas as the model for Japan's state building, and he hoped to leverage his experiences to increase his social and cultural capital thereby. In 1867, after he was suspended

6. *FYZ*, 1:10.

temporarily from his government translator job for importing books for private use during an official business trip to America, he decided to depart from his bureaucratic career for good. Besides starting his private academy, Keiō School, he devoted most of his energy to compiling books introducing all things Western, aiming to cash in on his overseas experiences to support himself and the academy.[7] Between 1867 and 1869, as the Tokugawa government lost power and imperial authority was restored, Fukuzawa also underwent a profound transformation from a pension-receiving samurai to a self-sustaining intellectual who made his living by publishing his works.[8]

In the midst of the Meiji Restoration, as the political leaders in Japan decided to launch a full-scale reform modeled after European nations to catch up with the West, his timely books provided Japanese readers with a simple and straightforward introduction of Western social institutions, political systems, and cultural norms. Appearing as an authority on the Western world (*seiyō*), he gained considerable political and social influence and became a popular author of his time. The success and fame of his books, however, also enticed others to reprint or plagiarize them for a quick profit. This put his publishing projects in jeopardy. For example, Fukuzawa estimated that he sold about four thousand copies of *Seiyō jijō* (Conditions in the West) within two years of its publication; at the same time, roughly nine thousand copies of three "counterfeit editions" (*gihan*) were sold in Kyoto and Osaka.[9] As a result, despite the great success of *Seiyō jijō*, Fukuzawa was for some time unable to accumulate enough capital to produce a sequel, *Seiyō jijō gaihen*, to further introduce basic ideas of European law and political economy. Widespread reprints of the five books he published in 1866–1867 had hurt his business so badly, as he complained to a bookseller friend, that he was forced to postpone the publication plan for months and even sell the printing blocks of one book to make ends meet.[10]

When *Seiyō jijō gaihen* was eventually released in the summer of 1868, readers found at the very end of the book several chapters on the correlation of economic development and private property rights. Among the different forms of property rights acknowledged in the "advanced" countries of Europe and America, Fukuzawa told his readers, there was this special thing called "*kopīraito/*

7. The school was the predecessor of today's Keiō University.
8. Nagao, *Fukuzawaya Yukichi no kenkyū*, 211–265. Mayuyama, "Shoseki shō Fukuzawaya Yukichi."
9. *FYZ beken*, 115.
10. *FYZ*, 17:50.

copyright," which he translated as *zōhan no menkyo*, license for processing blocks. This, he articulated, should be understood as an author's monopoly as stipulated by the law: authors, as rightful owners of their works, enjoy exclusively the proprietary profits arising from reproductions of copies of their works. Up until recently in human history, he further explained, the law treated only tangible objects as private property, but gradually people recognized that knowledge should also constitute a kind of personal possession. This was why copyright had recently been regulated in detail under official state law in Europe, and thus constituted, presumably, a progressive doctrine at the forefront of the Western world. After presenting a brief history of copyright and the different lengths of the pertinent statutes of limitation, he moved on to stress that the Western countries also meted out similar punishments to those who made unauthorized reprints—copies were confiscated and publishers fined.[11]

The brief description of copyright law that Fukuzawa gave was neither original nor unique; nor was it particularly significant in the book as a whole. What was meaningful was *how* it appeared in the book. When compiling *Seiyō jijō* and *Seiyō jijō gaihen*, Fukuzawa relied heavily on two popular introductory textbooks on political economy from the mid-nineteenth century—William and Robert Chambers's *Political Economy for Use in Schools and for Private Instruction* (1856) and Francis Wayland's *The Elements of Political Economy* (1856).[12] Most sections of *Seiyō jijō gaihen* were translations of passages from *Political Economy* with his creative interpretations, yet the Chamberses did not discuss copyright in their book. What Fukuzawa did was to insert two things into his translation of *Political Economy*'s chapters on private property to put copyright in context. He first inserted a discussion of different types of labor, which he excerpted from Wayland's book, and then added two subsections on patents and copyright, taken from *The New American Cyclopaedia*, into the Chamberses' discussion of private property.[13] By doing so, Fukuzawa knitted patents and copyright into the Chamberses' argument about the enhancement of economic development and the necessity of protecting not only private property but also profits stemming from the property. Wayland's discussion of physical and mental labor,

11. *FYZ*, 1:473–475.

12. For a detailed textual comparison between Chambers's *Political Economy* and *Seiyō jijō*, see Iida, "Reimei ki no keizaigaku kenkyū to Fukuzawa Yukichi (sono ni)," 689–95, 673–675. Sugiyama, "Fukuzawa Yukichi ni okeru keizaiteki jiyū," in *Meiji keimōki no keizai shisō*, 158–164.

13. Nagao, *Fukuzawaya Yukichi no kenkyū*, 270.

meanwhile, created a context in which Fukuzawa could situate copyright as a legitimate reward for mental labor.

In doing so, he cleverly scraped together an overarching narrative in the third tome of *Seiyō jijō gaihen* that could be used in an argument against unauthorized reprinting. The desire to create and protect private property is human nature, and it shaped the principles and the course of economic development. Civilized societies would have more sophisticated ways of defining and protecting both tangible and incorporeal property than would less civilized ones, because their economy was more advanced. Patent and copyright are the latest and thus the most advanced forms of property protected by Western law. Recognizing that ideas, literary creations, and inventions can be easily "stolen" by others owing to their incorporeal nature, the Western countries, therefore, instituted strict laws to punish infringement of copyright and patent. They did so to ensure that people would be willing to continue inventing and writing so that civilizations could keep evolving and the economy could progress perpetually.

Although it is not entirely clear whether the section on copyright was inserted because of the piracy issue Fukuzawa encountered at the time,[14] the description of copyright/*zōhan no menkyo* in *Seiyō jijō gaihen* closely corresponds to the series of petitions and public announcements he made in 1868 against those who produced unauthorized reprints of his works. It is worth noting that neither the Chamberses nor Wayland portrayed the development of private property explicitly as a "civilizing" process. It was Fukuzawa who created this evolutionist discourse to interconnect copyright, economic progress, and legal norms in the civilized nations, to empower his request for copyright protection. In a public announcement in *Chūgai shinbun* (Domestic and foreign news) in the spring of 1868, for example, he denounced those who reprinted his works without his consent by pointing out that such a practice "is strictly forbidden universally (*bankoku*) in principle."[15] In a polite but incredulous petition to the new Meiji government in autumn 1868, around the same time *Seiyō jijō gaihen* was released, he accused Kyoto booksellers who had reprinted his

14. Although most scholars now accept that there is a correlation between Fukuzawa's introduction of copyright and the piracy issues he faced, some argue that the draft of *Seiyō jijō gaihen* was finished before he started to worry about pirated imprints. Considering that Fukuzawa had been able to invest only enough money to make two-thirds of the blocks for *Seiyō jijō gaihen* when he started to complain about piracy in the spring of 1868, and the section on copyright appeared in the last part of the book, I think it is also possible that the section was not originally in the draft but added by him after his books were pirated.

15. Yoshino Sakuzō, ed., *Meiji bunka zenshū*, 17:243.

books of acting "greedily, only for personal profit, and inconsiderate of Civilization under heaven." Such conduct, he stated, "would not be tolerated by any enlightened government around the world," so if the government did not strictly punish those pirates, Japan would be looked down upon by the civilized countries that took copyright seriously.[16]

All about the Printing Blocks

Ironically, what was enshrined by this "civilization" discourse and practiced in early Meiji Japan was not exactly the Western, and thus "universal," doctrine Fukuzawa described, but certain conventions of the Tokugawa book trade. When Fukuzawa translated copyright as *zōhan no menkyo*, he did not, as he later claimed, create new terms to capture the essence of something alien to the Japanese. What he did was simply combine two preexisting terms in Japanese—"license" (*menkyo*) and "possessing printing blocks" (*zōhan*)—to define copyright as "license to possess printing blocks." Indeed, in his writings and petitions, Fukuzawa identified the author, the creator of the work, as the one holding the exclusive rights for its uses and distribution. His periphrastic translation of copyright, resting on Tokugawa book-trade terminologies, led his contemporaries (and even Fukuzawa himself) to associate copyright not with the ownership of intellectual creations, but more with the possession of *han*, the tangible printing blocks.

To understand how this misperception occurred, we have to look into the essential roles printing blocks played in cultural production during the Tokugawa period (1603–1867). Publishing had become highly commercialized during this period. Even books published by official institutions or private individuals, which were traditionally not compiled for commercial gain, could be found circulating in the marketplace. And they were produced in the same cultural and technological environment as were the commercially released books. To publish a book, one had first to hire engravers to make printing blocks, printers to produce imprints, and binders to bind loose pages into books. The publishing process in late imperial China was very similar.[17] Unlike movable-type

16. Concerning the incredulous tone of this petition, see Tomita's annotation of it in "Honyaku jūhan no gi ni tsuki negai tatematsuri sōrō kakitsuke: tatsu jūgatsu."

17. For a general overview of how woodblock imprints were made in premodern China, see McDermott, *A Social History of the Chinese Book*, 9–39. For a general account of Tokugawa book production, see Kornicki, *The Book in Japan*, 47–55.

printing in Europe, which required publishers to make large numbers of copies at once, the woodblock printing popular in East Asia allowed publishers to print on demand or make a custom copy. Once a set of printing blocks was made, it could last for decades or even centuries, depending on the quality of the wood planks and the cumulative number of copies printed over time. Those who possessed the woodblock set of a book could, in theory, make as many copies as they liked, whenever they needed to, as long as ink and paper were available. Since the cost and the technical requirements for printing were low, the real substantial investment to publish a book was in the carving of printing blocks.[18] As tangible property, these printing blocks could be passed down as family, government, or company possessions for generations. They could be shared, rented, borrowed, or used as security for a loan, just like land and houses.[19]

Regulating and protecting the ownership of printing blocks would, understandably, be in the interests of those who possessed them or invested in them. In 1698, booksellers in Kyoto and Osaka petitioned the municipal government to prohibit reprinting of their publications within the local jurisdiction. By the early eighteenth century, booksellers and publishers in Japan's three major book-trade centers—Kyoto, Osaka, and Edo—had further established booksellers' guilds, known as *honya nakama*, to register the ownership of printing blocks, determine what kind of books could be published, and mediate conflicts among their members.[20] After being formally recognized by the Tokugawa authorities, these guilds further assisted the government in censoring newly published books via their register of printing blocks, and, in return, they gained the power to arrange legally recognized monopolies of different titles. If a manuscript passed the guild's review, the member who planned to publish it would receive a license to make printing blocks (*kaihan*). With the license, he would then own the exclusive right to use this particular block set to produce imprints. This exclusive right, known as *hankabu*, literally "stock of printing blocks," was also

18. On the low cost and legal technical requirement of woodblock printing, see Chow, *Publishing, Culture, and Power in Early Modern China*, 33–38. For a comparative discussion of how the technical differences between East Asian woodblock printing and European movable-type printing shaped the working processes and capital investments in their production methods, see McDermott and Burke, eds., *The Book Worlds of East Asia and Europe, 1450–1850*, 11–16.

19. *The Book in Japan*, 244–247; Brokaw, *Commerce in Culture*, 180–185.

20. For the localized prohibition against reprinting, see Yamamoto, *Edo jidai santo shuppanhō taigai*, 272–278.

transmittable and shareable like the physical printing blocks.²¹ Such measures appeared to be strikingly similar to the copyright system in eighteenth-century England, but the subject of protection, as well as the creation and justification of ownership, were profoundly different.²²

Throughout the eighteenth and nineteenth centuries, these guilds exerted powerful regional regulation of *hankabu* and, with the endorsement of the Tokugawa authorities, arbitrated disputes over *hankabu*, mostly different kinds of unauthorized reprinting, ranging from *jūhan* (duplicated printing blocks), to *ihan* (fake/forged printing blocks), to *ruihan* (partially duplicated printing blocks).²³ While official institutions and private individuals could not join the guilds and have their ownership protected in the same way, they shared the same belief in the importance of possessing printing blocks and could register their ownership of block sets with local authorities. They distinguished themselves from commercial booksellers in the book trade as *zōhansha*, possessors of the printing blocks. If an author wanted to retain absolute rights in a work, the simplest way would be to invest in the carving of the printing blocks and to possess the blocks physically. In other words, he had to become the *zōhansha* of his works.²⁴

That was exactly what Fukuzawa was when he started his publishing operation. Between 1867 and 1869, his correspondence and personal notes were replete with details concerning the production and retention of the printing blocks. These detailed accounts revealed how he, as an author-*zōhansha*, interacted with artisans, printers, and booksellers. In the summer of 1867, he hired xylographers to make the printing blocks of his *Raijū sōhō* (Rifle instruction manual), *Seiyō tabi annai* (Travel guide to the West), and *Jōyaku jūikkokuki* (Affairs of eleven treaty countries) at his house.²⁵ Though possessing the printing blocks, Fukuzawa was not himself involved in printing, binding, or marketing;

21. Kornicki, *The Book in Japan*, 179–184.

22. Most scholars of Japanese book history and legal history do not consider the *hankabu* sound evidence for proving that any notion of copyright existed in early modern Japan. See Kornicki, *The Book in Japan*, 242–251; Suwa, "Kinsei Bungei to Chosaku ken."

23. For a general overview of different categories of unauthorized reprinting, see Natsuo, *Kinsei shoki bungaku to shuppan bunka*, 358–379.

24. *The Book in Japan*, 244; Inaoka, "Zōhan, giban, hanken," 6–15. Technically, only private publishers could be identified as *zōhansha* (in contrast to commercial publishers as *hanmoto*), but many commercially released books in the Tokugawa period also carry the statement "XX *zōhan*" in the colophon.

25. *Fukuzawaya Yukichi no kenkyū*, 219–220.

instead, he collaborated with commercial booksellers to "publish" these books together. Tokyo bookseller Izumi, the issuer of *Raijū sōhō*, for instance, took Fukuzawa's block set back to his workshop to print in September 1867. Anticipating the cost of paper, printing, and binding, Izumi received 20 percent of the total sale as his commission, and Fukuzawa, as the block-owner, would claim the remaining net profit. To ensure that Izumi didn't underreport the print run, Fukuzawa used a common practice known as *tomehan* to retain a portion of printing blocks with him during the printing process. This forced Izumi to print those particular pages under his supervision; in return, he would know exactly how many copies Izumi produced, and, if copies with missing pages were found in the market, he could tell that Izumi had cheated him.[26]

Indeed, Fukuzawa enjoyed a certain autonomy as a *zōhansha* in terms of choosing partner booksellers and supervising part of the printing process, but he did not have full control of publishing and distribution. Since the bookseller-partner was in charge of the production cost, he could not ensure or estimate his net profit. Noticing this systemic disadvantage for the *zōhansha* in such collaborations, by the spring of 1868 he started to set up a comprehensive publishing operation at his own place. He hired in-house carvers, printers, and binders; purchased paper in bulk to lower the production cost; and relied upon booksellers only for distribution. Some of the printing blocks he made at the time are still housed at Keiō University, the school he established in 1858.[27] This move, which he later described as "the greatest gamble" of his life, made him a cultural entrepreneur. When his publishing business reached its peak in 1873, its annual sales were so high, as he proudly noted in his autobiography, that even government ministers would envy him.[28] Indeed, this move allowed him to establish complete control over the production of his own books, but it also meant that unauthorized reprinting would have a more acute impact on his livelihood because he had now invested not only in block making but also in printing and paper.

Throughout 1868, he submitted petitions to various authorities in Edo/Tokyo and Kyoto on an almost monthly basis urging them to punish those reprinting his books. Although the local officials usually responded to his petitions and complaints promptly, Fukuzawa encountered enormous obstacles to having those who reprinted his work punished, especially when his opponents were

26. For the practice of *tomehan*, see Makita, *Keihan shoseki shōshi*, 85–92.
27. When I visited Keiō University in 2008–2009, these blocks were stored in the basement of their old library.
28. *FYZ*, 7:150–152.

aristocrats or well-established scholars.[29] Even though he repeatedly used the civilization discourse to exert pressure on local officials to protect his profit, how far these cases could go largely relied upon individual officials' goodwill and determination, because there was no formal law in Japan backing the author-*zōhansha*'s monopoly on publishing his books.

This situation changed when the Meiji government promulgated *Shuppan jōrei* (The publication regulations) in May 1869. For the first time, the "exclusive profit" of "people who published books" gained through book publishing was granted by state legislation. In some ways, this could be seen as a victory for Fukuzawa's civilization discourse, as *Shuppan jōrei* clearly adopted the wording of *Seiyō jijō gaihen*. However, its definition of the "patentee" as entitled to the "exclusive profit" was ambivalent: while it promised to protect the publisher's "exclusive profit," the protection would be valid only during the lifetime of the *chojutsusha*/author. For decades, legal scholars in Japan have been debating whether the author was the person whom the *Shuppan jōrei* was meant to protect.[30] The law, despite its "civilized" appearance in wording, was implemented through the old booksellers' guilds in Tokyo, Kyoto, and Osaka. Owing to the limited capacity of the Meiji government at the time, the enforcement of the law was outsourced to the managers of these early modern institutions.[31] The weak new state, like its predecessor, offered these guilds specific legal accreditation and relied upon them to sustain a certain social and market order. What we see in this new Meiji regulation was more a continuation of, rather than a break from, late Tokugawa book-trade customs.

Aware of the guilds' authority in arbitrating disputes over unauthorized reprinting, Fukuzawa had previously submitted a plea to the Osaka Booksellers' Guild against those pirating his *Seiyō jijō* in Osaka. As a "layperson *zōhansha*," he was not recognized by the guild as one of their own and, as a result, had to rely upon a bookseller friend to pass on his plea. After the promulgation of *Shuppan jōrei*, in order to ensure that he would receive the full protection of his "monopoly profits," Fukuzawa registered himself as bookseller Fukuzawa and joined the Tokyo Booksellers' Guild in November 1869.[32] From 1869 to 1874,

29. Kawauchi, "Fukuzawa Yukichi no shoki no chosaku ken kakuritsu undō."

30. For example, Katsumoto, *Nihon chosakuken hō*, 26. Itō, "Chosakuken seido shi no sobyō." Mizuno, *Chosakukenhō*, 9.

31. *Chosakukenhō hyakunenshi*, 46. Ōie, *Chosakuken o kakuritsushita hitobito*, 6–7.

32. *Fukuzawaya Yukichi no kenkyū*, 238–239. "Fukuzawa Yukichi no Shoki no Chosakuken Kakuritsu Undō."

in most of his petitions to government authorities, he also presented himself as a merchant-landlord, rather than an author.[33] In the view of his contemporaries, his appeals against unauthorized reprinting were justified and accepted, not because he wrote the books but because he was the publisher who made and possessed the printing blocks of those books.

When he introduced this doctrine, emerging from and shaped by European movable-type print culture, to Japan, he was unavoidably subjected to the xylographic environment in which his books were produced. As a result, as he translated copyright as *zōhan no menkyo*, the long-lived commercial practices and cultural norms Fukuzawa and his contemporaries subscribed to influenced profoundly how it was understood and enforced. For example, in almost all the legal actions Fukuzawa took against those who reprinted his books and "stole his intellectual fruit," while he emphasized the unique nature of copyright as intangible property, his ultimate goal was, nonetheless, to destroy the tangible blocks of the pirated editions, so that only he could produce his books.

Fukuzawa's status as a block-owner was also displayed on the actual copies he published. On the title page of *Raijū sōhō* (fig. 1.1), one finds in the left column a statement indicating that the blocks were "processed by Mr. Fukuzawa" (*Fukuzawa shi zōhan*). A red seal was stamped on top of this statement as an additional declaration of ownership and a certification of authenticity. This was a rare bilingual seal that reads, "Copyright of Fukuzawa" (Copyright of 福澤氏), suggesting that, for him, the notion of *zōhan* and the concept of "copyright" were practically interchangeable. At the end of the third volume of *Seiyō jijō gaihen*, Fukuzawa listed all his publications and declared his ownership as the head of Keio School. The seal carved into the printing block reads, "Keio School possessed the printing blocks [of these books]"; at the end of this list, he stated in extra large and bold characters, "Bootlegging the printing blocks is prohibited" (fig. 1.2).

The practice of placing "XX *zōhan*" in the colophon or on the title page of a book, as well as stamping a block-owner's seal on top of such statements to indicate who owned the blocks, was invented by neither Fukuzawa nor Tokugawa booksellers. This practice and the very phrase *zōhan* were both foreign conventions that the early modern Japanese learned from China. Until the mid-nineteenth century, China had been the predominant cultural authority in East Asia. For centuries, Japanese aristocrats and monks imported Confucian classics, Buddhist and Daoist scriptures, literary works, and other Chinese books from China. These Chinese books enjoyed particular prestige in

33. *FYZ*, 19:441–478.

FIG. 1.1. Title page of *Raijū sōhō* (Rifle instruction manual), 1864.
Source: Raijū sōhō (Tokyo: Fukuzawa Yukichi, 1864).
Courtesy of the Digital Collections of Keio University Libraries.

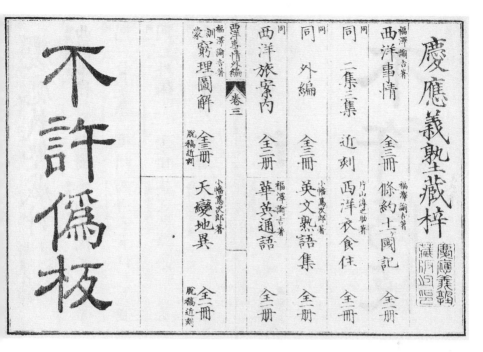

FIG. 1.2. Advertisement of Keio School's publication in the *Seiyō jijō gaihen*, 1869.
Source: *Seiyō jijō gaihen* (Tokyo: Keio School, 1869).
Courtesy of the Digital Collections of Keio University Libraries.

the Japanese book world, not only because the education most social elites received in Japan was mainly Chinese classical learning, but also because they were seen as the physical medium transmitting "Civilization" from its center in China to its periphery. During the Tokugawa period, while foreign trade was limited to Chinese and Dutch merchant ships, a large number of Chinese books, as one of the most significant imports, continued to be brought to Japan through Nagasaki by Chinese junks on a regular basis. The majority of these books would end up in the private collections of wealthy *daimyo*, but some of them were reproduced by Japanese booksellers or official institutions, with or without Japanese annotations.[34] When producing the local facsimile editions of Chinese books, Japanese publishers copied their original page layouts,

34. For the Sino-Japanese exchange of books, see Ōba, *Books and Boats*, chaps. 4 and 5; Matsuura, "Imports and Exports of Books by Chinese Junks in the Edo Period," in Nagase-Reimer ed., *Copper in the Early Modern Sino-Japanese Trade*, 175–195.

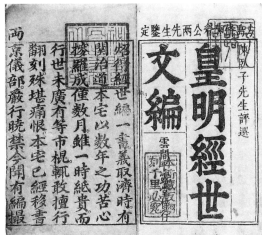

FIG. 1.3. Title page of *Huang Ming jingshi wenbian* (Collected essays about statecraft of the imperial Ming), printed by Pinglu Tang Studio between 1627 and 1644. Pinglu Tang Studio was the studio of late Ming literati-publisher Chen Zilong (1608–1647), also the compiler of this title. The seal on the top right corner reads, "Pinglu Tang Studio." The seal on the bottom left corner above the statement "carved and printed by Yunjian Pinglu Tang Studio" reads, "this office processes printing blocks [of this book]. [People who] reprint this book will be pursued and punished even if they live one thousand *li* away." It is followed by a harsh statement by Chen denouncing unauthorized reprints of this title.

the design of their colophons or cover pages, and the Chinese binding styles. Subsequently, works of traditional Chinese learning by Japanese scholars also imitated the Chinese books to borrow some of the cultural prestige they embodied. As a result, Chinese books were held up as models of what a proper book should look like in early modern Japan. The physical appearance of a considerable proportion of Japanese books produced in the Tokugawa period, especially scholarly titles, shared similar characteristics with the Chinese books produced in Ming-Qing China, including the phrase *zōhan* and the block-owner's seal (see figs. 1.3 and 1.4).

Zōhan was a loanword from Chinese *cangban*, which also literally means "possessing the printing blocks." As early as the late twelfth century, the term *cangban* had appeared in colophons or on title pages of printed books. In the Chinese bibliographical tradition, the statement "XX *cangban*" had been used to identify the publisher of a book, but recent Chinese rare book scholars have reached a new consensus that, considering that the ownership of printing blocks might change

FIG. 1.4. Title page of an early eighteenth-century Japanese edition of *Cangming chidu* (Correspondences of Mr. Azure-sea). The statement in the left column reads, "Edo Bookshop Suzanbō cut blocks for printing," and the seal reads, "suzan." Suzanbō was the publishing house owned by Kobayashi Shinbē in Edo (today's Tokyo). Courtesy of Harvard-Yenching Library Chinese Rare Books Digitization Projects.

over time, "XX *cangban*" was not to be viewed as infallible information to determine who the publisher was; rather, it was to be seen as a statement notifying readers that the blocks were retained by "XX" after the printing process.[35]

A standard title page found in late imperial Chinese books, as figure 1.3 shows, usually contains the essential information about a book—its title, name/byname of its author/compiler, its publisher, or who possessed the printing blocks of this book. Such title pages were, as Sören Edgren argues, used initially as commercial advertisements carrying basic messages for marketing purposes; they are now invaluable yet underused sources to help historians of the book understand the late imperial book trade and print cultures.[36] The title page was also a unique space where Ming-Qing publishers declared their ownership of books. In addition to stating "XX *cangban*," publishers/block-owners would stamp their seal on top of the statement. By the late Ming, some publishers designed seals or colophons with trademark-like decorative images or detailed information about the block-owner (address, motivation for publishing, etc.) as a way to increase their "branding" power or express their individuality (see fig. 1.5).[37] This kind of seal was most likely used, in addition to decorating title pages, as a simple device to help readers and customers differentiate an authentic copy from an unauthorized one. As a Hangzhou publisher declared in the block-owner's seal he stamped on his 1695 edition of *Chunqiu dan he xiyi* (The Dan-he style analysis of *Spring and Autumn*), "the printing blocks are retained at my studio. . . . [I]f this seal is missing [from a copy], then it means [the copy] is certainly an unauthorized reprint."[38]

Juxtaposing the title pages and the block-owner's seals produced in Ming-Qing China, in Tokugawa Japan, and by Fukuzawa Yukichi in the early Meiji era, one can easily see the similarity of their layouts, the information they contain, and presumably the idea of block-ownership they represented. The late imperial Chinese notion of *cangban*/possessing the printing blocks, as well as the practice of stamping the block-owner's seal as the declaration of authenticity and ownership, borrowed by Tokugawa Japan, became the crucial resources for Fukuzawa to translate and practice what he claimed to be a "new" and Western doctrine that had no local equivalent.

35. Shen, "Shuo 'benya cangban,'" *Shu yun youyou yi mai xiang*, 39–140.
36. Edgren, "The Fengmianye (Cover Page) as a Source for Chinese Publishing History."
37. Inoue, *Min Shin gakujutsu henshenshi*, 25–26, 36.
38. "Shuo 'benya cangban,'" 144.

FIG. 1.5. Title page of *Xinjuan zengbu quanxiang pinglin gujin lienü zhuan*, published by Yu Wentai Santaiguan, late sixteenth century. The *ding*-shape *cangban* seal in the middle column reads, ". . . customers please find this seal/mark to identify the authentic copies." This elaborate seal is a fine example of how such seals were used as an authentication device. Courtesy of Harvard-Yenching Library Chinese Rare Books Digitization Projects.

Retranslating "Copyright"

It is hard to assess whether Fukuzawa's series of efforts to promote and protect his copyright in the late 1860s was successful. Indeed, his introduction of copyright in *Seiyō jijō gaihen* had a positive impact on the making of the *Shuppan jōrei*, and most of his petitions and complaints against unauthorized reprinting garnered prompt response from government agencies and the Tokyo Booksellers' Guild. However, his ownership of his works was recognized by the booksellers' guilds and local officials mainly because of his status as a block-owner, a bookseller who happened to publish his works, rather than an author declaring the exclusive ownership of his writings. Although he managed to obtain favorable results in most cases, had pirates' blocks destroyed, and received some compensation from the pirates, these actions were not particularly cost-effective. It usually took months to settle a case, yet the compensation, compared to Fukuzawa's annual income from publishing, was insignificant. Booksellers around Japan also do not seem to have curtailed their reprinting of Fukuzawa's books because of his ruthless legal actions or the "civilization" discourse he created for copyright. While Fukuzawa continued expanding his publishing operation, others kept pirating his latest works, such as *Gakumon no susume* (The encouragement of learning). At least six different pirated editions of this book were circulated in the market soon after it was published in 1872.[39] Fukuzawa estimated that, while he sold around 200,000 authentic copies of the first volume, various pirates must have sold at least 100,000 "fake" copies.[40]

In the summer of 1873, maybe frustrated by the spreading piracy of his books all over Japan, Fukuzawa decided to further raise his fellow countrymen's awareness of copyright by introducing a new and more accurate translation of this doctrine. By combining "*han*/block" and "*ken*/right" together, he coined the new word *hanken* for copyright. The neologism *hanken*, some argue, reflects Fukuzawa's intellectual development on rights, social contracts, and liberalism, because he had replaced "*menkyo*/license" with "*ken*/right."[41] However, just as his introduction of "*zōhan no menkyo*" in 1868 aimed to make a case for his

---

39. Nagao, *Fukuzawaya Yukichi no kenkyū*, 267.

40. *FYZ*, 3:23. When stating how popular his books were, Fukuzawa often took the sale of pirated copies generously into account; however, it was never clear how he estimated the sale of pirated copies. Some scholars have pointed out the fact that Fukuzawa had a proclivity to hyperbolize his own influence; see Kinmonth, "Fukuzawa Reconsidered."

41. Nagao, *Fukuzawaya Yukichi no kenkyū*, 287.

countermeasures against unauthorized reprinting, his second translation was also on a specific mission. To understand what motivated him to replace *menkyo* with *ken*, we need to situate his second translation of "copyright" in its proper context and the new types of copyright infringements he was struggling with at the time.

By 1873, most pirates Fukuzawa encountered were operating in a legal gray zone. They no longer produced straightforward reprints of Fukuzawa's books. Some disguised a pirated edition as a different book by giving it a different title. For example, one Aichi bookseller made a pirated version of Fukuzawa's *Kairekiben* (Defending the changes in the calendar) with the title *Taiyōreki kōshaku* (On the solar calendar), and a Tokyo pirated edition of *Sekai kunizukushi* (To the end of the world) went under the heading *Chikyū ōrai* (Around the globe).[42] Sometimes they would combine contents to recast separate books as one "new" volume. A book found in Osaka entitled *Meiji yōbunshō* (Meiji writing manual), for example, was a collection of texts selected from Fukuzawa's *Kyūri zukai* (Illustrated introduction of physical sciences) and *Seiyō jijō*.[43] Because their contents and titles were not precisely the same as Fukuzawa's original works, it was difficult to label them as the standard *jūhan* editions. Also, these books were duly registered and licensed at their local booksellers' guilds, and thus they were, technically, legal publications protected by the *Shuppan jōrei*. Even worse, many of them were published not by commercial publishers, but by local governments, in the name of enlightenment and civilization. For example, the county governments of Aichi, Nagatsu, and Oda all published their own editions of *Gakumon no susume* as a textbook for use by the local elementary schools.[44]

In 1872–1873, Fukuzawa launched a series of legal actions and petitions aiming to combat these legally recognized "fake editions." Among them was a case against the Osaka government that particularly forced him to rethink the nature of copyright, as well as the relationships among the law, private property rights, and state power. In spring 1873, learning that the Osaka government had published a copybook that included some content from his *Keimō tenarai no fumi* (Enlightenment preliminary copybook), he petitioned the mayor of Tokyo, who happened to be his close friend, urging the city government to protect his property and destroy the blocks of that Osaka copybook. "There is no way in the world to enhance Civilization besides writing books": he employed

42. Ibid., 452, 471–477.
43. Ibid., 446.
44. "Postscript," *FYZ*, vol. 3.

his "civilization" discourse again and argued that to ensure intellectual advancement, "the civilized West enacted harsh laws against piracy to protect intellectual property."[45] In this petition, he emphasized that such strict laws are fixed; therefore the government, as the executor of the law, should not violate its rules. The exclusive profit of the officially licensed publication should be protected, and no matter where or who the pirates were, they must be prosecuted.

After receiving the Tokyo government's complaint on behalf of Fukuzawa, the Osaka government, in its reply to the Tokyo authorities, denied Fukuzawa's charges by arguing that they were not a profit-driven pirate but an enlightenment agent trying to bring modern civilization to students in Osaka. They made their copybook based on Fukuzawa's copybook, because Fukuzawa's original text was not applicable to their students, and not because they wanted to take any commercial advantage. Since this was an educational initiative for the greater cause of civilizing Japan, and the book was registered properly, they saw no reason for them to be labeled as felons. They also explained that they were unable to surrender the printing blocks to be destroyed because the copies had been printed by movable type and the type set had been disassembled. Given the fact that now the copybook was out of print and there were no printing blocks to be burned, the Osaka government suggested that the Tokyo authorities and Fukuzawa relax and withdraw the case.[46]

Fukuzawa did not want to back down. Between May and July, he and the Osaka government exchanged several rounds of correspondence via the Tokyo municipal government. Fukuzawa, to override the Osaka government's authority as a private citizen, proclaimed copyright as a "public law under the Heaven (*tenka no kōhō*),"[47] a universal principle superior to the Osaka government and its educational initiative. Enlightening Japanese schoolchildren was essential, he argued, but the Osaka government should properly purchase his copybooks instead of plagiarizing them.[48] The Osaka government, on the other hand, criticized Fukuzawa for exhibiting great selfishness and greed. They accused him of forcing poor children, in the name of "Civilization," to buy a book that was only partially useful to them. They further pointed out that their copybook was technically not a pirated edition because they reprinted only the selected

45. *FYZ*, 19:449.
46. Ibid., 457.
47. Ibid., 449–450.
48. Ibid., 457–458.

"forty-seven words" they considered useful, hinting that Fukuzawa's copybook was flawed. Since the rest of their book was original, it was legitimately a different work.[49] In return, Fukuzawa declared that all the excuses the Osaka government made would not change the very fact that their copybook contained words from his copybook. Even if the Osaka copybook had only forty-seven words from Fukuzawa's copybook, those forty-seven words belonged to him, he claimed, and therefore the Osaka copybook "is accordingly my own [Fukuzawa's] property!"[50]

In July 1873, as part of this exchange of letters, Fukuzawa submitted a unique petition to the Tokyo authorities—his translation of an entry on copyright from an American legal dictionary.[51] It was in this petition that a new term for "copyright," namely, *hanken*, first appeared. By presenting this dictionary entry, some scholars argue, it seems that Fukuzawa was attempting to prove once again that Western countries had strict laws and harsh punishments to protect copyright, just as he had noted in *Seiyō jijō gaihen*. But the real point he wanted to make might have been hidden in the annotation he attached with the dictionary entry. In the annotation, he carefully articulated the difference between the "real" meaning of copyright and the not-so-accurate Japanese reception of this concept, for which he was partly responsible. He tried to distinguish right (*ken*) from license/permission (*menkyo*).

"Copyright used to be translated as official permission (*menkyo*) to publish, but it is not quite an accurate translation," he explained in this annotation and indirectly admitted that his first translation of "copyright" might have led to misunderstandings of the notion. He then clarified that "[copyright] means that the author who writes a book enjoys the monopolistic right to make blocks to reproduce his work and others may not freely copy it." The legitimacy of copyright comes from authorship. An author's ownership of his works and the right to reproduce them came into being because the author is the creator and, hence, is the natural owner of the works. "So copyright is the exclusive right to publish, or could be abbreviated as the right to printing blocks, *hanken*."[52]

49. Ibid., 461–462.

50. Ibid., 462–464.

51. Ibid., 467–468. According to Fukuzawa, the section he translated is *Jon·haowirusu shi hōritsu infu* (ヂョン・ハヂウィルス氏法律韻府, Legal notes of Mr. Jon Haowirusu). However, even now, scholars remain unsure as to the identity of "Zuyon Haouwirusu ヂョン・ハヂウィルス" and as to what exactly the title should be.

52. *FYZ*, 19:468.

The role government should play, according to Fukuzawa, was simple: "The only duty government has [regarding copyright] is to, as a manifestation of the government's commitment, prohibit piracy."[53] By emphasizing the status of copyright as a kind of private property created by an author's mental labor rather than a kind of license or privilege granted by the state's grace, Fukuzawa attempted to separate *hanken* from the traditional licensing-registering system the Meiji government had adopted from the Tokugawa period. He argued that the state had a duty to protect people's property by strict enforcement of well-crafted laws and regulations, but this duty did not confer on the government the right to freely reproduce people's works whenever it saw fit. The essential intention underlying Fukuzawa's argument has to be understood within the context of his copyright-infringement struggles during that time—in this case, the government was the one pirating his works. If copyright were justified as a license granted by the government, the government that extended its will beyond the license and published authors' works without authorization might not be engaging in acts considered illegal. This was the fundamental problem that Fukuzawa identified when he stubbornly argued against the Osaka government. As he complained in one petition to the mayor of Tokyo, he knew he was just a commoner under the rule of government and had little power against it.[54]

After Fukuzawa submitted this translation and, once again, employed the rules of the "civilized" West to justify his claim, it seems that the Osaka authorities had been checkmated. If the Osaka and Tokyo governments would like to establish "civilized" rule, they were obliged to respect Fukuzawa's property rights and follow the law as well. By October, the only counterattack they could muster against Fukuzawa was his alleged offense against government authority. They complained that he had written too many petitions against the Osaka government, and the discourteous language in these petitions had effectively disgraced the government.[55] In December, the Ministry of Justice stepped in and decided this case. An Osaka official was punished for malfeasance insofar as he had reprinted Fukuzawa's works without official permission; he was fined four yen.[56]

Hanken, the new term Fukuzawa coined, was officially written into the state's law when the Meiji government revised *Shuppan jōrei* in 1875. According to the

---

53. Ibid.
54. Ibid., 469.
55. Ibid., 473.
56. The pronouncement is quoted from *Chosakukenhō hyakunen shi*, 53.

1875 revision of *Shuppan jōrei*, authors, translators, or publishers could apply for a *hanken* certificate for their book at the newly established Home Ministry. Once the certification was approved, the applicant would be granted a thirty-year exclusive monopoly on the book. Authors and publishers could also choose not to apply for a *hanken* certificate and allow their books to be reprinted freely. This new legislation represented a significant departure from the earlier versions that preserved more Tokugawa conventions. First of all, the government took over from the booksellers' guilds the business of ownership registration. These early modern institutions lost their legal power to arbitrate ownership disputes. Second, the subject of registration changed from the traditional *hankabu* closely associated with the possession of printing blocks to the general right granted by the law to the author. In addition to conventional, straightforward reprinting (*jūhan*), the new law also identified plagiarizing copyrighted content as an infringement.

Although the 1875 revision empowered authors to claim and protect their rights, in actual fact the majority of *hanken* applicants in the 1880s and 1890s were publishers or author-publishers like Fukuzawa. So it was not surprising that some of the old norms of the book trade continued to be practiced. Many booksellers who had possessed blocks since the late Tokugawa period identified themselves as the rightful *hanken* holder and considered *hanken* to be something like printing blocks that could be rented or shared. For example, bookseller Naitō Denemon actively signed contracts with other booksellers to share *hanken* (and the block set) of individual books. He also at one point sued the Ministry of Education for infringing his *hanken*, because the ministry had republished in its elementary school readers part of an old title whose printing blocks he held. The *zōhan* stamps and seals continued to be used as a device to declare ownership of books/blocks and to authenticate imprints. During this period, as letterpress-printing machines became more popular in Japan, more and more books adopted the "Western-style" layout and no longer had the traditional title page. *Zōhan* stamps and seals, by then, would appear more regularly at the very end of the book on a page known as *okuzuke*.[57] As a variation of the *tomehan*

---

57. The use of *okuzuke* could be traced back to the mid-Tokugawa period. The Tokugawa *bakufu* military government authorities, for censorship purposes, asked publishers and booksellers to print the names of author(s), printers, and distributors on every copy they produced, so that they could be held accountable. An extra page, known as *okuzuke*, containing this information was inserted at the very end of the book. For a brief overview of *okuzuke*, see Yagi, "Okuzuke gaishi."

practice, some authors would stamp their seal on the *okuzuke* as a way to cal-culate the print run and ensure that they received the right amount in royalties. For example, Fukuzawa Yukichi kept a record of how many sheets one of his authors (also a Keiō employee) had stamped, and how much royalty he paid based on the number of seals stamped. Famous Meiji author Natsume Sōseki (1867–1916) also had his own notes on copyright seals and royalties.[58]

This Meiji twist on the old practice of seal stamping was further popularized after the *Hankenhō* (Copyright Law) was issued in 1893. According to the law, to possess a copyright/*hanken* of a certain book, one must register the book with the Home Ministry. After registering with the government, the applicant would receive a copyright certificate. A holder of a copyright certificate was obligated to put the fixed convention *"hanken shoyū* (copyright retained)*"* on every actual copy of the book as an indication that the book had been properly copyrighted. This fixed convention, required by the law, usually appeared on the *okuzuke* page, along with the book's basic identification. It was illegal for individuals who had not registered the copyright of a book to put *"hanken shoyū"* on copies of that book; yet it was also impermissible for those who had a registered copy-right not to put this statement on their books. Japanese booksellers very quickly established a new custom by combining this legally mandatory conven-tion with the old practice of seal stamping. Gradually, *zōhan* stamps evolved into the *hanken* seal (*hanken no yin*) of the author or the publisher. One could often find the red copyright seal or stamp in an elaborately designed square stating *"hanken shoyū."* (fig. 1.6)

This practice was adopted by Japanese publishers so that they could continue stating *"hanken shoyū"* and stamping *hanken* seals on *okuzuke* pages even when the laws that enforced doing so no longer existed. In 1899, to meet the require-ment of joining the Berne Convention, the international agreement governing copyright,[59] the Meiji government abolished this copyright law and issued the new *Chosakukenhō* (Copyright Law), modeled after the French copyright law.

---

58. Inaoka, "Zōhan, giban, hanken," 97–100.

59. Joining the Berne Convention was one of the conditions European countries imposed on Japan in the 1890s when Japan was trying to alter the unequal treaties it had with European powers in the mid-nineteenth century. This convention was in fact the first "equal" international treaty Japan signed with European countries. Japan joined the Berne Convention as a nation-state and was treated as a member equal to European members. By comparison, the United States joined the Berne Convention only in 1988, and China did not join until 1992. The Berne Convention and its counterpart, the Paris Convention, are generally considered to be the origin of "international intellectual property laws."

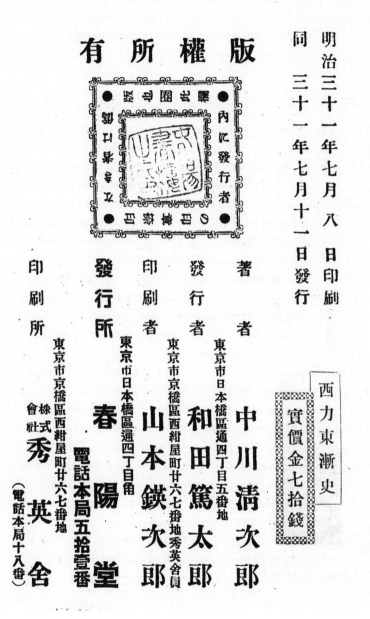

FIG. 1.6. Copyright page of *Seiryoku tōzen shi* (History of Western aggression in the Orient), 1898. Below the "*haken soyū*" statement is a frame reserved for the copyright seal. The statement in the decorative border declares, "If the publisher's seal is not found inside [this frame], this is a bootlegged copy." The seal in the frame reads "Shun'yō dō."
Source: *Seiryoku tōzen shi* (Tokyo: Shun'yō dō, 1898).

In this new law, the French term *droit d'auteur* was introduced, and the common-law copyright was replaced by the civil-law author's rights as the doctrine Japan officially followed.[60] After the new law was put into effect, *"hanken shoyū"* was no longer mandatory; this practice, however, remained very popular in Japan throughout the first half of the twentieth century.

From *Hanken* to *Banquan*

Hanken was introduced in China and adopted as the Chinese term for copyright at the turn of the twentieth century when the direction of the flow of books in East Asia was reversed after the Sino-Japanese War. China's shocking defeat in 1895 was interpreted by Qing elites at the time as definite proof that the top-down Meiji Restoration had successfully transformed Japan into a strong nation, but the series of reforms China underwent in the name of "self-strengthening" around the same time had been ineffective. This shock created profound intellectual doubt as to the superiority of Chinese "Civilization," as well as a deeper psychological complex toward Japan. As concerned scholars and the gentry started to call for more radical institutional reform, Japan, which had long been regarded as culturally inferior by Chinese elites, became a potential model. Japan's victory, they believed, demonstrated the possibility for a once-defeated and non-European country to "catch up" in a few decades via full-scale Westernization. For the first time, the Chinese intellectual community started to take Western knowledge seriously, and this sea change in intellectual trends was quickly reflected in their reading preferences.

As educated Chinese hastened to consume and adopt Western knowledge, to cope with the challenges posed by advancing imperialist powers, they discovered nearby Japan as a perfect shortcut to Western civilization. Before 1895, most Western knowledge was introduced in China via translation by European and American missionaries and their Chinese assistants. Although the Qing state did establish institutions like the *Tongwenguan* (Imperial Language College, est. 1862) in Beijing, teaching European languages and sending students to Europe to study since the 1860s, it took a long-term investment to cultivate enough qualified translators with a good command of both European languages and Chinese. Take Lin Shu's collaborator Wang Shouchang, for example. He

---

60. For the making of chosakukenhō and how the subject of legal protection changed from copyright to the *droit d'auteur* after Japan joined the Berne Convention, see *Chosakukenhō hyakunenshi*.

spent six years in Paris studying law and French before coming back to China as a French instructor at the Fuzhou Naval Academy. On the other hand, learning Japanese seemed to be an easier alternative owing to a large number of Chinese characters/*kanji* in standard Japanese at the time. Advocates for Japanese learning claimed that it was possible for educated Chinese to master Japanese within a few months. In 1896, the *Tongwenguan* set up its Japanese program, and some private individuals and provincial officials also initiated Japanese learning or translation projects. By translating books from Japanese as opposed to European languages, they believed, China would be able to accelerate its absorption of Western knowledge exponentially.[61] As the radical reformer Kang Youwei (1858–1927) promised in his *Riben shumu zhi* (Bibliography of Japanese books), "the Europeans were cattle and the Japanese were farmers," but by reading Japanese works on Western knowledge, "we [the Chinese] could just lie back and reap what they cultivated."[62]

Japanese officials and publishers also quickly noticed Japan's advantage in being the broker of Western knowledge for China. As the Japanese consul general in Shanghai Odagiri Masunosuke (1868–1934) stated in an 1898 interview, he believed now was a "good time" for the Japanese publishing industry to enter the Chinese book market. Since the "Chinese people's pride has been fairly shaken after the war," he claimed, they had become willing to learn from Japan's successful experience and to start "buying books—on all kinds of subjects from politics, law, and economy to industry, science, history, and geography—from Japan regularly."[63] Believing that Japan could benefit politically and commercially from exporting books to China, several major publishing houses, such as Hakubunkan, Fuzanbō, and Maruzen, as well as Pan-Asianists such as Azuma Heiji (1853–1917) and his *Zenrin yakushokan* (Friendly-Neighbor Translation Press), quickly set up branches in China and actively shipped books to the Chinese market.[64] Fuzanbō, at its peak, was able to export to China thousands of copies of their titles on Western knowledge on a regular basis for several years

61. Tam, ed., *Zhongguo yi ribenshu zonghe mulu*, 58–59.

62. Kang, *Riben shumu zhi*, in Jiang and Zhang, eds., *Kang Youwei quanji*,3:263–264. Similar arguments may be found in Zhang Zhidong's and Liang Qichao's writings as well. For further discussion, see chapter 2.

63. "Shinkoku bōeki no zento," *Taiyō* 4:21 (October 1898): 220.

64. "Shinkoku muke no shoseki shuppan gaikyō oyobi Tō-A kōshi setsuritsu jōkyō," *Tosho geppō* 3:5 (February 23, 1905). In this article, the author could find only fifty-three titles of Japanese works translated and published by Japanese publishers before 1904.

before they were overwhelmed by Chinese piracy and decided to withdraw from the mainland market.[65]

In addition to the considerable volume of Japanese titles (and their Chinese translations) exported to China by Japanese publishers, Chinese students and political activists based in Japan also played a key role in this Sino-Japanese circulation of knowledge and books. Forced into exile after the failed 1898 Reform, for instance, Kang Youwei's disciple Liang Qichao set up several presses to publish and promote their reform ideas as well as Western knowledge. Japanese books and journals were his main resources for "accessing" modern Western political ideas.[66] Beginning in 1900, Chinese students studying in Japan also organized translation-study groups, such as *Yishu huibian she* (Society for Book-Translation and Composition, est. 1900) and *Hunan bianyi she* (Hunanese Society for Translation, est. 1902), to systematically translate and publish Japanese titles to "enlighten" their fellow countrymen. These books and journals were mostly produced in Yokohama and Tokyo by local printing houses and then exported to China.

The centuries-long tradition of cultural exports from China to Japan was reversed. Japan was no longer on the receiving end in the East Asian book trade but now emerged as the principal provider of "new" knowledge in the region. Japanese works quickly became the overwhelming majority of foreign-language works translated into Chinese. From 1896 to 1911, according to Tam Yue-him's extensive survey, 958 titles were translated into Chinese from Japanese, for an annual average of 63.86 titles.[67] Between 1902 and 1904, 60.2 percent of all translations published in Chinese were translated from Japanese.[68] Accompanying the flood of translations of Japanese titles was a sudden influx of new terminology, mostly two-Chinese-character expressions coined by Japanese to translate Western concepts into the Chinese lexicon.[69] While these Japanese expressions provided a new cultural infrastructure for late Qing Chinese to discuss Western things and ideas, this unprecedented lexical exchange also altered the basic expressions and writing styles of Chinese.[70]

65. Fuzanbō, *Fuzanbō gojūnen*, 620.

66. Liang Qichao spent more than a decade in Japan during his exile there in 1898. See Fogel, ed., *The Role of Japan in Liang Qichao's Introduction of Modern Western Civilization to China.*

67. *Zhongguo Yi Ribenshu Zonghe Mulu*, 61.

68. Tsien, "Western Impact on Chinese through Translation," 315. Tsien's statistic was based on *Yishu jingyan lu.*

69. Shin, *Kindai Nitchū goi kōryūshi.*

70. Reynolds, *China, 1898–1912*; also see Wang Fansen, *Zhongguo jidai sixiang yu xueshu xipu,* 181–194.

The term *hanken* was one of these new Japanese terms picked up by Chinese at the turn of the twentieth century. *Hanken* in Japanese was borrowed into Chinese as *banquan*; it has been used as the Chinese translation for "copyright" since then. The words "copyright" and "literary piracy" had appeared in English-Chinese dictionaries as early as the 1860s. In the widely distributed and authoritative *English and Chinese Dictionary*, for instance, William Lobscheid translated "copyright" as *yinshu zhi quan* (right to print books), and "literary piracy" as *zei ren shu de* (one who steals others' book). His translation, however, does not seem to have caught on in China.[71] When the Society for the Diffusion of Christian and General Knowledge among the Chinese (*Guangxuehui*; hereafter, SDCK), the Shanghai-based missionary press, first started to promote the doctrine of copyright in 1896–1897 against Chinese unauthorized reprinting, they used the preexisting and more neutral term *fanke* (reproduce/duplicate [the printing blocks]) in Chinese to refer to literary piracy, or unauthorized reprinting. When referring to the doctrine of copyright in their petitions and announcements, they defined it as a "Western custom" (*xili*) that prosecutes people who "reprint another's works and sell them for profit" as robbers stealing another's property.[72] But they never gave a name to this "Western custom."

The first person to use the loanword *banquan* in Chinese texts to refer to the phenomenon of copyright may have been Kang Youwei. In spring 1898, he presented a chronicle of the Meiji Restoration, *Riben bianzheng kao* (A study of Japan's political reform) to the Guangxu Emperor, hoping to persuade the emperor to launch a full-scale institutional reform modeled after Japan. When discussing the promulgation of *Shuppan jōrei* in 1869, Kang argued that "the rise of Europe" could be attributed to Europeans' "encouragement" of learning and innovation—for example, something called *banquan* was awarded to those who "write books." Realizing how such an incentive had animated European intellectuals and inventors to create new ideas and machines, Meiji Japan issued laws to institutionalize copyright/*banquan* awards, and, Kang believed, that was one of the reasons that science and technology in Japan had rapidly advanced in the past decades.[73] Like Fukuzawa, Kang also emphasized the correlation between

71. Lobscheid, *English and Chinese Dictionary with the Punti and Mandarin Pronunciation*, 502.

72. "Guangxuehui yanjin fanyin xinzhu shuji gaoshi" [The SDCK's announcement that reprinting new publications is strictly forbidden], *Wanguo gongbao* 97 (February 1897): 16699–16700. For contextual discussion of this order and its historical origin, see chapter 4.

73. Kang Youwei, *Riben bianzheng kao*, 39.

copyright protection and the wealth and power of a nation. During the ill-fated 1898 Reform, the Guangxu Emperor did issue, among hundreds of new policies, an imperial edict to grant people who "write new books" the privilege to enjoy exclusively the profit generated by their books, but the term *banquan* did not appear in this edict.[74] It is also not clear whether this edict was ever executed; this radical reform program ended prematurely after the Empress Dowager Cixi and the conservatives retook power. Kang's discussion of *banquan* might not have circulated widely at all at the time, after all. *Riben bianzheng kao* was primarily written for just one reader—the Guangxu Emperor—and for decades it remained an unpublished manuscript held in the imperial library at the Forbidden City. Some handwritten copies may have circulated at the court and among Kang's coterie, but the work never reached a general audience.[75]

Between 1898 and 1903, the term *banquan* appeared sporadically in official correspondence, newspaper articles, and public letters about institutionalizing domestic and international copyright protection in China. For example, *Qingyi bao* (The China discussion), a political journal established by Liang Qichao in Yokohama in the aftermath of the 1898 Reform, translated an article from *Tōyō keizai shinpō* (Toyo economic news) on how the lack of copyright protection in China was hurting the business of Japanese publishers who wanted to "enlighten the Chinese." In addition to the translation, *Qingyi bao* also published an editorial supporting the idea that the Japanese government should pressure the Qing court into protecting copyright. The author, most likely Liang, expressed how "enraptured" he was when he learned about the Japanese attempts to "spread copyright to China." Restressing the correlation among copyright, the translation of "New Learning" knowledge from Japan, and progress in China, he hoped that such a Japanese incentive would help the Chinese to establish this new system that "didn't exist in China before."[76]

74. "Guangxu ershi si nian wu yue shiqi ri neige feng shangyu" [The imperial edict the ministry received on the seventeenth day in the fifth month of the twenty-fourth year of the Guangxu Emperor], *Guangxu xuantong liangchao shangyu dang*, 24:230b–231a.

75. Although this title had been referred to and mentioned in other documents during the 1898 Reform, and some of the ideas and arguments Kang presented in this manuscript had been recycled and modified by him in the 1900s when Kang reinvented the history of the 1898 Reform, it was never published. In 1947, Mary Clabaugh Wright saw a handwritten copy of it in Beijing and made a microfilm of that copy, but the original manuscript was not discovered until the 1980s.

76. "Du Dongyang Jingji Xinbao bu banquan yu Zhina lun" [Reading about Toyo economic news's discussion on how to promote copyright in China], *Qingyi bao* 13 (March 21, 1899).

When the issue of copyright protection for foreign publishers in China was brought up by the United States and Japan in the aftermath of the Boxer Rebellion, the term *banquan* was used by Chinese treaty commissioners Lü Haihuan (1843–1927) and Sheng Xuanhuai (1844–1916) to refer to copyright in their imperial memorials and their correspondence with governors-general. Unlike Kang and Liang, most top officials in the Qing court seemed to see the American and Japanese request to legislate international copyright protection as a threat rather than a blessing. Zhang Baixi (1847–1907), the highest official in charge of educational affairs, as well as major governors-general, such as Zhang Zhidong (1837–1909) and Liu Kunyi (1830–1902), all sent anxious telegrams to state their firm opposition to the request. Copyright was "irrelevant" to China currently, they argued, and it would slow down China's Westernization course, because, once treaties protected the copyright of foreign works, the cost of translating foreign books would increase so much that enlightening society would become impossible.[77] Owing to their strong opposition, when the Sino-US Renewed Treaties of Trade and Navigation and Sino-Japanese Renewed Treaties of Trade and Navigation were officially signed in early 1903, the copyright protection defined in the treaty clause was a compromised one. It protected only the copyright of books that were "prepared particularly for Chinese readers," and created a loophole for Chinese publishers freely to translate any foreign books written for a general audience.[78]

This treaty clause, despite its obvious flaw, was seen by Chinese publishers as a special privilege that could potentially put Chinese booksellers at a disadvantage. Worrying that now foreign booksellers were equipped with a legal weapon against them and Chinese pirates, some started urging the Qing state to recognize and protect Chinese booksellers' and authors' copyright. In 1903, for example, the proprietor of Civilization Books (*Wenming shuju*), Lian Quan (1868–1931), petitioned Zhang Baixi on copyright protection.[79] Because of *banquan*, "the privilege to monopolize the profit of certain publications was a general doctrine of the five continents," he argued; the Qing should, "like every other nation," establish "strict laws to reward those who exert their hard labor

77. Zhongyang yanjiuyuan jindaishi yanjiusuo ed., *Zhong-Mei guanxi shiliao: guangxu chao*, 5:3271–3272; Wang and Wang, eds., *Qingji waijiao shiliao*, 2712–2717.

78. Wu, "Qingmo Minchu Zhong-Mei banquan zhi zheng," in *Guoli zhengzhi daxue lishi xuebao*, 38, 97–136.

79. For more discussion of other aspects of this petition, see chapter 4.

[to produce books] and to prevent piracy and counterfeits."[80] A similar argument was made by Yan Fu in his public letter to Zhang as well. Although reprinting could in principle help popularize ideas quickly, he warned Zhang, it would acutely discourage authors and translators from producing new works; therefore, "in nations that do not have copyright laws, the publishing business is usually flat or even dead." He thus urged the Qing state to promote *banquan*, reward those who "import civilization" to China, and crack down on piracy before it was too late. If Chinese authors and booksellers enjoyed the "insignificant profit" of *banquan*, he believed that Chinese talents would shine and China would be able to catch up with European countries in twenty years.[81] In the same year, Commercial Press also published a small pamphlet entitled *Banquan kao* (On copyright), a Chinese translation of the "copyright" entry in the *Encyclopedia Britannica*. In its preface, the proprietor of Commercial Press stated that he was publishing this brief introduction on the development and the legal principles of copyright because he believed it to be urgent and necessary for China to establish its own copyright law, especially after the newly signed trade treaties with Japan and the United States had granted foreigners conditional copyright protection.[82]

The words of these early advocates of *banquan*/copyright in China read like Fukuzawa Yukichi's with a time delay. They mostly issued from the loose coterie of Kang Youwei and the radical reformers. Portraying copyright as a civilized, progressive, and universal doctrine that China needed to adopt in order to catch up with the rest of the world, they also attributed the intellectual and technological advancements of Europe to its nations' copyright legislation. Like Fukuzawa, they too believed that material rewards would motivate authors, inventors, and scholars to keep creating new ideas and things. The value and power of copyright, for these early Chinese promoters, was derived from its foreignness; and the "failure" of China could be attributed to the lack of such Western, thus forward-looking, doctrines. Those who opposed introducing *banquan*/copyright into the trade treaties, on the other hand, also recognized copyright as a "general law (*gongli*)" but considered China not "civilized" enough to embrace it yet. If the foreign countries' ultimate objective was to have China join the international legal regime of copyright so that Sino-foreign trade would

80. "Lian bulang shang Guanxue Dachen lun banquan shi," *DGB*, May 22, 1903.

81. Yan Fu, "Yu guanxue dachen lun banquan shu" [A letter to the commissioner of the Imperial University on *banquan*], in *Zhongguo banquan shi yanjiu wenxian*, 46–48.

82. *Banquan kao*, 1–2. For more discussion on these petitions, see chapter 4.

be better protected, Zhang Baixi argued, not having copyright would be a greater benefit for everyone. China could catch up with the West more rapidly if Western books could be translated and copied freely in China; therefore, for China's development, the government should resist any request for international copyright protection. Although the two sides saw the correlation between copyright protection and the progression of civilization differently, they shared the idea that copyright was an alien doctrine that had no indigenous equivalent in China. For the advocates, it needed to be artificially transplanted in China. For those opposed to legalizing copyright protection in treaties, its introduction in China was something that the government could block or resist.

Borrowing an Empty Convention to Reinvent Tradition

In February 1903, the Shanghai Polytechnic Institution, a European-style academy set up by British missionaries and overseen by the Shanghai Municipal Council, published the following questions in *Shen bao* for their monthly essay competition: "What is the Sino-Japanese *banquan* alliance? How does the *banquan* law in Western countries work? What are the pros and cons of them?"[83] The presentation of such questions as the topic for a public competition with a cash prize indicates that by 1903 there was a significant number of people in Shanghai with a genuine understanding of the term *banquan* and the Western copyright law equipped to discuss copyright in a meaningful way. Or at least the organizers believed so. If we browse China's major newspapers and journals, such as *Shen bao*, *Dagong bao*, and *Zhongwai ribao*, as well as Chinese books published at the time, indeed, we will spot the term *banquan* appearing on a regular basis. The term *banquan*, which was literally unknown in Chinese up until 1898, seems to have become part of the everyday language of China's cultural circle, especially among booksellers, journalists, and literati in the empire's vibrant new book-trade center, Shanghai, within few years.

Does this sudden popularization of *banquan* suggest that more and more people in the cultural sector were inspired by the early copyright promoters' initiative—enhancing intellectual and technological advancement in China by transplanting and promoting this strange doctrine? Most of the time in the 1900s, when the term *banquan* appeared in written texts, it was not used to articulate arguments for copyright protection as described above, but to make

---

83. "Gezhi Shuyuan eryue shuo keti" [The monthly topic from Polytechnic Institution for the first half of the second month], *SB*, no. 10722 (February 27, 1903): 3.

simple and brief declarations of ownership or authenticity in book advertise-ments or the actual copies of books.[84] Despite appearing highly frequently, such declarations or statements have received little scholarly attention. This is partly because they were often made by lesser-known cultural figures or publishers who left behind little documentation explaining their rationale for word usage, and partly because these statements were exceedingly formulaic and thus deemed to be less worthy of serious investigation than those more elaborate discussions by renowned and influential intellectuals, like Kang or Liang. How-ever, by closely examining where and how this kind of standardized *banquan* formula appeared, we will see that these lesser figures were not simply "influ-enced" or "inspired" by the leading intellectuals' and reformers' pro-copyright messages. They transplanted and practiced copyright/*banquan* from their own perspective, and they connected this seemingly foreign concept with something old and local.

If one could launch a keyword search for the term *banquan* in texts produced in late Qing China, one would most likely find it in the convention "*banquan suoyou*" (copyright retained). This was a direct borrowing of the popular Japa-nese convention "*hanken shoyū*" discussed earlier in this chapter. Although Chinese publishers borrowed the convention their Japanese colleagues used to declare their copyright, the legal and customary authorities attached to it were lost in the process of transplantation. Indeed, it was not unusual for a single word or phrase to be borrowed or loaned between languages and societies

---

84. Although a large-scale quantitative survey on late Qing books and book advertisements would reveal the exact quantity, frequency, and even patterns in the appearance of both *banquan* and this fixed convention, it is beyond the scope of this study. Based on the impression I have after browsing three major newspapers from that time, *Shen bao*, *Dagong bao*, and *Zhongwai ribao*, I believe it would be fair to estimate that at least one-third to one-half of the advertise-ments in newspapers at that time were for newly published books and periodicals. Either a public proprietorship declaration of *banquan* or this fixed convention could be found in over 50 percent of these book advertisements. As for actual books, based on my research on late Qing publications housed in the Shanghai Library, books that contained either a copyright page or this fixed convention obviously increased after 1902. Via private exchange, Xiong Yuezhi af-firmed that he had a similar impression when conducting research for his *Wan Qing xinxue shumu tiyao*. Proprietorship declarations of *banquan* or this fixed convention not only appeared in New Learning books or Western-binding books, but could also be found in more traditional titles and traditional-binding books. A pattern similar to the one I observed in book advertise-ments in late Qing newspapers and late Qing books in the Shanghai Library can also be found in the fourteen-volume catalog of Qing colophons published by the PRC National Library Rare Collection Department, Guojia tushuguan gujiguan, ed., *Qingdai banke paiji tulu*, vols. 1–14.

unaccompanied by the customs, norms, and local contexts that empowered it. Japan's 1893 Copyright Law, which legally empowered the *"hanken shoyū"* convention in the first place, had already expired. Even if the law had not expired, its efficacy would not have reached Chinese booksellers anyway. The customary credibility this statement had in Japan's book trade would not be valid in China of its own accord. In other words, what Chinese booksellers transplanted was a fixed yet empty convention. Without the 1893 Copyright Law and the Japanese publishers' shared consensus, Chinese booksellers had to give *"banquan suoyou"* its context and create their own ways to prove or to justify that they indeed "possessed *banquan.*"

When Chinese booksellers borrowed *"hanken shoyū"* from Japan, they did not and could not transplant the legal authority backing this statement, but they did successfully imitate its outlook. Many took a leaf out of Japanese books—the *okuzuke* page, where Japanese booksellers were required to state their possession of *hanken*—and inserted it into the Chinese books they published (fig. 1.7). This particular page, usually appearing at the end of a book, is now generally known as *banquan ye* (copyright page) in Chinese. While it is considered an essential part of Chinese books today, it was brand-new to Chinese readers at the turn of the twentieth century. This page first appeared in Chinese books that were printed in Japan by Japanese letterpress printing companies, and was later popularized in China when Chinese booksellers and printers started to produce "Western-style" (*yangzhuan*) books modeled after Japanese books of the time. By the end of the first decade of the twentieth century, almost all the "Western-style" books in China contained an extra page at the end of the book. Necessary information, such as the name (and occasionally address) of the author, the name and contact details of the publisher, the date of publication, list price, and points of distribution, could be found on this page.

When Chinese booksellers appropriated the *okuzuke* page and the *"hanken shoyū"* statement, they also imitated the square (often with fancy borders) reserved for authors or publishers to stamp their copyright seal(s). What they put in the square, however, suggests that Chinese booksellers might have had different ideas about the interrelationship of the seal, the authenticity of the copy, and the nature of *banquan.* In some cases, the square was left empty as if it was just for decoration. In some cases, the *"banquan suoyou"* statement was framed by the square, as if to highlight the statement. In many other cases, a seal or a stamp could be found inside the square. Having investigated a wide range of books published between 1902 and 1910, I believe it is fair to conclude that the majority of seals found on the *banquan ye* (and sometimes on the cover page) of books were the bookseller's rather than the author's, as in figure 1.6. The continuity between the Ming-Qing *cangban* seal tradition and the publisher's *banquan* seal is apparent.[85] Such a seal was used as a certification of authenticity in late Qing China too. One Shanghai publisher, Golden Millet Studio (*Jinshu zhai*), explained this to its customers in a 1906 advertisement: to distinguish their authentic copies from fake ones, it had "stamped a seal on the last page of every book [it produced]. 'Golden Millet Studio's *banquan* certificate' and seven words were engraved in seal script. [This seal] shall serve as the identification mark [of the authentic copies]."[86]

Chinese publishers did not merely copy "*hanken shoyū*" and the practice of stamping a copyright seal; they also added a twist to create a local context for this borrowed statement. The set phrase "*banquan suoyou*" is often found in newspaper advertisements or the actual copies of books as part of a fixed eight-character statement:

Banquan suoyou fanke bijiu.
版權所有翻刻必究 (Copyright is retained, and reprinting will be pursued and punished)[87]

Like the *banquan ye*/copyright page, this convention has become a default component of Chinese books today and is often regarded as the Chinese equivalent of "copyright reserved" or ©. But back in the 1900s, it was a reinvention of an old custom. "*Fanke bijiu*," the second half of this fixed statement, had a long history. It can be seen on the colophons and title pages of Chinese books published as early as the thirteenth century and found periodically in late Ming and early Qing books (see fig. 1.3).[88] While scholars like Edgren and Inoue

85. Based on my research at Shanghai Library, Regenstein Library at the University of Chicago, National Taiwan University Library, Fu Sinian Library and Guo Tingyi Library at Academia Sinica (Taiwan), Tōyō Bunko Library (Tokyo, Japan), Beijing University History Department Library, CASS Modern History Institute Library, Yale University Library, and Cambridge University Library. Published catalogs of Qing colophons, such as *Qingdai banke paiji tulu*, also provide a great deal of information.

86. "Jinsuzhai guanggao" [Announcement from Golden Millet Studio], *ZWRB*, March 22, 1906.

87. *Fanke* (reengraving) and the phrase *fanyin* (reprinting) were used interchangeably in the convention.

88. For examples of *fanke bijiu* statements in mid-to-late Ming books, see Shi et al., *Zhongguo chuban tongshi*, 5:341–342. Intriguingly, the section on "copyright" protection in the Ming in Li Mingshan's *Zhongguo gudai banquan shi* is almost identical to this book.

光緒三十一年七月十日印刷
光緒三十一年八月一日發行

版權所有

定價每部大洋八角

原著者　美國女士斯土活
翻譯者　閩縣林紓
　　　　仁和魏易
圈點者　桐城女士吳芝瑛
校閱者　金匱廉泉
印刷所　上海四馬路胡家宅文明書局

總發行所

漢口黃陂街
北京琉璃廠
上海棋盤街
金陵石壩街

文明書局

FIG. 1.7. Copyright page of *Heinu yutian lu* (A black slave imploring Heaven), 1905.
The frame in the upper middle part of the page states, "*banquan suoyou* [copyright is
reserved]." The seal stamped in the frame reads, "the seal of Civilization Books." The
Source: Heinu yutian lu (Shanghai: Wenming Shuju, 1905).
Courtesy of Shanghai Library.

consider this kind of warning to be a Chinese "pseudo-copyright,"[89] Chinese legal scholars, such as Zheng Chengsi and his disciples, would declare it to be the earliest copyright protection in human history.[90]

Indeed, on the surface, the declaration of "copyright reserved" and the warning that "reprinting will be pursued and punished" seem to serve the same objective—to state and ensure the statement issuers' monopoly on the printing of a certain book—but the rationales behind these two conventions were profoundly different. In late Ming and early Qing books, the warning "*fanke bijiu*" was often accompanied by the statement "XX *cangban*," which, as discussed earlier, reflects the idea that the ownership of a book is vested in the one who possesses the printing blocks. Examples that Inoue Susumu provides in his discussion of the late Ming "pseudo-copyright," such as Chen Zilong (1608–1647) and Chen Jiru (1558–1639), were authors and compilers from our contemporary perspective, but they were also publishers who hired craftsmen to make printing blocks and published their works.

Although the contemporary understanding of copyright and the notion of block possession are entirely different, the similarity between China's centuries-old "*fanke bijiu*" and copyright seem to have been apparent to people at the turn of the twentieth century. For example, the English Sinologist Herbert A. Giles considered "*fanke bijiu*" to be the closest Chinese equivalent to the English word "copyright." In his 1892 *Chinese-English Dictionary*, he defined "*fanke bijiu*" as "re-printer will be prosecuted," saw it as "a notice (= All rights reserved)," and asserted its uniqueness: "apart from which there is no copyright in China."[91] When the Chinese treaty commissioner Lü Haihuan explained in an imperial memorial that they had made their best effort to "ensure China's interests" during the treaty negotiation in 1902, he attempted to downplay the "foreignness" of the copyright protection that the United States and Japan requested by stating that "this is what we called '*fanke bijiu*.'"[92] By referring to this late imperial convention against reprinting as an equivalent of copyright, he hinted that the

89. Edgren, "The *Fengmianye* (Cover Page) as a Source for Chinese Publishing History"; Inoue, *Chūgoku shuppan bunkashi*, 255–261.

90. For similar arguments, see Zheng, *Zhishi caichanquan fa*; Li, ed., *Zhongguo jindai banquan shi*; Wang, *Jindai Zhongguo zhuzuoquan fa de chengzhang*, 7–12.

91. "Fanke bijiu," in Giles, *A Chinese-English Dictionary*, 342.

92. "Lü Sheng liang qinshi fudian" [The telegram reply from Treaty Commissioners Lü and Sheng], in *Zhongguo banquan shi yanjiu wenxian*, 43.

foreign powers' demand might not be that far distant from local contexts after all.

The popularization of the practice of stamping the *banquan* seal and the statement *"banquan suoyou fanke bijiu"* among Chinese booksellers in the 1900s, thus, might not be directly attributable to the reformers' promotion of *banquan* and the civilization discourse they employed. Although the Qing government did not officially promulgate its copyright law until 1911, the lack of a copyright law did not prevent Chinese booksellers from using the term *banquan* to proclaim their ownership of books. And they learned the usage of *banquan* via the physical copies of books imported from Japan across the Yellow Sea. While the early promoters of copyright in China emphasized how, as a new and foreign concept, copyright/*banquan* needed to be artificially transplanted and consciously adopted in China, the rapid popularization of the *"banquan suoyou fanke bijiu"* statement suggests that Chinese booksellers did not see *banquan* as a completely alien notion without a local counterpart. The marriage between *"banquan suoyou,"* a convention the late Qing booksellers borrowed from Meiji Japan, and *"fanke bijiu,"* a Ming-Qing customary warning against unauthorized reprinting, proceeded smoothly because the late Qing booksellers quickly saw the connection between *cangban*, *cangban* seal, *banquan*/copyright, copyright seal, the traditional convention *"XX cangban, fanke bijiu,"* with which they were familiar, and the Meiji convention *"hanken shoyū"* they saw in Japanese books. This familiarity had to do with the fact that the terms and customs to signify copyright ownership that they found in the newly imported Japanese books had their roots in Ming-Qing book culture.

2

The Business of "New Learning"

WHEN LIN SHU WAS approached by Wang Kangnian in 1899, the Shanghai publisher's request to purchase the right to (re)publish his work seemed peculiar to this provincial scholar. However, by the end of 1903, the Chinese term for copyright, *banquan*, appears to have become part of Chinese book-sellers' everyday language. It could be commonly found in book advertisements or propriety assertions in newspapers or in actual copies of books. Lin Shu, who once declared that he did not "own" his translation, also started to receive payments and royalties for his latest works. In the summer of 1905, he and his collaborator Wei Yi (1880–1930) even published a public announcement in *Shen bao* as the original *banquan* owners of *Heinu yutian lu* (A black slave imploring Heaven; their translation of *Uncle Tom's Cabin*) condemning any attempt to reprint this book.[1] Though Lin stated in the preface of *Heinu yutian lu* that they had translated this novel to provoke racial awareness in the Chinese, it was also undeniably a profit-making project for Lin now. As Civilization Books, the publisher of *Heinu yutian lu*, proclaimed in its advertisement, they had "paid a huge sum of money" to acquire Lin and Wei's *banquan*.[2]

Lin Shu's changing attitude toward literary property, as well as the sudden popularization in China of *banquan*/copyright at the turn of the twentieth century, was a direct result of the commodification of Western knowledge that

1. "Wenming shuju zuiyao xinshu guanggao heinu yutian lu shengming banquan" [Civilization Books' latest and most important title, *Black Slave Imploring Heaven*, declares its *banquan*], SB, July 1–31, 1905.

2. "Lin yi taixi mingzhu xiaoshuo heinu yutian lu" [Lin Shu's translation of the famous European novel *Black Slave Imploring Heaven*], SB, July 16, 1905, 1.

was defined as "New Learning" (*xinxue*) at the time.[3] Readers today might regard *La Dame aux camélias* or *Uncle Tom's Cabin* simply as literary works, but for late Qing Chinese intellectuals they belonged to the realm of New Learning knowledge just like chemistry and political economy, because they were foreign.[4] After Qing's unexpected defeat in the Sino-Japanese War, Chinese cultural and political elites hastened to consume this so-called New Learning knowledge to cope with the challenges posed by the advancing Western powers. Translating, producing, and reading New Learning texts, many considered, were crucial for China's national salvation. As Liang Qichao put it, "If a nation wants to strengthen itself, it should translate more Western books; if a student wants to stand on his own feet, he should read more Western books."[5] The influx of this new body of knowledge in the late Qing fundamentally reshaped how Chinese elites understood themselves and the world, led to the collapse of the cosmos of traditional Chinese learning, and redefined what counted as useful knowledge. Although this intellectual sea change has been one of the most extensively studied subjects in modern Chinese history, its socioeconomic impacts have yet to be comprehensively evaluated. This chapter will demonstrate how the profound intellectual shift triggered a commodification of New Learning knowledge and the sudden popularization of *banquan*/copyright at the turn of the twentieth century.

Missionaries' Cash Cow

When describing how the changing intellectual atmosphere in the aftermath of the Sino-Japanese War reshaped China's book market, editor and historian Lü Simian (1884–1957) recalled that at the time "the sale of books and

3. By "New Learning," I mean the general knowledge that was new and foreign for China at the time. It included foreign languages, natural sciences, modern manufacturing, international relations, Western military technologies, Western political thoughts, European history, foreign literatures, and the like. Other terms, such as "Western learning" (*xixue*) and "contemporary affairs" (*shiwu*), were also used to refer to this new body of knowledge. However, since not all new knowledge was from the West, I prefer to use "New Learning" in my discussion. On the complicated cultural exchange that occurred as New Learning knowledge emerged, see Lackner and Vittinghoff, eds., *Mapping Meanings*; Lackner, *New Terms for New Ideas*; and the WSC-Databases, http://www.wsc.uni-erlangen.de/wscdb.htm.

4. For example, Liang Qichao categorized Lin Shu's translations of fiction under New Learning in his overview of Qing China's intellectual landscape. See Liang Qichao, *Qingdai xueshu gailun*, 162–163.

5. *Xixue shumu biao*, 1b.

periodicals of 'New Learning' increased day by day, month by month."[6] Qing's defeat was a profound shock as well as a deep disillusionment for Chinese intellectuals across the spectrum, since many of them had long regarded Japan as an inferior neighboring country. This psychological complex provoked many of them to question the applicability of traditional Confucian teaching and worldviews in the competitive world of modern nation-states. For the first time, they started to consider Western knowledge and ideas worthy of investigation and study.[7]

The best way to grasp this new body of knowledge and ideas, for many learned Chinese at the time, was reading Western books or their translations. *Xixue shumu biao* (A reading list for Western learning) and *Do xixue shu fa* (How to read Western learning books), the twin brochures compiled by the young Liang Qichao, reflected this belief well. Listing 352 translations published between the Opium Wars and the Sino-Japanese War, and providing his brief annotations on individual titles and his instructions on how to approach them in proper order, Liang aimed to guide his readers to enter this unfamiliar world of Western knowledge by self-study.[8] He argued that the difference between a European schoolboy who was able to name major countries in the world and a man of letters in China who was ignorant of such matters was not their intelligence, but their access to the "new" knowledge.[9] His underlying assumption was that if educated Chinese had access to Western books, then they would be able to comprehend Western knowledge, including chemistry experiments, geometry, or agronomy, like their Western counterparts. This book was a timely supplement for those who were reevaluating the applicability of Western ideas in China. Two thousand copies were sold in the two months after its first publication by Wang Kangnian's *Shiwu bao* (The Chinese progress) in Shanghai in the autumn of 1896. Readers who failed to obtain a copy wrote anxious letters to Wang asking for help. And at least two reprinted editions became

6. Lü, "Sanshinainlai zhi chibanjie (1894–1923)," *Lü Simain yiwenji*, 1:373.

7. Concerning the impact of the Sino-Japanese War on Chinese intellectuals, see Chang, *Chinese Intellectuals in Crisis*; Schwartz, In *Search of Wealth and Power*; and Cohen, *Between Tradition and Modernity*.

8. It also listed 86 translations published before the First Opium War, 88 titles completed but not yet published, and 119 titles written by Chinese authors on "Western learning." Liang didn't comment on these books; he merely listed them for reference.

9. *Xixue shumu biao*, 1a.

available in less than one year.[10] While some readers earnestly followed Liang's instruction to collect and read the "Western learning" titles he recommended, some aspired to compile their own collectanea and introductory reading guides of "Western learning."[11] Between 1896 and 1905, more than a dozen similar reading guides and annotated bibliographies hit the market.[12]

Books on Western knowledge were available to Chinese readers long before the Sino-Japanese War. Since the late Ming, the Jesuits stationed in China had translated European religious, scientific, and mathematical works into Chinese.[13] After the Taiping Rebellion (1851–1864), Protestant missionaries in the treaty ports, as well as reform-minded officials, also started to translate books on international law, military technology, industry, and European history in a more systematic fashion. Throughout most of the nineteenth century, however, these books received almost no attention from the Chinese intellectual community. They remained niche readings at the periphery of the Chinese book world. English missionary John Fryer (1839–1928), who spent more than a decade directing translation projects for *Jiangnan jiqi zhizaoju* (Jiangnan Arsenal, est. 1867), estimated that between 1871 and 1881, the Jiangnan Arsenal managed to sell about 31,000 copies of its 98 titles. For him, this sale volume was acceptable but not encouraging, as their patrons were mostly limited to the state-run translation academy *Tongwenguan* and a few "modern" schools in the treaty ports.[14]

After the Sino-Japanese War, however, Chinese intellectuals seemed to suddenly "rediscover" these books, such as *Wanguo gongfa* (The public law of the nations)—William A. P. Martin's translation of Henry Wheaton's *Elements of International Law*,[15] and eagerly acquired more new titles on Western sciences, society, and culture. As they hastened to consume Western knowledge, the books on New Learning, moving from the margins of the traditional Chinese

10. For example, *Xixue shumu biao fu Du xixue shufa* [A reading list for Western learning with how to read Western learning books] by Wuchang zhixue hui (Wuchang Society for Chemistry) and *Xixue shumu biao* by Shenshiji zhai (Cautious Foundation Studio) in 1897.

11. For the reception of *Xixue shumu biao* in the late Qing, see Pan, *Wan Qing shiren de xixue yuedu shi*, 322–341.

12. Xiong, ed., *Wan Qing xinxue shumu tiyao*, 1–10.

13. For the Jesuits' translation activities in China, see Dunne, *Generation of Giants*; Elman, *On Their Own Terms*, chaps. 2 to 5; Li, *Zhongguo wan Ming yu Ouzhou wen xue*.

14. John Fryer, "Jingnan zhizaozongju fanyixishu shilue" [A brief overview of the translation of Western books in Jiangnan Arsenal], in Zhang ed., *Zhongguo jindai chuban shiliao*, 1:21–22.

15. For the reception of William Martin's translation of Wheaton's *Elements of International Law* in China, see Liu, "Legislating the Universal"; Howland, *Translating the West*, 124–125.

textual world to the main stage, became desirable readings. There may be no better example than the case of the SDCK to illustrate how New Learning books became commodities at the turn of the twentieth century. The skyrocketing sale of their books after 1895 changed the financial structure of this missionary press and turned it from a not-for-profit organization into an operation sustaining itself by book sales. The commodification of New Learning knowledge also prompted the SDCK to see their publications as profitable private properties. They became the first publisher in China to employ the concept of copyright to claim ownership of books and to condemn unauthorized reprinting as unlawful misconduct, just like stealing or robbery.

The SDCK was first formed in 1887 by the Reverend Alexander Williamson (1829–1890). As its Chinese name, *guangxue*, suggested, the SDCK took the spreading of Christian messages and Western "general knowledge" in China as its main objective. To make itself more acceptable to scholar-officials, civil service examinees, and their families, the SDCK consciously downplayed its religious mission and presented itself chiefly as a promoter of useful Western knowledge.[16] It compiled and published books introducing Western history, politics, and international affairs and distributed them mostly free of charge outside examination halls during the provincial-level civil service examinations. For the SDCK leaders, giving out free books was the best way to tempt the educated Chinese to develop an interest in Western ideas (and Christianity too, they hoped). In their 1893 and 1894 annual reports, for instance, the SDCK celebrated the tens of thousands of free copies, such as *Zhongxi si dazheng* (The four great policies in China and the West), that they had given to examinees along with religious pamphlets.[17]

Between the 1880s and 1890s, this publishing operation was mainly supported by overseas donations from American and English Protestant organizations and some private individuals. When Timothy Richard (1845–1919) assumed leadership of the SDCK in 1892, he was fully aware that only with stable financial support could they continue their publishing project, but he never saw selling their books for profit as a feasible or acceptable way to fund the SDCK. In the

16. Wang, "Qing ji de guangxuehui," *Jinshisuo Jikan* 4 (1973): 194.

17. Litimotai, "Guangxuehui di wu nian jilüe" [The brief version of the fifth annual report of the SDCK], *Wanguo gongbao* 49 (December 1893): 13417–13420; "Guangxuehui di liu nian jilüe" [The brief version of the sixth annual report of the SDCK], *Wanguo gongbao* 60 (December 1893–January 1894): 14119–14127.

1892 annual report, for instance, he reported the increase in book sales in an apologetic tone. He expressed regret for having to charge money for their publications because donations alone could not cover salaries for translators and expenses for printing and distribution. They would have circulated books free of charge if they had had sufficient donations, Richard stated. "Without the books, it would be impossible for [new] learning to be understood [by Chinese]; without money, it would be impossible for the books to be published." So he urged their foreign donors as well as the Chinese government to contribute more funds to keep the SDCK's books free to the Chinese.[18] What Richard didn't reveal to the SDCK donors was that their books were largely not appreciated by the Chinese even though they were free. In his memoir, he recalled that before 1895, most of their publications distributed outside examination halls were not read at all. They were "actually made into soles for Chinese shoes" or "collected and burned along with other papers containing Chinese characters in temple buildings."[19]

In 1895, the Chinese treatment of these books changed drastically. After the war had broken out, subscriptions to the SDCK's organ, *Wanguo gongbao* (A review of the times), doubled within one year. Many Chinese subcribed to it because of the articles about the war by Young J. Allen (1836–1907); they considered these articles "neutral" and thus more reliable. The overwhelming popularity of *Wanguo gongbao* forced the SDCK to reprint constantly to keep up with readers' demands. Several Chinese officials and government agencies also increased the number of copies for which they subscribed.[20] The series of articles and translations from foreign newspapers on the Sino-Japanese War that Allen compiled for *Wanguo gongbao* was published in book form as *Zhongdong zhanji benmuo* (The chronicle of the Sino-Japanese War) in 1896. Some statistics suggest that between 1896 and 1897, the SDCK sold more than 22,000 copies of this book.[21] Another SDCK postwar best seller was *Taixi shinshi lanyiao* (An overview of the new history of the West), which was Timothy Richard's translation of Robert MacKenzie's *History of the Nineteenth Century*. Xiong Yuezhi estimated that the missionaries sold more than 30,000 copies of *Taixi*

18. Ibid.
19. Richard, *Forty-Five Years in China*, 231–232.
20. Ibid., 231.
21. Cha, "Lin Lezhi de shengping yu zhishi," 150–151.

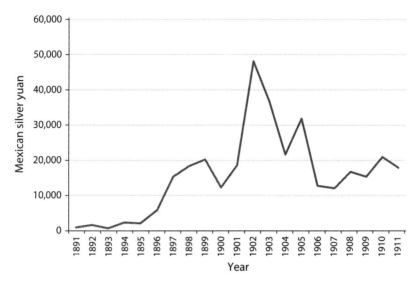

FIG. 2.1. The SDCK's annual sales, 1888–1905.
Source: The SDCK's annual reports (1888–1905).

shinshi lanyiao within a few years.[22] The sale volume of these two titles marked a new milestone for New Learning books in China: it took the Jiangnan Arsenal a decade (1871–1880) to sell 30,000 copies of their books, but *Zhongdong zhanji benmuo* and *Taixi shinshi lanyiao* needed only two to three years to exceed that number. Besides the impressive success of individual titles, the scale of the SDCK's overall sales also increased dramatically. As figure 2.1 shows, the SDCK's sales tripled in 1895–1896, then doubled again in 1896–1897. From 1893 to 1899, its sales volume expanded twentyfold.

Since the outbreak of the war, the SDCK had been among the first to argue that, despite the fact that the Qing had more advanced military equipment than did Japan, China's reluctance to embrace Western knowledge would cost it the war. They repeatedly promoted this argument in *Wanguo gongbao* and *Zhongdong zhanji benmuo*. Reaching the educated Chinese in the aftershock of China's defeat, this argument aroused Chinese interest in reading books on Western knowledge. As the SDCK benefited significantly from the shifting

22. *Xixue dongjian*, 601. The SDCK published a "common edition" of this book in 1899; four thousand of the five thousand first-edition copies were sold within in two weeks. Some even proclaimed that over one million copies of this book were sold at the turn of the twentieth century.

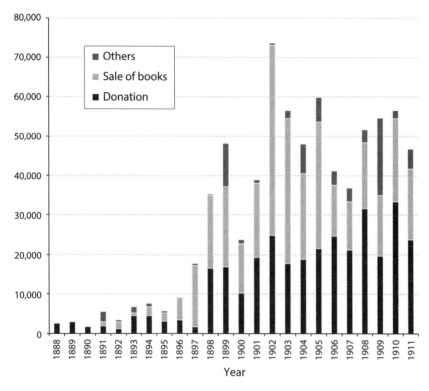

FIG. 2.2. The SDCK's sources of income, 1888–1911.
Source: The SDCK's annual reports (1888–1911).

intellectual trend they had helped to create, this sudden and soaring popularity of their books also reshaped their operational model. While it seemed that the SDCK had accomplished their goal of making Western knowledge and ideas prevail in Chinese intellectual circles, they were no longer able and willing to distribute most of their books for free. As figure 2.2 illustrates, book sales represented an increasingly dominant proportion of the SDCK's annual income between 1896 and 1903. Although the sums they received in donations also increased over time, their financial significance to the SDCK decreased. After 1896, sales of books in China replaced contributions from Britain and America to become the SDCK's primary source of income.

Making money from their enlightenment mission might not be what the SDCK intended initially, but the revenue from their publishing "business" ended up becoming the indispensable and essential resource for maintaining the institution's daily operations. Between 1896 and 1904, as the sales of the

SDCK's New Learning books burgeoned, the SDCK's operational scale had also expanded significantly to accommodate the rising demand for their publications and the expansion of their free-copy distribution. The increasing expenses for printing and salaries were covered by the sale of books rather than by donations from overseas. The financial loop created by the expansion in publishing projects resulted in the SDCK's needing (and maybe expecting) more and more bookselling revenue to sustain this growth. Indeed, they did not have an interest in accumulating capital and usually spent their surplus on printing more free Bibles, but the expanding operation started a chain reaction that drove them to look for ever more readers and higher revenue. As a result, this not-for-profit missionary press ended up acting intriguingly like a commercial publisher and started to treat their New Learning publications as commodities.

Juggling between their noble ideal of providing free books to enlighten China and the economic reality that the organization now depended on the bookselling revenue, the SDCK leaders had a bittersweet feeling about the newly discovered commercial value of their books. In their annual reports, they celebrated their record-breaking sales year after year as an encouraging sign that Chinese readers finally recognized the merit of Western knowledge.[23] Chinese booksellers, who used to consider the SDCK publications "unworthy to be handled," now approached them and indicated that they were "only too glad to sell" books for the SDCK. Chinese booksellers had strong incentive to sell the SDCK publications, as they were such hot commodities in the marketplace that customers were willing to pay extra to obtain a copy. For instance, Richard's *Taixi shinshi lanyiao* cost two yuan in Shanghai, but its selling price tripled in hinterland cities such as Xi'an. Chinese booksellers not only gained extravagantly by selling the "authentic" SDCK publications in inland regions, but they also reprinted them for profit. According to Richard, in the city of Hangzhou alone there were no fewer than six different editions of his *Taixi shinshi lanyiao*, including "one edition *de luxe* for the rich."[24]

When reporting to their donors in 1897, the SDCK presented Chinese piracy as an achievement of their enlightenment mission. "Although it is illegal

---

23. "Shanghai guangxuehui dijiuncinianhui lunlue" [The brief report of the ninth annual meeting of Shanghai SDCK], *Wanguo gongbao* 98 (March 1897): 16757; "Shanghai guangxuehui dishiniannianhui lunlue" [The brief report of the tenth annual meeting of Shanghai SDCK], *Wanguo gongbao* 108 (January 1898): 17415–17416; "Guangxuehui dishiyinianbao jilue" [The brief version of the eleventh annual report of SDCK], *Wanguo gongbao* 120 (January 1899): 18244.

24. Richard, *Forty-Five Years in China*, 231–232.

for these people to steal others' books to benefit themselves," the report stated, "considering their motivation, we were in fact very happy."[25] In his memoir, Richard also proclaimed that at the time they didn't worry about Chinese pirating their books because the sales of their "authentic" copies alone could be more than sufficient to support their daily operations.[26] What he neglected to reveal in his recollection of the China mission was that the SDCK, in fact, cared a lot about the profit "stolen" from them by Chinese publishers. Concurrent with their cheerful comments on Chinese piracy were their consistent and aggressive announcements in *Wanguo gongbao* declaring their exclusive ownership of their best sellers. In the winter of 1896, they petitioned the American consul general in Shanghai, T. R. Jernigan, and the Shanghai circuit intendant, urging them to condemn piracy. Acknowledging the efforts made by SDCK missionaries to "serve the world," Circuit Intendant Liu issued a specific prohibition outlawing any reprinting of the SDCK's popular titles. When announcing Liu's order in *Wanguo gongbao*, the missionaries also introduced the doctrine of copyright in the public statement they published along with the Chinese official's order:

> Now we know that some scurrilous publishers are reprinting these books for profit. According to Western custom, reprinting another's works and selling them for profit is the same as a robber stealing another's property. This is a crime that should be punished.[27]

In the actual copies of the SDCK publications, one could also find the same prohibition and statement, as if the missionaries were trying to brand a mark of ownership on every book they produced. In addition to announcing that their publications were now under the protection of both Chinese and Western authorities, in these statements the SDCK also firmly declared their determination to stop piracy: "if [people] dare to reprint [their books], they will be punished by authorities immediately."[28] With this special prohibition order in hand, the SDCK, the missionary press that once apologized for charging their readers money for books, became the first publisher in China to take legal action against those who reprinted their books. Their financial records indicate

25. "Shanghai guangxuehui dishiniannianhui lunlue," *Wanguo gongbao* 108 (January 1898): 17416.

26. Ibid.

27. "Guangxuehui yianjin fanke sinzhu chuji gaoshi," *Wanguo gongbao* 97 (February 1897): 16699–16700. For contextual discussion of this order and its historical origin, see chapter 4.

28. Ibid.

that the SDCK took legal action against Chinese publishers at least twice in the Shanghai Mixed Court and successfully received a 100-yuan compensation in 1897 and another 535 yuan in 1899.[29]

The power of the special "copyright" protection that the SDCK obtained was limited. Chinese booksellers across the empire continued making their reprints of *Zhongdong zhanji benmuo, Wenxue xingguo ce, Taixi shinshi lanyiao*, and other SDCK publications about the West. For example, in 1898 the SDCK claimed that they had found nineteen different reprinted editions of Timothy Richard's *Taixi shinshi lanyiao* in Sichuan alone.[30] It was estimated that at the turn of the twentieth century over one million unauthorized reprints of SDCK's publications were sold in China, which was five times the number of "authentic" copies the SDCK had produced.[31] The rampant piracy of SDCK publications was presented to American and European readers at the time by several "China experts," such as Robert K. Douglas, as a sign of "intellectual awakening in China."[32] One American review of Douglas's account commented on this phenomenon in a somewhat cynical tone: "Western civilization, we are told, was not needed to introduce literary piracy into China; and literary copyright being unknown, the publications have been largely reprinted by themselves whenever their success justified such a step."[33]

Late Qing Political Reforms and the New Learning Fever

The commercial value of Western knowledge that the SDCK discovered after the Sino-Japanese War reshaped not only the SDCK's operation but also the way the New Learning books in China were produced in general. Investing money and resources in translating, compiling, and publishing New Learning titles was no longer exclusively a matter of serving the enlightenment mission, national salvation, or personal intellectual achievement; it also constituted a profitable venture. Before 1895, most publishers of Chinese books on Western knowledge—missionary presses, government institutions, or individual

---

29. "Shanghai guangxuehui dishiniannianhui lunlue," *Wanguo gongbao* 108 (January 1898): 17415–17416; "Guangxuehui dishiyinianbao jilue," *Wanguo gongbao* 120 (January 1899): 18244. These are the earliest copyright lawsuits we can trace in China.

30. "Guangxuehui dishiyinianbao jilue," *Wanguo gongbao* 120 (January 1899): 18244.

31. See the SDCK's 1906 annual report.

32. Douglas, "The Awakening of China."

33. "The Awakening of China," *American Monthly Review of Reviews*, July–December 1900, 110.

scholars—were what historians of Chinese print culture categorized as "non-commercial publishers."[34] While donations supported missionary presses like the SDCK, government agencies, such as the Imperial Language College and the Jiangnan Arsenal, relied on the central or local government's funding.[35] Since the sale of books wouldn't affect their operations, in theory they could devote themselves to producing what they regarded as intellectually worthy rather than worrying about the balance sheet. This model, however, prevented them from being financially self-sustainable: the withdrawing of donations or government subsidies would easily paralyze these institutions. In the postwar years, when the SDCK became increasingly dependent on their bookselling revenue, several Chinese-owned noncommercial publishing enterprises for New Learning books were also expected to make a profit. For instance, when Liang Qichchao founded his Great Unity Translation Press (*Datong yishu ju*) in 1897, instead of collecting donations or asking for governmental sponsorship, he believed that the press could achieve self-reliance by selling shares and books.[36] During the 1898 Reform, the government took over the press as its new designated provider of New Learning books. To cover the cost of its expanding production scale, the government agreed to grant it a two-thousand-tael monthly subsidy but with the proviso that the state would withdraw the funding once the press became profitable again.[37]

The potential of this emerging New Learning book market in China was quickly noticed by Chinese "commercial" booksellers and printers. As some started to carry the SDCK's and other missionary presses' books on Western knowledge, others decided to reprint them or produced their own New Learning titles. For them, it was nothing but good business. For instance, Commercial Press, which would later become East Asia's largest publishing enterprise in the twentieth century, transformed itself from a small printing company to a cultural entrepreneur after it had a taste of this new market. Founded in 1897 by four former Chinese printers of a missionary publishing house, Commercial

<hr>

34. For a discussion of the tradition of noncommercial publishing in China, see McDermott, " 'Noncommercial' Private Publishing in Late Imperial China." The publishers of New Learning books prior to 1895 fit in the traditional categories of noncommercial publishing: private family publishers (*jiake*), religious publishers, and government publishers (*guanke*).

35. For example, the Jiangnan Arsenal was mainly funded by Zeng Guofan's Huai Army budget and tax income from the Shanghai Maritime Customs Service.

36. Liang Qichao, "Datongyishuju xuli" [The Contract of Great Unity Translation Press] (1897), in *Zhongguo jindai chuban shiliao*, 2:52–54.

37. "Gai yishuju wei yishuguanju zhe" [The proposal to transform Daton Translation Press to Official Translation Press] (1898), in *Zhongguo jindai chuban shiliao*, 2:50–52.

Press, as its name suggested, was initially a printing shop making business flyers and commercial documents for foreign firms in Shanghai. On the side, they also printed periodicals and books for missionary presses in town.[38] As a contractor employed by these missionary presses, they had firsthand experience of China's soaring demand for New Learning books as the volume of their printing jobs increased over time. In 1898, as an experiment, they commissioned a Chinese English teacher to annotate *Indian Reader*, an elementary English textbook published in India for Indian subjects, and published it as *Huaying chujie* (Primary English-Chinese reader) and *Huaying jinjie* (Advanced English-Chinese reader). Within a week, more than three thousand copies of these two English primers were sold. The profit they generated allowed Commercial Press to recoup their initial investment and move to a nicer location.[39]

Between 1896 and 1905, China witnessed an explosion of New Learning books. The intensified political and educational reforms launched by the Qing court beginning in 1898 created a New Learning fever among educated Chinese, as Western knowledge and ideas became the new subjects of the reformed civil service examination. Also, believing in the prospects of this new market, more and more Chinese publishers, like Commercial Press, started to systematically commission translations, purchase manuscripts, and hire editors to produce more trendy New Learning titles. Meanwhile, the Chinese, as briefly discussed in chapter 1, discovered an easier, cheaper, and faster way to produce more New Learning texts by translating Japanese books on Western knowledge. These changes in the supply and demand of Western knowledge drastically elevated the scale of the New Learning book market. Between 1900 and 1904, more than 899 new translations were published in China; this exceeds the total of all translations published in the previous ninety years combined.[40] When Liang compiled his *Xixue shumu biao*, he managed to collect about 300 translation works published in the previous half century (1842–1895), but now, on average, 226.5 new translations were published annually (1902–1904).[41] Besides translation

38. For an attentive discussion of its early years, see Tarumoto, *Shoki Shōmu Inshokan kenkyū*, 1–107.

39. Jiang Weiqiao, "Chuangban chuqi zhi shangwuyinshuguan yu zhounghuashuju" [The early years of Commercial Press and Chinese Bookstore], in *Zhongguoxiandai chuban shiliao*, 4:395.

40. Xiong, *Xixue dongjian yu wanqing shehui*, 13. Xiong compiled these statistics based on several bibliographies of that time and other statistics compiled in the early twentieth century. He acknowledges that the actual number of translations was higher.

41. Tsien, "Western Impact on China through Translation," 305–327. The 226.5 titles/year result is based on Gu Yeguang's *Yishu jingyan lu*.

works, there were also countless periodicals, edited volumes, indexes, bibliographies, textbooks, pamphlets, readers, and novels created by Chinese under the rubric of New Learning.[42] These books were mostly produced not by missionary presses or official presses, but by Chinese booksellers and cultural entrepreneurs. All of a sudden, newspapers were flooded with advertisements for the latest New Learning books as if they were the trendiest and most desirable appurtenances for educated Chinese.

In the preface of *Zhengzhi xue* (Political science), Feng Ziyou (1882–1958) vividly depicted how his contemporaries eagerly armed themselves with New Learning knowledge:

> After the acute trauma [of the Boxer Rebellion] in 1900, the whole society from top to bottom was shaken, thus the court decided to reform in order to strengthen itself; literati/gentry (*shidafu*) anxiously rushed to respond to the court's call for talent, and none of them were not saying, "New Learning, New Learning." However, A asked B, B asked C, and C came back to ask A— they just looked at each other with fear, and none of them knew what exactly "New Learning" meant. They, therefore, decided to go to the city and wandered around to look for the answer. Wherever they saw a bookshop's billboards stating "New Books on Contemporary Affairs," they crowded into [the bookshop] just like ants and grabbed whatever was available. Many shrewd merchants reprinted old books under trendy titles or used fake appeal to edit and repackage old stuff. Literati were so ignorant of such matters. They misidentified this junk as treasure, read them day and night, pointed them out and told each other happily: "This is New Learning! This is New Learning!"[43]

Was this almost blind yearning for New Learning driven by patriotism? As Feng hinted in his observation, the educated Chinese's desperate pursuit of New Learning books was "to respond to the court's call for talent." Such New Learning fever was, to a fair extent, a practical, if not utilitarian, response of the Chinese elites to the educational and examination reforms at the turn of the twentieth century.

In 1898, in response to China's defeat in the Sino-Japanese War, the young Guangxu Emperor (1871–1908, reign: 1875–1908) launched a series of top-down institutional reforms modeled after Japan's Meiji Restoration. To forge future

---

42. For example, *Yishu jingyan lu* listed 642 titles of New Learning books compiled or edited by Chinese and published between 1902 and 1904. The number of these "nontranslation" books is roughly equal to the number of translated works.

43. Feng, *Zhengzhi xue*, 1.

sociopolitical elites and imperial bureaucrats who could keep up with the world, the government was to reform the civil service examination and to make mathematics, sciences, international politics, and other Western knowledge the new school curriculum. Though it ended prematurely under Empress Dowager Cixi (1835–1908) and the conservatives' strong opposition, the ill-fated 1898 Reform, as Rebecca Karl and Peter Zarrow point out, shaped the overarching idea of late Qing reforms for years to come.[44] The full-scale reform the Qing court announced in the aftermath of the Boxer Rebellion in 1901, generally known as the New Policy Reform (1902–1911), was the Manchu monarchy's top-down Westernization and state-building project. The first and most symbolic step of the "New Policy" was the introduction of a new civil service examination format: the eight-legged essay, which had been the standard composition format for the past five centuries, would be officially abolished. Examinees would now be expected to deliver theses discoursing on "the history of Chinese politics" and "policy questions on world politics," in addition to the traditional *Four Books and Five Classics*.[45] The evaluation would be made based on how well candidates could offer substantial analysis on contemporary affairs and historical issues. Meanwhile, a school system following European and Japanese models would be established as a parallel path to recruit and produce future elites for the empire.[46] In the following three years (1902–1904), two provincial and two metropolitan examinations were held in this format.[47]

The "up-to-date" exam questions on contemporary issues, in theory, would enable the government to select the most suitable talents who had a basic

44. Karl and Zarrow, eds., *Rethinking the 1898 Reform Period*. It is worth noting that several young bureaucrats who left the government because of the 1898 coup d'état became cultural entrepreneurs in the late Qing and early Republican era. For example, Lian Quan, the proprietor of leading textbook and New Learning publisher Civilization Books; Zhang Yuanji, first the head of Nanyang Public School's Press Department, then the general manager of Commercial Press; Cia Yuanpei, the editor in chief of Commercial Press for a while and then a revolutionary were among this group of young elite officials.

45. Elman, *A Cultural History of Civil Examinations in Late Imperial China*, 596.

46. For the examination reform and its abolishment in 1905, see chap. 11 of Elman's *A Cultural History of Civil Examinations in Late Imperial China* and Franke, *The Reform and Abolition of the Traditional Chinese Examination System*.

47. The frequency of examinations in these three years is unusual. The 1902 examination was the makeup exam for the 1900–1901 examination that was canceled because of the Boxer Rebellion. The examination hall in Beijing was burned down during the Boxer Rebellion, so the 1903 metropolitan examination was held in Kaifeng. The 1904 examination was an extra (bonus) exam for Empress Dowager Cixi's seventieth birthday.

understanding of Western knowledge and were thus capable of transforming the empire into a modern state. By assigning New Learning knowledge as the subjects of examination and the school curriculum, this reform also granted it officially recognized cultural and ideological legitimacy. The reformed examination might be able to reshape the educated Chinese's mind proactively, but the belief in book learning and meritocracy, which had supported the examination system for centuries, was unchallenged. The life goals of the hundreds of thousands of literati-examinees also remained steadfast: succeeding in the civil service examination, becoming a degree-holder, and then entering officialdom. The tactics they employed to climb the ladder of success were also mostly the same. Just as they had memorized the *Four Books and Five Classics* and studied model eight-legged essays in the old days, they rushed to New Learning books to meet the new standard.

Personal and fictional accounts during this period revealed the fact that many educated Chinese started to read New Learning books because they considered these books to be the magical key to open the door to success. Take Zhu Zhisan (1886–1967), for example. As soon as the court announced the examination reform, his tutor asked this young man from Hubei to abandon the eight-legged essay formula and directed him instead to practice writing on mock essay topics such as "how to regulate commerce" or "the impact of railroads on China." When he went to Wuhan for the provincial examination in 1902, he tried to buy and borrow as many new books published in Shanghai on current affairs as possible, because he was convinced that "learning the writing style [of these kinds of books] would be the key to succeed in the exam. Essays that drew prizes recently are mostly modeled after this kind of writing style."[48] Liu Dapong (1857–1942) was another late Qing examinee who noticed the correlation between reading New Learning books and passing exams. For years this hinterland *juren* degree holder living in a Shanxi market town had been struggling to obtain the highest degree (*jinshi*). When trying his luck once again in 1902 in Kaifong, this earnest follower of Confucius's teachings was stunned by how his fellow examinees rushed to bookshops to grab books about current affairs and New Learning as their references. Booksellers also took the opportunity to profit from these desperate customers by raising book prices.[49] After another failure in 1903, Liu came to the conclusion that his contemporaries had "abandoned

---

48. "Zhu Zhisan riji (lianzai zhi yi)," 344, 326, 335, 285–288, 340, 335–337.

49. Liu, *Tuixiangzhai riji*, 121 and 609. For a biographical study of Liu, see Harrison, *The Man Awakened from Dreams*.

the learning of Confucius and Mencius and studied Western learning" just "for quick success" in the examinations.[50]

Fiction depicted the examination reform in a cynical yet realistic fashion. A stereotypical plot usually involved (a) an old-guard tutor, whose students have bitterly abandoned him after the examination reform, (b) ignorant and pretentious "elites" who have gained a big advantage from New Learning but in fact know little about it, and (c) anxious young men who rush from (a) to (b). These educated Chinese's utilitarian attitudes toward New Learning books, as well as their stubborn aspiration for officialdom, were a popular subject of literary satire. For example, in *Wenming xiaoshi* (A minor history of civilization) by Li Boyuan (1867–1906), Mr. Wang, the tutor of the three brothers of the Jia family,[51] stubbornly ignores the examination reform and keeps teaching the same old writing tricks for the eight-legged essay because that is the only subject he knows well. However, after the Jia brothers fail in the reformed examination, they bitterly blame Mr. Wang for impeding their "careers." They turn to another tutor, Mr. Yiao, who claims to be a "current affairs" expert and has an impressive record in helping his students pass the examination. Following Mr. Yiao's advice, they begin to order and read newspapers and new books from Shanghai to familiarize themselves with New Learning terminology, so that they may become "civilized" and succeed in the next one.[52]

An employee of Enlightenment Bookstore (*Kaiming shuju*)[53] also noticed the customers' shifting preferences when he sold books outside the examination hall in Nanjing in 1902 and Kaifong in 1903.[54] During his stay in Nanjing, he managed to sell an impressive number of copies of the New Learning books he had brought from Shanghai (see table 2.1). Though he stated that his main incentive to sell New Learning books outside the Nanjing examination hall was to "spread the seeds of Civilization" to the twenty thousand examinees, he was

50. Ibid., 126.

51. The three brothers of the Jia family are Jia Ziyou, Jia Pingxuan, and Jia Gemin. Their names are homonyms for words meaning fake freedom, fake equality, and fake revolution.

52. Li, *Wenming xiaoshi*, 109–116.

53. This Kaiming Bookstore was a Shanghai-based bookstore publishing and selling New Learning books. It had no connection with the later well-known Kaiming Bookstore established in the 1930s.

54. Gongnu, "Jinling maishu ji" [Selling books in Nanjing] (1902), and Wang Weitai, "Bianliang maishu ji" [Selling books in Kaifong] (1903), in *Zhongguo xiandai chuban shiliao*, 1:384–415. According to Zhang Jinglu, these two pieces have the same author, and he might be one of the employees or co-owners of this bookstore.

TABLE 2.1. Books Sold by Enlightenment Bookstore
outside the Examination Hall in Nanjing in 1902

Subject	Kinds	Copies
History	38	893
Geography	19	337
Politics and law	27	533
Economics	6	168
Education	7	94
Science	28	427
Periodicals	5	189
Edited essay collections	9	282
Examination companions	5	46

Source: Gongnu, "Jinling maishu ji" [Selling books in
Nanjing] (1902), in Zhang ed., Zhongguo xiandai chuban
shiliao, 1:385.

aware that his customers now preferred the New Learning books over traditional
examination companions for practical reasons. He noticed that books on world
history and modern history were particularly popular chiefly because rumor
had it that the "examiners would ask about foreign politics and history this time,"
so "examinees had to get a rough understanding of those subjects [to succeed
in the exam.]" Most customers who came to his book stand asked for quick-
to-finish and easy-to-use handbooks of New Learning that they could bring into
the examination hall as references. He and his friend thus joked that if they could
compile titles like *Wushi zitong waiguo shi* (Self-taught foreign history) or
Xizheng bu qiuren (Study-it-yourself Western politics), they could make a big
fortune.[55]

Whether reading New Learning books helped examinees to get ahead in the
old literati-official career path remains contested among cultural historians of
late Qing China.[56] That said, the educated Chinese at the time seemed to firmly
believe in the magic of New Learning books. Their anxiety and their desire to
pass the examination contributed to this cultural fever, which triggered a rapid
expansion of the New Learning market. A closer look at the growth rates of the
SDCK's book sales also allows us to see the strong correlation between its

55. Ibid., 383–385.

56. For discussion of whether people who read New Learning books had an advantage in
the reformed exams, see Pan, *Wan Qing shiren de xixue yuedu shi*, 298–322, and Cao, "Keju,
chuban yu zhishi zhuanxing," 188–253.

growth and the announcements of examination reforms: as figure 2.1 shows, its sales surged sharply in 1898, owing to the 1898 Reform. Sales increased 25 percent in 1900–1901, doubled again in 1901–1902 after the Qing court announced the abolishment of the eight-legged essay format, grew another 63 percent in the next year, and reached their peak in 1903 when the first reformed metropolitan examination was held in Kaifeng.

Shortcuts and Disorders at the New Frontier of the Knowledge Economy

This reform-induced New Learning fever created opportunities for adventurous cultural entrepreneurs and intellectuals with foreign connections; at the same time, it also unsettled the existing order of the Chinese book trade. Throughout the Qing dynasty, as Cynthia Brokaw points out, textual knowledge diffused throughout China from the cultural heartland to the hinterlands, and the printed books produced and circulated throughout the empire appeared to be surprisingly homogenous. An almost timeless body of the common core of texts—(1) educational and examination works (primers, classics, examination reference aids, and model essays); (2) how-to guides (manuals, daily encyclopedias, handbooks); and (3) entertainment works (fiction, songbooks, popular poetry collections)—were printed and read by Chinese in different regions over the centuries.[57] However, the examination reforms, as well as the educated Chinese's changing reading preference for New Learning books, unsettled this common core of texts and destabilized the Chinese book world. The prospects of traditional educational and examination works were gloomy because these seemingly "timeless" titles would soon become obsolete if educated Chinese no longer needed to study the *Four Books and Five Classics* and practice model essays for the examinations. For those who made their living comfortably by printing and distributing conventional examination references and aids, this was an unprecedented existential crisis. After having heard the rumors about the possible abolishment of the eight-legged essay in 1898, for instance, Yan Hai-lan, a Jiangxi bookseller, asserted pessimistically to his friend that if this policy was enforced, the prep books that he had invested thousands of taels in publishing would become wastepaper overnight.[58] Yan's concern was

57. Brokaw, *Commerce in Culture*, 553–559.
58. Pi, *Shifutang riji*, 3:262.

not groundless. As Enlightenment Bookstore's sales list indicated, customers outside the Nanjing examination hall in 1902 had lost interest in conventional companions and references. Only forty-six copies were sold. Readers now preferred to spend money on books about world history, science, and politics, which they believed to be essential to success in the reformed examinations.

In the last decade of the Qing dynasty, the business of those who specialized in classic education and examination prep declined as a consequence of the examination reform; the livelihood of many would be even more severely impacted by the abolishment of the civil service examination in 1905. On the other hand, those who could produce New Learning titles to meet the readers' increasing demand would likely reap profits from this emerging new market. However, the technical and intellectual entry barrier to the business of New Learning was high. People with a good command of both European languages and Chinese were rare in late Qing China; consequently good translations were always in short supply. Before the Sino-Japanese War, "Western learning" or New Learning books were mainly European titles translated and edited by foreign missionaries and their Chinese assistants. Most of the titles published by the Jiangnan Arsenal and the SDCK were products of such Sino-foreign collaborations. Some were translated by Chinese who had studied in Europe or America or learned European languages at treaty ports or in missionaries' schools. As one official estimated in an 1894 proposal for establishing a state-sponsored translation institute, it would take at least two years for a young Chinese to have a good enough command of English or French to become an effective translator.[59] For Yan Fu, who spent years studying at the British Royal Naval Academy, having command of foreign languages didn't automatically equip someone to be a qualified translator. A good translator, he argued, also had to grasp the cultural contexts and basic knowledge supporting the text he or she was translating. As a result, he stated, it could take years for one translator to carefully and accurately translate one book into Chinese.[60]

Given the imbalance between the shortage of capable translators and the soaring demand for New Learning books, compiling such books became a well-remunerated vocation. Chinese booksellers now began to hire in-house

59. Ma Jianzhong, "Nishe fanyi shuyuan yi" [A proposal to establish translation academy], *Zhongguo jindai chuban shiliao*, 1:32–33.

60. Yan Fu, "Lun yicai zhi nan" [On the difficulty of being a good translator] (1899), in *Yan Fu heji*, 1:165–167. Also see his correspondence with Zhang Yuanji in 1900 on the same subject.

translators or editors to deliver timely New Learning titles. Or they would pay a lump sum to popular translators or authors, such as Yan Fu and Lin Shu, to obtain their latest manuscripts. When Yan Fu and Lin Shu published their first (and maybe their most famous) translations soon after the Sino-Japanese War, neither of them received any remuneration. However, soon after their books became overnight sensations, booksellers in Shanghai, such as Wang Kangnian, Commercial Press, and Civilization Books, quickly approached them offering money for their next projects. The commercial value of New Learning books allowed these translators to become the first generation of Chinese authors to negotiate and receive copyright royalties, which I will discuss in greater depth in the next chapter.

That said, not every bookseller interested in the New Learning business was able or willing to invest lump sums of money for new translations of Western books. Looking for cheaper alternatives and shortcuts, they made several "breakthroughs" at the supply end that significantly lowered the entry barrier to the New Learning market. The first and foremost shortcut to Western knowledge that the Chinese "discovered," eliminating the burden of learning European languages, was Meiji Japan. Pointing to the prevalence of Chinese characters (*kanji*) in Japanese, many Chinese officials and intellectuals, from Zhang Zhidong to Liang Qichao, believed that it would be easy for educated Chinese to master reading Japanese within a few months.[61]

By translating Japanese books on Western knowledge instead of European books themselves, China could expedite the introduction of new knowledge with lower and shorter-term investment than would be required to cultivate proper translators of European languages. By 1902, it was estimated that more than 60 percent of translations published in China were translated from Japanese.[62] Most of these translations were produced and published by Chinese rather than Japanese. Although some Japanese intellectuals and publishers envisioned the great potential of the Chinese market, in reality Japanese publishers, such as Hakubunkan and Uzanbou, found it very difficult to enter China's New Learning book market.[63] Unauthorized reprinting of their books

61. For example, Liang Qichao, "Lun xue Ribenwen zhi yi" [On the benefits of learning Japanese], in *Yinbingshi heji* 3:1372–73. Originally published in *Qingyi bao*, no. 10 (April 1, 1899): 62.

62. Tsien, "Western Impact on Chinese through Translation," 315.

63. "Seigoku muke no shoseki shuppan gaikyou to Toa Koushi setsuritsu jokyo" [An overview of the publishing business, targeting Qing's market and the establishment of the East Asia Company], *Tosho geppo* 3:5 (February 23, 1905).

was one major challenge they faced, and the inability to compete with the army of Chinese translators was another. Beginning in 1900, study abroad was sponsored and encouraged by the government. Japan, owing to its geographical proximity to China, became the most popular destination for Chinese students; the flood of students traveling to Japan became the new troop of translators of the New Learning knowledge. The mainstream Japanese at the time, known as *futsūbun* (standard writing), contained a large number of *kanji* characters; as had been predicted, this allowed Chinese who had spent only a few months studying in Japan, or those who learned Japanese via self-teaching manuals, to manufacture translations without really mastering the language. Driven by patriotism or by economic reasons, many students started their translation projects soon after they arrived in Japan. Translating foreign knowledge, then, was no longer the monopoly of missionary presses, such as the SDCK, or a few exceptional Chinese, like Yan Fu, who spent years learning European languages. After reaching their peak in 1903, the SDCK's annual sales started to decline, while production of the New Learning books, in fact, was growing quickly. The missionaries, who had once been *the* authority on New Learning in post-Sino-Japanese-War China, could no longer stay on top of the game.

This shortcut to Western knowledge via Japanese books, as one bookseller described, had allowed the publishing of translations to accelerate "like rising wind and scudding clouds."[64] Soon the number of translations from Japanese became so numerous that even well-informed readers would feel overwhelmed. For instance, in 1903, Sun Baoxuan (1874–1924), son of a rich and influential official and an extensive reader of New Learning books, declared that there were so many new books and new periodicals translated from Japanese that "the Chinese were no longer able to shut their brains."[65] The number of translations from Japanese books that late Qing Chinese produced was impressive, but many of them fell short in their quality and readability. Since most of the translators had only elementary knowledge of Japanese, it was not uncommon to find that what they did was just to keep all the *kanji* and original Japanese grammatical structures and creatively fill in words for the *kana* characters.

Bao Tianxiao (1876–1972), a Suzhou native who forged his career in Shanghai's booming New Learning market, was such a translator. For three months he studied Japanese with a Japanese monk in Suzhou but eventually decided to quit. With this superficial training, nevertheless, he later started to translate

64. "Jinling maishu ji," 384–385.
65. Sun, *Wangshanlu riji*, 739.

Japanese translations of European novels, such as H. Rider Haggard's *Joan Haste* and Edmondo De Amicis's *Cuore*. Owing perhaps to his eloquent writing style, he somehow established a reputation as a "good translator."[66] Several of his friends who had studied in Japan were also translating books and asked Bao, now a "successful" translator, to find buyers for their manuscripts. In his memoir, Bao recalled that he often had to heavily revise friends' manuscripts before approaching booksellers because "some of them were simply too rough to sell."[67] During his time at Golden Millet Studio, a bookshop opened by a rich official between 1902 and 1904, Bao also claimed, he had to extensively revise and edit manuscripts by a well-known translator named Ye Han to make them comprehensible to readers. As a returning student from Japan, Ye operated not only a Japanese language school but also a translation company in Shanghai. His translations, according to Bao, usually still read like Japanese as Ye seemed to only replace the Japanese possession-indicating particle *no*/の with *zhi*/之, the Chinese character showing possession; as a result, his sentences often were too awkward to be understood at all.[68]

The uneven quality of such New Learning works was a concern to readers and booksellers at the time.[69] The poor readability of the clumsy translations from Japanese books, Liang Qichao argued, was a necessary evil if new knowledge was to be imported quickly and massively. He acknowledged that indeed many translations were no better than "root of grass, cortex of tree, frozen sparrow, and rotten rat," but for the Chinese, like a "hungry refugee suffering from famine," "crap" would be a timely lifeline.[70] Some rotten rat, however, was so bad that even the most desperate refugee wouldn't take it. When publishers purchased such translations for quick commercial return, they often were taking their chances, as most of them were not equipped with the knowledge and method to evaluate whether a manuscript was decent or debased. For publishers who specialized in publishing New Learning books, letterpress and lithography were frequently their preferred methods of printing. While these two methods allowed publishers to produce massive print runs and gave the books a "modern" appearance, they required more up-front capital investment. If a book they published turned out to be unreadable, they would be likely to

66. Bao, *Chuanyinglou huiyilu*, 158, 173–174.
67. Ibid., 241.
68. Ibid., 220, 222–223.
69. *Yishu jingyan lu*, 402; "Jinling maishu ji," 386–387.
70. Liang Qichao, *Qingdai xueshu gailun*, 162.

suffer a great loss of their investments in manuscript and printing. In 1901, for instance, Xia Reifang, manager of Commercial Press, spent ten thousand yuan to purchase the translation of a couple dozen translations from Japanese. It was a disaster because almost all the manuscripts were too bad to be published. [71] Because of this failed investment in atrocious New Learning manuscripts, Commercial Press incurred a financial deficit.[72]

Another alternative enabling the Chinese to produce timely New Learning books without investing in translating Western texts was to compile collectanea, references, and encyclopedic collections of New Learning knowledge using existing texts and periodicals. Most booksellers devoted to this alternative were Shanghai-based and had originally used lithography to produce traditional core texts. Lithography was introduced in China in the mid-nineteenth century by missionaries to produce the Bible and other religious materials locally. Since the 1880s, commercial publishers in Shanghai, both Chinese and foreign, had been using lithography to reproduce rare books and calligraphy, as well as to print illustrated news and novels. As Christopher Reed points out, the relatively low investment, the aesthetic appeal of imprints, the minimal changes in publishing outlook, and the capacity to shrink images and pages made lithography a popular printing method in late nineteenth-century China.[73] In the 1880s and 1890s, during what Reed calls the "golden age" of Shanghai's lithographic printer-publishers, it was estimated that half of their publications were civil service examination–related titles, especially the pocket-sized *Kangxi Dictionary*, the *Four Books and Five Classics* index, and model essays.[74] The rise of these lithographic printer-publishers unavoidably had an impact on the traditional woodblock publishers also specializing in the same body of core texts, but regarding the diffusion of knowledge, they shared and reinforced the very canon that the late imperial publishers and booksellers had established. To reduce the cost per copy, lithographic printer-publishers tended to produce a large number of

71. Tarumoto, *Shoki Shōmu Inshokan kenkyū*, 61, 87.

72. Learning from this lesson, in 1902, Commercial Press established its own in-house "trans-compilation" (*bianyi*) unit to translate, edit, and compile books. To ensure the quality and readability of their books, they hired former Hanlin scholars, Zhang Yuanji and Cai Yuanpei, to take charge of this "trans-compilation" unit. For the establishment of the "trans-compilation" staff, see Tarumoto, *Shoki Shōmu Inshokan kenkyū*, 87–93. For a discussion of the "semiotic modernity" that Commercial Press's *bianyi* practices created and represented, see Meng, *Shanghai and the Edges of Empires*, 33–42.

73. Reed, *Gutenberg in Shanghai*, 87–127.

74. Ibid., 104–122. Also see Sim, "Wan Qing shiyin juye yongshu de shengchan yu liutong."

units (10,000–50,000 copies) per print run, but this practice also made them vulnerable to sudden market shifts. When the examination reforms were enacted, they could not escape a sharp decline.

To cope with readers' changing tastes, some cleverly utilized their editorial experience in making conventional examination aids, leveraging the geographical advantage of treaty port Shanghai to enable them to gain access to new books and newspapers.[75] They started to compile collectanea, classified compilations (*leibian*), references, and encyclopedias of New Learning knowledge for the reformed examinations.[76] Between 1897 and 1904, at least fifty such collectaneas and encyclopedias were published by Shanghai's lithographic printer-publishers. Most of these books' titles included popular keywords, such as *Xixue* (Western Learning), *xinxue* (New Learning), *shiwu* (current affairs), *zhongxi* (Sino-Western), *fuqiang* (wealth and power), and *wanguo* (ten thousand nations/world), to attract eager readers who had succumbed to the New Learning fever. Some compilers of such works did not hesitate to admit that these works were prepared specifically for examinees. For instance, the compiler of *Wanguo zhengzhi congkao* (The international policies series) stated that it was difficult for readers who had spent all their time crafting eight-legged essays to know instantly how to discuss and analyze international policies. To help those struggling examinees, he had collected, classified, and annotated relevant works aiming to assist readers to "meet the government's new demands," as now "international policies" had become a new subject in the reformed examinations.[77] The preface of *Xixue santong* (Tri-comprehensions of Western knowledge) also declared that after the examination and educational reforms, it became "necessary" for students to study Western books, yet the number of translations was too immense for them to manage. So, the author asserts, he has compiled this book as a timely rescue for anxious examinees.[78]

Indeed, some late Qing New Learning encyclopedia authors and bibliographers did embark on ambitious projects to reorganize and classify Western knowledge based on a traditional Chinese bibliographical framework.[79] And

75. For further discussion of the geopolitical advantage of Shanghai, see chapter 5.

76. For the relationship between the emergence of New Learning encyclopedias and civil service examination reform, see Amelung, "The Complete Complication of New Knowledge."

77. "Xu" [Preface], *Wanguo zhengzhi congkao*, 1.

78. Xie Ruochao, "Xu" [Preface], in Yuan and Yan, eds., *Xixue santong*, 1–3.

79. Amelung, "The Complete Complication of New Knowledge."

some revived the tradition of collecting statecraft essays (*jingshi wenbian*) when editing and compiling collections of essays on current affairs, and they thus brought New Learning into the Chinese statecraft genealogy. It is, however, also true that many of these New Learning collectaneas and encyclopedias simply classified and indexed the extensive Western knowledge into searchable, topical, and thematic categories corresponding to the new examination subjects and format, without further intellectual reflection or reinterpretation.[80] In other words, they collected and rearranged existing New Learning texts but didn't produce new knowledge. Despite such compilations' impressive length and scale, the production of these New Learning collectaneas, references, and encyclopedias was often abridged. Their contents were highly duplicative as the "sources" of knowledge they relied upon were largely the same. To make their works stand out, authors and compilers often had to emphasize how their methods for collecting, selecting, and arranging these "common" sources were better than those of their competitors. For instance, in the preface of *Zhongwai cewen daguan* (Grand prospectus of policy questions regarding Chinese and foreign matters), Lu Runyang (1841–1914) stressed that the essays in this twenty-eight-volume collection were carefully selected and classified by qualified compiler Lei Jin, the chief editor of *Shen bao*, who was familiar with current affairs. And this made it "more useful" than other similar titles that were "scraped together randomly" just "for profit."[81]

There was yet an even simpler alternative for producing New Learning books than investing in this "great cut-and-paste enterprise (*ju jian zhi ye*)":[82] to simply reprint the New Learning titles that sold well.[83] Therefore, it was not uncommon to see multiple "editions" of the same New Learning books in late Qing China. The SDCK, for example, found almost twenty different reprint editions of its best seller *Taixi shinshi lanyiao* in 1898. It was estimated that there were at least seven editions of Lin Shu's *Bali chahua nü yishi* circulating in the market at the time.[84] Jiangnan Arsenal's *Zuozhi chuyan* (John Frye's translation of J. H. Burton's *Political Economy for Use in Schools, and for Private Instruction*)

80. For instance, the six volumes of the New Learning encyclopedia, *Xinzheng yingshi bidu* [Must-read new politics for examination], accorded with the six subjects of the reformed examination; see Sim, "Wan Qing shiyin juye yongshu de shengchan yu liutong," 262.

81. Lu Runyang, "Xu," in Lei, *Zhongwai cewen daguan*, 3–4.

82. Yao, *Shanghai xianhua*, 117.

83. For a discussion of different types of reprinting in the late Qing, see chapter 5.

84. Ah Ying, "Guanyu *Chahuu nü yishi*."

also spawned at least ten different reprint editions. It was not unusual to find books with almost identical titles but containing completely different contents, or books with distinct titles and authors that turned out to be the same work.[85]

The realm of New Learning knowledge was flourishing yet disordered; as new titles continued to be released rapidly, it became difficult, even for the well-read authors of New Learning bibliographies and reading guides, to keep up with the latest publications or to gather accurate publishing information. Within few years after 1895, Chinese readers experienced a transition from "information inadequacy" to "information overload." Some basic principles and techniques developed in China's bibliographic tradition to assess different editions and textual authenticity across long spans of time became increasingly invalid when it came to the New Learning books. Many publishers of these New Learning books were new; it was thus hard for readers to rely upon their knowledge about historical *shanben* (fine edition) publishers to judge whether one New Learning publisher was more trustworthy than another. Most of the New Learning books were also newly published titles. When multiple editions of the same book appeared in the marketplace simultaneously within a short period, the conventional technique to detect the earliest (thus the most "authentic") edition, by comparing publishing dates, paper stock, and fonts, was no longer applicable. To accommodate this reality, in his *Zengban dong xi xue shulu* (The expanded edition of bibliography of Eastern and Western learnings), Xu Weize listed different "editions" of the same titles. Although he managed to indicate some of the "authentic" editions of particular titles in his entries, he was deeply concerned about the absence of rules and trust in the book world since the influx of New Learning books. "When there are not enough translation books [available], advancing knowledge will be difficult," he stated, "but now we have too many and too miscellaneous new books. Booksellers scraped [texts] together into books or reprinted books under different titles for profit." Seeing unauthorized and unregulated reprints as harmful to the order of knowledge, he urged his fellow Chinese to regulate publications and suggested that the Chinese government adopt the law of *banquan*/copyright.[86]

For publishers and booksellers, reprinting was a severe threat to their business as well as to the book trade as a whole. In a 1903 pamphlet that Commercial

---

85. For a discussion of the editions of late Qing New Learning books, see Pan, *Wan Qing shiren de xixue yuedu shi*, 304–305.

86. Xu Weize, ed., *Zhengban dong xi xue shulu*, in *Jindai yishu mu*, 32–33.

Press published to promote copyright, the proprietor stated that "although now the intellectual circle is full of vitality, as soon as a book is published, profit-driven people rush to reprint it."[87] The harm done by unauthorized reprinting could sometimes be fatal. The majority of Japanese publishers withdrew from the Chinese market because of Chinese piracy. For instance, when Uzanbou first imported New Learning books they had translated from Japanese to Chinese, they could comfortably sell one to two thousand copies per order. However, their "authentic" copies were quickly overpowered by the cheaper Chinese reprints. Within less than two years, it gave up its operation in China.[88] Guangzhi Books (*Guangzhi shuju*), a Shanghai-based publishing house specializing in translations, also made a public announcement in the press declaring that piracy had caused the company a "serious deficit," so they were determined to take legal action against those who reprinted their books without permission.[89]

Similar announcements could be found on a daily basis in late Qing newspapers. Some publishers urged their readers to "distinguish" between their high-quality, authentic copies and shoddy reprints by "insincere" booksellers.[90] Others condemned unauthorized reprinting and threatened to report those responsible to the officials. Unauthorized reprinting, as discussed in the previous chapter, was not a new phenomenon in the Chinese publishing world, and proprietor statements declaring ownership of books could also be found periodically in the late imperial period. However, as the relatively stable order of late imperial core texts was shaken by the shifting intellectual trends and examination reforms, and as New Learning books became a profitable commodity, the volume and frequency of such proprietor claims and statements reached an unprecedented level. While such statements became a new norm in the late Qing book trade, they also indicated how common the problem of unauthorized reprinting may have been at the time. It was in this context that the convention "*banquan suoyou fanke bijiu*/copyright is reserved, and reprinting will be pursued and punished," and the *banquan*/copyright seals I discussed in chapter 1, became popular.

87. *Banquan kao*, 1–2.

88. Uzanbou, ed., *Uzanbou shuppan nen shi*, 620.

89. "Guangzhi shuju guanggao" [Guangzhi Books advertisement], *ZWRB*, February 1, 1904.

90. "Shanghai zhizaoju fashou tushu guanggao" [Shanghai Arsenal book-selling advertisement], *ZWRB*, November 15, 1904.

Conclusion

The conventional narrative about the introduction of copyright to China at the turn of the twentieth century is a story of how foreign powers imposed their Western legal doctrines and systems on China to protect their subjects' commercial interests. The Chinese were forced to "learn the law at gunpoint," yet the attempt failed because the Chinese state cared only about controlling the press and Chinese society did not appreciate this notion.[91] In this chapter, however, I argue that, at the turn of the twentieth century, what interested foreign booksellers also interested Chinese booksellers and authors. While treaty powers tried to make the Qing state adopt intellectual property laws at the negotiating table, the concept of *banquan*/copyright began to be embraced and promoted by Chinese booksellers and some authors for their commercial interests.

The series of sea changes in Chinese intellectual trends, education policy, and book market orders turned *banquan*/copyright into a popular concept for claiming ownership of publications and criminalizing unauthorized reprinting. China's defeat in the Sino-Japanese War initiated a change in educated Chinese's attitude toward Western knowledge; the Chinese intellectual community's suddenly increased interest in New Learning knowledge made New Learning books a desirable and profitable commodity, and further created a new cultural market. The commercial value of New Learning books not only prompted booksellers to invest money in publishing more new titles but, at the same time, also made them more concerned with unauthorized reprinting. In the SDCK's revealing case, it is clear that New Learning publications became a property worth protection only after they became valuable in the marketplace. It was in this context that not-for-profit missionary presses started to use the concept of copyright to declare their exclusive ownership and labeled Chinese pirates as the equivalent of thieves stealing others' property.

The Qing state's educational and examination reforms beginning in 1898 elevated the New Learning knowledge to the status of the state's new intellectual orthodoxy. Many educated Chinese rushed to adopt and consume new books for a practical reason: to pursue their old goal of officialdom in the changing new examination system. The Chinese book trade had been deeply interlocked with the state's education policy and trends in the literati

91. Alford, *To Steal a Book Is an Elegant Offense*, chap. 3.

community, because the educated Chinese had been the mainstream readership in China, and the educational and examination books had been the major
core texts and sure sellers in late imperial book production. So, when the Qing
state reformed its educational and examination system, educated Chinese responded to these reforms by rushing to the new "Way." When this occurred, the
dynamics and structures of the Chinese book trade were shaken
correspondingly.

Between 1900 and 1905, while the publishing scale of New Learning books
grew dramatically, the market for examination-related books declined and eventually collapsed after 1905. During this period, the production of New Learning books was no longer the monopoly of Western missionary presses or of a
select few Chinese who knew European languages. The Chinese "discovered"
Japan as an ideal economical shortcut to Western knowledge and began to mass-
produce New Learning titles by translating Japanese books into Chinese. At
the same time, booksellers changed production modes: they were now willing
to invest money in purchasing promising manuscripts and used lithography or
letterpress to produce New Learning books in large quantities. If the investment
succeeded, the booksellers generated considerable profit, but if their investment
in manuscripts failed, or others reprinted their famous titles, they could suffer
a more significant financial loss. The ups and downs of Commercial Press in its
early years showed that publishing New Learning books was a highly profitable
and highly risky business at the turn of the twentieth century in China.

During this period, Chinese booksellers progressively dominated the New
Learning market. Missionary presses like the SDCK and Japanese publishers
who envisioned an enormous Chinese market captured only a small part of the
market. The problems of reprinting that bothered the missionaries and forced
Japanese publishers to withdraw from the Chinese market also troubled these
Chinese booksellers. As illustrated in this chapter and the previous one, Chinese booksellers adopted these foreign publishers' arguments and began to promote the new concept of banquan/copyright to claim and justify ownership
of their publications. By the end of 1903, the term banquan, which was rarely
known or used by Chinese before 1900, had become part of Chinese booksellers'
common language. The various reprints of one book, which had previously
been viewed as "alternative editions," were now considered pirated editions
that should be banned. An example of this change in point of view can be seen
in the case of Lin Shu's *Bali chahua nü yishi* and *Heinu yutian lu*: after *Bali
chahua nü yishi* first appeared in 1899, there were several reprints circulating in

China, but the translator, Lin Shu, the original block-possessor, Wei, and the Shanghai bookseller, Wang, who bought its "right of printing blocks" seem never to have criminalized those who reprinted *Bali chahua nü yishi*.[92] When Civilization Books published *Heinu yutian lu* in Shanghai in 1905, the translators and the publisher announced their proprietorship and denounced the pirates publicly in the press.

92. Even when literature scholars like Ah Ying did his bibliographic study of *Bali chahua nü yishi*, the various reprints were simply regarded as different editions rather than pirated editions. It would be worthwhile in the future to investigate when and why bibliographers started to use "pirated edition" instead of "alternative edition" to label the reprints in their studies.

3

"The Everlasting Reward for My Labor of Mind"

THE EMERGENCE OF the New Learning cultural market not only affected how Chinese booksellers regarded the ownership of the new books they published, but also profoundly reshaped the economic lives of those who produced new works. The soaring demand for more New Learning titles made it possible for late Qing authors and translators to make a living, or even a fortune, by writing. When the concept of *banquan*/copyright became a powerful means that Chinese booksellers used to claim ownership of publications and prosecute unauthorized reprinting, authors and translators also began to invoke it to justify why they too, as the originators of the works they created, were entitled to the commercial profit their works generated. This chapter focuses on Yan Fu (1854–1921), one of the most influential translators in modern China, to illustrate how Chinese authors and translators developed a workable and sustainable *banquan* system to cope with their changing economic life at the turn of the twentieth century.

Yan Fu is often considered by contemporary legal scholars and intellectual historians to be one of the earliest Chinese intellectuals to promote *banquan*/copyright.[1] Like Fukuzawa Yukichi, Yan Fu has been known for introducing and articulating Western knowledge to his countrymen as the secret of Western wealth and power.[2] So it is no surprise that Yan's "pioneering" awareness

1. Scholars believe that Yan Fu's *Yuan Fu* was the first book involved in copyright negotiation. Sun, *Yan Fu nianpu*, 145; Li, *Zhongguo jindai banquan shi*, 20–27.
2. For Yan Fu's translation and his understanding of Western knowledge, see Schwartz, *In Search of Wealth and Power*; Huang, *Ziyou di suoyiran*.

of copyright would be attributed to his experience studying abroad and his exceptional command of the nineteenth-century European political economy.[3] Indeed, as briefly discussed in the preceding chapter, when, in 1902, Yan wrote to the Qing government's top educational administrator urging the state to protect *banquan*, he emphasized that *banquan*/copyright was key to the progress of modern civilization and a positive concept possessing universal moral value. It is worth noting, however, that Yan did not wave the flag of Western progressiveness from the very beginning of his translating career and ask for royalties. Rather, he commenced advocating for copyright only after his first translation work, *Tianyanlun* (The changes caused by Nature), became a timely best seller in 1897. Had Yan been motivated by an abstract belief in progress, he would likely have claimed his copyright of *Tianyanlun* from the beginning. His becoming an earnest champion of *banquan*/copyright coincided with the commodification of New Learning knowledge discussed in the previous chapter. Yan Fu was undoubtedly one of the leading figures in modern Chinese intellectual history, but we must bear in mind that he was also an active participant in China's changing knowledge economy. While Yan's everyday financial needs might have driven him to have increasing concern for copyright after he recognized how much profit his translations could bring, the popularity of *Tianyanlun* might also have convinced publishers that the money paid to buy Yan Fu's latest manuscripts would be a wise investment.

Making a case for *banquan*/copyright and progress in petitions was one thing; putting it into practice was a different matter. Unlike other contemporary translators, such as Lin Shu, Yan Fu did not relish the idea of simply selling his manuscripts for a onetime payment based on the length of the work and its market potential. He also was not keen to become a public intellectual/cultural entrepreneur, like Liang Qichao or Wang Kangnian, to run publishing enterprises in the interest of publishing his own works. What he wanted was to receive a long-term royalty for each copy of his works that was published and sold. Tracing the publishing of Yan's first four major translations between 1897 and 1904, this chapter will take a close look at how he changed his work pattern, negotiated with publishers for remuneration and royalties, developed various mechanisms to remotely monitor his publishers and calculate his royalties, and eventually achieved this goal. Both he and his publishers were searching for a workable system to enforce and practice *banquan*/copyright in the booming New Learning book market. What they ultimately developed would

3. Li, *Zhongguo jindai banquan shi*, 20–27

become the standard procedure for authors to ensure receipt of their royalties in modern China. By tracing Yan Fu's trials and errors in securing his long-term royalties, this chapter illuminates one little-known yet crucial aspect in the history of intellectual property rights in China: how *banquan*/copyright was owned and transferred by booksellers and authors as a kind of incorporeal property. How did authors like Yan Fu maintain ownership of their works even after their manuscripts were sold and published? And how did they secure their share of the profit from their publications as originators of the works and original owners of its *banquan*/copyright?

Selling Adam Smith

Before Yan Fu was known for his translations of European works on political economy, he was an anxious marginal figure in the late Qing intellectual community who took an atypical career path. Born and raised in Fujian in the aftermath of the Taiping Rebellion, Yan Fu, son of an herbal doctor, received the traditional education to prepare him for the civil service examination. The premature death of his father, however, forced Yan to drop out of the local academy and give up this "orthodox" pursuit of officialdom. At the age of fifteen, to get a free education, he enrolled in the newly established Fujian Naval Academy to become a naval officer. Later, in 1877, he and a handful of other students were sent to England to study at the Royal Naval Academy in Greenwich. During his two years of study in England, it became clear to him and his guardian, the Qing ambassador in London, that he might be more suitable to be a teacher, a diplomat, or a statesman than a naval officer. After returning to China, he embarked on what turned out to be a dead-end career at the naval academy as a language instructor, first in Fuzhou and then in Tianjin. Although he was one of the exceptional few Chinese who had studied abroad, he was unable to advance to a higher rank in the government because he did not have the proper *jinshi* degree in hand.[4]

During the Sino-Japanese War, a war that killed and injured many of his old classmates and students at the naval academy, Yan Fu started to translate Thomas Huxley's *Evolution and Ethics* into Chinese as *Tianyanlun*, as his response to China's defeat in the war. *Tianyanlun* was by no means a literal translation of *Evolution and Ethics*, as Yan significantly modified Huxley's original text and

---

4. For a general biographical account of Yan Fu, see Wang, *Yan Fu zhuan*, and Pi, *Yan Fu dazhuan*.

added his interpretation, comments, and references to Chinese classics to advocate social Darwinism in China. Like most of the literary and academic works by Chinese *wenren* literati, *Tianyanlun* was first circulated in manuscript. He hired personal copyists to make multiple copies, sent them to his peers and teachers, asked for feedback, and, most importantly, made this work available to others.[5] It soon became popular among Yan's friends and their cultural circles. Increasingly, Yan received requests from anxious readers who wanted to borrow the manuscript; some copies never made it back into his hands.[6] In 1896 Yan started to seriously explore the possibility of publishing it.[7] The book was finally published in 1898 as one volume of *Shenshijizhai congshu* (Cautious Foundation Studio collectanea). Later that same year, Yan Fu published his lithographic edition.[8] There was no claim of *banquan*/copyright in the Cautious Foundation Studio edition. In the letters in which Yan Fu discussed the publishing of *Tianyanlun*, there was also no mention of *banquan*/copyright or financial remuneration at all.

Like Lin Shu's *Bali chahua nü yishi* and Timothy Richard's *Taixi shinshi lanyiao*, *Tianyanlun* was the right book published at just the right time, as it aptly satisfied the appetite of educated Chinese readers hungry for more New Learning books. Various reprint editions quickly hit the market. It is estimated that there were at least eleven different editions available at the time.[9] Chinese readers were fascinated by Yan's elegant writing as well as Huxley's social evolutionism. Lu Xun and his brother, for instance, could still recall, decades later, how much they valued this book as schoolboys in Nanjing.[10] The success of *Tianyanlun* transformed him from a little-known instructor at Beiyang Naval Academy to a famous, admired intellectual in China. Not only did many progressive high-ranking officials start to befriend him and try to recruit him to their offices, but even the emperor himself summoned him to discuss current affairs.[11]

5. For a more detailed discussion of the various editions of *Tianyanlun* and the circulation of *Tianyanlun* manuscripts, see Wang, *Tianyanlun chuanbo yu Qingmo Minchu de shehui dongyuan*.

6. "Yu Wudi shu" [Letter to the fifth younger brother] (1897), in *Yan Fu he ji*, 1:117.

7. For example, he consulted with Liang Qichao and Yu Lulun on this matter. See "Yu Liang Qichao shu 1" [Letter to Liang Qichao 1] (1896), in Yan, *Yan Fu ji*, 3:513; "Yu Wu Lulun shu 1" [Letter to Wu Lulun 1] (1897), in *Yan Fu ji*, 3:522.

8. *Yen Fu ji*, 5:1317.

9. Sun, *Yan Fu nianpu*, 133.

10. Lu Xun, "*Suoji*" [Trivial notes], in *Zhaoha xishi*, 49–50.

11. Sun, *Yan Fu niapu*, 97–113.

All these new privileges were unthinkable for any member of the literati who, like him, held only the lowest civil degree, *xiucai*, at that time. *Tianyanlun* had made Yan Fu into an intellectual celebrity and helped him generate cultural and social capital.

Aware that the popularity of *Tianyanlun* also had a commercial dimension, Yan changed his working pattern when he embarked on his second translation project: to translate Adam Smith's *The Wealth of Nations* into Chinese. Before he finished his translation, he began to seek a "buyer" who could offer a good deal from the outset. When negotiating with potential buyers of *Yuan Fu*, his translation of *The Wealth of Nations*, he actively invoked the concept of *banquan*/copyright to justify to publishers why he should receive not just a lump sum in remuneration but also long-term royalties. In Yan's view, as the creator and thus the owner of *Yuan Fu*, he was entitled to sell it to anyone he liked and as many times as he could. Publishers who acquired the manuscript of *Yuan Fu* from Yan did not enjoy an exclusive right to publish it. As a matter of fact, he sold the publishing rights of *Yuan Fu* at least three times at the turn of the twentieth century and subsequently earned a considerable profit.

The first time the term *banquan* appeared in Yan Fu's writings was in 1899 when he tried to convince Zhang Yuanji, at that time the director of the Translation Department at Nanyang Public School in Shanghai and later head of the Trans-Compilation Department of Commercial Press, to buy his forthcoming *Yuan Fu*. Initially what Yan Fu wanted was a full-time job as an in-house translator for Nanyang Public School.[12] After failing to persuade Zhang to offer him the job, Yan shifted to a new proposal and asked Zhang to buy the manuscript of *Yuan Fu*, which was only half complete at the time. His asking price was 3,000 taels at first, and in 1900 the deal was closed for 2,000 taels. During his negotiations with Zhang, Yan at one point threatened to sell the work to another institution that allegedly was willing to pay more than 3,200 taels; Yan used this leverage to pressure Zhang to come up with a better offer.[13]

In addition to a lump sum of 2,000 taels, Yan Fu asked Zhang for an additional 20 percent royalty on *Yuan Fu* as a reward for his diligent work. He argued that *banquan*/copyright royalty, as a form of guaranteed financial returns, would encourage more people to devote time and energy to translating Western knowledge. Emphasizing that copyright was not a selfish monopoly of knowledge, he asserted that the "Westerners" opposed monopoly but celebrated

---

12. "Yu Zhang Yuanji shu 1" (1899), in *Yen Fu ji*, 3:526.
13. "Yu Zhang Yuanji shu 4–10" (1899–1900), in *Yen Fu ji*, 3:531–543.

the privilege of copyright because they knew how much their countries would lose if they failed to reward talented individuals.[14] In 1902, Yan Fu further developed this argument in a letter to Zhang Baixi, the commissioner of the Imperial University, urging him to acknowledge *banquan*/copyright by prohibiting unauthorized reprinting. Unauthorized reprinting would, he argued, reduce authors' and translators' motivation to produce new works. If the government gave free rein to "greedy publishers" to reprint valuable new works, authors and translators might become deeply disillusioned and abandon their efforts to enlighten the public; as a result, national progress would slow down, and China might be at risk of collapsing. Although copyright protection seemed to be an insignificant matter for the government, he boldly proclaimed that it was a crucial aspect of Enlightenment values and would determine whether China could strengthen itself.[15]

Yan Fu heavily employed the rhetoric of progress and civilization as well as the argument for wealth and power in his letters to tie together his economic interests and the future development of China. A closer examination of his economic life indicates that he was consistently struggling with his finances at the time: he had a large family in Fujian to feed, and his opium habit was expensive. However, his bureaucratic career had been hindered owing to his lack of a higher civil service degree. In his diary and family correspondence, he often complained that the salary of a middle-ranking bureaucrat was not sufficient to enable him to maintain the image of a *bella figura* in Beijing. In letters to his wife, the high price of tailor-made clothes and the cost of supporting both a household in Fujian and one in Beijing were often the subjects of his concern. When he ran short of funds, in the late 1890s, he would borrow money to maintain his lifestyle and feed the family.

Financial straits also drove him to use *Yuan Fu* as the vehicle for repaying a 3,000-tael debt. According to Bao Tianxiao, Yan Fu borrowed 3,000 taels from Kuai Guangdian, a wealthy official/intellectual, around 1900. Yan failed to repay the debt, so he offered the manuscript of *Yuan Fu* and some other translations instead. Kuai accepted those manuscripts as repayment of the debt because the success of *Tianyanlun* convinced him that Yan's works were valuable assets. As Kuai's private employee, Bao was directed to open a publishing house, Golden Millet Studio, in 1901 to publish Yan's manuscripts, sell them, and make a profit as soon as possible. For a few years, Golden Millet Studio was an active New

14. "Yu Zhang Yuanji shu 11–12" (1901), in *Yen Fu ji*, 3:543–546.
15. "Yu Zhang Baixi shu 2" [Letter to Zhang Baixi 2] (1902), in *Yen Fu ji*, 3:577–578.

Learning publishing house and organized public lectures to promote Yan Fu's translation of John Stuart Mill's *A System of Logic*, but its operation came to an end after Kuai's investment failed to generate a desirable return. After the closing of Golden Millet Studio, there was one thing that continued to bother Bao regarding *Yuan Fu*: Commercial Press had published a new edition of *Yuan Fu*, and apparently Yan Fu received payment from Commercial Press. In Bao's view, Yan should not have made such an arrangement: since he had given *Yuan Fu* to Kuai as repayment of his loan, *Yuan Fu* should be Kuai's possession rather than Yan's.[16]

There was one thing Bao did not know, however. When Yan used *Yuan Fu* to pay his 3,000-tael debt, he also sold it to Zhang Yuanji for 2,000 taels and a 20 percent copyright royalty. In total, Yan managed to generate considerable wealth by selling his translation of Adam Smith's *The Wealth of Nations* several times: a 5,000-tael remuneration, the 20 percent copyright royalty from Nanyang Public School, and later another copyright royalty from Commercial Press. Between the publication of *Tianyanlun* and the publication of *Yuan Fu*, Yan's involvement in this emerging New Learning cultural market had profoundly changed his economic life. His financial needs were fulfilled by this new stream of income as his translations became a popular commodity in the late Qing book market. Having failed to advance in the bureaucratic system, he now found that royalties from translations offered him an alternative career path: that of a translator working for profit.

Justifying the Author's Profits

Most of the discourses, phrasing, and rhetoric Yan Fu used in his letters to Zhang Yuanji and Zhang Baixi to make a case for copyright were neither original nor unique for the time. His argument stressing the correlation between copyright and progressive modern civilization echoes what Fukazawa Yukichi had written almost a half century earlier. His assertions in these letters were not distinctively different from those of his contemporaries, such as Young J. Allen of the SDCK or Lian Quan of Civilization Books, who also invoked the concept of *banquan*/copyright to request official protection against unauthorized reprinting. But neither Fukazawa Yukichi, Young J. Allen, nor Lian Quan was *just* a translator/author like Yan; they were cultural entrepreneurs who also invested money in producing the books they claimed. As discussed in chapter 1,

16. Bao, *Chuanyinglou huiyilu*, 218–223, 237–241.

Fukazawa's dual roles as translator and printing-block possessor injected ambiguity into his ownership of his books. He never entirely departed from his role as publisher, and thus the question of whether his authorship alone would constitute ownership of his works was never raised. Unlike them, Yan Fu had little or no interest in operating his own publishing business. Throughout most of his life, he trusted publishers to take care of the publication and distribution of his works, as long as he could receive remunerations and royalties. In other words, his possession of *banquan* did not originate from his ownership of the printing blocks or other means of publication. This set him apart from most contemporary promoters of *banquan*/copyright. To justify why his exclusive ownership of his works should be acknowledged and why he was entitled to receive royalties continuously, he emphasized the reward he was owed for the mental labor he put into translating important New Learning works.

Yan Fu's major works, like other popular New Learning books at the turn of the century, were translations of foreign books. This factor determined what kind of strategy he could effectively use to justify *banquan*/copyright ownership. Instead of focusing on artistic creativity and intellectual originality, he emphasized that the mental labor he devoted to translating, as well as his cultural contribution in enhancing the development of China, deserved to be rewarded in the form of royalties.[17] The core concept Yan Fu invoked to articulate this labor-reward logic was drudgery. In the first letter to Zhang Yuanji on his proposed royalty plan, he told Zhang he agreed that since Nanyang Public School had bought the manuscript of *Yuan Fu*, all the profit this book's sales generated should belong to the school. However, "because the translator [I] devoted so much time and energy [in work]," he argued, "I was wondering whether I could get a certain share from the sale as the royalty of the translator."[18] In 1903, when Yan wrote a public letter to Zhang Baixi, he also used the "hard work should be rewarded" rhetoric to urge the government to recognize *banquan*/copyright. Translating was the most difficult kind of labor, he asserted, and claimed that translators had to possess exhaustive reserves of energy and spirit to finish a project. Therefore, granting copyright to translators would be not only a fair

17. The argument that *banquan* protection is a privilege bestowed on booksellers and authors for their cultural contributions indicates that *banquan* could not come into being by itself but had to be granted by some authority. For more discussion of this process and its problems, see chapter 4.

18. "Yu Zhang Yuanji shu 1" (1899), in *Yen Fu ji*, 3:541.

reward but also an encouragement for future projects.[19] Similar words were uttered by Lian Quan, proprietor of Civilization Books, in his 1903 letter to Zhang Baixi. When arguing why his *banquan*/copyright needed to be protected, he pointed to the "tiny labor" (*wailao*) he had made as an editor of these textbooks. In responding to this letter with an announcement of protection, Zhang stated that "reprinting was strictly prohibited," because this was "a sign of respect for the drudgery (*kuxin*) endured by translators and editors."[20]

Like many of his contemporaries, other literati turned New Learning entrepreneurs, Yan also tended to assert his disinterest in profits. Although in his letters advocating *banquan*/copyright he repeatedly emphasized that royalty was a legitimate reward for his diligent work, he often used a dismissive tone to describe the material reward he was asking for, perhaps to maintain a sort of cultural dignity for being above worldly pursuits. For instance, in the letter to Zhang Baixi, Yan stated that he dedicated his time to translating new books into Chinese to introduce Western civilization to the Chinese public, and asked, "How could people ignore the labor I have put in and expropriate my tiny remuneration (*weichou*)?"[21]

The rhetoric of "tiny remuneration" was also part of Yan's passive-aggressive argument for authors' or translators' exclusive copyright ownership of their works. Presenting himself as a selfless agent of enlightenment, he had to elucidate why protecting copyright rather than allowing free reprinting was truly helpful to the dissemination of knowledge. "I ask for copyright not because I don't realize the considerable benefits of enlightened education that everyone would acquire if new books could be reprinted freely," Yan stated in his letter to Zhang Baixi. However, he further argued, if books could be reprinted freely, those who exhausted themselves in translation might feel that their intellectual contribution was devalued because greedy publishers could easily make a profit at their expense without any hard work. If unauthorized reprinting were allowed in the name of enlightenment, he asked, "Who would go to the trouble of translating [new books]?" Acknowledging and protecting copyright were crucial for a vibrant cultural environment. He asserted that as long as publishers were permitted by the government to reprint others' books, there would be fewer and

19. "Lian bulang shang guanxue dachen lun banxuan shi" (1902), in *Zhongguo banquan shi yanjiu wenxian*, 45.

20. Ibid.

21. "Yu Zhang Baixi shu 2" (1902), in *Yan Fu ji*, 3:577–578. This letter was also published in *Guowen bao* [National news] in May 1902.

fewer people willing to translate or publish new books. Eventually, there would be no more new books to be reprinted, and the Chinese cultural market would collapse. China would then lose the means to enlighten its people and transform itself into a modern nation. Considering the devastating consequences of not protecting copyright, what he asked for was neither avaricious nor unreasonable. He just requested a small reward and modest economic security.[22]

Selling a manuscript for a onetime remuneration was not unusual in the turn-of-the-century New Learning market, but Yan Fu demanded more. For him, the "tiny remuneration" he was entitled to should be a long-term share in the profit his books generated for years to come. In 1900, when he first advanced this idea to Zhang Yuanji, Yan was aware that what he proposed was not a conventional practice. "I knew that after [Nanyang] Public School spent 2,000 taels purchasing this manuscript," he stated, "it should become your property, and all the profit you get from publishing and selling it should belong to you." He was, nevertheless, still hoping that he, as the translator, could receive a certain percentage of the book's sales. Yan Fu called it the author's "permanent profit (*yongyuan zhi liyi*)."[23] Since Zhang did not respond to this suggestion at all, Yan made another attempt to convince him in 1901. Stating that copyright royalty was a convention in Europe, he tried to make a case for this "permanent profit" as a more advanced form of remuneration. He admitted that, in all fairness, he no longer possessed the right to publish *Yuan Fu* and should not covet any part of the profit made after he had sold the manuscript. However, he also believed that by granting him such "permanent profit," Nanyang Public School would benefit economically in the long run. In the aftermath of the Boxer Rebellion and the Qing court's call for "New Policy" reform, he argued, the value of his book *Yuan Fu*, along with the demand for good New Learning books, had increased significantly. Publishers now had to compete more intensively for new translation works of superior quality. Those who were willing to share a small proportion of the profit with the authors, he believed, would be able to attract better authors to publish with them. By granting a percentage of the sales profit to the creator of a book, publishers could also encourage authors and translators to work more conscientiously. Once their income and livelihood came to be determined by the sales of their works, authors and translators, Yan argued, would likely work more diligently to ensure the quality of their new manuscripts.[24]

22. Ibid.
23. "Yu Zhang Yuanji shu 8" (1900), in *Yen Fu heji*, 2:205.
24. "Yu Zhang Yuanji shu 11" (1901), in *Yan Fu heji*, 2:234–235.

Monitoring Royalty from Afar

Using his works' potential market influence as his leverage, Yan persuaded Nan-yang Public School to issue a memorandum promising that he would receive 20 percent of the profit from the sales of *Yuan Fu* for twenty years.[25] By doing so, he would maintain some form of ownership over *Yuan Fu* even though he had "sold" the manuscript to Nanyang Public School. In his mind, as the cre-ator of *Yuan Fu*, his ownership of this work would never cease to exist, and it would, in fact, extend to every copy of *Yuan Fu* produced and sold. This arrange-ment between Nanyang Public School and Yan Fu was unprecedented in China. Although Yan's request for copyright royalty was well-argued, he did not know how to execute it. After the publication of *Yuan Fu*, Yan quickly realized how difficult it was in reality to monitor his book's publication and sales from afar. At the time, Yan was working as both the Chinese general manager of the Kaiping Coal Mine, a British and Chinese joint venture, and the head of the Imperial University's Translation Office. Unhappy with his day jobs, Yan had been planning to become a full-time, independent author making a living solely by writing and translation. But before he could make such a career move, he needed to ensure that his income from writing would be reliable and sustainable. While he spent most of his time in northern China, mostly in Beijing and Tianjin, most of his publishers were based in Shanghai. How to remotely supervise and cal-culate copyright royalty, and how to establish mutual trust with publishers op-erating seven hundred miles away from him, became the key problems he had to face. Between 1901 and 1904, to secure the full amount of royalty to which he thought he was entitled, Yan Fu consistently negotiated, scraped, and strug-gled with his publishers. It took three books for him and his publishers to reach a consensus and work out a procedure to manage his "tiny remuneration."

In September 1901, after learning that Zhang Yuanji, Yan's contact person at Nanyang Public School, was leaving for Commercial Press,[26] Yan asked Zhang to produce a written *banquan*/copyright contract before his departure.[27]

---

25. Ibid.
26. Zhang Yuanji became the headmaster of Nanyang Public School in spring 1901, but quickly was at odds with the American principal. Their relationship was so bad that in May–June 1901, he attempted to resign. Although his resignation was not accepted by Sheng Xuan-huai, the patron of the school, Zhang's intention to leave was clear. Yan Fu alone knew of Zhang's plan to quit. See "Yu Zhang Yuanji shu 9" (June 11, 1901), in *Yan Fu heji*, 2:224–226.
27. "Yu Zhang Yuanji shu 12" (1901), in *Yan Fu heji*, 2:224–226.

Though it is not clear whether Yan successfully obtained the written agreement he wanted, Nanyang Public School did promise to give Yan a half-tael royalty for each copy of *Yuan Fu* sold (instead of the 20 percent royalty for twenty years Yan had initially proposed). It also agreed to settle royalty accounts quarterly.[28] Between 1901 and 1902, Nanyang Public School continually released *Yuan Fu* in Shanghai, volume by volume. However, the geographic distance between Shanghai and Tianjin left Yan unable to keep track of the publication of *Yuan Fu*. For instance, he didn't know when exactly it was released. He read Liang Qichao's review of the first two volumes of *Yuan Fu* in *Xinmin congbao* (New people) before he received the actual copies of those volumes himself.[29] When the publication of the whole set (five volumes) of *Yuan Fu* was completed in the winter of 1902–1903, he relied on his friend Xia Cengyou (1863–1924) to inform him that the first impression of *Yuan Fu* had been sold out in Shanghai within a month. When reporting this encouraging news to Yan, Xia also cynically remarked that he believed "only a few people could truly comprehend [*Yuan Fu*]" and most customers just wanted to "put one set on their desks to show off their familiarity with 'New Learning.'"[30]

As Yan's informant in Shanghai, Xia could illustrate how *Yuan Fu* was received in the marketplace, but it was nearly impossible for Xia, no matter how well-connected he might be, to know exactly how many copies of *Yuan Fu* were produced and sold by Nanyang Public School. Without knowing the exact sales volume of *Yuan Fu*, Yan could not confirm whether the royalty payment he received from Shanghai was accurate. This uncertainty became a major trigger of Yan's anxiety. On October 26, 1903, when the royalty for the summer quarter didn't arrive on time, Yan panicked and wrote a concerned letter to Zhang Meiyi (1857–1924), the headmaster of Nanyang Public School.[31] Ten days later, having received no reply, Yan wrote another anxious letter to Zhang demanding an explanation. Suspecting that Nanyang Public School might not be paying him honestly, Yan asked Zhang to let Yan or his representative audit Nanyang Public School's account book. He told Zhang that he had been informed that "the sales of *Yuan Fu* this summer were so great that over tens of thousands of copies had been sold," so he would like to learn the exact sales numbers from Zhang: how many times had Nanyang Public School reprinted *Yuan Fu* this

---

28. "Yu Rangsan shu 1" [Letter to Rangsan 1] (1903), in *Yan Fu ji bubian*, 266–267.
29. "Yu Zhang Yuanji shu 14" [Letter to Zhang Yuan ji] (1902), in *Yan Fu heji*, 2:282–283.
30. *Yan Fu nianpu*, 194.
31. "Yu Rangsan shu 1," in *Yan Fu ji bubian*, 266–267.

year? How many copies did they print each time? And how many copies remained unsold?[32]

On November 23, Yan finally received the royalty payment for the summer quarter that Zhang had sent over two months earlier. The delivery was delayed owing to China's inefficient postal service. This payment eased Yan's anxiety slightly, assuring him that Zhang had no intention of cheating Yan of his rightful royalty. Perhaps as a reluctant apology for his earlier panicky letters, Yan later praised Zhang for being an "honest and reliable gentleman who respected and protected *banquan*/copyright," and applauded him for his efforts to crack down on the unauthorized reprinting of *Yuan Fu* in Hangchow. Nevertheless, he reminded Zhang, precisely because he respected *banquan*/copyright, he should not object to permitting Yan or his representative to examine the sales account of *Yuan Fu*; he should at least tell Yan exactly how many copies had been sold.[33]

After realizing that a written contract alone could not guarantee him "accurate" royalty payments, Yan became more cautious and demanding when he sold his translation of Herbert Spencer's *The Study of Sociology, Qunxue yiyan*, in the winter of 1902. For years Yan had been working on this book. As an intellectual and political project, his introduction of Spencer's more moderate work could, he hoped, somehow "balance" the extreme social Darwinist sentiments in China's public discourse that had been inspired by his *Tianyanlun*.[34] *Qunxue yiyan* was also a test case for Yan to see whether he could make his living solely by translating. "I came to realize that I could no longer stand to work for others," Yan confessed to Xia Cengyou. "If this could be the means of livelihood, [I] would abandon everything to go for it."[35]

In February 1903, Yan Fu sold *Qunxue yiyan* to Civilization Books, a leading publisher of New Learning books in Shanghai. As a publicity campaign as well as a propriety proclamation, from late February until the release of *Qunxue yiyan* in May, Civilization Books published series after series of advertisements in major newspapers in China to declare that the famous translator Yan Fu had granted them the *banquan*/copyright of his latest work, *Qunxue yiyan*.[36]

To better monitor the sales of *Qunxue yiyan*, Yan Fu adopted the practice of seal stamping, which, as discussed in chapter 1, had become popular in China

32. "Yu Rangsan shu 2" (1903), in *Yan Fu ji bubian*, 267–268.
33. "Yu Rangsan shu 3" (1903), in *Yan Fu ji bubian*, 269–270.
34. "Yu Xiong Chunru shu 63" [Letter to Xiong Chunru 63], in *Yan Fu ji*, 3:678.
35. "Yu Xia Zengyou shu 1" [Letter to Xia Zengyou 1] (1902), in *Yan Fu ji bubian*, 262–263.
36. For example, *DGB*, February 23, 1903.

at the turn of the century as a means to declare *banquan* ownership and certify the authenticity of actual copies. In theory, the *banquan* seal would enable Yan to keep track of the production and sales of his book even if he had no access to the booksellers' financial records. As Yan Fu could use the number of seals he (or his representative) stamped to calculate how many copies of *Qunxue yiyan* Civilization Books had produced, the seal was an anticheating device. If any copy of *Qunxue yiyan* without Yan Fu's seal was found in the marketplace, it meant that Civilization Books had secretly produced extra copies without notifying Yan. Such a seal-less copy then could be handily used as evidence to prove that the publisher was violating their contract. Ideal as this method may sound, when Yan Fu tried to implement it, he once again found the geographic distance between him and Shanghai a major barrier. Still holding a full-time appointment at the Imperial University, Yan could not travel to Shanghai frequently to stamp his seal on each copy of *Qunxue yiyan* in person. It was also equally infeasible for Civilization Books to ship all the copies to Beijing for Yan Fu's inspection and authentication. As a compromise, Yan stamped his seals on small stamps and sent them to Shanghai according to Civilization Books' request.

The number of *banquan* stamps Civilization Books requested did not reflect the exact print run or accurate sales numbers, but likely just the estimate in Civilization Books' publication plan. This uncertainty prompted Yan to suspect his publisher's honesty. In October 1903, around the same time that Yan was irritated by the delayed royalty payment from Nanyang Public School, he was also dubious of Civilization Books and started to make inquiries about the "reality" of its operation. From Zhang Yuanji, now the editor in chief of Commercial Press, Yan learned the stunning news that Civilization Books had printed 6,000 copies of *Qunxue yiyan*. Since Yan had sent Civilization Books only 4,000 stamps, he was convinced that the publisher must have secretly printed and sold thousands of extra copies. Considering Zhang's disclosure to be substantial evidence of cheating, Yan wrote an angry letter to Lian Quan, the proprietor of Civilization Books, to break the publishing contract for *Qunxue yiyan*. He also demanded that Lian pay him royalties for 6,000 copies at once.[37]

At the time, Lian was preoccupied with the opening of Civilization Books' Beijing branch as well as the unauthorized reprinting of their books that had

37. "Lian Quan yu Yan Fu shu 3" [Lian Quan to Yan Fu 3] (1903), in *Yan Fu ji bubian*, 374–375. Unfortunately, the letters Yan Fu wrote to Lian Quan on this matter were lost. Yan Fu's attitudes and demands during this dispute were reconstructed from the letters Lian wrote to respond to Yan's accusations and requests.

been discovered. Stating that he was not in charge of the Shanghai headquarters at the moment, he politely suggested that there must be some misunderstanding between Yan and Yu Fu, the co-owner of Civilization Books and the manager in Shanghai. He told Yan that he believed that Civilization Books had not broken the contract, and it was impossible for them to pay Yan the lump sum of royalty at once because they didn't have that much cash on hand.[38]

The actual contract for *Qunxue yiyan* between Yan Fu and Civilization Books has been lost in the torrent of time, but its gist can be reconstructed through the letters Lian wrote to Yan during their dispute over royalty payments for *Qunxue yiyan*. The contract for *Qunxue yiyan* was neither a time-limited nor a long-term one. Yan Fu granted Civilization Books his permission to print and sell 6,000 copies of *Qunxue yiyan*. After the first 3,000 copies were sold, it was Civilization Books' responsibility to pay Yan Fu the royalty for 6,000 copies in full. Once the remaining 3,000 copies were sold out, the contract would automatically expire, and the *banquan*/copyright of this book would revert to Yan Fu. For each copy sold, Yan would receive a half-tael royalty. Whenever Civilization Books made new imprints, it was required to ask Yan Fu for the requisite number of author's stamps. If Civilization Books violated the contract, it would be subjected to a 2,000-tael penalty.[39]

Part of the confusion about how many copies of *Qunxue yiyan* Civilization Books printed was caused by Lian and Yu's changing production plan. Initially, Lian planned to make 6,000 copies at once, but Yu, who had a more conservative view of the market, felt that a 2,000-copy print run for the first impression would be enough. Believing 2,000 copies to be far from sufficient, Lian ordered to Yu to increase the print run for the first impression to 4,000, and accordingly asked Yan for 4,000 stamps. What Lian didn't know, however, was that Yu held back at the last moment and printed only 3,000 copies. After realizing that the demand for *Qunxue yiyan* was higher than he expected, Yu wrote to Lian about printing more copies and requesting more stamps from Yan. Lian, however, delayed his response to Yu as he believed that Civilization Books still had substantial reserves of *Qunxue yiyan*. Worrying that they would run out of books, Yu proceeded to print 3,000 more copies of *Qunxue yiyan*. With only 1,000 stamps left, 2,000 copies of this second impression did not have Yan Fu's stamps on them.

---

38. Ibid.
39. "Lian Quan yu Yan Fu shu," in *Yan Fu ji bubian*, 373–375.

Although Lian tried to explain to Yan that this was the result of simple mis-communication and ad hoc changes in the publication plan, Yan Fu insisted on seeing it as Civilization Books' secret plot to avoid paying him the proper royalty he deserved. Arguing that Yu's decision to reprint *Qunxue yiyan* was a sign that Civilization Books had reached the sales target of 3,000 copies, he de-manded that, according to the contract, a 3,000-tael royalty be paid right away. On the other hand, Lian stated that Yan's accusations were unfounded. He at-tributed the problematic 2,000 copies of *Qunxue yiyan* without Yan Fu's stamps to Yu's "overly conservative way" of doing business and his inaccurate estimate of reserves. Yu had never intended to take advantage of Yan, Lian argued; other-wise he would not have revealed the actual print run to Zhang Yuanji and would never have written to Lian requesting more *banquan* stamps. To calm Yan Fu's fury, Lian proposed to pay a partial royalty and give him the 2,000 copies in question as a substitute for the remaining royalty.[40]

Upon receiving the 1,000-tael royalty from Civilization Books, Yan Fu re-mained furious. He wrote another angry letter to Lian threatening to withdraw from the contract. Insisting that Civilization Books was being dishonest about the actual print runs and sales figures, Yan demanded that Lian let him audit both their account book and their stock. Increasingly irritated by Yan's never-ending demands and accusations, Lian stopped trying to please this New Learn-ing cultural star. In his reply to Yan on January 16, 1904, he firmly stated that they would not allow Yan to examine their financial records. He told Yan that Civilization Books was willing to cancel their contract for *Qunxue yiyan* if that was what Yan wanted, but they refused to take the blame as cheaters or contract-breakers. Civilization Books insisted that since the questionable 2,000 copies were not released to the market, they did not violate the terms of the contract. Those 2,000 copies were sitting in the warehouse waiting for the extra author's stamps to arrive.

As for Yan's request for the full 3,000-tael royalty, Lian told Yan that they would never pay it. After inspecting their own sales records, Lian stated that so far only 1,200–1,300 copies of *Qunxue yiyan* had been sold. According to the contract, Civilization Books did not need to pay Yan the full royalty for 6,000 copies as they had not met the 3,000-copy sales target. If Yan didn't believe him, Lian told Yan that he was welcome to count the number of remainders himself. "To clear your doubt," Lian stated, "we will ship all the remaining copies in our Beijing branch and recall all the released copies back to Shanghai [for your

40. "Lian Quan yu Yan Fu 3" (1903), in *Yan Fu ji bubian*, 374–375.

inspection]. Meanwhile, we will also announce in major newspapers that from now on, *Qunxue yiyan* is removed from the market."[41]

Like Yan Fu, Lian was also an active advocate for *banquan*/copyright in late Qing China. He wrote petitions to local and metropolitan officials promoting *banquan*/copyright as a universal progressive doctrine and asking them for *banquan*/copyright protection. He unstintingly paid handsome remunerations to leading New Learning authors like Lin Shu and Yan Fu, and his Civilization Books was not hesitant to publicize in their newspaper advertisements the "high prices" it paid to obtain famous translators' *banquan*/copyright By 1904, however, he seemed to be increasingly impatient with Yan's demands regarding royalties. This changing attitude might be attributed to the daunting problem of unauthorized reprinting that he was struggling with at the time. He had become disillusioned with *banquan*/copyright. Their publications, especially textbooks and New Learning best sellers, including *Qunxue yiyan*, were widely reprinted by other publishers. Since September 1903, Lian had been trying to crack down on one reprint edition of *Qunxue yiyan* in Hangchow. In a letter to Yan Fu, he claimed that by January 1904 he had spent over 3,000 taels tracing and hunting down different publishers reprinting their works for quick profit. The daily operation of the company prevented him from devoting all his time and resources to the costly antipiracy expeditions, and, as a result, the cheap reprint editions flooding Shanghai and Beijing crowded out their authentic copies in the market. For months, its Beijing branch had failed to sell any authentic copies of *Yuan Fu*. Lian revealed to Yan that this was the real reason why the popularity of *Qunxue yiyan* in the marketplace was not directly reflected in the actual sales of their "authentic" copies. Although Lian asked government officials to issue *banquan*/copyright protection orders, they did not seem very keen to take strong actions to enforce these protection orders. Even worse, in fact, as Lian had just learned, one of the most influential officials who had granted Civilization Books such a protection order was reprinting their books too.

Frustrated and disillusioned, Lian began to see *banquan*/copyright as a burden and demanding authors like Yan Fu as troublemakers. They put author's or bookseller's seals on the *banquan* page to authenticate a copy, but this would not prevent or stop unauthorized reprinting. Readers seemed to see little difference between the "authentic" copies and the "fake" ones, and they simply went for whatever was cheaper. For New Learning publishers like Lian, paying

41. Ibid.

banquan royalties increased their production costs considerably and made it harder for them to initiate a cutthroat discount war.[42] Considering deep discounts to be the only effective tactic to counteract the cheap reprints, at one point Lian even suggested that they should cancel the contract at once, give all the remaining copies to Yan, and let Yan sell those books himself. Since an author didn't need to pay himself royalties, he claimed, Yan could afford to sell the books at lower prices.[43]

This dispute spoiled the trust between Yan Fu and Civilization Books. Lian bitterly blamed Yan's bold accusation for his financial difficulties. "If you needed money urgently, I am willing to lend some to you as I told you before in Beijing," Lian grumbled, "but you accused me of secretly printing 2,000 more copies . . . I would rather die than willingly submit to your accusations." He also blamed Commercial Press for stirring up trouble. In a letter to Yan, he indicated that Zhang Yuanji had deliberately informed Yan of the "actual" print run of *Qunxue yiyan* to make mischief, out of envy. Stating that a business like Civilization Books that "persisted in honesty" would not want to "associate with Commercial Press," Lian recommended, in a fit of pique, that Yan sign a new contract for *Qunxue yiyan* with Commercial Press once the old one was canceled. "Commercial Press has greater capital, with which we could not compete," Lian told Yan, and argued that that press should be able to cope more easily with both the damage caused by unauthorized reprinting and Yan's capricious demand for huge amounts of money. For less wealthy enterprises, like Civilization Books, *banquan*/copyright contracts had proved to be too exorbitant to entertain. Lian confessed to Yan that he would be more than happy to cancel the *banquan*/copyright contract for *Qunxue yiyan* with him, because "when I signed the contract, I did not know it would be so hard to protect *banquan*."[44]

Sharing Ownership with Publishers

Yan Fu finished his translation of Edward Jenks's *A History of Politics, Shehui tongquan* (The general illustration of society), in November 1903, the very month he was aggressively demanding of both Nanyang Public School and Civilization Books that they give him the "proper" amount of royalty payments.

---

42. "Lian Quan yu Yan Fu shu 4," in *Yan Fu ji bubian*, 376.
43. Ibid.
44. Ibid., 378.

Learning a lesson from his unpleasant confrontations with publishers, Yan might have become more aware of the difficulty involved in putting *banquan*/copyright into practice. When he eventually sold the *banquan* of *Shehui tongquan* to Commercial Press, it comes as no surprise that the two parties stipulated detailed instructions and procedures regarding payment and ownership. The publishing contract for *Shehui tongquan* that Yan Fu and Commercial Press signed in December 1903 was the earliest *banquan*/copyright contract I have found so far that thoughtfully defined the rights and obligations of both the author and the publisher, the nature of *banquan*, and how the author's seal should be used:

1. For each copy of this book printed and sold, the author/owner of the manuscript will get a net profit of one-half Mexican silver dollar. The sale price of this book can be adjusted accordingly. How the copies will be made with different papers or different binding, [as well as] how much the wholesale discounts will be, are all at the publisher's discretion, and are not of concern to the author.

2. The author's stamp has to be stamped on every copy of this book. If copies without a stamp [are found] and proved to have been made by the publisher privately [without the author's consent], [the publisher] has to pay a penalty of 2,500 silver dollars [to the author], the contract will no longer be valid, and the *banquan* of this book will automatically be returned to the author's possession.

3. The *banquan* of this book is a property shared by both the author and the publisher. If the contract becomes invalid, the *banquan* belongs to the author.

4. If the author discovers that the publisher is behaving deceptively in the publishing [of this book], or the publisher fails to pay the profit the author is entitled to, then the contract will be canceled.

5. Every time [the publisher] plans to print [this book,] [the publisher] should notify the author as to how many copies [the publisher] intends to publish, so that [the author] can prepare stamps accordingly.

6. The royalty of translation is based on the actual sales of this book and should be liquidated monthly by the end of the month. The author will send his representative to collect the royalty.

7. Before the contract becomes invalid, the author cannot authorize others to publish this book.

8. If the format and layout, the inks and papers, or the editing and proofreading of this book do not meet very high-quality standards, the author can ask the publisher to improve them anytime.[45]

According to this contract, the *banquan*/copyright of *Shehui tongquan* was jointly owned by the author (Yan Fu) and the publisher (Commercial Press) based on the principle that the author created the manuscript and the publisher is the principal in charge of printing and circulation. The actual copies of the book were the products of both the author's intellectual labor and the publisher's capital investment. The bond between the author and the publisher came into being when the author granted the publisher the permission to print his work, so although the author created the literary text, he could not interfere with the production and circulation of the book apart from stamping his copyright seal. It was also up to the publisher to decide the price of the book. In other words, printed copies of the book, as physical objects, were produced by the publisher and thus belonged to the publisher. Instead of requesting 20 percent of the sale price as royalty, as in the *Yuan Fu* case, in this contract Yan Fu asked for a fixed amount of money (0.50 silver dollar) for each copy sold. Then no matter how much or little Commercial Press charged for *Shehui tongquan*, and no matter whether Commercial Press offered a discount to compete with the cheap reprints, Yan's royalty would remain stable and secure. In fact, a royalty of 0.5 dollar per copy was over 40 percent of *Shehui tongquan*'s sale price (1.2 silver dollars), twice the percentage Yan Fu had asked for from Nanyang Public School when they published *Yuan Fu* one year earlier.[46]

Considering that he was not, and was unable to be, physically present in Commercial Press's printing facility in Shanghai to monitor the print run and the printing process, Yan continued to use the author's seal/stamp as a simple, low-cost device to calculate how many copies were made and how much royalty he should have received. Perhaps Lian's angry comment during their quarrel about how easy it was to counterfeit Yan Fu's seal had provoked Yan;[47] the copyright stamp he designed and stamped on *Shehui tongquan* in the spring of

---

45. Liu and Zhang, eds., *Zhang Yuanji nianpu*, 47–48.

46. The current standard royalty in China, Taiwan, Hong Kong, and the United States is between 10 and 20 percent of the list price; 40 percent is unbelievably high in comparison with today's standards. Natsume Soseki's royalty was 30 percent, the highest among his Meiji contemporaries.

47. "Lian Quan yu Yan Fu shu 2," in *Yan Fu ji bubian*, 375.

FIG. 3.1. Yan Fu's copyright stamp on *Shehui tongquan*
(The general illustration of society), 1904.
Source: *Shehui tongquan* (Shanghai: Shangwu yishuguan, 1904).
Courtesy of Shanghai Library.

1904 was a lavish and complicated one (fig. 3.1). The same seal could also be found on *Fayi* (Meaning of the law), his translation of Montesquieu's *De l'esprit des lois*, *Yingwen hangu* (English grammar explained in Chinese), and other books he published with Commercial Press. Three annuli compose the stamp: the outer annulus was the Western apothegm "Know thyself." The middle annulus was a Chinese copyright statement: "Mr. Yan of Houguan reserves copyright (of the book)" (*Houguan yanshi banquan suoyou*). And in the center of the stamp, one finds an image of a swallow, the word for which is pronounced just like Yan's family name. (Swallow/燕 *yan*, 嚴 *yan*). It was Yan Fu's personal trademark. It is worth noting that the ideal of shared ownership was manifested in this stamp as well. Commercial Press stamped its seal at the fringes of Yan's stamp (the outer circle in fig. 3.1), indicating that the copy had been authenticated by both the author who created the work and the publisher who turned it into tangible print copies.

Commercial Press turned out to be the best partner Yan could have. Beginning in 1904, it became the almost exclusive publisher of Yan's new works. It also gradually bought the *banquan*/copyright of Yan Fu's earlier works. In late February 1904, Yan Fu resigned from the Imperial University, moved to Shanghai, and started his new life as an intellectual making his living by writing and translating. In a letter to his student Xiong Jilian (?–1906), he described his newfound freedom and the uncertainty in his economic life. When he worked for the Keiping Coal Mine and the Imperial University, he received a fixed salary but felt confined to the job. Now he could control his own time, and the royalty that Commercial Press promised him was exceptionally high. Yet he lacked a sense of security since now he "made a living [exclusively] by the pen." And since the sales of his book would determine his income, his fate was tied to the book market. Worrying that the flood of cheap reprints of his books might lead to a decrease in his royalty income, he urged Xiong to seek out potential pirates of his works and ask them not to violate Yan's *banquan*/copyright.[48] As Lian Quan suggested to Yan Fu, Commercial Press indeed had deep pockets that he could rely on even when multiple publishers reprinted his books, or when he wanted to withdraw a considerable amount of royalty in advance. In the winter of 1904–1905, for instance, Yan Fu traveled to London to assist in a lawsuit between Chinese owners and British owners of the Keiping Coal Mine, and later to Paris to visit his son. Commercial Press paid all the travel expenses (3,000 taels in total).[49]

Conclusion

The *banquan*/copyright system that Yan Fu and Commercial Press developed in 1903–1904 became a standard procedure. Commercial Press set up a royalty account for Yan Fu, reckoned his royalties two or three times annually, and deposited the money into his account. To manage his royalties, Yan and his family received an account book from Commercial Press; with this account book, they were able to withdraw money at any Commercial Press branch they

---

48. "Yu Xiong Jilian shu 25" [Letter to Xiong Jilian 25] (1904), in *Yan Fu ji bubian*, 251–252.

49. "Yu Zhang Yuanji shu 15.16.17.18," in *Yan Fu heji*, 2:358–362, 384–385.

chose, anytime they wanted. After Yan Fu passed away in his birthplace, Fuzhou, on October 27, 1921, Yan's family inherited his royalties. Hastening home from Beijing upon his father's death, for instance, Yan Fu's first son, Yan Qu (1874–1942), stopped in Shanghai and made a withdrawal of 3,000 yuan from his late father's royalty account at Commercial Press.[50] To get a sense of the value of this lump sum at the time, consider that Lu Xun and his brothers had just spent 3,000 yuan to buy a *siheyuan* compound with a courtyard in Beijing for their three families.[51] Yan Qu's ability to withdraw such a significant amount of money from his late father's royalty account provides an inkling of how much royalty Yan Fu might have accumulated over the years. To a certain extent, Yan Fu did achieve the goal of receiving "permanent profit" as the creator of his works.

Yan Fu's case is significant in the history of intellectual property rights in China, not because he was an influential translator and intellectual, or because he managed to earn a handsome royalty, but because his understanding and practice of *banquan*/copyright marked a crucial departure from the outlook of his contemporaries. For him, his translations were the products of his intellectual labor, and this justified his ownership of these works as their creator. It is true that much of the language, the rhetoric, and the arguments he employed to make his case in the 1900s strikingly resembled what Fukuzawa Yukichi had said in the 1860s and 1870s. Both of them presented copyright as a kind of property right that belonged to authors and should be protected by the state. Both of them linked copyright with the Western powers' strength and progress, and argued that the monopoly of profit would encourage intellectual innovations. Nevertheless, there is a fundamental difference between Fukuzawa and Yan: as discussed in chapter 1, although Fukuzawa made these arguments to promote *hanken*/copyright as an author, his ownership of his publications was recognized by his contemporaries mainly because he was the possessor of printing blocks used to manufacture copies of his books. Yan, on the other hand, had little interest in involving himself in the publishing business and attempted to

50. "Zhi wang xian hua jin ping bo" [To Wang Xianhua and Jin Pingbo] (1921), in *Zhang Yuanji quanji*, 1:266. According to Zhang Yuanji, Yan Qu's plan was to first withdraw 1,000 yuan in Shanghai and then another 2,000 yuan when he arrived in Fuzhou.

51. At the time, Lu Xun's monthly salary as a midranking bureaucrat at the Ministry of Education was three hundred yuan. According to Lu Xun's youngest brother, Zhou Jianren, Lu Xun's salary was ten times that of a common worker. Zhou Jianren's monthly salary as a college-graduate and an editor at Commercial Press was sixty yuan in 1921. And the salary of a middle school teacher was around twenty yuan at the time.

justify his ownership based solely on the fact that he *created* his translation works. For him, *banquan*/copyright was the author's ownership of his intellectual creation rather than the ownership of the means of production discussed in the preceding chapters.

The physical embodiment of his intellectual creation was the manuscript. In Yan's negotiations with Zhang Yuanji over whether the author was entitled to a long-term royalty, it is clear he knew that what he proposed was contrary to the conventional manuscript deal of the time. When an author sold his manuscript, its ownership was transferred from the author to the buyer (publisher), and the author could no longer claim it was his property. For example, as Michael Hill's study on Lin Shu's translation career suggests, most of his manuscripts were sold outright, and he received only a onetime payment from publishers for his *banquan*/copyright.[52] Although Lin Shu was a well-paid bestselling author, he received remuneration based on the length of his manuscripts rather than the sales of his books. One of Lin's friends called his house "the Mint" to describe the income that Lin derived every moment that he wrote,[53] but to keep generating money, Lin had to keep translating new novels at his "mint."

Lin Shu saw the finished manuscript as a cultural product that, once sold to the publisher, would no longer be the author's possession. The profit generated from the sales of books, therefore, should not also be enjoyed by the author. For him, selling off the manuscript for a lump sum was the norm, and there was nothing more an author could ask. For this reason, he stated in the preface of *Yuxue liuhen* (Leaving a mark on the snowy skin), his translation of H. Rider Haggard's *Mr. Meeson's Will*, that the "writing and publishing businesses are two entities . . . it would be impossible for writers to become rich." He thus criticized the plot of *Mr. Meeson's Will*—a female author who got a terrible copyright deal ends up marrying the rich publisher's heir—and called it Haggard's "laughable fantasy."[54]

Yan Fu, however, considered that, as an author, he maintained his ownership of his works even after he sold the manuscripts. His *banquan*/copyright did not completely transfer to the publishers; rather it extended to every physical copy produced from his manuscripts. This made his understanding of

52. Hill, *Lin Shu, Inc.*

53. Qian Zhongshu, "Lin Shu de fanyi" [Lin Shu's translation], in his *Qizhuiji* (Taipei: Shulin chubanshe, 1990), 97–98.

54. Rider, trans. by Lin and Wei, *Yuxue liuhen*, 2.

banquan as *intellectual* property very different from the view of most of his con-temporaries, who tended to associate *banquan* with the possession of the means of production. However, Yan did not realize his conception of *banquan/*copyright by promoting it, in writing, as civilized doctrine but through his practices. As this chapter illustrates, Yan and his booksellers groped their way to figuring out how to share the *banquan* of a book. The final workable system that he and Commercial Press developed in 1903–1904 would become the standard procedure for other Chinese authors and publishers to calculate proper royalties. Commercial Press applied it to other authors, such as Liang Qichao, Cai Yuanpei, and Lin Yutang, and issued a "royalty account book" (*banshui ping-zhe*) to its top authors to keep records of their royalty accounts. Other publish-ers also signed publishing contracts modeled after *Shehui tongquan*'s contract with their authors. For example, Lu Xun also calculated the royalties he was due from his publisher, Beixin Books, in the 1920s by counting the author's *banquan* stamps and recording them carefully in his diary.[55]

---

55. Lu Xun, *Lu Xun riji*, vol. 2. Lu Xun and his publisher Li Xiaofeng started to exchange correspondence extensively and had been dealing with Lu Xun's royalty since 1923. Although Li was able to pay Lu Xun his royalty regularly at the beginning, it became difficult for him to keep up. From 1929, Li started to miss payments and his relationship with Lu Xun soured.

4

Between Privilege and Property

THE CONCEPT OF *banquan*/copyright was promoted by booksellers, translators, and progressive intellectuals, in response to the changing landscape of China's cultural economy at the turn of the twentieth century. The rapid commodification of New Learning knowledge, together with the decline and eventual collapse of the civil service examination prep market, reshaped the dynamics of the relatively stable and homogenous late imperial book trade. The booming New Learning book market prompted publishers to invest money in purchasing *banquan* of the latest works from promising translators and authors, such as Yan Fu and Lin Shu. At the same time, new printing technologies, especially lithography, also made reproducing (identical) copies cheaper, faster, and easier than ever before. It was at this particular moment, when publishing new books became both a highly profitable and a highly risky business in China, that the very concept of *banquan*/copyright was embraced by Chinese booksellers and authors as a new means to claim, justify, and protect their newly earned profits from selling new books. Upholding *banquan*/copyright as a new doctrine, they condemned unauthorized reprinting as the equivalent of stealing or robbing.

Chinese booksellers and authors not only *talked* about *banquan* as a progressive and fashionable New Learning idea, but they also put it *in practice*. Drawing from both Meiji Japanese conventions and late imperial customs, they developed various measures to declare what they believed to be *banquan*/ copyright. As the convention *"banquan suoyou fanke bijiu"* started to appear in newspaper advertisements and on title pages on a regular basis, the carefully designed *banquan* seals were stamped on the actual copies of books as proprietary claims. However, it remained questionable whether all these measures created an effective sanction against unauthorized reprinting. Since there was no common consensus or general authority that Chinese publishers and readers could rely on to verify the credibility or authenticity of these claims and seals, all those so inclined could publicly claim that they possessed *banquan* of certain books or stamp their seals on the copies they printed. In the absence of the legal backing and institutional support required to really "pursue and punish" the pirates, the threats booksellers made in newspapers against piracy were likely to be empty words. That booksellers persisted in their efforts to make proprietary claims and issue warnings against unauthorized reprinting indicated that piracy remained a pressing issue and, ironically, also suggested how little real impact these measures had.

Worrying that the Chinese book market might become so disordered that it would eventually collapse, some prominent New Learning publishers began to campaign for domestic *banquan*/copyright legislation. In the late spring of 1903, for instance, in one of his petitions, Lian Quan of Civilization Books argued that the government, to encourage intellectual innovations and advancement in China, ought to issue laws to protect *banquan*/copyright as soon as possible; otherwise, China's book market and intellectual circle might be ruined by the lack of order and standards.[1] In the preface of its 1903 pamphlet *Banquan kao*, the proprietor of Commercial Press shared Lian's anxiety; he stated that they were motivated to publish such a book as a timely stimulus to the government to draft a formal *banquan* law, which they considered to be urgent and necessary.[2]

These Chinese publishers' requests for a domestic copyright law are noteworthy. The promulgation of intellectual property law in early twentieth-century China has been considered by scholars to have been solely the result of foreign pressure;[3] however, these domestic efforts urging the creation of a Chinese copyright law show that Chinese booksellers cared as much about their ownership of publications and their commercial interests as their foreign counterparts did. Before Lian Quan petitioned the state in support of the enactment of a formal law, however, he and his fellow booksellers had already started practicing and claiming *banquan*/copyright according to their understanding of this "general doctrine of the five continents." What they expected from the state was a formal and more systematic regulation of *banquan*/copyright that they

1. "Lian bulang shang Guanxue Dachen lun banquan shi," *DGB*, May 22, 1903.
2. *Banquan kao*, 1.
3. For example, Alford, *To Steal a Book Is an Elegant Offense*, chap. 3.

could rely upon to distinguish the authentic from the counterfeit, as well as to combat and punish those who reprinted their books without authorization.

Lian and his peers would have to wait seven more years before China's first copyright law was eventually instituted. In the meantime, booksellers could acquire *banquan* protection from the Qing state in one of the following two forms: (1) *banquan* protection orders issued by local or metropolitan officials to individual booksellers as a type of privilege for their cultural contributions to society; (2) *banquan* certificates issued by first the Imperial University and then the Ministry of Education (*Xue bu*) to authors and booksellers after their books, especially textbooks, passed the state's review. Booksellers hoped that these orders and certificates, issued, acknowledged, and empowered by the state, could authenticate and ensure their book ownership right. However, as this chapter illustrates, the Qing officials mainly understood *banquan*/copyright as a privilege granted exclusively by the state to reward publishers or authors for their outstanding works rather than a form of property that the state was obligated to protect. These two forms of state-issued *banquan*/copyright protection interlocked the state's authority and the cultural value of a book with the protection of a book's exclusive profit, as well as the proprietorship recognition of a book. When these two mechanisms were put in practice, publishers and authors quickly learned that these privileges might not necessarily deliver the kind of state protection they had envisioned and expected. The quarrels between them and the very state authorities granting them *banquan* protection against unauthorized reprinting committed by the government provoked a series of discussions in late Qing China on the nature of *banquan*/copyright: Was it a form of property that comes into existence by itself? Or was it a privilege that had to be granted by a state authority?

The Inflation of *Banquan* Privilege

"Was there any formal law in China against piracy?" Japanese sinologist Naitō Konan (1866–1934) raised this question in one of the "brush conversations" he had with Chinese literati during his visit to China between 1899 and 1900. Excited about the Japanese contribution to China's recent intellectual shift, he was simultaneously worried by the Chinese reprints of Japanese books that he saw in Shanghai. "We don't have a fixed law to regulate publishing," a young Chinese scholar told him. "However, if [one] petitions Chinese officials for a protection order and receives it, the impossible would become possible. Afterward, if others reprinted the [petitioner's] books, not only could pirates be uncovered easily, but also pirates would be punished harshly."[4] What he referred to here was a particular kind of simple order granted by individual local officials in reply to petitions asking for specific acknowledgment of the petitioners' proprietorship of a particular title, as well as for a general prohibition against the unauthorized reprinting of such titles.

When the SDCK demanded in 1896 that Chinese officials recognize and protect their copyright, what they received from the circuit intendant of the Suzhou, Songjiang, and Taicang region was an exclusive prohibition of unauthorized reprinting of SDCK titles. In this protection order, Circuit Intendant Liu stated that "missionaries [at the SDCK] worked conscientiously on their books . . . , [and] finally publish them to serve the world. Since [they] have announced in public their opposition to reprinting [their books], how could others take advantage of their efforts and reprint [their books] for profit?"[5] He therefore forbade any unauthorized reprinting of the SDCK's ten most popular titles and promised the missionaries that local Chinese officials would accordingly punish those who violated this order. Although the missionaries of the SDCK considered this particular order to be the copyright protection they had requested,[6] it seems that, for Circuit Intendant Liu, others should refrain from reprinting the SDCK's books not because the missionaries *owned* their publications, but rather because they made a noble contribution to society through publishing.

This "copyright" protection order that the SDCK received in 1896 was not invented by Circuit Intendant Liu to respond to the missionaries' unusual request. As with the *banquan* seals used by authors and publishers to declare ownership and authenticity, as well as the *"fanke bijiu"* discussed in chapter 1, the history of this sort of reprinting prohibition order can be traced back to as early as the late twelfth century.[7] One of the earliest examples of this kind of prohibition was an order issued in 1248 by the *Guozigian* (Imperial Academy) upon the request of a minor official named Duan Weiqing. It prohibited others

4. Naitō, *Naitō Konan zenshu*, 2:60–61.

5. "Guangxuehui yianjin fanke sinzhu chuji gaoshi," *Wanguo gongbao* 97 (February 1897): 16699–16700.

6. Ibid.

7. The earliest known reprinting prohibition order in China may be the one found in Wang Cheng's *Dongdu shilüe* [Alternative history of the "Eastern Capital" Kaifeng], published in Meishan (Sichuan) between 1190 and 1194. Some Chinese historians have used this as evidence to argue that the Chinese had developed their own intellectual property right as early as the Song dynasty.

from reprinting *Conggui maoshi jijie* (Mr. Conggui's collected commentary on the *Book of Poems*), a title compiled by Duan's late uncle and published by the Luo family. Stating that this title was "the fruit" of his late uncle's lifework in classics, and the Luo family edition was the "finest" and "most accurate" one, Duan worried that "if other publishers reprint this book for money, they undoubtedly will change the texts, misspell the words, and make mistakes." To prevent inferior reprints of this book from "dishonoring [his] late uncle's classic study," he thus petitioned the Imperial Academy to ban others from reprinting it. Acknowledging the scholarly value of this title, the Imperial Academy issued a reprinting prohibition order, stating that whoever violated this order would be punished by the authorities, and their printing blocks would be confiscated and destroyed.[8]

Throughout the late imperial period, individually issued reprinting prohibition orders with a similar format, rhetoric, and "intellectual contribution–reward" justification could be found periodically on Chinese books.[9] The nature of this kind of order, however, is ambiguous. While Niida Noboru and Inoue Susumu consider them to be a sort of "proto-copyright,"[10] William Alford sees them as an "interesting by-product" of the Chinese state's publication review system that aimed to control publication rather than protect it, given the fact that most titles mentioned in this sort of order were Confucian classics.[11] Based on the dozens of examples bibliographical scholars have found, it seems that the petitioners' commercial profit was not the order-issuers' primary concern. As Ye Dehui suggested, these orders were mainly issued on the presumption that reprints produced by careless private bookshops would compromise the authenticity and accuracy of the text and thus be harmful to the intellectual community.[12] What the petitioners and the order-issuers wanted to achieve by forbidding unauthorized reprinting (of specific books), at least nominally, was to maintain the intellectual order of knowledge rather than to protect individual petitioners' property ownership. Nevertheless, this kind of order entitled

8. "Guozigian jinzhi fanban gongju" [Reprinting forbidden statement from the Imperial Academy], quoted from *Ye Dehui shu hua*, 53.

9. *Ye Dehui shu hua*, 52–57; Tsien, *Paper and Print*; Poon, "The Printer's Colophon in Sung China, 960–1279."

10. Niida, *Chūgoku hosei shi kenkyu*. Inoue, *Chūgoku shuppan bunkashi*, 255–261.

11. Alford, *To Steal a Book Is an Elegant Offense*, 14.

12. *Ye Dehui shu hua*, 53.

publishers/block-possessors to seek the assistance of local officials when combating unauthorized reprinting of their works. The order thus indirectly protected the monopoly of their publications (and the profit they generated). In this context, the textual perfection and intellectual contribution of a book became important criteria for its ownership to be recognized and protected by the government. Such reprinting prohibition orders might aim to strengthen the state's control of publication and its intellectual agenda, but they could also be seen as privileges that only those who produced outstanding and useful books could enjoy.

Given the relatively small sample that bibliographers have found, it remains unclear whether this kind of protection order was a common practice in Ming-Qing China, and whether it can rightfully be considered "proto-copyright." It is clear, however, that in the view of some late Qing officials, this was equivalent to the "copyright" protection foreigners wanted. In 1900–1901, for example, local officials in the treaty ports of Niuzhuang and Chongqing issued to Japanese booksellers Maruzen and Rakuzendou several reprinting prohibition orders similar to the one the SDCK received in 1896.[13] When missionaries of the SDCK and Japanese booksellers urged American or Japanese consuls to request copyright protection from Chinese officials, they wanted reprinting of their books to be banned because they considered these books to be their property. The reprinting prohibition orders they got from Chinese officials seemed once again to stress the textual excellence and intellectual contribution of a book as the primary reason why it deserved special protection. As a result, these two justifications for forbidding unauthorized reprinting intertwined with each other; the quality of a book became bound up with *banquan*/copyright.

After the Qing state renewed its trade treaties with foreign powers in the aftermath of the Boxer Rebellion, protection of international copyright, trademark, and the patent was brought up as an issue and was written into the treaties in formal clauses. The Qing state and foreign countries agreed in specific terms to recognize and protect the intellectual properties belonging to each other's subjects.[14] Some Chinese booksellers believed that this special privilege

13. Gaimushō kiroku 7.2.2.5–2 (4) and (5); 7.2.2.5–1 (43).

14. In the Sino-US Renewed Treaties of Trade and Navigation of 1903, and the Sino-Japanese Renewed Treaties of Trade and Navigation of 1903, registration and protection of American and Japanese citizens' copyright, patent, and trademark were written into formal clauses. However, in these two treaties the terms for copyright protection were constructed in a very unusual way

to which the foreign booksellers were now entitled could potentially put Chinese booksellers at a disadvantage. In particular, some Chinese New Learning publishing firms in Shanghai, such as Enlightenment Books (*Guangzhi shuju*), registered themselves as foreign companies to enjoy this privilege that was denied to other Chinese booksellers.[15] The proprietor of Commercial Press, for example, stated explicitly in the pamphlet *Banquan kao* that the best way to reverse this unfair competition would be domestic copyright law. Lacking a domestic copyright law, he asserted, China's book market and intellectual circles would soon be cornered by foreign booksellers who enjoyed copyright protection.[16] While some urged the state to issue its copyright law to regulate and protect Chinese ownership of publications, others just decided to request the same kind of protection orders from local authorities. The circuit intendant of the Suzhou,

---

such that the treaty protected only copyright of books that were "prepared particularly for Chinese readers." For a discussion of the flaws of these two treaties, see Wu, "Qingmo Minchu Zhong-Mei banquan zhi zheng," 97–136, and Wang, "Partnering with Your Pirate."

15. The proprietor of Enlightenment Books, Feng Jingru (?–1913), was a Chinese man with British nationality living in Hong Kong. Feng requested that the British consul in Shanghai urge the circuit intendant of the Suzhou, Songjian, and Taicang region and the Shanghai county magistrate to issue orders protecting his publications. These orders were reproduced on every copy they published. For example, "Qinming erpin dingdai Jiangnan fen xun Su Song Tai bingbei dao Yuan wei geisha" [Prohibition announced by Yuan, the imperially appointed second rank circuit intendant of the Suzhou, Songjiang, and Taicang regions] (1902.4.9), in Ichimura Sanjirō, Chen Yi, trans., *Zhina shiyao*, back of copyright page.

16. *Banquan kao*, 1. In fact, in 1905, the board of Commercial Press decided to register the company in Hong Kong in order to enjoy the copyright protection to which British subjects were entitled. Registering as a Hong Kong company, however, brought some unwanted consequences: as a British company, Commercial Press would have to follow the British copyright law and would have to pay an authorization fee to foreign authors and publishers if they wanted to translate and publish foreign books. So the board quickly changed their minds and within months withdrew Commercial Press's registration. See "Guangxu sanshi yi nian wu yue Shangwu Yinshuguan feichang gudong hui" [Commercial Press shareholders special meeting in the fifth month of the thirty-first year of Guangxu Emperor] (1905.6), "Guangxu sanshi yi nian shi yue Shangwu Yinshuguan feichang gudong hui" [Commercial Press shareholders special meeting in the tenth month of the thirty-first year of Guangxu Emperor] (1905.11), and "Guangxu sanshi yi nian shi yi yue Shangwu Yinshuguan feichang gudong hui" [Commercial Press shareholders special meeting in the eleventh month of the thirty-first year of Guangxu Emperor] (1905.12) in Song, ed., *Zhongguo chuban shiliao jindai bufen*, 3:9–10. Via personal conversation, Billy So told me that Commercial Press might never have registered as a Hong Kong company: there was no record of its registration in the Hong Kong colonial archives.

Songjiang, and Taicang regions, the Shanghai county magistrate, and other officials had no problem with granting Chinese booksellers the same kind of prohibition against reprinting they issued to foreign booksellers.

As a result, the quantity of such prohibition orders suddenly soared in 1902–1903. By the end of 1903, this unique "privilege," previously rarely seen or given only to foreigners, seems to have become a popular and common process in the Chinese book trade. A new convention, "*shujing cunan fanke bijiu* ([this] book has been registered, reprinting is prohibited)," began to be commonly used by Chinese booksellers interchangeably with "*banquan suoyou fanyin bijiu*" in newspaper advertisements and on copyright pages. The interchangeability of these two conventions suggested that, for Chinese booksellers, petitioning officials and obtaining a prohibition order would be one way to secure their *banquan*. To display the official backing they now had, they often reproduced the prohibition order in their newspaper advertisements as well as in the actual copies of books they published.

Usually, the protection order included two sections: the bookseller's petition requesting prohibition of the unauthorized reprinting of his publications and the official's reply granting the prohibition order. Both the bookseller's appeal and the official's response were composed around the agreed understanding that the *banquan* was a special privilege issued by the state to booksellers for their contribution in enhancing society's intellectual development. For instance, when Lian Quan petitioned Zhang Baixi urging a more systematic *banquan*/copyright protection, he argued that Civilization Books was not asking for *banquan*/copyright protection for their "selfish" interests. Rather he considered *banquan*/copyright to be a just reward that the state could give to Civilization Books for its "contribution to enlightening [society]" so that its editorial staff's "insignificant labor" would be validated.[17] In his reply, Zhang praised the exceptional quality of translations it published, such as Yan Fu's translations. He promised that the Imperial University would register Civilization Books' latest publications; and "to encourage editors who made painstaking efforts," he would prohibit others from reprinting their books. In return, he hoped that Civilization Books could continue their meticulous work on publications for the intellectual community.[18]

17. "Lian bulang shang Guanxue Dachen lun banquan shi," *DGB*, May 22, 1903.

18. Zhang Baixi, "Guanxue dachen pida Lian Huiqing bulang chengqing mingding banquan you" [The commissioner of the Imperial University's reply to the former vice-director (of the Board of Revenue) Lian Huiqing's petition to issue a formal copyright regulation], *DGB*, June 4, 1903.

With the rapid increase in quantity, however, the content and format of these individually issued special prohibition orders quickly became formalized or even generic.[19] A typical general protection order looked like this:

Imperially appointed Circuit Intendant of the Suzhou, Songjiang, and Tai-cang region in Jiangnan, Yuan [Shuxun] (1847–1915) has issued the follow-ing prohibition as requested:

Merchant Meng Zhixi petitioned: "We believe that fiction is the best way to infuse civilization and to enlighten society. We gather together and raise capital, and we translate and publish the novel and honorable fiction of Europe and America, to enhance the Chinese's intelligence, as well as to assist the inadequate educational system. We rented a house on Chessboard Street in Shanghai and named our company Fiction Forest. We continually pub-lish fiction [works] and sell them at reasonable prices. We are in great fear that other booksellers might reprint our books for profit, change the con-tent of our books, or change their titles to confuse readers. Thus we plead to prohibit other people from reprinting our publications from now on. In addition to asking the Office of Commerce for registration permission and the strict prohibition of reprinting, we also plead for your protection. To pro-tect and secure *banquan*, please issue a prohibition to the county offices, and inform concession leaders and consuls general in Shanghai of our reg-istration. We also provide a recognizance to guarantee that our books, *Sh-uang yen ji* (Story of two beauties), *Meiren zhuang* (A Beauty's Adornment), *Fuemosi zaisheng an er an san an* (The Return of Holmes I, II, and III), etc., are all compiled by us and not pirated from others. We are willing to be pun-ished if our statement is found false." Responding to this petition that has come to my office, I instruct all the branch offices and county offices to ac-knowledge the petitioner's registration and issue a prohibition. Thus book-sellers should be informed that they cannot reprint various books published by Fiction Forest to gain profit. If people violate this ban, once found, they will be punished without mercy. Do follow this order and not break it.

Announced on the eleventh day of the third month in the thirty-first year of Guangxu[20]

---

19. In fact, the same format and justifications against piracy could also be found in protection orders issued by the same local officials to other types of businesses (medicine, soap, etc.) to protect their brand names and products.

20. Xiaoshuo Lin, trans. and ed., *Huangjin gu Fuermosi zhentan an*, back of copyright page.

The structure of this order and its rationales were not unlike those of the other examples discussed previously. The term *banquan* was used by the petitioner to refer to the subject of protection. Although he mentioned the considerable fortune and labor invested in operating Fiction Forest, the main reasons why his *banquan* deserved protection are familiar: (1) the potential compromise of textual accuracy caused by cheap reprints needed to be stopped, and (2) the intellectual and cultural contribution of excellent books deserved to be rewarded. When the intellectual contribution or textual excellence argument was too frequently advanced, however, it was in danger of becoming generic verbiage. As the proprietor of Fiction Forest stated, they translated and published "the novel and honorable fiction of Europe and America, to enhance the Chinese's intelligence, as well as to assist the inadequate educational system," but could *Return of Holmes* really "infuse civilization and . . . enlighten society"? Also, supposedly only outstanding and useful books deserved to be protected from unauthorized reprinting, but if all booksellers could make the case that their publications were greatly beneficial to Chinese society, then this privilege might no longer be exclusive.

The credibility of these individually issued *banquan* protection orders is questionable too. In principle, by petitioning local officials to request *banquan* protection, the bookseller left an official record in the government's register. His ownership of the book was then certified in this way and acknowledged by the government. In addition to gaining the state's credibility to back their *banquan*, theoretically booksellers also invoked the state's power to crack down on pirates. Between 1902 and 1911, hundreds of such orders seem to have been issued by different officials separately without coordination. One might assume that before publishing them, officials checked the authenticity of petitions requesting *banquan* orders, reviewed the titles addressed in the appeal, ensured that their quality was outstanding, and perhaps also sought to determine whether similar titles had been registered at other offices. It seems that, in reality, local officials rarely verified the petitioners and their statements. If Circuit Intendant Yuan had taken the time to review Fiction Forest's petition, he would have found that the petitioner "merchant Meng Zhixi" was not a real person but a fictional figure. He was created by the three major partners of Fiction Forest: Ceng Mengpu (1872–1935), Ding Zhicun, and Zhu Jixi. They combined characters from their names to create the pseudonym when they registered their company in 1904 and petitioned Circuit Intendant Yuan for *banquan* protection in 1905.

Although the quick popularization and inflation of these individually issued *banquan* protection orders made them less distinctive and less prestigious, they nevertheless promised booksellers one thing: since the state authorized their *banquan*/copyright, the state would also enforce the prohibition against reprinting. Pirates would be subject to the state's punishment. In the *banquan*/copyright protection order Circuit Intendant Yuan issued to Fiction Forest, for example, Yuan displayed the state's authority by stating the harsh warning "If people violate this ban, once found, they will be punished without mercy." But would pirates be punished without mercy? And if the state violated this kind of *banquan* protection, would those responsible be punished as well?

When the State Was the Pirate

In the spring of 1904, Chinese booksellers learned the answer by witnessing how Civilization Books, a high-profile and well-connected New Learning publisher, struggled to protect itself from the very authority that had granted it *banquan* protections while simultaneously pirating its books. This incident not only exposed the structural flaws of these generic *banquan* protections, but also revealed the tensions between the state and the publishing community, as well as between different government agents, on publishing control, market regulation, and property protection. At the core of this dispute, one would find several conflicting interpretations of the term *banquan*. The same question that had haunted Fukuzawa Yukichi thirty years earlier in Tokyo was now tormenting late Qing booksellers: Was copyright a property right or a state-granted privilege?

Civilization Books was established in the summer of 1902 in Shanghai by a group of Wuxi literati and officials enthusiastic about educational reform. Owing to its carefully compiled textbooks, beautifully printed model paintings, and the latest works of Yan Fu and Lin Shu that it published, it quickly became a rising star in the highly competitive New Learning market. Within one year, it had not only opened a branch in Beijing but also publicly floated shares to raise capital.[21] Like its peers, keen on securing its exclusive profit, it actively practiced all the available means to claim and protect its *banquan*: it stamped *banquan* seals on printed copies of books, made public *banquan* announcements in newspapers, signed *banquan* contracts with leading authors, and asked officials to issue special *banquan* protection orders. Lian Quan, the brains behind

21. "Shuru wenming" [Importing civilization], *DGB*, February 19, 1903; "Shanghai Wenming bianyi yinshu ju xu zhao gufen zhangcheng" [The constitutions of the Shanghai Civilization Books for floating shares], *DGB*, August 7–8, 1903.

Civilization Books, was the vice-director of the Board of Revenue before he withdrew from officialdom and reinvented himself as a cultural entrepreneur. As a former metropolitan administrator, he was able to solicit *banquan* protection orders not only from Shanghai local officials, but also from the empire's top administrators, including Yuan Shikai (1859–1916), the grand guardian and superintendent of trade for the northern ports (*Beiyang dachen*), and Zhang Baixi, commissioner of the Imperial University.[22] Lian also registered Civilization Books at the newly established Ministry of Commerce (*Shang bu*). And his correspondence with Zhang Baixi on establishing a more systematic *banquan*/copyright protection was published and reprinted in several newspapers, thus highly publicizing Lian Quan and Civilization Books as the leading advocate of this new doctrine.[23]

By repeatedly reproducing the *banquan* protections granted to it in both newspapers and its books, Civilization Books demonstrated and stressed that powerful officials had patronized this firm and all its publications. In one advertisement, for example, it declared that "the superintendent of trade for the northern ports has informed all the provincial authorities, public or private institutes that the *banquan* of all books compiled and published by us are registered. Reprinting [Civilization Books' publications] is thus prohibited." The advertisement went on to threaten pirates that local authorities would surely be made to confiscate all the pirated copies once they were uncovered. Pirates would have to pay fines to the local authorities and compensation to Civilization Books. Presenting itself as a promoter of better education for China, it promised that all confiscated copies would be donated to local schools; half of the compensation would go to the informant as a reward, and the other half would go to the local government to support education.[24]

22. This post was newly created after the Boxer Rebellion. The commissioner of the Imperial University was in charge of the civil service examination reform, the establishment of new-style schools, the operation of the Imperial University, and supposedly other affairs related to education and learning. In 1904, the Qing court established the Ministry of Education. The minister of education (*Xuewu dachen*) was in charge of this new board. For general history of *Xue bu*, see Guan, *Wan Qing xuebu yanjiu*.

23. "Lian bulang shang guanxue dachen lun banquan shi," *DGB*, May 22, 1903, and "Guanxue dachen pi da Lian Huiqing bulang chengqing mingding banquan you," *DGB*, June 4, 1903.

24. "Wenming shuju jinyao guanggao" [An urgent announcement by Civilization Books], *DGB*, February 24, 1903.

Ironically, while the *banquan* protections Civilization Books received seemed to establish a precedent referred to by other officials or publishers,[25] the firm gradually learned that, in the face of real threats, these protections might not be as effective or trustworthy as they had once believed. In his letters to the firm's star author, Yan Fu, between 1903 and 1904, Lian was not hesitant to display his increasing disillusionment with this kind of *banquan* protection order. In September 1903, Lian reported to Yan that they had found a bookseller in Zhejiang called History Studio (*Shixue zhai*) reprinting Yan's two latest works, *Qunxue yiyan* and *Yuan Fu*. Notifying Yan that he had sent a telegram to Sheng Xuanhuai, and urging Sheng, the president of Nanyang Public School that had just published *Yuan Fu*, to join forces to "protect *banquan*," Lian promised Yan that he would crack down on the pirates and protect Yan's interests. "Your Excellency's book [*Qunxue yiyan*] is an unprecedented and unrepeatable work in our country," Lian assured Yan. "We cannot but do our utmost to fight [against piracy.]"[26]

The result was disappointing. As the relationship between Yan Fu and Civilization Books quickly soured in December owing to a dispute over royalties,[27] Lian was also troubled by the fact that local officials were not keen on enforcing the *banquan* protections granted by Yuan and Zhang. Lian claimed that they had uncovered at least ten different reprinted editions of their popular textbook *Mongxue duben* (Elementary reader), but it was impossible for their staff to travel around hunting pirates without the government's backing. "There is no way to stop piracy," Lian confessed to Yan, and went on to tell him that it was the pirates, not him, who had critically compromised Yan's potential income. According to him, the Beijing branch of Civilization Books had stocked several hundred "authentic" copies of Yan's *Yuan Fu*, but, failing to compete with cheap reprints flooding into town, they hadn't sold any in recent months.[28] The dispute between Yan Fu and Civilization Books worsened, and so did Lian's

---

25. For example, in a petition to the minister of education on protecting the textbooks this school had published, the petitioner explicitly asked the minister to grant him protection "according to the precedent of Civilization Books." See "Jiangsu Shiye Xuetang jingdong Yang xialian Mo cheng guanxue dachen bing gao xu" [The petition to the commissioner of the Imperial University by the director of Jiansu Industrial Academy Xiaolian Yang Mo, continued], *DGB*, September 14, 1903, 2–3.

26. "Lian Quan yu Yan Fu shu 2," September 2, 1903, in *Yan Fu ji bubian*, 373–374.

27. Concerning the conflict between Yan Fu and Civilization Books on their contract, the author's seal, and royalty calculation, see chapter 3.

28. "Lian Quan yu Yan Fu Shu 3," December 18, 1903, in *Yan Fu ji bubian*, 374–375.

struggle with piracy. Promises and endorsements from high-ranking officials did not authorize Civilization Books as the exclusive proprietor of its books, nor did they coerce local authorities into enforcing those protections actively. Lian was so pessimistic that he started to see *banquan*, "the general doctrine of the five continents" he had once praised, as a burden. When Yan Fu failed to get the royalty payment he requested in advance, he threatened to cancel their contract now to get his *banquan* back and square up all the payments. On January 14, 1904, Lian replied that he was in fact very willing to void the contract and return the *banquan* to Yan because "when signing the contract, I [Lian] did not know that it would be so hard to protect *banquan*." He further declared, "If the government could not protect *banquan*, how could they prohibit us from canceling our contract arbitrarily?"[29] Toward the end of this long and depressing letter to Yan Fu, Lian revealed to him his latest and biggest threat: *Beiyang guanbaoju* (Northern Ports Official Press) was pirating every textbook published by Civilization Books. It had reprinted at least 5,000–6,000 copies of each title. He was so anxious about this case that he hadn't been able to sleep in the past three days, Lian told Yan, and cried out, "Our bookstore is doomed!"[30]

The reason Lian thought that Civilization Books was doomed had to do with the particular pirate he was facing: Northern Ports Official Press. Not only was it an official publishing enterprise, but it was sponsored by none other than Yuan Shikai, the superintendent of trade for the northern ports, who had generously issued them *banquan* protections just months ago. The problem Lian faced, then, was not just whether local officials were keen to acknowledge *banquan* protections, but how he could confront the authority that both granted the *banquan* protection and violated it.

Instead of confronting Yuan and directly accusing his subordinate of unauthorized reprinting, Lian reported to the Ministry of Commerce and urged them to notify Yuan that a "fake" Northern Ports Official Press was reprinting Civilization Books' textbooks.[31] Listing all the titles and the number of copies pirated by this "fake" Northern Ports Official Press, Lian claimed that the reprints made by this copycat were widely known in the book market. This piracy

29. "Lian Quan yu Yan Fu shu 4," January 16, 1904, in *Yan Fu ji bubian*, 375–379.

30. Ibid., 379.

31. "Lun Zhi du qing chexiao banquan zhi miu" [On the absurdity of the Hebei governor's order to cancel [Civilization Books'] *banquan*], ZWRB, March 3, 1904, 1. Yuan was at the time also the governor of Hebei.

compromised not only Yuan's authority and Lian's business, but, more importantly, also the government's reform plan to encourage learning and commerce. In his petition, Lian called on the "real" Northern Ports Official Press to catch the copycats and punish them, but he knew all along that there was no "fake" Northern Ports Official Press. In a notice to Civilization Books' shareholders, Lian disclosed another side of his effort to handle this thorny problem. Besides petitioning the Ministry of Commerce, Lian had also attempted to settle privately with the man behind this reprinting operation—the general director of Northern Ports Official Press, Intendant Zhang Xunzhi—via a common friend in Tianjin.[32]

Zhang's response showed little amicability. He insisted that Lian had exaggerated the scale of their reprinting, and that their reprints were not commercially released and so wouldn't be Civilization Books' competition. Claiming that they had never received any official order regarding *banquan* protection, Zhang further pointed out that those official *banquan* protections upon which Civilization Books relied had no legal basis because there was as yet no copyright law in China. Moreover, he criticized Lian for making the situation unnecessarily complicated and putting Yuan in a difficult spot by getting the Ministry of Commerce involved. If Lian wanted to appeal against Northern Ports Official Press, Zhang threatened to publicly expose all the mistakes in Civilization Books' publications to ruin its intellectual reputation. At the same time, Zhang urged Lian to consider him as a fellow official and not to precipitate an open break in their friendship.[33]

Despite both Lian's and Zhang's efforts to resolve this dispute privately, neither of them was willing to make any concessions. In early February 1904, Yuan Shikai officially responded to Lian's petition. In the telegram he sent to the Ministry of Commerce, he decided to support his subordinate and urged both authorities to revoke the *banquan* protections that Civilization Books had received. This telegram was quickly reproduced and misinterpreted by several newspapers as the government's stand against *banquan* protection in general.[34] This seems to have caused immediate panic among booksellers; it forced

32. Ibid.

33. "Lun Zhi du qing chexiao banquan zhi miu xu zuo gao" [On the absurdity of the Hebei governor's order to cancel [Civilization Books'] *banquan*, continued], *ZWRB*, March 9, 1904, 1.

34. "Lun Zhi du qing chexiao banquan zhi miu," and "Nili banquan gonghui" [Proposing the establishment of a *banquan* guild], *DGB*, March 6, 1904, 3.

newspapers to publish the complete version of Yuan's telegram to clarify that Yuan's request for the abrogation of *banquan* protections applied only to Civilization Books.[35] The full version of Yuan's reply, however, didn't ease the booksellers' panic. On the contrary, revealing more details as to why Civilization Books' *banquan* protections were revoked, it provoked even harsher criticism of Yuan and the government.

The main body of Yuan's reply was a statement made by Zhang, in which he elaborated the main reasons why Civilization Books was not a victim of piracy but the subject of punishment. First of all, he argued, Northern Ports Official Press was an exclusive publisher of the grand guardian and superintendent of trade for the northern ports providing textbooks for schools in Zhili (Hebei) province according to the grand guardian's orders. It was not a commercial publisher and was thus exempt from the *banquan* protections. Second, Civilization Books' claim on the *banquan* protections they had received from Yuan and the minister of education was problematic. Zhang pointed out that Civilization Books had not sent all 170-plus titles they published to Yuan and the Imperial University for review and approval, yet they claimed publicly that both authorities had granted protections to *all* titles they published. The subjects of these *banquan* protections were indeterminate, and thus Lian's claim on the full coverage of these protections was a lie. For Zhang, since most books had not been reviewed by either of these two authorities, Civilization Books didn't possess the *banquan* protection of those books.

He went on to attack Civilization Books' credentials as an outstanding provider of New Learning books by questioning the quality and ideological correctness of its publications. Just as he had once threatened Lian he would do, Zhang now did expose the flaws in Civilization Books' textbooks. Although the textbooks themselves were well-edited and ideal for students, he complained, these books contained many factual and ideological mistakes that they had to correct before they could reprint these books. "*Banquan* was originally a fine policy in the West to encourage literature," he stated, "but books submitted to the Imperial University have to be flawless to be granted *banquan.*" Based on this principle, he considered many of Civilization Books' publications unworthy of *banquan* protection. He further listed five particularly problematic titles that needed to be banned: *Zhongguo lishi* (Chinese history), *Liuyang erjie*

---

35. "Chaban shuju ziwen" [Order to investigate [Civilization] Bookstore], *DGB*, March 3, 1904, 3.

wenji (The collected writings of two heroes from Liuyang),[36] *Li Hongzhang,
Faguo geming* (French Revolution), and *Ziyou yuanli* (Principles of freedom).
These books, he argued, either promoted antigovernment ideas or included
contents that slandered or mocked the court, and thus should be banned. In-
stead of protecting Civilization Books' *banquan*, this report concluded that the
Ministry of Commerce and the Imperial University should not only revoke
Civilization Books' *banquan* protections but also punish them for circulating
flawed and subversive texts.[37]

In early March, Yuan Shikai ordered that Civilization Books be shut down.[38]
This decision immediately elicited further criticisms of Yuan Shikai. These criticisms displayed both bitter disappointment with the state authorities and
anxious uncertainty about *banquan* itself. Xia Cengyou, a reform official and
historian, published a long editorial on behalf of *Zhongwai ribao* on March 8
and 9 to express the press's support for Lian.[39] While reemphasizing the correlation between copyright and progress, he raised three points regarding the
relationship between *banquan* and the state. To counter Zhang's claim that *banquan* protection had no legal basis, he pointed out that there was, in fact, a law
for *banquan* in China. Citing a little-known imperial edict on patent protection
issued by the Guangxu Emperor during the 1898 Reform, he claimed that
booksellers were empowered by this edict to ask for *banquan* protections from
officials. Although the 1898 Reform failed quickly, and most reform policies
were reversed right away, this minor edict was neither realized nor canceled.
By bringing up this particular edict, Xia was able to invoke the (nominally)
highest authority of the empire in support of Lian's requests for *banquan* protection, as well as to overwrite Yuan's order.

Xia's second comment questioned Yuan's and the state's authority and credibility. He argued that when Yuan had granted *banquan* protections to Civilization Books, on the one hand, and allowed his staff to pirate their books, on the
other hand, not only was Yuan's reputation compromised but the dignity of the
government as a whole was also impaired. This incident, he claimed, would un-
dermine future officially issued *banquan* protections, because it revealed how

36. The "two heroes from Liuyang" is usually understood to refer to revolutionary Tang
Caichang and radical reformer Tan Sitong. The writings of both were banned by the Qing court.

37. "Chaban shuju ziwen," *DGB*, March 3, 1904, 3.

38. "Shuju tingban" [Bookstore was shut down], *DGB*, March 6, 1904, 4.

39. "Lun Zhi du qing chexiao banquan zhi miu," *ZWRB*, March 8, 1904, 1; "Lun Zhi du qing
chexiao banquan zhi miu xu zuo gao," *ZWRB*, March 9, 1904, 1.

quickly the government and its officials changed their orders, contradicted themselves, and failed to keep their promises.

Xia also attempted to clarify the ambiguous association between censorship and *banquan*. He suggested that the government should understand censorship and *banquan* as two different matters, rather than mixing them together. Using as an example the censorship campaigns of the Qianlong Emperor (1711–1799), he argued that Yuan's punishment of Civilization Books was by comparison unnecessarily harsh and unreasonable. If books published by Civilization Books contained subversive words, Yuan could ask the publisher to remove the problematic passages just as Qianlong ordered subversive authors' words to be removed from all kinds of books. There was no need to ban the whole book or to go so far as to shut down the firm. He further reminded Yuan that using censorship to punish Civilization Books was a double-edged sword: if the textbook at the center of the storm, *Zhongguo lishi*, was so ideologically incorrect that they had to shut down Civilization Books for good, then why had Northern Ports Official Press reprinted such a problematic work? If Civilization Books' publications were so offensive to the authorities, why had Yuan granted them *banquan* protections in the first place? Didn't this suggest that Yuan had failed to screen these contents at the time?

Xia's criticism was a political one. Speaking as a literati-official, he was employing authorities and examples familiar to other literati-officials to make his case. He didn't directly discuss the nature of *banquan* but primarily attacked Yuan's poor governing. For him, the fundamental problem lay in the credibility of *banquan* protections, not their form. In other words, he didn't question Yuan's issuance of *banquan* protection orders; instead, he criticized Yuan's failure to stick to his own rules and promises. He was upset by the state's stance on revoking Civilization Books' *banquan* protections; that said, he still considered the state to be the only legitimate authority granting and enforcing *banquan*.

American missionary Young J. Allen, meanwhile, viewed the incident differently. Back in 1896, Allen's famous *Zhongdong zhanji benmo* was, along with other best sellers of the SDCK, one of the first books to receive individually issued *banquan* protections from local Chinese officials. At that time, *banquan* protection orders of that sort were rare and thus considered exceptional and privileged. The term *banquan* or the idea that human intellectual creation should be seen as property was still new and foreign to Chinese, even within the book-sellers' community. As discussed in chapter 2, Allen and other missionaries affiliated with the SDCK aggressively campaigned between 1895 and 1898 to promote this new concept in China to have their books protected. Since then the climate of the Chinese book market had changed drastically. The SDCK's sales declined after 1900 as more and more Chinese firms, such as Civilization Books and Commercial Press, joined the New Learning business. Although, by 1904, such *banquan* protection orders had become increasingly common and generic, the SDCK, as a pioneering advocate of copyright in China, continued to petition Chinese officials and made sure that their books contained officially issued *banquan* protections.

The Civilization Books case would be a shock to these missionaries. Two days after Civilization Books was ordered to close, *Dagong bao* reported that a missionary from an American missionary press had paid a visit to the firm, asked for details about the whole incident, and expressed his disaffection toward the government's decision.[40] Many scholars believe that this missionary was none other than Young J. Allen. During his visit to Civilization Books, he not only expressed his anger but also made an unusual proposal: booksellers in Peking and Shanghai should form an independent *banquan* guild to register and regulate *banquan* instead of relying upon the government.[41]

Not long after his visit to Civilization Books, in April, Allen published a short article entitled "Banquan zhi quanxi" (On the nature of copyright) in the SDCK's organ *Wanguo gongbao*.[42] This short and odd piece, published nearly a decade after the peak of the SDCK's copyright campaign, was Allen's animadversion against Yuan's decision in particular and the Chinese misconception of copyright in general. Although he didn't name any specific individuals or firms, such as Yuan Shikai, Zhang Xunzhi, Lian Quan, or Civilization Books, this piece was about the ongoing dispute. It started by hinting at the struggle that Civilization Books faced. Textbooks in China were in high demand, Allen claimed; thus any better-edited one would sell widely but would also be pirated right away. Booksellers reported unauthorized reprints to government authorities, but usually those who made reprints wouldn't be prosecuted. Even worse was the fact that "powerful and strong figures also want to repeal booksellers' *banquan*." The core of the whole dispute, he believed, was that "they believe that copyright is something that authority can give and take away as they like, and they see this as the common practice in the Western countries." As someone coming from "the Western countries," he felt the need to clarify this

40. "Nili banquan gonghui," *DGB*, March 6, 1904, 3.

41. Ibid.

42. Lin Lezhi, transcribed by Fan Yi, "Banquan zhi guanxi" [On the nature of copyright], *Wanguo gongbao* 183 (April 1904).

misunderstanding because, "in fact, there was no such law in the Western countries."[43]

The so-called Western copyright, he explained, is the private property right of authors and publishers. "Protecting [copyright] is the responsibility of the state, not a courtesy it could choose to extend or withhold." He further pointed out that any author's and publisher's copyright should be protected, no matter what kind of books they produced. Copyright came into existence once the book had been produced. The state regulated copyright via registration, but this didn't mean that books not registered would have no copyright. "Authors spend their time and energy in writing. Publishers invest their capital. Together, they produce books for the society. The whole society benefits from their books, so in return authors and publishers have copyright." The state should see itself as an agent of society to protect copyright, not a higher authority above society and the law. If the state authorities granted booksellers *banquan* protections but took them away whenever they wished to do so, Allen argued, authors and booksellers would be so disheartened that they might quit publishing altogether because it would be impossible for them to protect themselves.[44] By articulating the "real" principles and rationales behind European copyright law, Allen attempted to "correct" Yuan's and Zhang's misinterpretation of *banquan*. According to him, individual *banquan* protection orders, although prevalent at that time, had a crucial structural flaw because the protections were granted in the wrong context. As long as the legitimacy and credibility of *banquan* derived from the state's authority, and as long as *banquan* was granted individually according to the content of the book or the preference of the officials, *banquan* would never be copyright.

Young J. Allen's animadversion ended on a high note by reminding the Qing state that "it is the people who make the country prosper; it is the state that protects its people."[45] Although he stressed that the "right" of "copyright" should be seen as a natural property right that couldn't be invalidated by the state, his Chinese contemporaries seemed to be more interested in finding a higher political authority to support their ownership claims than in arguing for *banquan*/copyright as an individual right. At the end of the day, Lian Quan still counted on the existing power structure to save his Civilization Books. The primary strategy of Lian's counterattack was to find an official equal to or higher

43. Ibid.
44. Ibid.
45. Ibid.

than Yuan Shikai to support him. He appealed to the young and powerful Manchu prince Zaizhen (1876–1947), president of the Ministry of Commerce and
first son of Prince Qing Yikuang (1838–1917), the most powerful Manchu royal
in court politics at the time. Prince Zaizhen was only twenty-eight in 1904, but
he had been to Great Britain to attend the coronation of King Edward VII (1902)
on behalf of the emperor. Traveling extensively in Europe and Japan, this young
prince was keen on reform and on the West. And he had the backing of his father,
Prince Qing, the chief minister of the Grand Council. Since Civilization Books
had just published Prince Zaizhen's diary of his trip to Great Britain, Liang had
a good connection on which to build.[46]

   In his appeal to Prince Zaizhen, Lian refuted all the accusations Zhang had
made. He argued that a "reprinting prohibited" statement had been printed on
the last page of every copy that Civilization Books produced; on copies of those
books that Zhang and his Northern Ports Official Press had pirated, there was
even a reproduction of Yuan Shikai's complete *banquan* protection order. It was,
therefore, impossible for Zhang not to have noticed that these books had been
under Yuan's protection. Second, although Zhang claimed that his reprints were
not released commercially, local officials and schools had to "donate" to his press
"to cover the cost of printing." Since Zhang and his press gained financially
through these "donations," his operation was not purely not-for-profit as he had
asserted. Third, if Zhang knew of the flaws in Civilization Books' textbooks, he
could have just notified the publisher so that those mistakes might be corrected;
instead of notifying Civilization Books, Zhang's press went on to reprint the
books they considered too problematic to use in schools. Lian further claimed
that the edition Zhang had pirated was the first edition; most of the mistakes
he complained about had been fixed in the improved second edition, so there
was no reason to accuse them of being irresponsible. As for those "antigovernment" titles, none of them were published by Civilization Books, nor had they
ever entered into a consignment arrangement to sell such books. Offering their
account books as evidence, Lian insisted that this was a false accusation. He then
asked Prince Zaizhen to urge Yuan to punish Zhang for his misconduct and false
accusations.[47]

---

46. Zaizhen, *Yinyao Riji*.

47. "Lian bulang shengfu Shangbu qing zouding banquan falü chenggao bing pi" [Lian
Quan's petition to the Ministry of Commerce requesting copyright law and the ministry's
reply], *DGB*, April 17, 1904, supplementary page.

Besides asking Prince Zaizhen to overrule Yuan's order, Lian reiterated the proposal he had made to Zhang Baixi in 1903: following in the footsteps of Western countries and Japan, the Qing state also needed to enact a copyright law to impose order on the domestic publishing business. Prince Zaizhen replied positively to his appeal, overruled Yuan's order, and allowed Civilization Books to reopen for business. He promised that the Ministry of Commerce would establish more systematic publishing regulations, but urged Lian to continue to publish after Zhang granted him *banquan*.[48]

Examining the True Value of a Book

Prince Zaizhen's final ruling settled the dispute between Civilization Books and Yuan Shikai but resolved none of the fundamental issues that had initially caused the conflict. He never explicitly addressed the question of whether the government should be exempted from the *banquan* protections they had issued. He, as the minister of commerce, also showed little interest in overseeing the process by which Civilization Books, and other publishers alike, could obtain government-issued *banquan*/copyright protections in the future. He handed these issues over to Zhang Baixi, the commissioner of the Imperial University. This decision reflects an interesting and vital understanding of *banquan*/copyright at that time: *banquan*/copyright was a matter of culture and learning, rather than a matter of commerce.

Since its establishment in 1903, the Ministry of Commerce had regarded itself as the Qing state's official authority on patents and trademarks. However, Zaizhen did not seem to have regarded *banquan*/copyright, which was then commonly grouped with patents and trademarks in modern intellectual property law, as the ministry's primary business. The Ministry of Commerce presided over Qing's policy making and regulation of patents and trademarks by reviewing applications for patents, drafting patent and trademark laws, and making preparations for the establishment of an independent trademark office.[49] When booksellers or authors petitioned the Ministry of Commerce to request *banquan*/copyright protections, however, the ministry tended to forward their petitions to the commissioner of the Imperial University (and later to the

48. Ibid.
49. Wang, *Qingmo Shangbu yanjiu*, 189–201

Ministry of Education).[50] Moreover, even though the Ministry of Commerce did draft a copyright law around 1905–1906, it never publicized that draft. On the contrary, it handed the draft over to the Ministry of Education for further revisions.[51]

All decisions that the Ministry of Commerce made regarding *banquan*/copyright were based on the understanding of a book's value in late imperial China. There was something special about books that made the *banquan* of a book fundamentally different from a patent for a match, or the trademark of a tobacco brand. For this reason, it appeared to be beyond the Ministry of Commerce's remit. Certainly, printed books had been produced and sold in the marketplace in China since the Song dynasty. However, for their producers and consumers, books were no ordinary commodities. The true value of a book could not be measured solely in monetary terms. Books had special importance and exceptional prestige in China. The tradition of book learning had been central to the identity and legitimacy of China's cultural and political elites for at least one millennium. The civil service examination system made literacy and a classical education the ladders to success, social status, wealth, and political power.[52] To a certain extent, possessing books, or having access to them, was the key to social mobility in late imperial China. Writing, reading, publishing, and collecting books, therefore, were not only essential to the elite Chinese literati's world of learning and their self- and communal identity, but also crucial to nonliterati, such as merchants and landowners, who were aspiring to higher social and cultural status.[53]

While the sociocultural significance of the book was seen in late imperial Chinese society as its true and primary value, its economic value, on the other

50. For example, "Pi Hua shang Wu Dabang bing suozu yueyin kuaizi yinzi Guantong yishu zhun Xuebu fucheng yu jiaoke wu shen guan she you" [Reply to Chinese merchant Wu Dabang's request to protect his *Thorough Instruction for Cantonese Phonetic System*]: the Ministry of Education dismissed the forwarded petition because the book was not a textbook [thus ineligible for *banquan* protection], *Shangwu guanbao* 28 (January 18, 1907): 14.

51. "Shangbu zou niding shangbiao zhuce shiban zhangcheng shi" [Ministry of Commerce's memorial for drafting a provisional trademark registration statute], *SB*, no. 11256 (August 18, 1904): 1. In this memorial, the minister of commerce referred to a draft copyright law in the making.

52. Ho, *The Ladder of Success in Imperial China*.

53. For a discussion of the cultural and social prestige of books in Chinese society and how the book-learning tradition shaped the elite Chinese literati's culture and life, see McDermott, *A Social History of the Chinese Book*.

hand, was consciously depreciated. Authors, compilers, and booksellers tended to portray their material gains from books as the "minor bonus" for their sincere contributions to the world of learning or an extra "reward" to affirm their cultural achievements, rather than as their source of income. This view held true even when they, in fact, made a living and fed their families through writing and publishing. Late Qing authors, like Yan Fu and Lin Shu, consistently referred to their newly received copyright royalties as a "tiny remuneration." According to this logic, authors' and booksellers' material gains were attached to and, in theory, determined by their intellectual contributions or artistic achievements. Therefore, *banquan* could not be separated from the intellectual, creative, and educational value of a book, and thus it should be supervised by educational and cultural administrators rather than officials in charge of commerce.

This seems to have been a consensus shared by both imperial bureaucrats and authors and booksellers in late Qing China. Not only did the Ministry of Commerce refer most *banquan*-related petitions and rulings to Zhang Baixi, the commissioner of the Imperial University, but the treaty commissioners also first approached Zhang when the issue of foreign copyright protection was brought up in the Sino-American negotiation for treaty renewal in 1902.[54] Booksellers' petitions for establishing a written copyright law or other kinds of systematic *banquan*/copyright regulations were usually addressed to Zhang as well. For those who sought individual *banquan* protection orders, it was taken for granted that Zhang was the most likely metropolitan official to ask. His orders regarding *banquan*/copyright or publishing were also believed to have had a notable impact on society.[55]

In the first few years of the twentieth century, Zhang was considered Qing's official authority on *banquan*/copyright, not only because he was in charge of education administration, but also because the Imperial University—like its

54. Zhang Baixi, "Zhi Riben shichen Neitian Kangzai shi han" [To Japanese ambassador Uchida Kōsai], in Deng Shi, ed., *Guangxu renyin (nian ba nian) zhengyi congshu* [The collectanea of political writings in the twenty-eighth year of Guangxu (1903)] (Taipei: Wenhai chubanshe, 1976), 799.

55. This can best be illustrated by an ironic accident that took place in the spring of 1903. Earlier in the winter of 1902, the Imperial University issued a pamphlet listing over one hundred titles in sixteen subjects that were approved and recommended by the university as suitable textbooks for new schools. Accompanying this pamphlet was an order from Zhang Baixi urging local and provincial governments to reprint the pamphlet. This order, however, was misunderstood (or intentionally misinterpreted) by booksellers and some local officials as an order to encourage people to freely reprint the titles listed in the pamphlet.

early modern predecessor, the Imperial Academy—represented the state's supreme intellectual credibility. As Lian Quan stated in his petition to Zhang in 1903: "[I] personally believe that the Imperial University is the pivot of knowledge under the Heaven. People devoted to learning under the heaven, if they do not rely upon and comply with the university, will hesitate about which direction to go and what course to follow." Identifying the Imperial University as the supreme authority in the world of learning, he further argued that the university had the responsibility and legitimacy to set standards to evaluate the quality and authenticity of books. He believed that "uncertain systems" and "undefined standards" had encouraged piracy in China and thus caused the current crisis: "[people in] the world of learning are confused, and authentic talents cannot stand out." To keep the world of learning in order, therefore, "standards [of knowledge] have to be carefully established; the measures of reward have to be publicly advocated."[56]

In his reply to Lian's petition, Zhang promised that the government was going to issue a copyright law shortly. As for the "reward" he was requesting, Zhang urged him to present those books to the Imperial University for examination (*shending*). The Imperial University would then grant an "approval seal" to those deemed worthy and "officially publicize that reprinting of these books is prohibited," as an "encouragement to those who put painstaking effort into writing and translating."[57] The "examination" procedure Zhang introduced here would become a standard method for Chinese booksellers and authors to obtain *banquan* from the Imperial University and later the Ministry of Education. When booksellers and authors presented a book to the Imperial University, their petition was kept in the official records of the Imperial University, thus making the university the guarantor of proprietorship of that book. Approval as such was not simply a reward; it was also an honorable privilege because it indicated that the content of the book was certified and endorsed by "the pivot of knowledge under the Heaven." This examination procedure bundled the quality of a book with whether its proprietorship would be acknowledged, connected the artistic or intellectual value of a book with its commercial value, and established the state as the authority to judge the former and protect the latter.

56. "Lian bulang shang Guanxue dachen lun banquan shi," *DGB*, May 22, 1903.

57. "Guanxue dachen pida Lian Huiqing bulang chengqing mingding banquan you," *DGB*, June 4, 1903. It was echoed by Civilization Books in "Wunming Shuju yiyin Qunxue siyan Licai xue jiangyi chengshu chengcing Guanxue dachen shending chenggao" [Civilization Books presented its newly translated and printed *Qunxue siyan* and *Licai xue jiangyi* to the commissioner of the Imperial University for review and examination], *DGB*, July 19, 1903.

To fully understand why and how Zhang and other top officials envisioned this state-led examination system, we have to take a close look at *Xuewu gangyao* (Outline of educational principles), a detailed guideline compiled in 1902 by Zhang Baixi, Rong Qing (1859–1917), and Zhang Zhidong, as part of their grand proposal for Qing's new educational system. For them, not all books were equal. What "the pivot of knowledge under the Heaven" cared about the most was one particular kind of writing: textbooks for the new schools. Granting *banquan*, in their proposal, was a means by which the state could control not only the quality but also the intellectual and ideological agendas of textbooks published by private publishers.

When the Qing state determined to launch a full-scale reform in the aftermath of the Boxer Rebellion, education was their first and foremost focus. With the notorious eight-legged essay examination format abolished in 1901, degree candidates now had to answer questions dealing with both Chinese and Western learning. At the same time, new schools were established as an alternative to examination for future Chinese elites. Top educational administrators believed that to set up the state's orthodox agenda and prevent chaos and confusion in intellectual circles, textbooks used in these new schools had to be compiled and issued exclusively by the state.[58] In the *Xuewu gangyao*, however, these top officials also admitted that "the textbooks to be compiled are too extensive, too diverse," so it was "certainly impossible" for any single institution to accomplish this task in a short period.[59] In a realistic compromise, these officials thus advanced an alternative: the Qing state would allow and encourage private individuals and institutions to compile textbooks to meet the needs of new schools, along with the "official edition" of textbooks published by the government. "If provincial literati compile usable textbooks following the official guidelines," *Xuewu gangyao* promised, "they will also be allowed to present their books to the state for review and approval. [Once approved by the state,] these books can be used in schools as official textbooks. As reward and encouragement, *banquan*/copyright will be granted, and authors will be allowed to produce and sell these books."[60]

Some officials saw the bundling of *banquan*/copyright protection and textbook review as a clever way to control the content of textbooks, as well as to

58. Zheng Hesheng, "Sanshi nian lai zhongyang zhengfu duiyu bianshen jiaokeshu zhi jiantao," 3.

59. Zhang Baixi, Rong Qing, and Zhang Zhidong, "Xuewu gangyao," in Zhang, *Zhang Baixi ji*, 53–54.

60. Ibid., 54.

ensure the quality of privately compiled textbooks. In early 1903, for example, treaty commissioner Lü Haihuan urged the emperor to make this review procedure obligatory for all textbook producers, to "correct the social trend." In one of his memorials, he expressed concern that private booksellers, with their profit-seeking motivation, might easily follow some "wrong" trends, such as Darwinism and Rousseauism,[61] or present numerous and subversive ideas that would bring "severe harm to the society." It was the state's job to "rectify them urgently" to "save society" and "correct the intellectual trend." He therefore urged the emperor to enforce a general review of all privately compiled textbooks. After a careful, strict examination and review, books that "had pure and correct objectives and were suitable for students" would be granted *banquan* privileges and would enjoy the status of official publications. As for those that were "shallow, disordered, and useless for education," or those that "contained false ideas and harmed the learned," he suggested that the state should ban them for good.[62]

The bundling of *banquan*/copyright and the examination procedure would further enable the state to screen and control the content of books. This might easily be seen by early twenty-first century readers as the government's crafty way of taking advantage of booksellers' commercial concerns to carry out its oppressive censorship mission; however, at the time, this bundle was generally welcomed by both booksellers and the presses. It was considered a fair, or even necessary, procedure to ensure the quality of books and to keep the world of learning in order, especially after the court announced the abolition of the civil service examination in 1905.

The abolition of the civil service examination marked two fundamental shifts in the Qing state's educational system and destabilized the world of learning, which was deeply intertwined with the examination system: new schools replaced the centuries-old examination system as the primary means to forge China's future sociopolitical elites and imperial bureaucrats, and the New Learning took the place of the classical canon as the new intelletual orthodoxy.[63] In

61. What Lü referred to here as Darwinism should be understood as social Darwinism; and what he meant by Rousseauism might be Jean-Jacques Rousseau's ideas of the social contract, freedom, and equality. It was common for late Qing Chinese intellectuals to believe that Rousseau's ideas had inspired and caused the French Revolution.

62. "Zou wei guanban jiaokeshu ken zao banfa sizuan keben ji ying lizheng yi duan quxiang er mian qitu gong chen guan jian yangqi shengjian shi," in *Lü Haihuan zougao*, 548–558.

63. For the social and intellectual impact of the abolition of the civil service examination, see Elman, *A Cultural History of Civil Examinations in Late Imperial China*, 569–623. See also Borthwick, *Education and Social Change in China*.

December 1905, the Ministry of Education was established to supervise a new educational system. Lacking sufficient budget and staff to realize their ideal of state-monopolized textbook production, the Ministry of Education regulated textbook production mainly by reviewing privately compiled works. The Review Office (*Shending si*) was quickly set up as the formal agency to examine these textbooks. Only titles that passed the agency staff's review were granted *banquan* and authorized for use in schools as "textbooks."[64] Meanwhile, the ministry also expanded the Imperial University's publishing arm into the Press Office (*Bianyi tushu ju*) to compile and publish the "official" editions of textbooks.

It seemed that both the officials and the public generally embraced a formal office in charge of the examination procedures at that time. Discussing the establishment of the Ministry of Education, several editorial pieces in Shanghai newspapers argued that it was necessary for the Ministry of Education to examine all the "private" textbooks and apply a carrot-and-stick policy to control and regulate booksellers who jumped into the textbook business.[65] Even Yan Fu, the self-proclaimed champion of copyright, suggested that *banquan*/copyright should be awarded only to "examined and approved" books; those "unexamined" or "dismissed" by the ministry should not be allowed to market themselves as "textbooks," and their purveyors should be punished.[66] This firm belief in the necessity of a carrot-and-stick policy was inseparable from the debased reputation of booksellers. "Most booksellers are driven by profit," as an editorial in *Shen bao* argued; "they are good at calculating." If they claimed that they published textbooks "to define the epitome of citizenship," "seven out of ten" were concerned only with their "business achievement." As a result, they produced textbooks that were "messy, miscellaneous, and full of mistakes," and did "great harm to society."[67] The assumption was that the profit-seeking nature of booksellers would prevent them from publishing textbooks of good quality and correct content.

64. "Xuebu di yi ci shending chudeng xiaoxue zhanyong jiaokeshu fanli" [The Ministry of Education's general guideline for the first review of the primary elementary school provisional textbooks], *XBGB* 3 (October 7, 1907).

65. For example, "Zhuanzai Nanfangbao lun she xuebu fangfa," *Dongfang zazhi* 2:12 (January 1906).

66. "Zhongwai ribao Yan Fu lun xiaxue jiaokeshuji yi shending," *Dongfan zazhi* 3:6 (July 1907).

67. "Shenbao xuewu chuyan," *Dongfang zazhi* 3:11 (December 1907).

Ironically, the bundling of copyright and content review was also welcomed by booksellers precisely because of their "profit-driven nature." The educational reform created not only hundreds of thousands of new schools but also a brand-new textbook market that hadn't previously existed in China. According to the Ministry of Education's first empire-wide education survey, new schools spent nearly one million taels on books in the 1906–1907 academic year alone.[68] A state-issued *banquan* protection would, in principle, help booksellers secure the exclusive profit of their textbooks. Also, if a title passed the ministry's review, its content and quality were understood to have been endorsed by the state. For booksellers, this could be a good selling point for their publications. In late Qing textbook advertisements, booksellers often highlighted the fact that their textbooks had been "reviewed and authorized by the Ministry of Education (*Xuebu shending*)"; thus they should be any school's top choice.

In total, from 1906 to 1911, over four hundred titles passed the Ministry of Education's review and were authorized for use in schools as textbooks within a fixed term. Most of them were published by Shanghai-based publishers, such as Commercial Press and Civilization Books.[69] The results of reviews were announced publicly in *Xuebu guanbao* (the official newsletter of the Ministry of Education), which was issued every ten days from the summer of 1906 to the end of the empire in 1911. The review of a book usually came with one or two short paragraphs of comments about its quality, why it deserved to be authorized or not authorized as a textbook, and what the author/publisher should revise to improve it. Sometimes, to set an example, the ministry published lengthy and detailed instructions in *Xuebu guanbao* demanding that booksellers alter the content or wording of their books. From these comments and guidelines, we can sort out the basic principles and standards the ministry applied when they examined and evaluated the hundreds of books sent to their office.

The quality of its content was the ministry's prime concern when reviewing a textbook. Although the review was bound together with the *banquan* protection, a book's originality or authenticity was not a determining factor. Instead, the main criteria were whether the content was well-written and whether it was carefully compiled. When the ministry commented on titles that passed the examination, for example, expressions such as "pellucid structure," "fluent

68. Xuebu Zongwusi, *Guangxu san shi san nian fen diyici jiaoyu tongtong ji tubiao.*
69. Wang, *Minzu hun*, 36.

writing style," and "excellent wording" were often used to support the judgment that these titles were "fine books" (*shanben*) deserving *banquan* privilege.[70] Interestingly, these criteria were very similar to the criteria for success in writing civil service examination essays.[71] On the contrary, books that failed the review usually did so because they had "vulgar diction," "poor and incoherent translation," "careless proofreading," or simply "too many typos."[72]

The practicability of the book was another criterion. Books that were too long, too complicated, or too hard to break into small sections were considered unsuitable for school, so they were often rejected by the ministry. Whether the book could provide up-to-date knowledge or skills for society's immediate needs was also crucial to the ministry. For example, Commercial Press's *Diguo yingwen duben* (Imperial English reader) was highly praised as a model English textbook to serve Chinese students' needs simply because "there was not a single poem in this book." "The main goal for our fellow countrymen when studying European languages is the ability to read their science books," the ministry's reviewer stated. "Not only is the irregular grammatical structure of poetry hard for beginners, but poetry also won't help us to read science books."[73]

Although it seems that the overwhelming majority of the Review Office's evaluative comments and revision instructions were devoted to "quality control," this doesn't mean that the reviewers didn't care about ideological correctness. When they learned that a certain title contained potentially subversive messages, not only did the title fail the review, but the ministry also banned it. Books mentioning equality, freedom, rights, or Han racism were considered problematic too.[74] For example, in 1908 a textbook prepared for girls' primary

---

70. For example: "Zhejiang juren Jiang Zhiyou cheng zhongxue xiushen jiaokeshu qing shending bing pi," *XBGB* 5 (November 7, 1906): 9a–9b; "Xingbu langzhong Hu Yulin zibian suanshu liang zhong chengqing shending kenyu banquan bing pi," *XBGB* 11 (January 5, 1907): 13a–13b; "Mengxue duben di wu qi bian er ce Wenming shuju," *XBGB* 23 (June 11, 1907): 27b.

71. I would like to thank the anonymous reviewer who pointed out the similarity between the ministry's textbook review criteria and the examination essays.

72. For example: "Guangdong Jiaying zhou yousheng Xiao Riyan cheng Xinxue Zhengzong yishu kenqing daizou bing qing shending zhun yu banquan bing pi," *XBGB* 5 (November 7, 1906): 19a; "Xiaoxue xin like shu shengtu yong jiaoyuan yong ge si ce," *XBGB* 23 (June 11, 1907): 30a; "Shengyuan Xu Weitao cheng zizhe ziran dili xue qing shending bing pi" *XBGB* 25 (July 1, 1907): 37; "Yingyong dongwen fa jiaokeshu yi ce," *XBGB* 57 (June 19, 1908): 19.

73. "Diguo yingwen duben san ce Shangwu Yinshuguan ben," *XBGB* 24 (June 21, 1907), 35a.

74. "Xuebu zou zunzhi hefu Zhi du zou jingchen guanjian zhe," *XBGB* 129 (July, 1910).

elementary schools failed to gain the ministry's approval simply because the word *pingdeng* (equality) appeared in the book; it was subsequently banned by the ministry. Having a preface written by the wrong person might bring serious consequences as well. One of Civilization Books' ethics textbooks was banned by the ministry because it had an "absurd" preface written by Cai Yuanpei (1868–1940), a Hanlin official turned revolutionary.[75] Books that had once passed the ministry's review might be banned later if they stirred up unexpected controversies. For instance, *Guangdong xiangtu jiaokeshu* (Guandong native-place textbook), approved by the ministry in 1906, was recalled in 1907 after its statement that Hakka and Hoklo were not of the Han race caused public disturbances in Guangdong. Its *banquan*/copyright was also immediately canceled. The ministry ordered its publisher to change this controversial statement and banned the sale of this edition.[76]

The Review Office did not serve only as the quality-controller to prevent "messy, miscellaneous" privately compiled textbooks from doing "great harm to society." They further actively proofread titles sent to them and changed undesirable contents. For those titles that contained minor problems, the Review Office sometimes made revision suggestions and asked the original authors or booksellers to submit textbooks for reexamination after the revisions were incorporated. In some cases, the Review Office published the complete revision instructions in the Ministry of Education's official newsletter and explained one by one why the parts should be revised. Although their revision instructions were most frequently small corrections that aimed to standardize confusing Chinese translations of foreign names and objects or to fix grammatical problems caused by literal translation (from Japanese texts), sometimes they asked booksellers to redact unwanted or politically sensitive phrases or even adjust the tone of a narrative. For example, in the 1908 revision instructions for *Wanguo lishi* (World history), compiled by the *Zuoxin she* (Knowing-New-Knowledge Society), the Review Office asked the authors to replace all occurrences of the word "revolution" with "rebellion," "reform," or "great chaos," and to excise all the positive descriptions of the French Revolution. They even rewrote the conclusion of one section: replacing the passive stance

---

75. "Zi Zhe fu chajin He bian nüzi xiaoxue guowen jiaokeshu wen" and "Dachi gesheng tixueshi jinyong Mai yi zhongdeng lunlixue wen," *XBGB* 66 (September 16, 1908): 1a–1b.

76. "Zi Jiang du qing Shanghai dao chi da guoxue baocunhui gaizheng Guangdong xiangtu jiaokeshu wen," *XBGB* 31 (August 19, 1907), 45a.

of the original ending, which suggested that the Europeans would conquer the world and destroy other countries, the new passage proclaimed that the world would come to see China and Japan standing up in East Asia as powerhouses.[77]

The Discrediting of the State as Supreme Authority of Knowledge

The tone the Review Office used in their comments, rulings, and revision instructions is a top-down authoritative, and sometimes omniscient, one. Chinese booksellers and authors were willing to revise the content of their books according to these demanding guidelines not just because they wanted to get *banquan*/copyright protection from the Ministry of Education. They also believed that the Review Office, as part of the Ministry of Education—the supreme authority in all matters of knowledge—would have more sophisticated and "correct" intellectual taste and a superior command of New Learning knowledge. This assumption, however, was challenged in 1907 by another office in the Ministry of Education.

Since 1898, the vision of a state-monopolized textbook production had been reiterated in every educational reform the Qing planned or launched. In reality, to promptly fulfill the immediate need of new schools across the empire, textbook production had been opened to private booksellers and authors. That said, the state never relinquished their goal to one day monopolize textbook production. When the Ministry of Education temporarily opened textbook production to private publishers and set up a procedure that intertwined *banquan*/copyright and textbook review, they also established their own Press Office to compile the official edition of textbooks. These "official editions," the ministry hoped, would soon be used empire-wide to ensure that students received a standard and homogenous education. This dual policy created an inevitable tension between the ministry and the private textbook publishers. It made the Ministry of Education both a player competing with other booksellers in this textbook market—a market generating one million taels per year—and, simultaneously, the visible hand regulating and monitoring textbook production via the Review Office.

77. "Wanguo Lishi Zuoxinshe bianyi," *XBGB* 24 (June 21, 1907), 7b; "Wanguo Lishi jiaoshou ximu," *XBGB* 61 (July 28, 1908), 3–9.

Many publishers worried that the flourishing business they enjoyed would be gone as soon as the Ministry of Education released its "official" textbooks, as it would be impossible for private individuals to compete with the government agency that defined orthodox knowledge for the state. "Believing the government's authority is our default mentality," as one bookseller expressed this common concern: "If an official edition [of textbooks] is released, no one will dare to criticize it, and it will be popularized nationwide. Even if there were well-made textbooks published by private booksellers, people are not going to use them."[78]

In 1907, after a series of delays, the Ministry of Education's Press Office finally released the first volumes of the "official" Chinese and moral textbooks for elementary school. To everyone's surprise, they were obvious imitations of Commercial Press's and Civilization Books' textbooks, especially in their design and format.[79] Unlike the books compiled and published by the Hanlin Academy or the Imperial Academy (both of which were praised for their quality and accuracy in late imperial China), textbooks published by the ministry were immediately harshly criticized by both the media and other officials. These criticisms cast further doubt on the intellectual and cultural superiority of the state.[80]

Shortly after the release of these first "official" textbooks, a young editor at Civilization Books named Lufei Kui (1886–1941)[81] openly criticized them in a Shanghai-based progressive newspaper. As one contemporary later recalled, Lufei's harsh review was praised and widely circulated at the time; it opened the floodgates and allowed readers to criticize the ministry's textbooks from different perspectives.[82] Examining them from an educator's perspective, he concluded that these "official" textbooks were simply too hard to be used in real classrooms. In his review, Lufei described in detail how "unsuitable to a child's mentality" these two textbooks were, how "illogical" the narratives were, how "bad" the illustrations were, and so forth.[83] Contrary to the Review Office's criterion of textual excellence, he judged these two textbooks based on their usability: whether their structure was compatible with school schedules, their

78. Bohong, "Lun guoding jiaokeshu."

79. Wang Jiarong, *Minzu hun*, 31–35.

80. Jiang Mengmei, "Qian Qing Xuebu bianshu zhi zhuangkuang."

81. Ludei Kui later established Chung Hwa Books, the second-largest publishing company in China, in 1912 and became the leader of the Shanghai book trade in the 1920s and 1930s.

82. Jiang, "Qian Qing Xuebu bianshu zhi zhuangkuang."

83. Bo, "Lun Xuebu biancuan zhi jiaokeshu," *Nanfang bao*, April 4 and May 4, 1907.

content accessible for schoolchildren, and whether their design could apply to other subjects.

Lufei's comments on the ministry's "official" textbooks are significant not only because he used a different set of standards to examine the value and quality of textbooks, but also because he suggested that the official editions of textbooks, just like privately published ones, *could* be subject to criticism and examination. Later in the same year, Huang Shoufu (1878–1911), a textbook editor and schoolmaster in Jiading, echoing Lufei's agenda, published a pamphlet entitled *Jiaokeshu piping* (Textbook review). He closely examined the ministry's Chinese textbooks for elementary schools side by side with eleven other "private" textbooks. As Huang stated in his review of the ministry's Chinese textbook, although he acknowledged the ministry's effort to offer standard textbooks for Chinese students, "that doesn't mean that their content cannot be discussed."[84] The comments of these reviewers signaled the possibility of challenging the state as the supreme authority in determining what kind of knowledge would be taught in schools and in evaluating the intellectual/artistic value of literary works.

The vital problem of the ministry's "official" textbooks, Lufei stated in his criticism, was plagiarism. He pointed out not only that the format and structure of the "official" textbooks were modeled after Civilization Books' and Commercial Press's textbooks, but that staff in the Press Office also plagiarized the contents of privately compiled textbooks verbatim, merely replacing a few words with synonyms, and yet pretended these were their original works. He claimed that, based on his quick survey, the contents of at least twelve lessons in the ministry-compiled Chinese textbook were copied from private textbooks, and he believed that many similar cases would be found if a careful review were launched. "The Ministry of Education has the role of examining books and granting *banquan*. It is thus clear that no one is allowed to plagiarize or counterfeit books that are under *banquan* protection." He further questioned: "If commoners pirated or reprinted these books, they would be punished. How then is the Ministry of Education going to justify itself?" He claimed that he was "anxious about the future of China's education if this is how the Ministry of Education compiles textbooks."[85] Lufei's criticism challenged the state's supreme authority over knowledge. If the left hand of the Ministry of Education, the Press Office, failed to produce excellent textbooks and plagiarized privately

84. Wang, *Minzu hun*, 33.
85. "Lun Xuebu biancuan zhi jiaokeshu," *Nanfang bao*, May 4, 1907, 1.

compiled textbooks, how could the right hand of the Ministry of Education, the Review Office, have the authority and ability to judge and examine privately compiled textbooks, or even grant them *banquan*?

Separating *Banquan* from Content Review

In 1905–1906 Chinese booksellers and literati had high expectations of the Ministry of Education's *banquan* review system, but it quickly became clear that the Ministry of Education was interested in reviewing only one kind of books: textbooks. Many found that their petitions to the ministry asking for *banquan* recognition were dismissed because the titles they submitted were not textbooks for new schools. For example, when a Chinese medical expert in Sichuan presented to the ministry the medical textbooks he had compiled and asked for *banquan* recognition, he was infomed that "the intention of compiling this book is very nice, but this is not a textbook [for new school students]. There is thus no need for review. [We] now return the book to you."[86] Even though the word "textbook" appeared in the submitted title, the request for *banquan* was still dismissed because medicine was not a subject in the new schools' curriculum. This reply suggests that the ministry followed an unwritten policy: *banquan*/copyright was exclusively reserved for textbooks of subjects in the school curriculum. Other books, no matter how well-written and useful they might be, would be excluded from the review and would also not be entitled to receive *banquan*/copyright from the ministry. Booksellers and authors seem not to have been fully aware of the limited scope of the ministry-issued *banquan* and kept submitting their books to the Review Office for *banquan* review. Beginning in 1907, the Review Office started to instruct applicants who submitted non-textbook titles to wait for the institution of the formal copyright law,[87] but the copyright law was not issued any time soon. As a result, booksellers and authors who wanted to obtain *banquan*/copyright of their non-textbook titles were left in limbo.

In May 1910, a young editor at Commercial Press named Tao Baolin published an editorial in its *Jiaoyu zazhi* (Education magazine), urging the Qing

---

86. "Sichuan juren Mei Guangding cheng bianji yixue jiaokeshu qing shending bing gei banquan bing pi," *XBGB* 5 (November 7, 1906): 9a.

87. For example, "Juren Xu Hongbao deng bianji wuji huaxue qingshi jin fanyin bing pi," *XBGB* 26 (August 9, 1907): 40a; "Nanyang guanshuju zhi dong Chen Zuolin cheng shu san shi wu zhong qing shending bing pi," *XBGB* 31 (August 29, 1907): 44a.

state to issue its copyright law without further delay. Tao was not merely pleading with the state to realize the promised *banquan* legislation; he further proposed that the state should take this opportunity to break up the bundle of *banquan* and content review. China's copyright law, he argued, should protect the *banquan* of all books, regardless of their quality and usefulness. This was an attempt to separate *banquan* and censorship, as well as to depart from the convention that supported the two forms of state-issued *banquan* privilege. Tao pointed out that Chinese officials and booksellers seemed to misunderstand the nature of copyright law and publishing law because they had always considered *banquan*/copyright to be a reward granted by the state recognizing the author's and publisher's contribution to society. The "*banquan*/copyright as reward" theory, he summarized, argues that "authors' creations contribute the most to a nation's cultural development. The progress of the society, as well as the happiness of humanity, rely on and benefit from authors' creations. Therefore, [authors] should, of course, be rewarded [for *banquan*]."[88] This theory, he argued, forever intertwined the protection of *banquan*/copyright with the review and even censorship of any given text.

The logic that authors who contributed to the progress of society should be rewarded with *banquan*, he argued, implied that authors whose works were useless to society should not be rewarded with *banquan*. According to him, this was a profound misunderstanding of the nature of *banquan*/copyright, because, according to current copyright laws in other countries, "no matter what kind of literary work it is, as long as it is a literary work, it will enjoy the right to be protected." In other words, the ownership of a literary work as a property came into being automatically when it was created, regardless of its intellectual quality or artistic value.

Tao further attributed his contemporaries' misconception of *banquan* to the late imperial practices discussed in the previous section. He pointed out that indeed the "reprinting prohibited" convention was similar to European copyright, but those Chinese prohibitions were meant to protect the purity of texts rather than the rights of property owners. This notion was now embedded in the minds of Chinese booksellers, officials, and authors when they talked about *banquan*. And this was why even though most books in Chinese were produced for profit, people still tended to associate *banquan* with the quality and "usefulness" of a book. The time had come, he suggested, for China to consider

88. Tao Baolin, "Lun zhuzuoquan fa chubanfa jiyi bianding banxing," *Jiaoyu zazhi* 2:4 (May 1910): 39.

banquan simply as an economic matter that should be regulated by the Ministry of Commerce rather than the Ministry of Education, because "the publication of a literary work has to rely on printing, and the printing business is commerce."[89]

He didn't oppose the necessity of review or censorship but thought review and *banquan* should be seen as two separate issues. "For example, imagine that there is an extremely disgusting thing in a public space," he elaborated; "the police can remove or ban this thing because it impairs public hygiene, but this doesn't mean that the ownership of this extremely disgusting thing is forfeited accordingly."[90] While the state could employ publishing laws to control public opinions and promote its cultural values, the mission of copyright law was to proactively protect an individual's intellectual creations as his or her private property. Therefore, Tao argued, "the state cannot prohibit a book's publication based on whether it is [intellectually] valuable or not."[91] Even the worst-written or the most useless works should be copyrighted and protected by the state because these books were also properties that belonged to their creators.

Conclusion

Between 1902 and 1911, Chinese publishers, authors, and the Qing state used two expedient mechanisms to regulate *banquan*/copyright before a formal copyright law was instituted. These two devices—the generic *banquan* protection orders issued individually by local officials and the *banquan* privilege/license granted by the Ministry of Education—were derived from the late imperial tradition of reprinting-prohibition orders based on a shared notion of the sociocultural significance of books. *Banquan*/copyright granted via these two mechanisms was understood by both their issuers and their recipients as a state authority's reward to individuals who produced outstanding titles that achieved intellectual excellence or made great sociocultural contributions. At the same time, the state saw granting *banquan* as a powerful way to attract private individuals and booksellers to provide urgently needed textbooks for new schools while simultaneously setting and controlling the intellectual and ideological agenda of the New Learning knowledge. The Qing government's intention was welcomed by Chinese authors and publishers at the time, as they

89. Ibid., 41.
90. Ibid., 40.
91. Ibid., 41.

considered the state to be the ultimate authority in the world of learning. In this context, *banquan* was thus also an indication of official approval and endorsement of their works, and it enhanced both their economic gain and their cultural capital.

In these two *banquan* mechanisms, the nature of *banquan*/copyright and the state's role in enforcing it were never clearly defined. When Chinese authors and booksellers wanted actually to exercise the *banquan*/copyright protection, they encountered challenges and consequences caused by this ambiguity. The bitter dispute between Civilization Books and Yuan Shikai's Northern Ports Official Press in 1904, for instance, revealed that individually issued *banquan* orders could be easily revoked by the very authority that issued them since these orders were considered "rewards" in the form of privileges. Northern Ports Official Press also considered that the state was not bound by its laws and regulations; following this logic, the press insisted that their decision to reprint Civilization Books' titles should be exempt from the government *banquan* orders. The idea of *banquan* as a reward for intellectual excellence also put publishers and authors in a vulnerable position when they asked state authorities for *banquan* protection or had a *banquan* dispute with the state, because the putative "ultimate authority in the world of learning" had the final say on whether these private publications were "good enough" to have their *banquan* recognized and protected. In the case of Civilization Books, one can see how the standard for intellectual excellence and usefulness could be changed arbitrarily for or against the same books in different situations.

The bundle of intellectual excellence and *banquan* protection by the state was a double-edged sword. The Qing state's legitimacy in reviewing books and granting *banquan* was based on the belief in the state as a supreme intellectual authority. However, when the state was found to be pirating and plagiarizing private firms' titles, its supremacy in intellectual and cultural matters was inevitably discredited. If those who had jurisdiction over the New Learning knowledge pirated and plagiarized profit-driven booksellers' imperfect books, did they then really have the ability and legitimacy to determine the value of a book and to grant a *banquan* privilege?

The challenge that Civilization Books and other private publishers faced in the 1900s when government agencies reprinted their works is essentially the same one that Fukuzawa Yukichi struggled with in the 1870s. While the frustrated Fukuzawa decided to coin the term *hanken* to stress copyright as an individual "right" that comes into being without the state's "endorsement," late Qing authors and publishers, in comparison, never fully made such a departure.

In the dispute between Civilization Books and Yuan Shikai's Northern Ports Official Press, Lian Quan and his supporters tried to flip the case by bringing in higher political authorities to overrule Yuan, but they never questioned the reasoning behind the officially issued *banquan* orders. One does see comments from Young J. Allen and Tao Baolin that identified the difficulty of protecting oneself from government reprinting given the Chinese general misconception of *banquan*. *Banquan*/copyright, they argued, was a type of property rather than some sort of privilege attached to content review as the Qing state understood it to be. Their emphasis on *banquan*/copyright as an individual "right" and literary creations as a type of private property, however, does not seem to have been echoed by their contemporaries; as a matter of fact, most of the discussion on *banquan*/copyright in late Qing China was not about "rights," but about the interrelationship of progress, the writing, translating, and publishing of books, and the publishers' and/or authors' exclusive material gains derived from the books. Even "progressive" intellectuals like Yan Fu and Liang Qichao rarely elaborated on the "*quan*/right" part of *banquan*/copyright in their writings. The rhetoric that many modern Chinese cultural figures employed in their campaign for *banquan*/copyright protection instead emphasized their disinterest in individual gain and their selfless devotion to textual perfection and the public good, as these were associated with higher intellectual authenticity and cultural reputation. Such rhetoric, to an extent, also made it difficult for them to make a case for *banquan* as an individual right and to detach it from the state (the reward-giver on behalf of the society) and from certain forms of content review (certifying the textual perfection and usefulness of their books).

In November 1910, when the Qing's newly established Imperial Senate (*Zizheng yuan*) approved and issued the long-anticipated *Da Qing zhuzuoquan lü*, it aroused very little public discussion. Heavily influenced by Japan's 1899 Copyright Law, this first copyright law in China largely adopted the Berne Convention's definition of copyright and granted to the creators of original works the exclusive right to reproduce their works. Once a work had been registered with the Ministry of Civil Affairs (*Minzheng bu*), the work's copyright would be protected by the law throughout the lifetime of the author and for another thirty years after his or her death. Violations of copyright, such as unauthorized reprinting or counterfeiting, were subject to fines of ten to two hundred yuan. In an annotation of *Da Qing zhuzuoquan lü* published by Commercial Press soon after the law's promulgation, Qin Ruijie (1874–?), a Japan-trained jurist, stressed repeatedly to his readers that *zhuzuoquan*/copyright was an "individual's private right (*geren zhi siquan*)" and should be understood as a particular type of intangible property.[92]

For Chinese booksellers and authors who had been hoping for a state copyright regulation to protect them from unauthorized reprinting, *Da Qing zhuzuoquan lü* was too little, too late. Although they did not stop sending their textbooks to the Ministry of Education for review and approval, as early as 1905 Chinese booksellers in Shanghai had decided to take matters into their own hands to form their own system of *banquan*. In the next chapter, we will see how they established their customary *banquan* regime parallel to the state's copyright law. In this regime, *banquan* was defined and practiced as a very tangible form of private property.

92. Qin, *Zhuzuoquan lü shiyi*, 2.

5

The "Copyright" Regime of Chessboard Street

FOR ANY LATE QING Chinese wanting to "enlighten" themselves, Shanghai was the place to go. If people's intellectual quality could be measured according to how well they read, they believed, the progress of a society would be determined by how many new books it published. As a 1903 Shanghai guidebook proclaimed, the unparalleled density of publishing houses and bookshops in the city, therefore, made it the "pivot of Civilization in China."[1] Going to Shanghai, in both autobiographical and fictional accounts, was often described as the inciting event in one's intellectual development, a point of departure, or a moment of revelation. In the satiric novel *Wenming xiaoshi*, for instance, the *real* story—the pseudo-reformers' laughable and pathetic encounters with modernity—begins only after the insignificant Jia brothers have embarked on their grand tour to Shanghai to "open their eyes to the world." In Shanghai, these three country bumpkins are quickly taken by their "progressive" mentor to a place that will "enrich their knowledge." The Jia brothers, who have been trying to "enlighten" themselves at home by reading newspapers and New Learning books, are brought to the site where most of them were produced. They have arrived at *Qipanjie* (Chessboard Street).[2]

Right in the middle of Shanghai's International Settlement, the commercial district stretching four to five blocks from the intersection of Chessboard Street/ Henan Road and Fuzhou Road was the home of more than three hundred booksellers and publishing houses throughout the late nineteenth and early twentieth centuries. If Shanghai was the "pivot of Civilization in China" at the

1. Zhang Zhongmin, "Cong shuji shi dao yuedu shi," 168.
2. *Wenming xiaoshi*, 125–126, 133–138.

time, the Chessboard Street neighborhood was the exact center of that pivot. Occupying the southeast corner of the intersection were Commercial Press (est. 1897), Chung Hwa Books (*Zhonghua shuju*, est. 1912), and Civilization Books (est. 1902). When the Qing Ministry of Education announced in 1906 the first batch of "ministry-certified" textbooks, 85 of the 102 titles on the list were published by either Commercial Press or Civilization Books. In the 1920s and 1930s, Commercial Press and its neighbor Chung Hwa Books controlled over 90 percent of the nation's primary and secondary school textbook market. One block south of the intersection, on Chessboard Street, visitors would encounter a series of lithographic presses, such as *Saoye shanfang* (Sweeping-Leaves Studio) and *Guangyi shuju* (Benefit-Enhancing Books). At the turn of the century, they dominated the lithographic reprinting of traditional texts and popular works.

Almost all the leading publishing companies in modern China set up their headquarters or flagship stores in the Chessboard Street neighborhood at some point. For intellectuals and authors who wanted to embark on a career in writing, provincial wholesalers who needed to replenish their stock with the latest best sellers, and readers who hoped to enlighten themselves, Chessboard Street was their ultimate destination. From the 1890s to the 1950s, the bookshops and publishing houses in the Chessboard Street neighborhood were the leading force shaping China's publishing industry and cultural trends. Street-level happenings in this overcrowded small neighborhood would often trigger a greater impact nationwide. Many of the innovations in the modern Chinese cultural economy had their start on Chessboard Street, including the popularization of *banquan*/copyright.

Many of the early *banquan*/copyright advocates in China were publishers and booksellers from the Chessboard Street neighborhood. It was they who first adopted the Japanese loanword *hanken* to define and declare their ownership of books. They coined the *"banquan suoyou fanke bijiu"* statement and stamped *banquan* seals on the actual copies of books. Investing in the publishing of New Learning titles, they began to pay high remuneration to authors and translators to obtain *banquan* of the latest manuscripts. They petitioned local and national officials not only asking for individual *banquan* protections but also calling for a formal and systematic ban on unauthorized reprinting. They were the victims of piracy at the turn of the century, yet simultaneously they were also engaged in reprinting and plagiarizing others' best sellers for profit.

To advance these individual efforts to protect *banquan*/copyright, in 1905 Chinese booksellers in Shanghai established their own extralegal "copyright" regime through two civic organizations: the Shanghai Booksellers' Guild (*Shanghai shuye gongsuo*; hereafter, SBG) and the Shanghai Booksellers' Trade Association (*Shanghai shuye shanghui*; hereafter, SBTA).[3] This chapter traces how the Chinese booksellers in the Chessboard Street neighborhood utilized the tradition of merchant guilds and the Qing government's reform initiative to create their quasi-legal institution aiming to regulate and protect what they believed to be *banquan*/copyright. It illustrates in particular how the SBG, a civic organization with no legal jurisdiction or official authorization, enforced its *banquan*/copyright regulation and punished pirates according to their ideas of morality, norms, and customs. The SBG's rich records on how they defined, registered, and protected their *banquan*/copyright also open a unique window to enable us to look into the everyday economic life of the booksellers at a micro level. They reveal not only the daily operation and conflicts in the modern Chinese cultural economy, but also the booksellers' conceptions of property ownership, civility, and trust that were articulated and contested in those routine transactions.

The second half of the chapter focuses on how they interacted and negotiated with the state's formal legal system after the promulgation of China's first copyright law in 1911. Throughout the 1910s and 1920s, although new legislation regarding the protection of copyright appeared, I argue, it was rarely enforced in reality because consistent political upheavals had prevented the Chinese central state from establishing sufficient legal control over its territory. The SBG nominally followed the state's formal laws, but in reality they continued to operate their own customary "copyright" regime parallel to the state's law. While the state's copyright law had legal standing, the guild's copyright regime was the one that functioned on the ground.

---

3. These two organizations coexisted from 1905 to 1928. The membership and the leadership of these two organizations, however, overlapped, as most of the SBTA members were also SBG members. In general, the SBG was the dominant actor in Shanghai regulating and mediating *banquan* disputes, and the SBTA tended to be more enthusiastic about petitioning the state. In 1928, these two organizations merged with other smaller guilds related to the book trade and formed a new Shanghai Booksellers' Guild (*Shanghai shuye tongye gonghui*). The new guild continued regulating and protecting fellow booksellers' copyright and tried to expand its copyright regime beyond Shanghai. To stress the institutional continuity of the old SBG and the new one, in this book, I will refer them both as the SBG. Although the SBTA also stated that *banquan* protection was its main objective, most of the *banquan* cases I find in the Shanghai Municipal Archives were mediated by the SBG, so the discussion in this chapter will focus mostly on the SBG's mechanisms and procedures.

"A Sheet of Loose Sands"

Before becoming one of the first five treaty ports opened to foreign trade and residence in 1842, Shanghai was at the margin of China's book world. This then small administrative and commercial town on the bank of the Huangpu River had only a handful of bookshops within its walls. The titles compiled and published by local cultural elites during the Ming-Qing period received only minor recognition in the Chinese community of learning.[4] By the turn of the twentieth century, as Shanghai was growing into the busiest port of East Asia, it also had emerged as *the* new publishing center of the empire. The rise of Shanghai exemplified the geographical shift of China's cultural centers from the interior to the coast. During the devastating Taiping Rebellion (1850–1864), as civil war brought about the fatal decline of the cultural and commercial hubs of the Yangtze region, Shanghai was unscathed, thanks to the presence of foreign powers in the treaty port concessions and the security forces they organized against the rebels. After Suzhou and Hangzhou were turned into battlefields, booksellers, scholars, and social elites from these prestigious urban centers fled to the International Settlement for shelter, along with hundreds of thousands of Chinese refugees. The war destroyed the libraries, schools, publishing houses, and rare book collections that had been the pride of the literati communities in Suzhou and Hangzhou for centuries, but the Jiangnan print culture and book-trade tradition survived as their heirs reestablished themselves in Shanghai.[5]

This rising Shanghai book trade, however, should not be seen as a straightforward relocation of the late imperial Jiangnan book culture to an alien metropolis. In the second half of the nineteenth century, as more and more Chinese booksellers and literati were drawn to the International Settlement, they utilized the geopolitical advantages of the foreign concessions and created their own kinds of cultural economy. First and foremost, the flourishing economy in the post-Taiping years promoted an explosive development of new types of urban entertainment and readership in Shanghai. This thriving and highly commercialized cultural market attracted literati to the city to explore alternative career possibilities in publishing, journalism, and theater. Second, the foreign concessions provided these Chinese cultural entrepreneurs easy access to the latest printing technology, information, capital, and modern

4. *Shanghai chuban zhi*, 3.
5. Meng, *Shanghai and the Edges of Empires*, 3–30.

transportation. This infrastructure allowed them to become the pioneers in China in adopting modern industrial printing methods and corporate capitalism, as well as the leading producers and promoters of the New Learning knowledge. The relatively liberal and stable civic environment, outside China's jurisdiction, created by the self-governing foreign settlements, meanwhile, made Shanghai the ideal location for adventurous authors and radical activists to publish sensitive and unorthodox content, such as subversive political comments or pornographic social satires, which might otherwise be banned by the Qing government.[6]

While enjoying these geopolitical advantages that the treaty port Shanghai offered, Chinese booksellers also had to face new challenges that their late imperial predecessors had never experienced. Operating in the International Settlement, they had to compete not only with each other but also with foreigners. European and American missionary presses, such as American Presbyterian Mission Press (est. 1860) and the SDCK, as well as for-profit enterprises, like Ernest Major's *Shen bao* (est. 1872), had also been publishing books in Chinese. They were, for several decades, equipped with more advanced printing machines, greater capital, and a more authoritative command of the "Western" knowledge. While the Chinese booksellers benefited from the freedom and stability of the concessions, they were also subject to the foreigner-run governing bodies of the concessions and the multiple jurisprudences of the city. While their foreign competitors enjoyed the privileges granted by the treaties, they did not. As discussed in chapter 4, after copyright protection was written into the 1903 Sino-American trade treaty, many Chinese booksellers, especially those from Shanghai, felt that they had been forced into a losing and unfair competition.

These new challenges were not unique to Chinese booksellers in Shanghai but a common concern for all Chinese sojourners in town. They recognized the power of regional and vocational cohesion to improve their competitive position in this alien metropolis. Native-place associations and common trade guilds, as well as criminal gangs, were formed by Chinese businessmen and workers to create and strengthen communal ties and identities. By the end of the nineteenth century, there were more than one hundred guilds and civic associations in Shanghai. They provided welfare services to their members,

---

6. For Shanghai print culture and mass media in the late Qing, see Reed, *Gutenberg in Shanghai*; Meng, *Shanghai and the Edges of Empires*; Yeh, *Shanghai Love*, 178–219; Wagner, ed., *Joining the Global Public*.

regulated their own trades and businesses, and also served as intermediaries to help their members negotiate with the multiple civic and political authorities in Shanghai.[7]

Since the 1880s, like other Chinese sojourners, the first generation of Chinese booksellers in Shanghai, though acknowledging the importance of having their own guild, were just unable to organize. In 1886, the Shanghai manager of Sweeping-Leaves Studio and several others who had relocated their business from Suzhou proposed to revive the centuries-old Suzhou booksellers' guild—*Chongde gongsuo* (Venerate Virtue Guild)[8]—in Shanghai. However, after purchasing real estate in the Chinese City (also known as the "Old City) to build the future guildhall, these booksellers were deeply in debt. Owing to the lack of sustainable financial support, as well as the low level of participation, they never managed to maintain a functioning guild for any substantial period.[9] They gathered only twice per year as a community to worship their patron god, Wenchang.[10] As the book trade in Shanghai expanded rapidly after 1895, booksellers, especially those who specialized in lithographic printing, were no longer satisfied with this arrangement and started to meet in a teahouse at the corner of Fuzhou Road in the afternoons to exchange information, trade books, and attempt to establish some market order among themselves. In 1897, hoping to institutionalize this daily teahouse meeting, some returned to the idea of establishing a booksellers' guild and pooled their money to rent a small house near Chessboard Street as their temporary guild office. The group was unable to convince others to regularly contribute, and this attempt failed within two years.[11]

7. For a history of the guilds in Shanghai and their roles in the city and national political and economic development, see Goodman, *Native Place, City, and Nation*.

8. The history of Chongde gongsuo in Suzhou can be traced back to 1662. The old guildhall was destroyed during the Taiping Rebellion in 1860. For the history of Chongde gongsuo in Suzhou, see McDermott, "Rare Book Collections in Qing Dynasty Suzhou," 172–173.

9. Based on the SBG accounts, there were at least four attempts (1886, 1897, 1898, and 1899) to build a booksellers' guild, but they all failed quickly.

10. SMA S313-3-1 Ye Jiuru, "Shuye Gongsuo chuangli jingguo shishi lüeji" [Brief account of the establishment and development of the bookseller's guild] (January 9, 1953); S313-1-2-1 "Shanghai Shuye Gongsuo luocheng quanti dahui kaihuici" [Opening remarks for the general meeting at the opening of the new SBG hall] (1914).

11. In 1953, Ye Jiuru recalled that it had been routine for many booksellers, especially those who specialized in lithographic printing, to meet daily in a teahouse at the corner of Fourth Avenue to trade books and exchange information with each other. See SMA S313-3-1 "Shuye Gongsuo chuangli jingguo shishi lüeji."

These attempts failed mainly because Chinese booksellers in Shanghai at the time were hardly a homogeneous community. They did physically congregate in the thriving and compact Chessboard Street neighborhood, but the magnitude of their assets, the structure of their businesses, and the printing methods they employed were as diverse as one could imagine. The leading bookseller of Chessboard Street around 1900 was Sweeping-Leaves Studio. Founded in Suzhou in the late sixteenth century by the Xi family, it transferred its primary operation to Shanghai in the 1880s. While carrying on its centuries-old woodblock-printing operation, the firm also started to use new lithographic technology to reproduce their fine editions of classic and literary titles and published some New Learning books on the side.[12] While Sweeping-Leaves Studio was representative of the late imperial commercial publishing tradition, the nearby Commercial Press was a champion of China's modern print capitalism. In 1902, this publishing firm reorganized itself into a modern corporation after attracting Japanese investment. At the other end of the spectrum, there were micro-publishers and jobber printers, who often set up their small operations at the margins of the neighborhood. The author of *Wenming xiaoshi*, Li Boyuan (1867–1906), for example, ran his tabloid-literature kingdom as a cottage industry. He wrote almost every piece in his entertainment journals and published his own novels. One printer would work downstairs with one rental printing machine, as he and his widowed mother lived upstairs in a small house.[13] They were joined in this periphery by other types of business, such as newspaper publishers, antiquarian book dealers, and stationers, which published and sold books as side jobs.

Books sold in the Chessboard Street neighborhood were printed by a wide range of methods too: woodblock printing, cast-type matrices, electrotype, letterpress, stone-based lithography, collotype, and zinc-plate, among others. Most printers and booksellers learned their craft from their masters; others, especially those who specialized in Western-style printing, received their training in at presses and in missionary schools. The traditional master-apprentice social bonds were still valued by the former but insignificant to the latter. Proprietors of the bookshops and presses in Shanghai came from various regions of China and diverse social backgrounds. Though there was a strong presence of Suzhou booksellers, Zhejiangnese and Fujianese were also influential in the Shanghai book trade. Some came from traditional publisher families, like the Xis; some joined the business as printing workers and artisans; some were

12. For a history of Sweeping-Leaves Studio, see Yang, *Saoye shanfang shi yanjiu*.

13. Wei Shaochang, ed., *Li Boyuan yanjiu ziliao* (Shanghai: Shanghai guji chubanshe, 1980), 40.

former officials, like Lian Quan and Wang Kangnian; and some were political reformers or revolutionaries. The Shanghai book trade thus was too diverse for the native-place associations or common trade civility alone to induce everyone in the trade to stand in solidarity.

A Guild for *Banquan*

Between 1905 and 1906, it seemed that the Chinese booksellers in Shanghai had found a sense of solidarity all of a sudden. They established not one but two civic organizations—the SBG and the SBTA—and managed to keep them running for the decades to come. Some scholars attribute this success to the national campaign by Qing's Ministry of Commerce to institutionalize merchants' organizations and associational networks at the time.[14] Some argue that it was the investment in Western-style printing technology that prompted Chinese print capitalists to seek protection and market order.[15] When Shanghai booksellers later recounted the history of their guilds, however, they stated that they were unified by their newfound common enemy: unauthorized reprinting. After the popularization of New Learning books and the abolition of the civil service examination, one SBG leader recalled in 1914, "there were more and more disputes about reprinting among us. Fellow booksellers thus felt that we should unite together as an organization to protect our *banquan* profit."[16] When the SBTA celebrated its tenth anniversary in 1915, they also stated that this association was formed mainly to "protect fellow booksellers' *banquan*."[17]

The idea of utilizing civic organizations to regulate and protect *banquan*/copyright seems to have been first proposed in China in the spring of 1904 by Young J. Allen. When visiting Civilization Books a few days after Yuan Shikai shut down the firm and revoked all its previously granted *banquan* protections, Allen allegedly suggested that, instead of counting on the state's unreliable protection orders, Chinese booksellers should organize their own "*banquan* guild."[18] The idea of a "*banquan* guild" was a paradoxical yet practical solution

14. Jiang Yaohua, "Shanghai shuye tongye gonghui shiliao yu yanjiu" [A study of the Shanghai Booksellers' Guild], in *Shanghai shuye tongye gonghui shiliao yu yanjiu*, 263.

15. Reed, *Gutenberg in Shanghai*, 171.

16. SMA S313-1-2-1 "Shanghai Shuye Gongsuo luocheng quanti dahui kaihuici."

17. SMA S313-1-4-1 "Shuye Shanghui shi nian kaikuang" [An overview of the first decade of the Booksellers' Trade Association] (1915).

18. "Ni li banquan gonghui" [Proposal to establish *banquan* guilds], *DGB*, March 6, 1904. For Allen's promotion of copyright, see chapter 2; for his comments on Chinese officials' *banquan* protection, see chapter 4.

to the unauthorized-reprinting problem in China at the time. *Huiguan* (meeting hall) and *gongsuo* (public office) in late imperial China were urban associations formed by people from the same region and in the same trade or craft. These native-place and common-trade organizations provided mutual assistance, promoted collective interests, and maintained the trade/craft communities' internal order. Since the late nineteenth century, the word "guild" had typically been used to refer to *huiguan* and *gongsuo* in foreign accounts; as a result, these late imperial Chinese organizations have often been seen in scholarly discussions of the period as comparable or equivalent to the early modern European guilds.[19] For Max Weber and later some Weberian scholars, these Chinese "medieval" establishments represented the reason why Chinese society had not transformed into a "rational" or "modern" one like Europe, as well as evidence that such a transformation did not occur.[20] It was a common belief among Western observers and scholars at the turn of the twentieth century that the Chinese guilds enforced brutal bylaws to regulate their trades and had enormous control over their members. Weber argued that the Chinese guilds had traveled this "road of relentless and incomparable self-help" because Chinese public authority had failed to create "fixed, publicly recognized, formal and reliable legal foundations."[21]

Historical studies of Chinese merchants' organizations and their roles as self-regulating institutions and quasi-legal authorities in late imperial Chinese cities, however, suggest that the rise of such mediation mechanisms and civil governance should not be attributed to the state's failure but were a result of the evolution of imperial institutions. They argue that the merchants' groups in Qing urban centers served as the administrative intermediaries with the state's permission and, counter to the Weberian assertion, formed interguild

19. The first text using "guild" to translate Chinese *huiguan* and *gongsuo* is a short piece written by D. J. Macgowan in the 1880s. In this book, for the sake of convenience, as well as to stress the continuity of these civic organizations' extralegal customs, I use the English word "guild" to denote the Chinese merchants' and craftsmen's organizations *huiguan* and *gongsuo* in the late imperial period as well as their later forms *shanghui* and *tongyegonghui* in the early twentieth century. It is worth keeping in mind that these organizations were similar to European guilds, but not exactly like them.

20. H. B. Morse's *The Guilds of China* was the first work to compare Chinese guilds with medieval English guilds with the implication that Chinese urban society had stagnated in the Middle Ages. Morse's book laid the foundation for Weber's discussion of Chinese cities and guilds. See Weber, *The Religion of China*, 13–20.

21. Weber, *The Religion of China*, 20.

alliances to weigh in on public affairs.[22] As the imperial codes did not address the subjects of most commercial disputes, local magistrates had to rely on, if not outsource to, the merchants' guilds to mediate and resolve them. This, in return, granted the merchants' groups particular legal authority and at the same time allowed the economic actors to establish order in the market while maintaining flexibility in commercial agreements.[23]

Recognizing the important role they played in market and social regulation, in 1904 the newly formed Ministry of Commerce called for a formalization of the merchants' organizations throughout the empire. Using the *Shanghai shangwu huiyi gongsuo* (Shanghai Commercial Consultative Association) as the model, it urged Chinese merchants to (re)organize their guilds and trade associations, and to establish regional chambers of commerce. Through this campaign, the ministry not only planned to standardize a hierarchical structure of merchants' civic organizations, but also hoped to formalize these groups' rights to contact the government, self-regulate local markets, and mediate commercial disputes.[24] As Maura Dykstra and Billy So point out, the Ministry of Commerce's call to establish a chamber of commerce was not just a transplantation or borrowing of the Western institution. The system recommended by the ministry accommodated numerous features of the existing extralegal commercial dispute resolution structure, and thus what it offered, in reality, was a formal and institutional recognition of the merchant organization's role in mediating commercial disputes, something they had been doing in the past.[25]

22. For example, see Rowe, *Hankow: Commerce and Society in a Chinese City* and *Hankow: Conflict and Community in a Chinese City*.

23. See Rowe's two books on Hankow; Golas, "Early Ch'ing Guilds"; Goodman, "Democratic Calisthenics." Negishi Tadashi, Niida Noboru, and Imahori Seiji all briefly discussed the Chinese guilds' role as a quasi-legal authority regulating market order and resolving commercial disputes in urban areas. For more recent studies on guilds' quasi-legal or extralegal practices in Suzhou and Szechwan, see Zhang, *Qing dai zhong qi Chongqing de shang ye gui ze yu zhi xu*; Qiu, *Dang falü yushang jingji*; Qiu and Chen, eds., *Ming Qing falü yunzuo zhong de quanli yu wenhua*, 275–344; and Dykstra, "Complicated Matters."

24. For the Ministry of Commerce's campaign in 1904 and the establishment of guilds and chambers of commerce after the campaign, see Chen, *Modern China's Network Revolution*, chap. 1.

25. For a survey of the Chamber of Commerce's newly institutionalized power in mediating commercial disputes, see Fan, *Ming Qing shangshi jiufen yu shangye susong*, chap. 5. For discussions of the continuity of the dispute-mediation mechanism of late imperial merchant groups and the "new" model introduced by the Ministry of Commerce, see Dykstra, "Complicated Matters," 390–391, and Billy So and Sufumi So, "Commercial Arbitration Transplanted."

Indeed, the timing of the SBG's and the SBTA's establishments, as well as their institutional structure, indicated that the Ministry of Commerce's campaign might have inspired the founding of these two organizations. Like other guilds or chambers of commerce established or reorganized during 1904–1907, the SBG's and the SBTA's bylaws closely followed the 1904 *Jianming shanghui zhangcheng* (Concise regulation of the chamber of commerce) that the ministry had issued. Their institutional structure also mimicked that of the Shanghai Commercial Consultative Association, which the Ministry of Commerce recommended as the model for other merchants' organizations: the membership was exclusively Chinese; each member contributed a membership fee and was granted a number of votes based on the scale of its business. The leadership (e.g., president, board members) and administrative staff (e.g., accountant, inspectors, and secretaries) were elected annually by its members; and the guild could address local book-trade issues and establish processes through regular or ad hoc meetings, as well as mediate disputes between its members.[26]

The Ministry of Commerce's campaign might have provided Shanghai booksellers with the platform, framework, and timing to establish their organizations, but the ministry could not guarantee the booksellers' zealous participation, the guild's financial stability, or its long-term success. In fact, the SBG quickly ran into financial trouble. Since most members were located in the Chessboard Street neighborhood, they rented a pricey Western-style house there as the guild's office, instead of using the old estate they possessed in the Chinese City.[27] The membership contribution to the Shanghai General Chamber of Commerce was another added cost for the guild. Even with increasing contributions from its members, the SBG constantly failed to make ends meet. To secure a sustainable source of income, in 1906 they decided to make the publication of *Guanshang kuailan* (Quick reference for officials and merchants) the guild's monopoly and used the profits to cover various expenses.[28] The financial burden of operating a guild was as onerous as what booksellers had experienced in their previous attempts to organize in the 1880s and 1890s, if not

26. SMA S313-1-1, SMA S313-1-3.

27. The rent for the Henan Road house eventually became unbearably high, so in 1914, the SBG decided to move their operation to the estate in the Chinese City. See SMA S313-3-1 "Shuye Gongsuo chuangli jingguo shishi lüeji."

28. See SMA S313-1-122 and S313-1-3. The SBG later also monopolistically produced two popular primers, *Youxue Qionglin* [Jade forest of children's primer] and *Baihua sishu* [Vernacular four books], to raise more money.

more so, but this time they neither quit nor let the guild dissolve. Something very close to their hearts had motivated booksellers in Shanghai to keep the guilds alive and bound them together as a community in 1905.

It was the need to protect their ownership and profit, and the longing for order in this booming yet chaotic cultural market, that kept Shanghai booksellers together this time. And they saw *banquan* regulation as the first and most crucial step to fulfill these needs. When the SBG and SBTA were established in 1905–1906, both wrote *banquan* registration and punishing piracy into their bylaws as the primary objectives. By inserting articles and procedures on *banquan*/copyright protection into the generic bylaws recommended by the ministry, the SBG appropriated the state-recognized arbitration function to establish their *banquan*/copyright regulation. The first article of the SBG's 1905 bylaws, for instance, echoing the Ministry of Commerce's guidelines, declared its mission to be "unifying fellow merchants and enhancing public prosperity in the trade."[29] Then when elaborating how the guild would unify booksellers, it stated that the mission would be accomplished by "setting up rules [of the book trade], eliminating unauthorized reprinting, policing privately reprinted copies, and adjudicating disputes between members."[30]

Several detailed measures in the 1905 bylaws delineating how the SBG was to achieve these objectives reflected the vision of its founders—mostly former Suzhou booksellers and lithographic publishers—to establish an inclusive *banquan* regulation. Regardless of the nature of the business, one article stated, all merchants in Shanghai "related to the book business, no matter whether they are woodblock, lithographic, copperplate [or] lead-type [printers], publisher-printers, or bookshops, as well as newspaper presses or stationers who sell books on the side," would be acknowledged as "fellows in the common trade (*tongye*)." As long as proprietors or managers were Chinese, they would be eligible to join the guild and register their *shudi* (master copy) and *banquan* at the guild. Based on this general register, the guild would mediate *banquan*/copyright disputes between members upon their request. The SBG prohibited unauthorized reprinting of any registered publication. Those who violated the guild's rules and printed either banned books or registered titles, once found, would have their imprints and printing blocks burned by the guild in

29. SMA S313-1-1 "Shanghai shuye shanghui zhangcheng" [Shanghai Booksellers' Trade Association bylaws] (1905).
30. SMA S313-1-1 "Shanghai shuye gongsuo chuci dingding zhangcheng" [The first bylaw of the Shanghai Booksellers' Guild] (1905–1906).

public, and the bookseller would also be fined according to the scale of the reprinting.[31] Established mostly by booksellers specializing in New Learning books, the SBTA, like the SBG, also declared "protecting *banquan*" to be their primary mission.[32] They even issued their own "*Banquan* Rules" (*Banquan zhangcheng*). This "*Banquan* Rules," which reads almost like a mini–copyright law, carefully defined how the SBTA would register, review, and protect *banquan* for its members and what kind of penalties pirates would incur if they were found violating the rules.[33] These *banquan*-related articles and measures that booksellers tailored for their needs indicate that they were not merely following the Ministry of Commerce's guidelines. They also actively employed this newly available platform and state recognition as the foundation of their *banquan*/copyright self-regulation.

Though the SBG proclaimed itself to be an institutional heir of the old Suzhou Venerate Virtue Guild and inherited the estate of the Venerate Virtue Guild in the Chinese City, it was no longer the sort of mutual aid organization that Suzhou booksellers like the Xis had initially envisioned. When they attempted to revive the old guild in the 1880s, they identified the guild primarily as a social safety net institution that would look after elderly members and their families, and pay members' funeral and burial expenses. It would also be in charge of the annual rituals of the booksellers' community, such as worshipping the guild god Wenchang. As ethical gentry-merchants, they would also support charitable causes and censor pornography.[34] These prominent mutual aid and religious traditions became almost invisible in the new bylaws. Instead, *banquan*/copyright regulations were foregrounded and emphasized. Although the god Wenchang still played an important symbolic role in the SBG's *banquan* regime, and the SBG leadership still periodically discussed charitable causes and the well-being of their senior members, these concerns no longer topped their agenda.[35]

31. Ibid.

32. SMA S313-1-1 "Shanghai shuye shanghui zhangcheng."

33. SMA S313-1-1 "(Fujian yi) banquan zhangcheng" [Appendix 1: copyright rules].

34. "Chuangjian Shuye Gongsuo qi" [Announcing the establishment of the bookseller's guild] (1886), *Shanghai shuye tongye gonghui shiliao yu yanjiu*, 5–6.

35. It seems that this transition from a mutual aid organization to a quasi-legal institution did not occur in other booksellers' guilds in China. For example, when the centuries-old *Beizhi wenchang gonghui* (Wenchang Guild for Hebei booksellers) in Beijing renovated its guildhall in Liulichang in 1908, it remained primarily a mutual aid organization. See Saeki, ed., *Niida Noboru hakushishu Pekin kōshō girudo shiryōshū*, 1:59–60 and 75–76.

Establishing an Order of Ownership

Before the SBG and the SBTA could act to protect their members' *banquan* from unauthorized reprinting, they would first have to be able to identify and define who owned the *banquan* of what titles. When creating a new register of the ownership of books in this ever-changing market, Shanghai booksellers were forced to articulate *banquan*/copyright, as well as the very nature of a "book": Who was eligible to register? What kinds of imprints could be registered? How should the ownership of a book be made accountable and verifiable? How could they determine that a book was different from other books? What were the criteria to for an "authentic" book and an "original" owner of that book?

In late March 1906, the SBG announced in major Shanghai newspapers that they welcomed fellow booksellers in Shanghai to join the guild and register both their businesses and *shudi*. Echoing the vision of an inclusive *banquan* regime highlighted in the bylaw, the SBG assured readers that this general register would accept all kinds of books, regardless of their content, printing methods, or publication dates. Once a book was registered at the guild, "reprinting [of it] will be prohibited." Altogether, booksellers could "jointly enjoy the protection of their profit."[36] What was registered was not a particular form of *banquan*/copyright, but the rather ambiguous *shudi*. In the minutes of early SBG meetings, *banquan* seemed to be understood as a type of privilege or license booksellers obtained from a state authority through petition or registration. *Shudi*, on the other hand, was something very tangible. It denotes "the means booksellers used to produce copies"—printing blocks for woodblock printing, lithographic limestone for lithography, and type plates or paper stereotype for letterpress. Different *shudi* could be identified by their physical appearance, such as the number of pages, the style of letters, and the size of the printing blocks or plates.[37] This kind of *shudi* master copy was the main subject of the SBG general register. The SBG also asked its members to submit a copy of each book they published to the SBG's exhibition room, creating a depository for future reference.[38]

Although the SBG tried to carefully distinguish between *banquan* and *shudi* in its bylaws, interestingly, according to the same bylaws, books that were

36. "Shanghai shuye tongye yaojin guanggao" [Shanghai Booksellers' Guild important announcement] and "Diaocha shudi guanggao" [Shudi register announcement], *SB*, March 29–April 6, 1906.
37. SMA S313-1-1"Shanghai shuye gonsuo chuci dingding zhangcheng," Article 6.3, 6.6.
38. Ibid., Article 6.5.

granted *banquan* by the state and those whose *shudi* were registered at the guild enjoyed the same kind of protection from the SBG.[39] In a meeting discussing the penalties for piracy, members decided that "for those titles without [state-issued] *banquan*, once their *shudi* are registered at the guild, they cannot be freely reprinted either. They would have accredited *banquan* publicly acknowledged by the community (*gongsuo tongren gongren banquan*)."[40] The SBG later formalized the use of "accredited *banquan*" and wrote it into their bylaws in the 1910s to replace *shudi*.[41]

Shanghai booksellers responded enthusiastically to the SBG's appeal. When this registration campaign ended ten days later, 119 booksellers, including 23 "new booksellers" from the SBTA represented by Civilization Books, had joined the SBG.[42] The guild then compiled a general register (*Shudi guahao*) that included 2,478 entries of master copies that 57 booksellers had registered during the campaign.[43] Titles appearing in this general register ranged from traditional novels, classical primers, and practical manuals to medical texts, New Learning titles, translations, and everyday encyclopedias. While some small booksellers might have fewer than five entries in the register, the well-established ones, such as Sweeping-Leaves Studio, Wenyi Bookshop (*Wenyi shuzhuang*), and the Thousand-Hectare Studio (*Qianqing tang*), claimed hundreds of master copies as their own.

This record, however, by no means reflects the panoramic landscape of the turn-of-the-century Shanghai book trade. Many titles available in the marketplace at the time were not listed in this general register. The hundreds of titles published by New Learning booksellers, such as Civilization Books and Commercial Press, were recorded at the SBG but not included in this general register.[44] In some cases, firms registered their business and their publications, but their registrations were dismissed because of the firm's ineligibility to join the guild. For example, the SDCK, the missionary press that first urged the Chinese government to protect copyright and received individual *banquan*/

39. Ibid., Article 6.3.

40. SMA S313-1-132 "Nian san ri" [23rd], May 16, 1906.

41. SMA S313-1-1 "Shanghai Shuye Gongsuo xianxing zhangcheng (guihai zhongding)" [Shanghai Booksellers' Guild current bylaws (revised in 1923)].

42. SMA S313-1-76.

43. SMA S313-1-77.

44. Although these twenty-three "new" booksellers' *shudi*/*banquan* were not listed in SMA S313-1-77, from SBG's mediation records and internal correspondence, it is clear that their *shudi*/*banquan* were registered at and recognized by the guild.

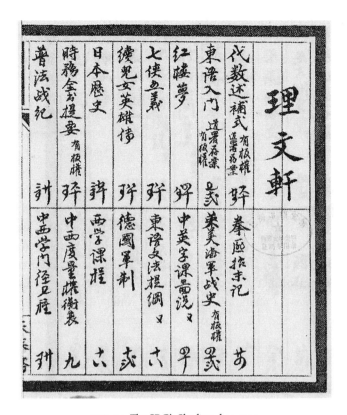

FIG. 5.1. The SBG's *Shudi guahao*, 1905.
Source: Shanghai Municipal Archives, S313-1-76.

copyright protection in the 1890s, also sent the list of their publications to the SBG to register. Ironically, although it had been the SDCK's long-term associate, Young J. Allen, who first proposed the idea of a "*banquan* guild" to Chinese booksellers, the SDCK's attempt to register their *banquan*/copyright at the guild was dismissed because none of its proprietors were Chinese.[45]

This general record shows only titles that Chinese booksellers successfully registered at the SBG. It is possible that booksellers decided not to register titles they had pirated from others or those they deemed to have less value. It is also possible that the guild rejected some of the entries during the registration process. For instance, Sweeping-Leaves Studio did not register every title they had published at the time. Comparing the sales catalog that Sweeping-Leaves Studio issued around 1904–1905 to their *shudi* entries in the SBG's 1906 general

45. SMA S313-1-76.

record, one quickly notices that they registered far fewer titles at the SBG than they listed in the sales catalog. They did not register any of their civil service examination references, likely because the abolition of the civil service examination the previous year had rendered these books (and their *shudi*) valueless. They also did not register "Court Editions (*dianben*)" of the classics or imperial edicts they reprinted, perhaps because they did not dare to claim the ownership of those texts. Neither did they register the titles they printed without proper authorization, such as the SDCK's best seller *Zhongdong zhangji benmo.*[46]

The SBG's general register of *shudi* might not be a comprehensive record of late Qing publications, but it offers us a valuable insight into the way Shanghai booksellers and the guild identified and organized the ownership of books. Each entry in the SBG's general register contains information considered crucial to determining the authenticity of a publication in the material form of its *shudi* master copy: name of the firm, title of the book, its printing method, and block or stone numbers; sometimes also its size and volume. It seems that for Shanghai booksellers, a book's physical features, such as the number of constituent elements, size, and material of its *shudi*, were more important than its content, the author's name, or the publication date when they wanted to identify a title. In many ways, the SBG's register of *shudi* looks similar to the London Stationers' Company's record. But while the London Stationers' Company recognized the manuscript as the essential thing that made a book come into being, the SBG seems to have acknowledged only the means of production as the object of ownership and associated it with *banquan*/copyright.[47]

The SBG's regulation of *shudi*, like the bookseller's *banquan* seals, reflects an understanding of ownership that was rooted in the early modern notion of *cangban*—possession of the printing blocks. Whoever possessed the means to print a book owned the *banquan* of that book; whoever invested capital to produce the copies was justified in monopolizing the profit generated by these copies. Following this logic, the SBG's general register was open to all kinds of booksellers, publishers, printers, and bookstores, but not to authors or

46. SMA S313-1-76 "Saoye shanfang nanji" [Sweeping-Leaves Studio South Branch] and "Saoye Shanfang beiiji" [Sweeping-Leaves Studio North Branch]; "Shanghai Saoye shanfang fadui shiyin shuji jiamu" [The sale catalog of Sweeping-Leaves Studio's lithographic books," in Zhou, ed., *Wan Qing yingye shumu*, 387–400.

47. For the London Stationers' register system, see Johns, *The Nature of the Book*, 213–230.

TABLE 5.1. Different Versions of *Wanguo Gongfa* Registered at the Shanghai Booksellers' Guild

Bookseller	Title	Block/ page numbers	Printing method
Jiahui shulin 嘉惠書林	*Quantu wanguo gongfa* 全圖萬國公法 (Fully illustrated public law of nations)	n/a	lithography
Zheyi tang 著易堂	*Wanguo gongfa* 萬國公法	192	woodblock
Guxiang ge 古香閣	*Wanguo gongfa* 萬國公法	122	lithography
Meihua Binji 美華賓記	*Wanguo gongfa* 萬國公法	119	letterpress
Qianqing tang 千頃堂	*Wanguo gongfa* 萬國公法	n/a	stereotype, quarto
Liuyi shuzhuang 六藝書莊	*Wanguo gongfa* 萬國公法	144	n/a
Guangyi shuju 廣益書局	*Xiao wanguo gongfa* 小萬國公法 (Pocket public law of nations)	81 (4 volumes)	lithography, pocket size

Source: SMA S313-1-77.

translators, unless they self-published.[48] For the guild, the key criterion defining ownership of a publication was the material manifestation of a book—not its content, but its physical appearance.

For the SBG, since the subjects of its register were tangible properties, when registering *shudi*, several booksellers could register the same title. As long as the books' physical features were distinct, they could be acknowledged by the guild as different publications, even if their contents were identical. In other words, it was the physical features of *shudi*, not the content, that would be used as the measurement to determine the authenticity and uniqueness of a book. In the SBG's general *shudi* register, we thus can find multiple entries for the same popular titles, such as *Quanxue pian* (Encouragement of learning) and *Liaozhai zhiyi* (Strange tales of Liaozhai). Seven different booksellers registered a *shudi* of *Wanguo gongfa* (Public law of nations) at the SBG in 1906.

48. For example, in the early 1910s, Xu Zhenya (1889–1937), the author of the best-selling novel *Yuli hun* (Jade pear spirit), appealed to the SBG, accusing his previous employer, the People's Rights Daily, and other publishers of having published his *Yuli hun* without his authorization. The SBG turned down Xu's appeal and told him they wouldn't handle his case because an author couldn't be a guild member. Later, when Xu decided to open his own press and publish the enlarged and revised edition of *Yuli hun* to compete with the pirated ones, he was recognized by the SBG as a bookseller and thus eligible to join the SBG and register his books. For Xu's interaction with the SBG, see SMA S313-1-121.

From the descriptions recorded in the SBG's general record, we know that these seven *shudi* were not alike, even if their contents might have been the same (see table 5.1).

The SBTA's "*Banquan* Rules," on the other hand, reflected an alternative vision of *banquan*. Unlike most similar commercial organizations that exclusively protected only their members' interests and properties, the SBTA opened their *banquan* register to all Chinese booksellers in Shanghai regardless of whether they wanted to join the SBTA, and as long as the title they planned to register was published after 1898.[49] While the SBTA members could register the *banquan* of their publications without extra cost, nonmembers paid a *banquan* fee (the sale price of ten copies) for each title they registered with the SBTA. Once a title was successfully registered, the SBTA acknowledged and protected its *banquan* and assisted its owner in dealing with pirates. Although the "*Banquan* Rules" might be recognized only by its members, the SBTA promised that if nonmembers pirated a registered title, the SBTA members would work together to locate the pirate and impose punishment on the offender on behalf of the *banquan* possessor.[50] Unlike the SBG, which emphasized in its *shudi* register the uniqueness of a publication's physical appearance, the SBTA's "*Banquan* Rules" identified originality of content as the prime justification for protecting a book's *banquan*. According to these rules, the main criteria for successful *banquan* registration of any given title were these: (1) the book's content must be authentic, not a product of plagiarism or parody; (2) the book must not contain reactionary ideas or debased content, such as pornography.[51] When referring to the authenticity of content, the SBTA was speaking less about the author's unique intellectual or literary creation and more about whether others had previously published the title or its content.

In principle, once a title was registered at the SBTA, the bookseller would be issued a *banquan* certificate as proof of registration, a copy of the title would be archived in the SBTA's exhibition room for reference, and "Copyright Possessed (*banquan suoyou*)" would be stamped on every copy of this title printed

49. It is not clear exactly why SBTA set the year 1898 as the divide, but that year may have been chosen because that was when the 1898 Reform occurred. As discussed in the previous chapter, the imperial edict that the Guangxu Emperor issued during the 1898 Reform protecting invention and intellectual works was referred to by some intellectuals in 1904 as the legal justification of *banquan* protection to support Civilization Books.

50. SMA S313-1-3 "Banquan Zhangcheng (fujian yi)" (1905).

51. Ibid.

to ensure its physical authenticity.[52] If any member was found to have pirated a registered title, the SBTA had the power and authority to confiscate all pirated copies and burn them. In addition to destroying the pirated copies, the SBTA could fine the pirate according to the scale of the piracy. If a member was caught pirating registered books a second time, not only was the fine doubled, but the repeat offender was also expelled from the guild and subsequently boycotted by all its members.[53]

It is worth noting that the SBG and the SBTA, despite their overlapping membership, had slightly different ideas as to what made a bookseller the exclusive owner of the *banquan* of a certain publication. Founded primarily by New Learning booksellers, the SBTA designed its *banquan* register mostly for newly published books and books that would be issued in the future. For the SBTA the primary criterion determining a publication's eligibility for *banquan*/copyright was the authenticity of its content, or whether it had been previously published. On the other hand, the SBG was keen to sort out first the ownership of publications already available in the marketplace. It used the term *shudi* interchangeably with *banquan*/copyright and identified the ownership of a publication based on the possession of the means of production.

Punishing Pirates in the Booksellers' Court

Although the SBTA proudly claimed that they had handled several dozen *banquan* infringements in the first decade of its history, there is little archival documentation about how SBTA enforced its "*Banquan* Rules."[54] On the other hand, the SBG's records reveal that SBTA members (who also held SBG membership) regularly asked the SBG to settle piracy disputes. Using the SBG's archival records, I have reconstructed the guild's daily enforcement of its *banquan* regime. These cases also illuminate another crucial aspect of the economic life of the

52. Ibid. and "Pi Shanghai shuye shanghui bing she shuye shanghui yingzhun lian suoyou banquan ziyang yin ji zunchi gengzheng bei fu mingshi er shi qubie you" [Reply to the SBTA's registration and its petition: the registration was granted but it should change the "Copyright Possessed" wording to correspond to its name], *Shangwu guanbao* 10 (July 25, 1906): 22-b.

53. SMA S313-1-3"Banquan Zhangcheng (fujian yi)."

54. This doesn't mean that the SBTA did not enforce its "*Banquan* Rules." It is possible that when the SBTA and the SBG merged into the Shanghai Booksellers' Guild in 1930, they did not provide all their records to this newly formed guild. It is also possible that the records simply did not survive.

Chessboard Street neighborhood: how the booksellers pirated each other's books.

To understand how the SBG got things done, we must first visit its office on Henan Road where the guild board received booksellers' complaints, mediated ownership disputes, and punished those who pirated registered titles.[55] Suppose you were a member of the SBG and had just learned that another bookseller had pirated your registered titles. Although you could appeal to the Shanghai county magistrate for justice, the simpler way to stop the illicit reprinting was to report the infraction to the guild's office and ask the guild to "judge (*pingli*)" for you. The guild's "judgment" proceeded efficiently; most cases going to the guild's office could be settled within a week, if not sooner, and interested parties accepted and respected the decision made by the guild.

When reporting to the guild's office, you would submit a written statement to the duty officer. The SBG's board members took turns spending a day in the guild's office serving as the duty officer to receive members' appeals and mediate disputes. To make your case, you would have to provide evidence proving that the bookseller(s) you were accusing had indeed reprinted your title(s). The duty officer, on behalf of the guild, would then require the accused bookseller to respond to your account, also in a written statement. After examining the statements (and evidence) from both sides, the guild would ask the plaintiff and the accused to be present for the formal decision at the guild's office. Once proven guilty, the pirate would be asked by the board to pay a fine based on the established penalties for piracy, as well as to surrender his piratical *shudi* master copy and all the piratical printed copies to the guild. In principle, the plaintiff would get half of the fine, while the other half went to the guild. To conclude your case, the guild would publicly burn the pirated *shudi* and books at the Wenchang god's temple to ensure that only you had the material capacity to publish your registered titles.

The SBG leaders seem to have relied more heavily on written words and physical evidence than on cross-examination or oral testimony. The duty officer or the board decided the "truth" of the dispute and made a decision based on the written statements presented by the interested parties, along with physical evidence such as actual copies of books and receipts. In fact, the guild's rules for adjudication explicitly prohibited the interested parties from talking

---

55. The guild mediated and ruled in all manner of commercial disputes among Shanghai booksellers daily, ranging from unpaid debts and runaway clerks to shipping delays, but the majority of cases that came to the SBG's private court were disputes related to *banquan*.

to each other directly or speaking without permission at the guild meeting at which the case was heard. Considering verbal communication too irrational and conflict-provoking, the SBG instructed the interested parties to "quietly listen to the duty officer's comments and decision."[56] Assuming that a truthful statement would be consistent and logical, the SBG believed that "if the statement is incoherent, it must be telling a lie."[57]

Owing to the Shanghai booksellers' special trust in written words, booksellers' reports on piracy, the accused members' defenses or confessions, and also the correspondence between the guild and its members on *banquan* disputes were kept in the SBG's archives along with the guild's decisions in these disputes. Using this rich documentation, I next focus on the different types of *banquan*/copyright disputes that Shanghai booksellers reported to the SBG and how the guild handled them in its early years before the Qing state issued its formal copyright law in 1910.

Abuse of Rental Blocks

One of the most common forms of *banquan* dispute in the late Qing was unsanctioned use of rental *shudi*, mostly wooden printing blocks or lithographic limestone plates. In these cases, the "pirated" copies were identical with the "authentic" ones because they were produced from the same set of *shudi*. Since this type of production was done without the original *shudi* owner's consent, Shanghai booksellers considered it a violation of *banquan*/copyright. As discussed in chapter 1, printing blocks, as physical means for book production, were regarded by Ming-Qing publishers and literati as transferable assets that could be shared, exchanged, purchased, and rented. To maximize the profit a printing block set could generate, block-possessors frequently rented out their idle *shudi* to others for a fixed period or a specified number of copies; in return, they received payment known as "block rent (*banzu*)." Such an arrangement could easily lead to bitter disputes if the "block tenant" secretly violated the leasing agreement and produced more copies than he was authorized to make.

Many of the early *banquan* disputes that the SBG adjudicated involved such *shudi* rental issues. Since these "pirates" didn't create their own set of *shudi*, the penalty the guild imposed on them for violating others' *banquan* was usually

---

56. SMA S313-1-100 "Pingli zhangcheng" [Mediation procedure]. One member was actually fined for speaking without permission in the ruling meeting.

57. Ibid.

a smaller sum labeled as "delayed rent." For example, in June 1906, Mind-Enlightening Book Studio (*Biaomeng shushi*) reported to the SBG that someone was selling unauthorized reprints of their *Su tongling zifa*. The guild's inquiry into the retailer selling this title revealed that the copies alleged to have been pirated were produced by Grant-Letters Books (*Hongwen shuju*). As it turned out, that firm had rented the *shudi* of this title from Mind-Enlightening Book Studio years before. Although Grant-Letters's proprietor first claimed that all the copies produced at the time had been sold, he later confessed to the SBG that one of their clerks had secretly made two thousand extra copies. The problematic copies that had been discovered were those secretly printed books. After the guild's mediation, Mind-Enlightening Book Studio agreed to view these additional copies as part of the print run permitted under the initial *shudi* rental agreement. Grant-Letters Books was ordered by the SBG to pay the cost of four hundred copies as "late rent" to Mind-Enlightening and to surrender all the remaining copies to them as compensation. The guild received half of the "late rent" as the pirate's "contribution" to the guild.[58]

Those who secretly printed extra copies using rental *shudi* without paying adequate "block rent" to the original *shudi* possessor were considered by the SBG to be relatively minor and offenders, because they did not create *another* set of means of production but merely abused the *shudi* they rented. The "real" pirates about whom the SBG and its members worried most were those who produced a duplicate *shudi* or partially replicated a registered title. The new printing technologies, especially photoengraving and lithography, enabled Shanghai booksellers to quickly make their own set of *shudi* and print as many copies as they liked. Many accused "pirates" were found guilty by the SBG for possessing their own lithographic limestone plates or collotype glass plates of titles registered by others. For the registered possessor of the original *shudi*, incinerating the piratical *shudi* would be most crucial.[59]

58. SMA S313-1-100 "Bingwu nian shuye gongsuo jiaoshe baogao yuanyou" [Reports of the SBG mediations for the year of Bingwu (1906)], 36–38, and SMA S313-1-100 "Bingwu nian yuance shuye gongsuo tongye jiaoshe shijian gongpan cungen" [The original ruling receipts of the SBG's mediating the disputes between members for the year of Bingwu (1906)], 12.

59. SMA S313-1-100, SMA S313-1-75.

Duplicating Shudi

Since the SBG recognized ownership of publications based on their *shudi* rather than their content, the same title could be registered by multiple booksellers, as long as the physical appearance of their *shudi* and the printing methods they used were different. From the guild's perspective, each of these booksellers was allowed only to produce copies of this title using the set of *shudi* they possessed because the ownership registered at the guild was that of a particular *shudi*, not the ownership of the title. In February 1908, for example, Flying-Swan Studio (*Feihong ge*) requested that the SBG check to see whether *Zhuibaiqiu* (Embellishment of white furs), an illustrated selection of favorite plays, published by Zhou Yue's (*Zhouyueji*) was a reprint edition of their *Zhuibaiqiu*. Responding to this accusation, Zhou Yue's declared that they were a legitimate publisher of the title because they possessed an old set of woodblocks of *Zhuibaiqiu*. However, they also admitted that the copies they were now selling had been printed not from this old woodblock *shudi* but from a set of lithographic limestone plates they had duplicated based on Flying-Swan Studio's lithographic edition of the same title. The SBG ruled that although Zhou Yue's possession of an old woodblock set of *Zhuibaiqiu* was well-known in the Chessboard Street community, their possession of this woodblock set entitled them to use only this means to produce copies of *Zhuibaiqiu*. Since Flying-Swan Studio had been the first to register the lithographic *shudi* of *Zhuibaiqiu* at the SBG, they were the rightful owner of the lithographic edition of the book. Zhou Yue's was deemed to have infringed on Flying-Swan Studio's ownership of the lithographic edition of *Zhuibaiqiu*.[60]

The unauthorized reprinting that Shanghai booksellers encountered at the time was often not such easily spotted straightforward duplication, but a partial copy or imitation of their "authentic" titles. In July 1906, for instance, Preciously Virtuous Studio (*Baoshan zhai*) reported to the guild that several illustrations from their vernacular *Four Books* had been appropriated by Grand-Letters' Prosperous Branch (*Hongwen xingji*) in its reading primer. Comparing the two titles, the SBG ruled that the accused had "scooped" only sixteen illustrations from the victim's publication; still the act violated "the standards of the book trade." Nevertheless, since the firm had not reprinted the whole book, the guild requested only the surrender of the problematic imprints and the master

---

60. SMA S313-1-100 "Yuanyue ershibari qipanjie feihongge baogao," February 29, 1908.

copy of those sixteen illustrations for incineration.[61] Fancy illustrations or maps in textbooks were a favorite target of such partial reprinting, likely because the cost of original illustration platemaking was steep, but reproducing them via photoengraving and lithography was easy.

Copycats

Copycatting was a common problem in early twentieth-century Shanghai when urban consumers were suddenly exposed to a wide range of new commodities and services. The front pages of Shanghai's major newspapers were frequently full of advertisements published by anxious booksellers, patent medicine manufacturers, and even insurance companies, condemning cunning copycats. They urged consumers to carefully identify bona fide trademarks and authorized retailers to ensure the authenticity of the products they bought. In the view of the SBG, copycats producing counterfeit titles that could mislead or confuse readers were an exceptionally abominable type of piracy, because copycats compromised not only the exclusivity of the genuine products but also the credibility of the brand name.

For some booksellers, protecting their brand was more important than recovering the profit lost to piracy. In October 1907, for instance, the Editorial Department of the Scientific Society (*Kexuehui bianyibu*) reported to the SBG that there was a copycat calling itself the "Scientific Editorial Institute" (*Kexue bianyiju*), which was very similar to their name in Chinese. This copycat, they stated, had published a mathematics textbook entitled *Suanshu jiaokeshu quanzhang* (Full textbook of arithmetic), which was a pirated edition of their *Chen Wen suanshu jiaokeshu* (Chen Wen's arithmetic textbook). The names of the two firms and the titles of these two books were so similar, they claimed, that their business had been noticeably affected, and the sales of their books were down. In response to the SBG's inquiry, the copycat admitted that they had plagiarized the Editorial Department of the Scientific Society's books; they agreed to surrender the remainders and the *shudi* master copy of this title to the guild.[62]

But this was not what the Editorial Department of the Scientific Society wanted. Burning all the remainders wouldn't rehabilitate their brand name, which they considered to have been corrupted and compromised by the

61. SMA S313-1-100 "Bingwu nian shuye gongsuo jiaoshe baogao yuanyou," 42; SMA S313-1-100 "Bingwu nian yuance shuye gongsuo tongye jiaoshe shijian gongpan," 19.

62. SMA S313-1-100 "Bingwu nian yuance shuye gongsuo tongye jiaoshe shijian gongpan," 23.

copycat. To restore this victim's reputation, the SBG then demanded that the "Scientific Editorial Institute" pay two hundred yuan in compensation for the damage they had done. The guild used half the money to publish a public announcement on the front pages of *Shen bao* and *Eastern Times*, two leading newspapers in Shanghai, for three consecutive days. In this statement, the SBG declared that the "Scientific Editorial Institute" had confessed to being a copycat, and then endorsed the Editorial Department of the Scientific Society as the "authentic" entity.[63] So pleased were they by the SBG's announcement, the Editorial Department of the Scientific Society decided to donate the compensation they received from the copycat as an extra contribution to the guild.[64]

Flexible Punishments

In principle, the SBG punished pirates according to its standard bylaws and "penalties for piracy." In practice, however, the guild's mediation and punishment procedures were very flexible. The interested parties also had considerable agency and power to negotiate with the guild for its final decision. For instance, by default, once found, finished or semifinished reprints, along with the piratical *shudi* master copy, were to be burned or destroyed at the Wenchang god's temple. This was done to secure the exclusivity of the authentic copies. Some "authentic" *banquan* owners, nevertheless, preferred to confiscate unauthorized reprints for resale instead of burning them to ashes. Deeming these unauthorized reprints to be commercially valuable commodities, the guild itself would sometimes request that the alleged offenders surrender their imprints as "compensation." For instance, in May 1906, when mediating the dispute between Grand-Letters Studio (*Hongwen tang*) and Thousand-Hectare Studio over *Jiezi Yuan huapu* (Mustard-seed Garden manual of painting), the SBG ruled that Grand-Letters Studio should provide to the plaintiff two hundred copies of their pirated *Jiezi Yuan huapu* as "block rent" and another fifty copies to the guild as their "financial contribution."[65] In the case of Zhou Yue's reprinting the

---

63. SMA S313-1-100 "Shuye gongsuo guanggao" [Announcement by the Booksellers' Guild]; also "Shuye gongsuo guanggao" [Announcement by the Booksellers' Guild], *SB*, November 7, 1907.

64. SMA S313-1-100 "Bingwu nian yuance shuye gongsuo tongye jiaoshe shijian gongpan," 23.

65. SMA S313-1-100 "Bingwu nian yuance shuye gongsuo tongye jiaoshe shijian gongpan," 8–9.

lithographic edition of *Zhuibaiqiu*, the SBG also did not impose a fine on Zhou Yue's but asked them to turn in fifty pirated copies to the guild instead.[66]

Piracy victims would sometimes even compensate the guild to obtain reprints and piratical *shudi* from the alleged pirate. In August 1909, for instance, Brilliant-Letters Books (*Huanwen shuju*) discovered that Haizou Books (*Haizuo shuju*) had produced massive reprints of their *Shangwu jiaoke chidu* (Commercial letter-writing teaching manual). Reporting to the SBG, they claimed that "every word in the [pirated] edition is the same [as in theirs]."[67] Initially, the SBG decided that the pirate should not only surrender the four hundred fifty remainders of their *Shangwu jiaoke chidu* and their piratical collotype glass plates to be destroyed, but also needed to pay a sixty-three-yuan fine to the guild. Nevertheless, the complainant, Brilliant-Letters Books, preferred to have the pirate hand over the remainders to them for resale. After further negotiation with the pirate and the SBG, the "victim" provided a twenty-three-yuan subsidy to the pirate to "help them pay the fine" to the guild. In return, they received the 450 pirated copies and were able to sell them as their own.[68]

Collective Justice in Chessboard Street

In the 1900s, the SBG successfully established an efficient and flexible *banquan* regime in the Chessboard Street neighborhood via its general *shudi/banquan* registration system, mediations in the guild's office, and its punishments of the pirates. But none of these strategies aimed to aggressively "catch" the pirates in action. Though the SBG strove to create and maintain order in the book trade, they did not consider regular patrolling of the marketplace to be their duty. It was the individual booksellers' responsibility to watch out for suspicious copies that might infringe their *banquan*. While relying on its members to "catch" those who reprinted their registered titles, the SBG nevertheless did not have clear written rules on how far members could go to "catch" the alleged pirates.

Oftentimes when Shanghai booksellers brought their *banquan* cases to the guild, they had already tracked down the alleged pirate's identity and even the scale of his piracy scheme. Physical evidence, like actual copies of the unauthorized reprints or the defendant's advertisements or flyers, were enclosed with the complainant's statements. In their statements to the SBG, they

66. SMA S313-1-100 "Yuanyue ershibari qipanjie feihongge baogao."
67. SMA S313-1-100 "Xuantong yuannian qiyue chusi."
68. Ibid.

occasionally revealed scattered details of how they had received tips about the alleged piracy schemes or what happened during their pursuit of the pirates. Such details need to be understood in the context of the Chessboard Street neighborhood, where booksellers operated their businesses, printed books, and socialized in a close and intimate setting. The inhabitants of the Chessboard Street neighborhood shared information and leads with each other regularly; not infrequently a bookseller's statement to the SBG began with "Someone told me that there's a pirated edition of my book(s) in the marketplace." With the leads, booksellers would try to obtain the alleged pirated copies to make their case solid. So as not to alert the suspected pirate, cautious booksellers often hired someone unfamiliar to Chessboard Street's inhabitants as their undercover buyer or informant. For instance, after Mind-Enlightening Book Studio received the lead about a potential pirate reprinting its *Su tongling zifa*, its proprietor asked a regular customer from Shanxi to purchase fifty copies of the suspicious title for him. He was thus able to get the needed evidence and confirm that these were indeed unauthorized reprints of his book.[69]

When some of its members presented their cases for the SBG's "judgment," they had already uncovered and appropriated the remainders of pirated editions and unfinished products, as well as the *shudi* master copy used in production. In several cases, before reporting to the guild, booksellers had asked the Shanghai Municipal Police (SMP) to inspect the suspect's printing studio or warehouse and confiscate the suspicious copies. However, it seems that the SBG's leaders preferred to keep *banquan* disputes within their community instead of going to the police first. The guild once asked Civilization Books to withdraw a case from the SMP and called off the police's scheduled raid.[70] In another instance, the SBG even informed the SMP that the complainant had dropped the case, and requested that the SMP hand over the books and *shudi* held in the police station to the guild because "the guild had taken over the case and would burn those copies."[71]

Tracking down pirates based on hearsay, entering others' storefronts or warehouses for inspection, or confiscating suspicious copies haphazardly—such actions were tricky in a busy and crowded space like the Chessboard Street neighborhood. Pirates in early twentieth-century Shanghai were not

69. SMA S313-1-100 "Bingwu nian shuye gongsuo jiaoshe baogao yuanyou," 36–38.

70. SMA S313-1-75.

71. SMA S313-1-75 "Shuye gongsuo zhi xunbufang zhishi xiansheng" [Booksellers' Guild to Mr. Police Director].

sinister-looking criminals operating their shadowy business in the underworld. As the SBG's archives indicate, most alleged "pirates" were "legitimate" booksellers and printers who lived and worked in the same sphere with their "victims." Many were also regular members of the guild. The same bookseller could be the victim of piracy in one case but the accused in another. While the well-established ones had their facilities and storefronts, many small-time booksellers shared printing studios and warehouses with others or hawked books at public spaces like teahouses and opium dens. In such a densely populated environment where the boundaries between businesses were ambiguous, it would be easy to misidentify an innocent neighbor as a pirate. For some booksellers, being misidentified as pirates and having their store and workshop searched by others were annoying harassments. For those previously convicted, being wrongly accused could have serious consequences. A minor bookseller named Jian Qingzhai, for instance, was accused by Civilization Books of pirating their geography textbook in the autumn of 1906. Since Jian had been found pirating another Civilization Books textbook the previous month, both Civilization Books and the SBG considered this repeat offender to be "scum in the book trade [and] a malefactor to the guild." The SBG thus decided to suspend Jian from the guild and expel him from the Shanghai book trade. As it turned out, Jian was innocent this time. It was another bookseller sharing the same printing studio who was guilty of the wrongdoing, and Jian's printing machine happened to be next to the real pirate's. Because of his previous record, however, Civilization Books mistook him as the one responsible.[72]

Relying on individual booksellers to catch pirates could potentially create another kind of chaos, as some members took more brutal measures to gather the needed evidence. The SBG did not have a written procedure specifying the acceptable actions its members could take to make their cases. As is illustrated by the following account of an abduction, the crowded Chessboard Street neighborhood made it possible for its inhabitants to achieve a certain collective justice by participating in the guild's investigation to reveal the truth.

In the summer of 1906, Li Difan reported to the SBG in despair. He accused Xia Ruifang (1871–1914), the general manager of Commercial Press and also an SBG trustee, of kidnapping him on the street. Li, a salesman for Commercial

---

72. SMA S313-1-100, SMA S313-1-75 "Jian Qingzhai baogao" [Report by Jian Qingzhai], September 22, 1906.

Books (*Shangye tushubu*),[73] a different firm, stated that he was approached by two men in *Xinchangxiang*, a popular opium den near Chessboard Street, on August 31. Identifying themselves as representatives of provincial schools coming to Shanghai to purchase textbooks, these two men told Li that they had been informed that Li could offer them a good deal on the books they wanted. As a salesman specializing in provincial customers, Li knew this would be a big order and agreed to help. Later, when these two parties met again at a nearby teahouse called Green Lotus (*Qinglian ge*),[74] Li brought samples of the requested books: seven titles from Shina Books (*Zhina shuju*) and several Commercial Press textbooks, such as *Zhongguo lishi* (Chinese history). The provincial buyers were pleased by the quality of the books and the price Li offered. They signed the contract on the spot and arranged the delivery and payment for the afternoon: the books were scheduled to be delivered by Li to room 11 of the Raising-Steps Hotel (*Gaosheng zhan*),[75] where the two men, Mr. Shen and his friend, were staying.

Li and his books, however, never arrived. Around three o'clock in the afternoon, Li and his friend Chen Yunsheng, a freelance book dealer, were on their way to deliver the books to the Raising-Steps Hotel. When they passed with their handcart in front of Left-Bank Books (*Jiangzuo shuju*) in Chessboard Street, a group of people suddenly appeared from nowhere, surrounded them, and dragged them to the building next door. In that building, which turned out to be Commercial Press's headquarters, Xia Ruifang was waiting. Xia angrily accused Li of pirating his firm's books and seized all the books on the cart.

After Li and Chen somehow managed to escape from Xia about an hour later, instead of reporting the incident to the police, they went directly to the SBG's office nearby seeking justice. Li accused Xia of setting a trap to abduct him and appropriate his commodities.[76] In his statement, Li expressed his suspicion that

73. See SMA S313-1-75, SMA S313-1-100. He identified himself as an employee of *Shangye tushubu*, but the investigator Chen Yonghe reported that Li was employed by Shina Books and specialized in dealing with provincial customers.

74. The Green Lotus was an important social spot in the neighborhood. While its first floor offered various entertainments, such as Chinese operas and storytelling, the second floor also served as a merchandise exchange hub for merchants to review samples and sign deals.

75. This popular Chinese-style hotel in the Heping Lane of Fuzhou Road also appeared in several late Qing social-realist novels as the place where protagonists or minor figures stayed when they visited Shanghai for business.

76. SMA S313-1-100 "Bingwu nian shuye gongsuo tongxing jiaoshe baogao yuanyou," 15, September 3, 1906.

Mr. Shen and his friend were not real provincial buyers but bait sent by Xia to lure him. The arrangement for him to deliver books to the Raising-Steps Hotel, he believed, was a trap: the hotel was located in a blind alley, and the only way to get there was to pass the headquarters of Commercial Press.[77]

For the SBG, Li's accusation against Xia was thorny in two respects. First, Xia was an influential bookseller and also a trustee of the SBG. When dealing with a suspected pirate, instead of collecting the needed evidence and appealing to the guild for adjudication, he decided to kidnap the suspect and seize the books in question. Such a move could be seen as Xia's depreciation of the guild's authority, even though he was in a leadership position in the SBG. To confirm its newly established authority as a dispute mediator and the booksellers' bastion against piracy, the guild would need to make this case a shining example of its ability to resolve piracy litigation cases more equitably and justly than individual booksellers could manage to do by taking measures on their own. On the other hand, to rule justly in this matter was difficult, as the prestige and credibility of the two parties were obviously not in the same league. Although it was indeed unusual or even suspicious for a small-time salesman like Li to be able to provide a large number of Commercial Press's textbooks with a handsome discount, it didn't automatically prove Li and his friend Chen to be pirates. If the guild deemed Xia more trustworthy because of the capital and size of Commercial Press, then there was a danger that the concerns of lesser booksellers in the community would be dismissed and innocent members would be wrongly convicted of piracy.

To figure out whether Xia had set a trap to kidnap Li, the board of the SBG sent an inquiry to a crucial third figure in this case: the provincial buyer Mr. Shen. On September 3, Shen replied and offered an entirely different story. He claimed that the original delivery destination had always been Commercial Press, not the Raising-Steps Hotel, as he and his companion had planned to package and ship the books from Commercial Press. The dispute, according to him, was not between Xia and Li, but between Li and him, because the books Li had delivered did not tally with what they had ordered. That was also why they had seized the books and refused to pay Li. Insisting that his book order was not a trap, he speculated that the absurd kidnapping story had been fabricated by the unknown freelance bookseller Chen, and he urged the SBG to find out the truth.[78] Following conventional procedure, the SBG board would examine and

---

77. SMA S313-1-100.

78. SMA S313-1-75 "Shen Shaoji zhi gongsuo" [Shen Shaoji to the guild], September 3, 1906.

compare the written statements presented by the interested parties to decide the case, but the accounts given by Li and Shen were equally dubious: Li never explained why he possessed a large quantity of Commercial Press's textbooks. And Shen could not explain why, if he intended to have Commercial Press package and ship his order, he had not ordered the books from them directly.

Facing this deadlock, the SBG sent out six of their eight elected *diaocha yuan* (investigators) on September 3 to collect information in the Chessboard Street neighborhood about this strange piracy and kidnapping case. The position of investigator had initially been created by the SBG to replicate a similar position in the Shanghai General Chamber of Commerce. The original mission of the investigators, according to the Shanghai General Chamber of Commerce's by-laws and the Ministry of Commerce's guidelines, was to survey the market; collect useful information, such as market trends and price fluctuations; and enhance the chamber of commerce's and the state's understanding of the economy. The eight investigators of the SBG, however, rarely devoted their time and energy to researching the market; they were called on by the guild to determine the truth in disputes when the written statements provided by the interested parties were too much at odds to permit the board members to rule in the case. Two days later, these investigators reported their findings back to the guild. They had collected more than two dozen witnesses' accounts that collectively made it possible to reconstruct what had happened to Li, Shen, Xia, and others on Chessboard Street between August 30 and 31, 1906. They broke the case wide open.

First and foremost, these investigators discovered that the provincial customer in room 11 of the Raising-Steps Hotel had never existed. None of the current guests in that hotel had come to Shanghai to purchase books.[79] Neither was any of them surnamed Shen.[80] According to the hotel bookkeeper, room 11, where Shen and his friend told Li they were staying, had been occupied by Mr. Xu from Ningbo for more than a month.[81] This debunked Shen's account of coming to Shanghai to buy textbooks. Consequently, his statement about the conflict in Commercial Press's headquarters also became questionable. Since the SBG was able to reach him and he did reply to their

---

79. SMA S313-1-100 "Rong Shaofu baogao" [Rong Shaofu's report] and "Chen Xiaohu baogao" [Chen Xiaohu's report].

80. SMA S313-1-100 "Rong Shaofu baogao," "Xu Heyun baogao" [Xu Heyun's report] and "Ye Jiuru baogao" [Ye Jiuru's report].

81. SMA S313-1-100 "Xu Junhe baogao," and "Ye Jiuru baogao."

inquiry promptly with a statement, undoubtly Mr. Shen was a real person in Shanghai. Then the question was this: Who exactly were these two "customers" who had approached Li in the first place in the opium den *Xinchangxiang*?

What had happened in *Xinchangxiang* the evening before the mysterious Mr. Shen approached Li, as multiple investigators' reports indicate, would be the key to solving this puzzle. Earlier in August, Xia Ruifang had learned about the existence of some cheap reprints of their best-selling textbooks, especially *Zhongguo lishi*, in the marketplace. These reprints cost between one-third and one-half less than the authentic copies; and several booksellers and shareholders had heard Xia anxiously complaining about the damage these pirated copies might cause.[82] On the evening of August 30, when Commercial Press employees Cheng Shenfu and Zhu Guanting went to *Xinchangxiang* and saw some suspicious-looking copies of textbooks, including *Zhongguo lishi*, on the next opium bed, they quickly associated these with the cheap reprints their boss had been complaining about. Learning that these books belonged to Li, who was not present then, Cheng and Zhu took advantage of Li's absence to inspect his belongings.[83] Their act was witnessed by several booksellers who also happened to be in *Xinchangxiang* that evening. The proprietor of Literary-Seas Studio (*Wenhai ge*), Yuan Zhicai, for instance, was smoking opium there at the time. He informed the investigator, Xue Junhe, that the two Commercial Press employees had told him those books were pirated copies and asked Yuan whose merchandise they were. Yuan also told Xue that when he noticed some strangers showing up next day at the same spot, specifically asking for Li Difan and seeking to buy textbooks, he was convinced that this must have something to do with the two Commercial Press employees he had chatted with the night before.[84]

Indeed, these two clerks immediately reported to Xia that they had found the pirate he was looking for. According to Rong Shaofu's investigation, the next day Xia sent two office accountants, Shen Jifang and Bu Shengtong, to *Xinchangxian*. They approached Li, posing as provincial customers from Hangzhou.[85] These two undercover buyers quickly reached a deal with Li worth six

---

82. SMA S313-1-75, SMA S313-1-100 "Cheng Yonghe baogao."

83. SMA S313-1-75, SMA S313-1-100 "Cheng Yonghe baogao," "Rong Shaofu baogao," "Xu Heyun baogao," and "Ye Jiuru baogao."

84. SMA S313-1-75, SMA S313-1-100 "Xu Heyun baogao."

85. SMA S313-1-75, SMA S313-1-100 "Rong Shaofu baogao." Shen's face may not have been familiar to Li because he was in charge of foreign contracts at Commercial Press.

hundred silver dollars, with a 40 percent discount. They later met again at the Green Lotus to examine the sample and finalize the deal. A waiter at the Green Lotus confirmed this episode: he had brought pen and paper to Li and Shen to make their contract.

The detailed information these investigators were able to collect suggests that there might have been no secrets in the Chessboard Street neighborhood. People working in other businesses, such as the staff of the Raising-Steps Hotel and the Green Lotus, provided helpful accounts to verify Li's and Shen's reports. But the most valuable information came from what other guild members had overheard and witnessed in the opium den and teahouses, the public spaces where booksellers and other merchants conducted their business, exchanged information, and relaxed. The fact that Yuan Zhicai and other booksellers were able to provide the SBG's investigators with details—the titles of the books on or under Li's opium bed, the exact titles Shen had ordered, the deal and the discount, how Shen and Bu had identified themselves, and where they claimed they were staying—suggests that Shanghai booksellers might always have kept an eye on what their fellow booksellers were doing.

The "kidnapping" on the afternoon of August 31 in front of Left-Bank Books was witnessed by numerous people because it took place in the middle of the Chessboard Street neighborhood. Xu Hongyun, the proprietor of Left-Bank Books and also one of the guild's investigators, testified in his report that he had been working at his office until he heard some unusual noises outside. When he went out, he saw a handcart in front of his shop, and Li was embroiled in an argument with several Commercial Press employees. He heard Li yelling, "Did you think I stole these books?" The Commercial Press staff members then dragged Li's cart full of books to their headquarters. When Xia Ruifang showed up, Li yelled again, "Did you think I stole your books?" Xia stemmed Li's rage and replied: "We didn't say you stole these books. We take it that you bought them, OK?" but then he dragged Li to his office.[86]

Other nearby booksellers also witnessed the confrontation between Li and the staff of Commercial Press. Li's outraged "Did you think I stole these books?" was apparently heard by many people, as it appeared in five of the six reports. Ye Jiuru also reported that some others heard Li yelling, "Do you guys think my books are books of questionable origins? I have proof [of their authenticity]!"[87] The authenticity and origins of the copies Li possessed

86. SMA S313-1-75, S313-1-100 "Xu jun Hongyun baogao" [Mr. Xu Hongyun's report].
87. SMA S313-1-75, S313-1-100 "Ye Jiuru baogao."

seemed to trigger the conflict on the spot. Several booksellers testified that they had heard the word "piracy" during their argument.[88] Two investigators' reports also substantiated Li's assertion that he was not originally heading to Commercial Press: the handcart was initially going south to the Raising-Steps Hotel, but during the conflict in front of Left-Bank Books the cart was pulled, and its direction was changed. It ended up facing north and then was dragged to Commercial Press.[89] These booksellers also observed what later took place inside Commercial Press's headquarters, as they were able to pack into the building to watch the tumultuous scene. Chen's and Rong's reports detailed how Xia then examined the books Li possessed to determine whether Li was the pirate they suspected. After carefully comparing Li's copies and their own authentic ones, Xia concluded that the copies Li had obtained were indeed "real."[90] But why would Li have such a large quantity of Commercial Press's textbooks in hand?

Shina Books provided the receipt of Li's order to prove that the Shina Books textbooks Li possessed were authentic,[91] but there was no record at Commercial Press indicating that Li had ever ordered books from them. According to Chen's, Rong's, and Ye's reports, Li told Commercial Press staff on the spot that he had obtained those books from a Cantonese customer. Commercial Press then sent a manager to accompany Li to a sugar company in the South Market of the Chinese City to verify Li's statement. The Cantonese owner of the sugar company confirmed that he had sold Li those books. They had been returned to him by another Cantonese who had ordered the books but failed to make the payment.[92] Allegedly, when Li and his friend Chen went back to Commercial Press's headquarters, Xia apologized to Li for misidentifying him as a pirate but refused to return Li's books to him.[93] Upset by Xia's retention of his books, Li went to the SBG for justice after he managed to leave Commercial Press.

Several days after these investigators turned in their reports to the SBG, an "insider" from Commercial Press visited investigator Xu Heyun's home at night to solve the last puzzle of this intriguing case. Cheng Shenfu, the clerk

88. SMA S313-1-75, S313-1-100 "Xu Heyun baogao."

89. SMA S313-1-75, S313-1-100 "Xu Heyun baogao," and "Xu Hongyun baogao."

90. SMA S313-1-75, S313-1-100 "Cheng Yonghe baogao" and "Rong Shaofu baogao."

91. SMA S313-1-75, S313-1-100 "Ye Jiuru baogao."

92. Ibid.

93. SMA S313-1-75, SMA S313-1-100 "Xu Hongyun baogao."

who had "discovered" Li's "pirated" copies in the first place, the "insider" told Xu, was desperate to make a big contribution to the firm to cancel out a major accounting mistake he had made earlier. So when he saw the copies of *Zhongguo lishi* on Li's opium bed, he rushed to report this to Xia to impress his boss.[94] As it turned out, Cheng's misinformation caused an embarrassing mix-up. In mid-September, the SBG validated Li's innocence. It ruled that Commercial Press should not only compensate Li's loss but also publicly apologize to him and the whole book trade for the disturbance they had negligently created.[95]

In the SBG's early years, these elected investigators were occasionally sent by the guild to collect information crucial to the cases but not included in book-sellers' formal statements to the guild. These investigators utilized their connections in the Chessboard Street area to gather leads and eyewitness accounts about individual disputes. They provided an additional means for both the guild and its members to "do justice," even though this was not what the position "investigator" had originally been created for. Just as they exploited the ministry's campaign and the standard bylaws for their own *banquan*/copyright regulation, the SBG board members used the means the Ministry of Commerce had designed to collect commercial intelligence to help them in adjudicating complicated cases like the abduction of Li Difan. By providing their witness accounts to the SBG investigators, booksellers who shared the streets, opium dens, teahouses, printing studios, warehouses, and other social spaces in this overcrowded Chessboard Street neighborhood were able to participate in the guild's dispute-resolution mechanism even though they were not the interested parties. They were able to maintain some collective justice and social order because they kept watching and being watched by each other.

When the SBG moved their guild office from Chessboard Street to the Chinese City in 1915, they decided to confer more power on the investigators to regulate pirate-hunting conduct. Instead of letting members search for suspicious copies and pirates on their own and report to the guild later, the SBG president assigned one or more board members as investigating/reviewing trustee(s) (*shenchadong*) to determine the authenticity of suspicious titles as well as to investigate disputes. The board then would decide how to mediate

<hr>

94. SMA S313-1-75 "Xu Heyun erci baogao" [The second report by Xu Heyun]. Ye Jiuru also received a similar lead from another employee of Commercial Press.

95. SMA S313-1-75, SMA S313-1-100.

piracy disputes according to their reports.[96] After the SBG and SBTA merged into the new Shanghai Booksellers' Guild in 1928, the guild further established a "piracy-inspection committee" to more actively clamp down on pirates, using the guild's resources, in and beyond the Chessboard Street neighborhood. This committee would eventually become the Shanghai booksellers' private police force, hunting pirates and enforcing the rules of Chessboard Street in Beiping and its vicinity.

The Parallel "Copyright" Regimes

The enforcement of the Shanghai booksellers' *banquan* regime illustrated in the two previous sections relied upon the guilds' register of *banquan* and *shudi* as their documentary foundation. Nonetheless, from the Qing state's perspective, the booksellers had no legitimacy to establish their *banquan* registers. When the SBTA proudly submitted their "*Banquan* Rules" to the Ministry of Commerce for official recognition in 1906, for example, the ministry rejected their "legislation" and stated clearly that *only* the state had the authority to grant *banquan*/copyright to others. It not only asked the SBTA to rename their "*Banquan* Rules" as "Publication Conventions" (*Chuban gongyue*) but also declined to endorse the SBTA's plan of stamping a "*banquan suoyou*" seal on its members' publications.[97]

The Ministry of Commerce's 1904 guidelines for chambers of commerce indeed authorized merchant organizations to mediate and settle internal conflicts or commercial disputes themselves. Simultaneously, the Qing state also promulgated its commercial codes, company law, bankruptcy law, and trademark regulations, aiming to formalize the state's regulation of the economy. After 1904, when facing commercial disputes, late Qing merchants could decide whether to bring their case to the court, to be ruled according to the state's commercial codes, or to the merchant organization for mediation. Fan Jinmin and the Sos' research suggests that merchants, as rational-legal actors, often preferred to settle their disputes at the merchant organization because it was

---

96. SMA S313-1-2-8 "Shanghai shuye Chongdetang gongsuo xianxing guize caogao" [Draft of the Shanghai Chongde Hall Booksellers' Guild current procedures] (1915).

97. "Pi Shanghai shuye shanghui bing she shuye shanghui yingzhun lian suoyou banquan ziyang yin ji zunchi gengzheng bei fu mingshi er shi qubie," *Shangwu guanbao* 10 (July 25, 1906): 22-b.

cheaper and often more efficient compared to formal lawsuits.[98] For disputes over *banquan* ownership, the most common type of dispute in the late Qing Shanghai book trade, however, the option of employing the state's formal law did not exist, as the domestic copyright law was yet to be issued. The government-issued individual *banquan* protection orders, as chapter 4 shows, were deemed by the booksellers to be ineffective and problematic. To exercise their state-acknowledged power to adjudicate *banquan* disputes, the SBG and the SBTA recognized the need to establish certain rules to define and document their members' *banquan* ownership. Such provisions were deemed necessary in the book trade as most of the *banquan* disputes were not disputes over documented commercial agreements, but conflicting claims of book ownership; unlike other forms of property, such as land, estates, or goods, book ownership was at the time not registered or recorded systematically. But the Ministry of Commerce's reply to the SBTA indicates that it considered these booksellers to have gone beyond propriety in coming up with such law-like *banquan* procedures, even though the booksellers might be doing so out of necessity.

The SBTA's internal records suggest that the Shanghai booksellers ended up feigning compliance with the Ministry of Commerce's order. The association did retitle its "*Banquan* Rules" as "Publication Conventions" to register itself at the ministry successfully, but in other internal documents, it continued claiming that the SBTA registered and protected *banquan* for its members. On the other hand, in its bylaws, the SBG carefully differentiated the state-authorized *banquan* from the guild-registered *shudi* master copy, which they later referred to as "*gongren banquan* (accredited *banquan*)." In practice, however, the state-authorized *banquan* and the SBG "accredited *banquan*" were treated the same way by the guild. This suggests that for the SBG members, these two enjoyed equal validity. In March 1910, the SBG even pushed their "accredited *banquan*" one step further; its members decided in a general meeting that the SBG would "grant a *banquan* patent" to new titles for a fixed term, and it would strictly prohibit unauthorized reprinting, imitating, or distribution of such titles. *Banquan* disputes would now be resolved in the general meetings by board members collectively. The detailed procedure for the SBG's "*banquan* patent" was decided by its members as follows. The SBG would charge a small fee/tax (0.2 percent of the sale price for each copy printed) for new titles registered at the guild. Traditional primers or classics, such as *Four Books and Five*

98. Fan, *Ming Qing shangshi jiufen yu shangye susong*, 285–288; Billy So and Sufumi So, "Commercial Arbitration Transplanted."

Classics, would be seen as public property shared by the community, and everyone in the Shanghai book trade could freely publish them as long as they notified the guild in advance. Meanwhile, for those who possessed the *shudi* master copy of "old and fine manuscripts, rare titles [owned by] famous people," and manuscripts of "newly written works and translations," after they registered their books with the guild, they would "be granted the exclusive monopoly of *banquan.*" To prevent these booksellers who possessed the exclusive *banquan* of certain valuable titles from excessively inflating the sale price, the guild also decided that the prices of such books should be decided collectively by the community in the guild's general meeting. They also considered opening their register to non-Shanghai-based booksellers.[99]

Despite the state's order asking them to stop using the term *"banquan"* in their register, Shanghai booksellers continued operating their *banquan* regimes by maintaining an intriguing distance from the state. On the one hand, the SBG was reluctant to have any government authority interfere with their piracy mediation and discipline. It discouraged its members from reporting fellow Shanghai booksellers to local officials, arguing that such action would not only cause trouble to the victim of piracy but also cause Shanghai booksellers as a group to lose face in the public sphere.[100] On the other hand, to ensure that they were recognized by the state, on paper, as legitimate civic organizations, the SBG and the SBTA also duly, if not religiously, followed the state's latest instructions to register themselves, presenting themselves as obedient subjects observing the law. When the Qing state finally announced its long-anticipated copyright law in December 1910, the SBG board quickly printed free copies of the new law for their members to "study." Writing "following the copyright law" into the guild's new bylaws, the SBG then promptly presented the document to the newly established Ministry of Civil Affairs (*Minzheng bu*) to ensure their own government recognition in the post-copyright-law era.[101]

In the revised bylaws, the guild stated that it would from now on follow the state's copyright law, but it didn't give up its "accredited *banquan.*" The Shanghai booksellers' *banquan* regime persisted in parallel with the state's copyright

99. SMA S313-1-120-15.

100. SMA S313-1-100.

101. SMA S313-1-120-48 "Xinhai san nian ershiyi ri kaihui tiyi gezhong wenti lie hou" [Issues discussed and suggested in the meeting on the twenty-first day of the year of Xinhai]; SMA S313-1-120-60 "Minzhengbu Xuantong san nian si yue bingqi zhuce lugao" [Draft registration petition to the Ministry of Civil Affairs in the fourth month of the third year of Xuantong].

regime. This was not only a parallel between a customary law and a state's code but also a parallel between a bookseller-centered conception of copyright and an author-centered conception of copyright. The Copyright Law of the Great Qing Empire, as many scholars have pointed out, closely imitated Japan's 1899 *Chosakukenhō* (Copyright Law).[102] It formally introduced new intellectual property terminology—*zhuzuoquan/chosakuken* (the right of the author)—to the Chinese.[103] The term *chosakuken* was coined by Japanese legal scholars in the 1880s to refer to the Continental conceptions of intellectual property, especially *droit d'auteur* (author's right) in French and *Urheberrecht* in German. When Mizuno Rentaro (1868–1949) drafted the new Japanese copyright law in the late 1890s to fulfill the requirement for the Berne Convention for the Protection of Literary and Artistic Works, he chose *chosakuken* over *hanken*, the term coined by Fukuzawa Yukichi in 1873 for "copyright." Considering *hanken* as "the right to copy" that referred only to printed materials, Mizuno used *chosakuken* to cover all kinds of literary and artistic works, such as music, drama, and images. At the same time, by coining this term, he recognized an author as both the creator and the owner of his/her intellectual property in this new law.[104] When the Qing state issued its copyright law, copyright was officially defined in the formal law as *zhuzuoquan*—the ownership of intellectual and artistic creation. The state would no longer grant special *banquan* protections or privileges to booksellers and authors. Instead, booksellers and authors needed to register their works with the state to obtain *zhuzuoquan* protection. *Banquan*, since it was not adopted in the formal law, was not a valid legal term; nonetheless, it was not replaced by *zhuzuoquan* in the Chinese publishing world after the

102. Wang, *Jindai Zhongguo zhuzuoquan fa de chengzhang*, chap. 3. Li, ed., *Zhongguo jindai banquan shi*, 108–111.

103. Although the phrase *zhuzuoquan* appeared in some Chinese legal dictionaries published in the late Qing, such as *Riben fazheng cijie* (Dictionary of Japanese legal and political terms) (1907) and *Hanyi riben falü jingji cidian* (Chinese Translation of Japanese law and economic dictionary) (1909), it was rarely used by the public. *Banquan* was still the most common term used by booksellers, authors, and officials to refer to "copyright" during this period. For a discussion of late Qing legal dictionaries, see *Jindai Zhongguo zhuzuoquan fa de chengzhang*, 30–35.

104. Joining the Berne Convention was one of the terms European powers requested of Japan in exchange for revoking the unequal treaties Japan had signed with them in the mid-nineteenth century. In 1899, Japan joined the Berne Convention as the first non-European member. For Mizuno's drafting of Chosakukenhō and his interpretation of *droit d'auteur*, see Ōie, *Chosakuken o kakuritsushita hitobito*, 117–130. For Japan's rewriting of its copyright law to join the Berne Convention, see *Chosakukenhō hyakunenshi*, 83–137.

promulgation of the Copyright Law of the Great Qing Empire. The term *banquan* continued to be used more commonly than *zhuzuoquan* in China throughout the twentieth century. In the Chessboard Street neighborhood, it was always what the SBG aimed to register, regulate, and protect, no matter how the political landscape changed or how many new copyright laws and regulations the various political regimes issued in the coming decades.

The actual enforcement of the Copyright Law of the Great Qing Empire is hard to evaluate because just months after it was put into effect, the Qing Empire was overthrown by the revolutionaries. During the 1911 Revolution, Shanghai booksellers were among the earliest merchant groups in town to offer their support to the newly established Republic. They quickly organized a small posse comitatus called *Shanghai shuye shangtuan* (Shanghai Booksellers' Posse) to patrol the city and promote the new Republic.[105] For the Chessboard Street neighborhood, the regime change brought business opportunities rather than political disturbances. Many booksellers quickly adjusted to the new Republican agendas, just as they had responded to the Qing educational reform a few years earlier, and rushed to publish new textbooks, calendars, and manuals for "new Chinese citizens." For instance, Lufei Kui and several other editors at Commercial Press seized the opportunity and established Chung Hwa Books in January 1912; they promptly released a series of textbooks to introduce the new Republic of China (hereafter, ROC) and its nationalist agenda. Taking advantage of Commercial Press's hesitation to update its textbooks after the revolution, Chung Hwa Books was able to carve out its market share and emerge as the second-largest textbook provider in the Republic Era.

The copyright legislation in China did not change much after the revolution. In March 1912, the new ROC government announced that the Copyright Law of the Great Qing Empire would remain valid provisionally. It also decided to acknowledge the *zhuzuoquan* register before 1911.[106] The SBG and the SBTA modified their bylaws to recognize the regime change and promptly registered themselves with the new government. While the ROC Ministry of the Interior proudly stated that they had recorded more than one hundred *zhuzuoquan* just months after its establishment, the scale of the official register was still dwarfed by the SBG's *shudi* register. For the time being, Shanghai booksellers

---

105. For the rules, budgets, and activities of *Shanghai Shuye Shangtuan*, see SMA S313-1-52. This organization also had theme songs and a small drama club.

106. "Neiwubu tonggao" [The public notice from the Ministry of the Interior], *Zhengfu gongbao* 543 (November 7, 1913).

seemed to have high expectations that this new government could bring about effective domestic copyright protection. After all, the SBG might be efficient in dealing with local *banquan* disputes, but its authority did not extend too far beyond the Chessboard Street neighborhood. Hoping that the state could help it to crack down on provincial piracy, Commercial Press launched a series of lawsuits against thirty-two booksellers in seventeen cities and provinces between 1912 and 1913.[107] The outcome of these lawsuits appears to have resulted in profound disappointment. In 1914, through the Shanghai General Chamber of Commerce and the National Alliance of Chambers of Commerce (*Quanguo shanghui lianhehui*), Yin Youmo (1863–1915), who succeeded Xia Reifang as Commercial Press's general manager,[108] pleaded with the Ministry of Justice regarding the flood of reprints of Shanghai publications in various provinces. He urged the ministry to reaffirm the legitimacy of the Copyright Law of the Great Qing Empire by ordering local courts to "seriously enforce the Copyright Law of the Great Qing Empire's penalty rules when ruling piracy cases," and "not exculpate [pirates] easily."[109]

In 1915, the Beijing government issued its *Zhonghua Minguo zhuzuoquan fa* (hereafter, the 1915 ROC Copyright Law) to replace the Qing copyright law. Not only were the articles of this new Republic's copyright law almost identical to those of its predecessor,[110] but the fate of this new law was also very similar to the old one's. As the SBTA pointed out in a petition in 1922, they were not even sure whether the 1915 ROC Copyright Law was a valid law duly passed by the National Assembly.[111] Indeed, like its predecessor, the 1915 ROC Copyright Law barely had a chance to be fully realized: in November 1915, when the law supposedly went into effect, the National Assembly agreed to change the form of government, and President Yuan Shikai installed himself as the emperor of the Chinese Empire. Yuan's attempt to revive imperial rule was short-lived, and his death soon after the failure of the Chinese Empire was followed by a decade of civil wars among regional military leaders. Although they fought against each other for control of Beijing and the ROC central government, none

---

107. Ibid.

108. Xia was assassinated in January 1914.

109. "Sifabu tongchi yanban fanban anjian" [The Ministry of Justice ordered [local courts] to deal with piracy cases severely] (June 4, 1914), in *Zhongguo banquan shi yanjiu wenxian*, 135.

110. For a comparison of *Zhonghua Minguo zhuzuoquan fa* and *Daqing zhuzuoquan lü*, see Li, ed., *Zhongguo jindai banquan shi*, 165–169.

111. *Zhongguo banquan shi yanjiu wenxian*, 162–166.

of them ever actually controlled the whole nation for a substantial period. The 1910s and 1920s were an interregnum when state power reached its low point, and for most of the time the central government existed only in name.[112]

In Shanghai, booksellers' economic life, as well as the SBG's daily operations, carried on despite these national political upheavals. Indeed, the SBG and SBTA periodically modified their bylaws and (re)registered themselves with the new governments to accommodate the changing administrations in Beijing. But the way Shanghai booksellers identified and recorded their ownership of publications did not change significantly. Though the SBG and SBTA asserted that they followed the state's copyright law, they never stopped registering their members' new books. The SBG continued to acknowledge the *shudi*/*banquan* registered at the guild as the communally accredited *banquan*/copyright, even if, from the state's point of view, the guild's entry and acknowledgments had no legal basis. Shanghai booksellers seem to have continued to prefer appealing to the guild instead of filing copyright lawsuits in court. Pirates in Shanghai were still brought to the guild's office, and their penalties were decided in the guild's general meetings according to the guild's rules rather than by the copyright law they claimed they were following. In the SBG's records and minutes from the 1910s to the 1930s, one sees that the pirated copies and their *shudi* were continuously surrendered to the guild and then burned in public under the supervision of the guild's leaders or the authentic *banquan*/copyright owners.[113] The SBG's confiscation and burning of unauthorized reprints and their *shudi* were entirely extralegal from the state's point of view because the only formal penalty for piracy assessed in the Qing copyright law and later the 1915 ROC Copyright Law was a cash fine. Interestingly, the question of whether the SBG's confiscation and destruction of a pirate's possessions violated the pirate's property rights was never brought up in the guild as an issue.

In theory, by stating that the guild followed the state's copyright law, the SBG protected both titles copyrighted by the state and titles registered at the guild in the same way during the 1910s and the 1920s. But what if the state's *zhuzuo-quan* register and the guild's *banquan* register conflicted with one another as to the ownership of the same publication? On July 21, 1920, the SBG faced just such a dilemma. Benefit-Enhancing Books appealed to the guild, asserting that their *Tongzi xin chidu* (The new model of letter writing for children) had been

---

112. As the SBTA stated in its inquiry to the Jiangsu High Court in 1923, whether this law was valid was an issue in 1920. See SMA S313-1-139-27.

113. SMA S313-1-86, S313-1-87, S313-1-88, S313-1-89, S313-1-90, S313-1-121, and S313-2-11.

pirated by another guild member, Sweeping-Leaves Studio, under the title *Putong xin chidu* (The general new model of letter writing). Benefit-Enhancing Books claimed that the copyright of this title "had been registered at and protected by the Ministry of the Interior." Listing in detail the similarities between these two titles, it urged the guild to punish Sweeping-Leaves Studio.[114] Sweeping-Leaves Studio, as it turned out, had had their *Putong xin chidu* registered at the SBG a considerable time earlier. According to the SBG's record, Sweeping-Leaves Studio had come forward in 1917 accusing Benefit-Enhancing Books of pirating this very title. At the time, Benefit-Enhancing Books, admitting their wrongdoing, had promised to change the title and content of their copycat book to avoid future confusion. On July 30, Wu Renfu, an SBG board member since 1905, who had served as mediator in the earlier dispute between these two firms, presented to the SBG a photoengraving copy of the agreement both sides signed at the time to confirm Benefit-Enhancing Books' confession in 1917. This piece of evidence proved that in the SBG's *banquan*/copyright regime, Sweeping-Leaves Studio was the victim rather than the pirate in this dispute.[115] Three days later, Benefit-Enhancing Books modified their statement. Instead of emphasizing the similarities between the two titles to show that Sweeping-Leaves Studio had pirated their book, now they stressed the differences in layout and format between the two to show that *Tongzi xin chidu* was an entirely original work.[116]

Which copyright registration should the SBG validate? According to the guild's entry and rules, Sweeping-Leaves Studio possessed the accredited *banquan* of *Putong xin chidu*, so Benefit-Enhancing Books was the pirate. But it was Benefit-Enhancing Books that had formally registered the copyright of *Tongzi xin chidu* at the Ministry of the Interior. According to the state's law, then, Sweeping-Leaves Studio was the one infringing other's copyright. After comparing these two almost identical titles, the board members, probably to avoid turning this dispute into a confrontation between the guild's *banquan* regime and the state's law, decided to host an informal mediation meeting. Instead of holding the meeting at the SBG office, the two parties met at a teahouse; a respected "elder" in the book trade was invited by the SBG to serve as a mediator. The agreement reached in the teahouse was later approved by the

---

114. SMA S313-1-88 "Bu liu yue chu liu ri guangyi laihan" [Compliment for the sixth day of the sixth month: letter from Benefit-Enhancing Books], July 21, 1920.

115. SAM S313-1-88.

116. Ibid.

guild's board: while both firms could keep the remainders of these two titles and sell them as they liked, they were required to hand over the *shudi* master copy of their title in question. The guild would then publicly burn these two sets of *shudi*.[117] Thus both "pirates" were punished, while justice was served for both "victims." The possibility of a future dispute between the two booksellers over these two titles was precluded, as after their *shudi* were destroyed, both firms lost their ability to produce these two titles. However, by acknowledging both the guild's register and that of the Ministry of the Interior, in this case, the SBG elevated their *banquan*/copyright bylaws to a position of equality with the 1915 ROC Copyright Law—as both Sweeping-Leaves Studio and Benefit-Enhancing Books received consideration and punishment. And by applying the guild's default punishment to pirates (burning their means of printing specific title) instead of cash penalties, the SBG showed that it was the functional enforcer of *banquan*/copyright protection in the Chessboard Street neighborhood.

In the spring of 1923, the SBG board members strove to gain formal recognition from the state for the guild's "accredited *banquan*" when they revised their bylaws once again to accommodate the latest warlord government in Beijing. In these new bylaws, the SBG stated that they would "conduct business according to the law (*yifa banshi*)."[118] By "the law," the SBG board meant *Gong-shang tongye gonghui guize* (Regulations for Manufacturers' and Merchants' Civil Associations), which had been issued by the Beijing government in 1918 to institutionalize guilds, trade associations, and chambers of commerce. When Wu Peifu (1874–1939) took control of the central government in the autumn of 1922, the Shanghai General Chamber of Commerce urged its members, the SBG included, to revise their bylaws and organizational structure according to this long-ignored 1918 regulation so that they could be properly registered and acknowledged by the new government. When modifying their bylaws, the SBG members also updated their *banquan* regulations and submitted them to the Ministry of the Interior hoping to gain their approval.

The most noticeable feature in the SBG's 1923 new bylaws was the further institutionalization of its *banquan* dispute-resolution procedure and its ostracizing of convicted pirates. Instead of taking turns hosting ad hoc adjudications for *banquan* disputes, the SBG board members would decide *banquan* disputes

117. SMA S313-1-88 "Liu yue ershi ri tehui" [Special meeting on the twentieth day of the sixth month], August 4, 1920.
118. SMA S313-1-1 "Bianyan" [Foreword], 1923.

collectively in regular meetings. By doing so, they promised to "save the interested parties from the harm and suffering of complicated litigation." Members who intentionally infringed on fellow booksellers' *banquan*, once reported by five members, would be expelled from the guild and would lose the protection and social safety net provided by the guild. If a nonmember or expelled former member were found reprinting books registered at the guild, the guild and its members would break off business relations with him. The SBG would announce its boycott in major Shanghai newspapers to make the expelled bookseller's name known to the public.[119]

When the guild board members revised the SBG's bylaws in 1923, what they discussed the most was the nature of the guild's "accredited *banquan*." The term "accredited *banquan*" was first used in 1906 to refer to *shudi* registered at the guild; it was formally written into the SBG's bylaws in 1916. When revising the bylaws to meet the latest regulations in 1923, several board members thought that, for the greater good of the book trade, it would be necessary to define "accredited *banquan*" and to confer on it a legal status equal to that of the copyrights registered with the state.[120] One board member, for example, argued that "accredited *banquan*" should be defined as something "granted by the guild after the board reviewed a newly published title and affirmed that it had never been published by others before." A bookseller who possessed the "accredited *banquan*" of a certain title would then enjoy the exclusive right to reproduce this title and monopolize any profit it generated. He also suggested that the SBG should issue certificates to booksellers as tangible proof of their "accredited *banquan*."[121] Although this proposal was not written into the final version, the new bylaws still firmly stated that the SBG would "protect *banquan* according to the Copyright Law, and [at the same time] . . . regulate *banquan* collectively accredited by fellow booksellers."[122]

The SBG's attempt to give its "accredited *banquan*" the same legal status as state-recognized copyright was declined. The ROC Ministry of the Interior, just like the Qing Ministry of Commerce in 1906, requested that the

119. SMA S313-1-1 "Shanghai shuye gongsuo xianxing zhangcheng (guihai zhongding)" [Current bylaws of Shanghai Booksellers' Guild (revised in 1923)], Article 3, 18, 19, 25, and 26.

120. SMA S313-1-1 69 "Shanghai shuye gongsuo zhangcheng chuni caogao" [First draft of the bylaws of Shanghai Booksellers' Guild].

121. Ibid.

122. SMA S313-1-1 "Shanghai shuye gongsuo xianxing zhangcheng (guihai zhongding)," Article 3-2.

booksellers' guild drop the term *"banquan"* in their bylaws because only the state could grant and register copyright.[123] On paper, the SBG accordingly changed *"banquan"* to *"faxing quan* (right to publish)"* in this particular article to meet the government's requirement.[124] In reality, however, the SBG still used the term "accredited *banquan"* in their daily conduct and even issued its *banquan* certificates in the 1920s and 1930s.[125]

Author's Due

The author-centered copyright laws issued by the Qing and Republican governments might never have been seriously enforced, owing to the consistent political upheavals, but they provided authors a voice in the guild's *banquan* regime as authors were now the rightful original copyright owners recognized by the state's law. In the 1910s and 1920s, there were instances in which authors appealed to the SBG for help. They urged the guild to punish booksellers who abused their contracts, or to clear their names and confirm their rights in works abused by pirates. Not keen on asisting these nonmembers, the SBG often recommended that they seek justice in the state's court.[126] Though the guild tended to stand aloof from such cases, it would sometimes interfere with authors' attempts to exercise their legal right to file lawsuits against its members by exerting pressure on the author's publisher. In 1926, for instance, when Liang Qichao, one of the most influential public intellectuals and politicians of early twentieth-century China, wanted to file lawsuits against those reprinting his early works, he had to drop his legal pursuit because the SBG did not support it.

In 1926, Chung Hwa Books' founder Lufei Kui was asked by Liang, their leading author, to bring lawsuits against several Shanghai booksellers who published Liang's *Yinbingshi wenji* (The collection of the Drinking-Ice Studio) without his authorization. However, Lufei Kui, who had been an active participant in both

123. SMA 313-1-1 24–29 "Shanghai xian zhishi gongshu xunling di liushi yi hao Ling" [Shanghai county master's office order no. 61] (March 19, 1925).

124. SMA S313-1-1 "Shanghai shuye gongsuo zhangcheng (Minguo shisi nian ba yue Nongshangbu Neiwubu hezhun beian)" [Shanghai Booksellers' Guild bylaws (approved by the Ministry of Agriculture and Commerce and the Ministry of the Interior in August 1925)].

125. One of the certificates survived in the guild's archives. See SMA S313-1-121.

126. SMA S313-1-121, SMA S313-2-11.

the SBG and the SBTA since 1912, did not want to sue his fellow booksellers for violating Liang's copyright. So he came to the SBG for help.[127]

Yinbingshi wenji was first published in 1902 by Enlightenment Books. It is a collection of Liang's political essays, criticism on the Confucian classics and history, and his translations of and introductions to New Learning knowledge. Liang's semiclassical, semivernacular "new style" of writing and his active role in major political and cultural movements made *Yinbingshi wenji* a widely circulated and well-read title at the turn of the twentieth century. Although there were several unauthorized reprints of *Yinbingshi wenji* available in the marketplace at the time, Liang, as both the author and also later the proprietor of Enlightenment Books, seemed to pay little attention to them. In 1925, when he decided to republish *Yinbingshi wenji* with Chung Hwa Books in a new format (thematically rather than chronologically arranged) and new layout (letterpress, Western binding), he changed his mind. Liang, now a professor at Tsinghua University, the head of National Library, and the director of the Judge Training Institute in preparation, had recently been hospitalized. His declining health prompted him to take the economic value of his copyright more seriously; in correspondence with his family, he consistently expressed anxiety and worried about the financial well-being of his young children.[128]

When the new and improved edition of his writings was released, Liang decided to take action against those who had reprinted the Enlightenment Books edition of *Yinbingshi wenji*, since these unauthorized copies were still widely available in the marketplace. As the publisher of the new edition, Lufei did not think it was a good idea to bring legal action against those who printed and sold the old version. First of all, the early version had been published many years earlier, and its original publisher, Enlightenment Books, was no longer in business. Second, although the contents of these two editions were the same, their arrangement and layout were distinctively different. Liang was in every respect the original creator of both publications; however, following the SBG's convention in determining *banquan*, the two versions were considered to be two different entities because they differed in physical appearance. Thus labeling the unauthorized reprinting of the old edition as pirating of Chung Hwa Books' version would not be a welcome move in Shanghai publishing circles. In his

127. SMA S313-1-121 "Lufei Kui zi Cai Jiuru Gao Hanqing" [Letter from Lufei Kui to Cai Jiuru and Gao Hanqing], June 5, 1926.

128. Liang Qichao and Pinxing Zhang, *Liang Qichao Jia Shu* (Beijing: Zhongguo wenlian chubanshe, 2000), 389–412.

letter to Cai Jiuru and Gao Hanqing, the president and vice president of the SBG, on June 5, 1926, Lufei told them that, although Liang had requested that Chung Hwa Books represent him to "solve [the problem] according to the law" (*falü jiejue*), he personally was reluctant to do so because "we also have to consider the well-being of our fellow booksellers." Afraid that launching massive lawsuits against multiple booksellers would make him unpopular in the book trade, Lufei hoped that the SBG could intervene and negotiate an alternative resolution to settle the issue without going to court.[129]

On behalf of the SBG, Gao proposed a plan that would allow both parties to benefit from the unauthorized reprinting of his *Yinbingshi wenji*. To make the distinction between these two editions firm and definite, those who had been publishing the old version should retitle their book. From now on, only the new version published by Chung Hwa Books was allowed to use *Yinbingshi wenji* as its title. This would, in theory, help readers to differentiate the new edition from the reprints of the old version. To ensure the quality of their reprints of the early version, their publishers should also carefully proofread their original *shudi* master copies to correct all the possible mistakes and typos. This settlement applied only to booksellers who had published the old *Yinbingshi wenji* before 1925.[130] Since Lufei refused to file lawsuits against those who had reprinted the early edition, Liang had no choice but to accept the guild's proposal as the resolution. Even though at the time Liang was the director of the Ministry of Justice's Judge Training Institute, he could not make the state's copyright law work to his benefit. Upon accepting the guild's resolution, Liang made several demands to those who had been, and now were allowed to continue, printing the Enlightenment Books edition of *Yinbingshi wenji*, including paying him an annual *banzu* (printing-block rent) as a substitute for copyright royalties.[131] Under the SBG customary *banquan* regime, Liang did have a right to do so because he had once been the proprietor of Enlightenment Books and thus was entitled to ask those who infringed on his exclusive ownership of the *shudi* master copy to compensate him in the form of *banzu*. When the SBG, in a consultative meeting, conveyed Liang's demands to those who had reprinted the old *Yinbingshi wenji*, they were willing to satisfy all of Liang's requests regarding the paper stock they used and the title change, but they refused to pay him any form of royalty. "This title was published a long time ago," they argued;

129. Ibid.
130. SMA S313-1-121 "Zi Cai Jiuru" [To Cai Jiuru], June 26, 1926.
131. SMA S313-1-121 "Zi Gao Hanqing Cai Jiuru" [To Gao Hanqing Cai Jiuru (from Lufei)], November 13, 1926.

"since Mr. Liang had been so generous and never fussed about [royalty], please do not ask for [it] now."[132]

Liang, nonetheless, insisted on the "rent" as his deserved reward. He could accept the existence of multiple pirated editions of *Yinbingshi wenji*, as long as he received his share of the profit these pirated versions accrued. On March 10, 1927, Lufei presented Liang's plan to the SBG: Liang decided to adopt the common practice of *banquan* stamps to ensure that he received his fair share of the profit, and he asked the guild to serve as the guarantor to supervise the use of stamps. He would give the SBG ten thousand stamps, which the guild would then dstribute to the booksellers. Each stamp cost five cents, and individual booksellers could purchase them from the guild according to their needs. Embodying Liang's authorization, these stamps would turn "pirate" reprints into "authorized" ones. When booksellers acquired Liang's approval stamps from the guild, it was the SBG's responsibility to collect that five cents per copy "rent" from them for Liang.[133] This resolution was arranged neither according to the ROC Copyright Law nor entirely following the SBG's bylaws. It was a result negotiated among the author, the "authorized" publisher of the new edition, the SBG, and those who had pirated the old version. Though it increased the SBG's workload, it successfully settled a potentially complicated and massive "piracy" lawsuit.

Conclusion

This chapter reconstructs the customary "copyright" regime that Chinese booksellers in Shanghai established and enforced in the early twentieth century though their civic organizations. In 1905, their shared interests in protecting their profits and their shared concern about piracy unified the booksellers in town; and two booksellers' organizations—the SBG and the SBTA—were established. Though Shanghai booksellers had been petitioning local officials for individually granted *banquan* protection privileges since 1902, they did not embrace *banquan* solely as a privilege awarded to booksellers or authors for a book's exceptional quality or sociointellectual contributions. In the SBG's *banquan* regime, tangible *shudi* master copies and later manuscripts for new titles

132. SMA S313-1-121 "Zi Lufei Kui" [To Lufei Kui (from Gao Hanqing and Ye Mingfa)], January 26, 1927.

133. SMA S313-1-121 "Zi Cai Jiuru Gao Hanqing" [To Cai Jiuru and Gao Hanqing (from Lufei Kui)], March 10, 1927.

were the main subject of its registration, and the booksellers who possessed these means to produce books were the *banquan* owners it recognized. Incinerating in public at the Wenchang god's temple the unauthorized reprints and the material means pirates used to produce them, following the same logic, was essential for the SBG to enforce its *banquan* protection, as only by doing so could the guild eliminate the pirates' capacity to reproduce more unauthorized copies in the future. The *banquan* owner's monopoly of a particular book was achieved and ensured by the fact that he possessed the *only* means to produce that book.

While it is true that the law-like procedures, regulations, and rules that the SBG and the SBTA developed in the absence of a formal copyright law at the turn of the century had no legal validity, they continued to be enforced by the guild even after the promulgation of the Copyright Law of the Great Qing Empire. Throughout the 1910s and 1920s, this flexible *banquan* regulation mechanism remained robust in the Chessboard Street neighborhood while formal copyright laws were never fully realized owing to the continuous political chaos. Although the SBG repeatedly stated in its bylaws that it followed the "central" state's copyright law, in reality they operated their *banquan* regime parallel to the state's law and as its equal in the Chessboard Street neighborhood. "Booksellers respect each other's *banquan*," one bookseller stated in 1935. "Not only because this is part of [our] morality, but also because *banquan* accredited [by the guild] is equal to the law."[134]

The SBG's capacity for punishing pirates was recognized not only by the inhabitants of the Chessboard Street neighborhood but also by foreign publishers and authors operating in the city. In the first half of the twentieth century, the copyright of foreign publishers and authors was protected in China according to the Renewed Sino-American Treaty of Commerce and Navigation of 1903. The copyright clause in this treaty, as I discussed in chapter 4, spurred some Chinese publishers on to request a domestic copyright law, as they worried that the treaty protection exclusively for foreigners would put them at a competitive disadvantage. As it turned out, however, this copyright clause was flawed and did not outlaw the unauthorized reprinting of most foreign books in China.[135] Unable to receive the legal protection they desired from the treaty, some

134. SMA S313-2-11 "Zi Shanghai shi shuye tongye gonghui" [To Shanghai City Booksellers' Guild (from Ding Yunting)], March 8, 1935.

135. For a discussion of the flaws in this treaty and the foreign publishers' struggle with Chinese piracy in the early twentieth century, see Wang, "Partnering with Your Pirate."

frustrated Anglo-American publishers, authors, and book dealers in Shanghai decided to imitate the SBG's self-regulation mechanism and copyright register. In 1914, they set up the International Publishers' Association—a copycat of the Chinese guild—to protect their copyrights against local piracy on their own. In its prospectus and news releases, it proclaimed that since 80 percent of the Chinese publishing community had joined their organization, their Chinese members would constitute a "strong enough" presence in the "local guild" and thus extend the SBG's copyright protection to the members of the International Publishers' Association. It also promised its members that copyright infringements would be stopped under the rules of the local guild.[136] This copycat organization was never fully realized because no Chinese actually joined it.[137] Nonetheless, this intriguing proposal indicates the perceived power of the SBG's *banquan* regime, in comparison with the formal treaty and law—a power so great that foreign publishers were willing to abandon their treaty privileges for copyright, and to adopt the customary and local mechanisms to deal with piracy.

This vibrant self-regulation mechanism established by Shanghai booksellers was, however, very local. The SBG's *banquan* regime, as shown in this chapter, relied on the Shanghai booksellers' common civility and interpersonal connections, intertwined with the social fabric and the compact sphere of the Chessboard Street neighborhood. Without these shared interests, bonds, and customs, it would have been difficult for the guild to attract the level of collaboration outside of Shanghai that they enjoyed in Li Difan's case. The dissatisfactory outcome of the lawsuits Commercial Press filed against provincial pirates in 1912–1913, on the other hand, shows that, even though the formal copyright law might have had little real force, it was the only legal means for Shanghai booksellers facing pirates beyond the Chessboard Street neighborhood.

In 1928, when the SBG, the SBTA, and some smaller guilds merged to become the new Shanghai Booksellers' Guild, this new organization carried on the SBG's *banquan* regime and inherited its geographical limitation. Having little

136. "The International Publishers' Association: Prospectus," 03-43-013-04-006; Waijiao bu dangan.

137. "Shanghai shuye shanghui huitong bing yi jian: waiguo shushang yaoqiu xiangyou banquan fanghai jiaoyu gongshang qiantu kenqing boju yo" [Petition from the Shanghai Bookseller's Trade Association Directorates: Foreign booksellers' request for copyright protection is harmful to the future of education and commerce; please reject their request], July 27, 1914, 03-43-013-04-001; Waijiao bu dangan.

faith in the state's enforcement of copyright law, in the 1930s Shanghai booksellers urged the new SBG to extend its *banquan* protection to other parts of China. As the Shanghai booksellers now became *the* dominant force in China's domestic publishing industry, the new SBG decided to take unusual measures to crack down on pirates outside of Shanghai to protect its members' property and interest: it established a private detective force in northern China to hunt those who violated the *banquan* rules of Chessboard Street.

6

Hunting Pirates in Beiping

IN AN INCONSPICUOUS house located in a side alley of the antique-book district *Liulichang* (Lazurite workshop) in Beiping,[1] the SBG set up an unusual private police force to combat piracy. Throughout the 1930s, its Beiping Office of the Piracy Investigation Committee (*Shanghai shuye tongye gonghui chajiu weiban weiyuanhui zhuping banshichu*, abbreviated as the Detective Branch hereafter) hunted down pirates in the old capital and beyond. Even though these would-be law enforcers had no legal jurisdiction over such matters, the Detective Branch staff tirelessly pursued those who violated the SBG members' copyright, and punished them with their own means.

Indeed, similar private-policing units to protect IPR had just emerged in early twentieth-century England and the United States, but the Detective Branch may have been the first attempt of this sort in East Asia. Equally unusual is the fact that it was a branch the SBG established in *another* city. Traditional guilds and trade associations in China, profession- or native-place-oriented, were known for their strong territoriality. They looked after only their own members and regulated markets exclusively in their own city and its vicinity. Although city-wide collaboration among guilds for the public interest could be spotted in the late Qing,[2] the goings-on in another municipality would be considered the business of that city's civic organizations. What the SBG did in the 1930s, however, goes beyond our conventional understanding of Chinese guilds: they

1. The name of this city, now known as Beijing北京, changed through time. In this book, I use "Beiping" (Northern Peace 北平), the term used from 1928 to 1949; when mentioning its past as the capital city of China, I use "Peking."

2. See William Rowe's two books on Hankow, especially *Hankow: Conflict and Community in a Chinese City.*

stepped into the center of another book trade and policed nonmembers, despite the fact that Beiping had its own booksellers' guilds.[3]

The Detective Branch's antipiracy operation in Beiping constitutes in itself a unique story, but its real significance lies in the possibility it opens up for us to understand the detection, enforcement, and negotiation that mediated the intellectual property law and its effect in early twentieth-century China, when different conceptions and practices of copyright grew intertwined. Operating in the gray area between legality and illegality, the staff of the Detective Branch inspected bookshops in the old capital city and surrounding market towns; launched raids, partnering with local police, to crack down on piracy; and, sometimes, resorted to criminal activities themselves, such as fraud, bribery, or home intrusion, to ensure their success. To impose the SBG customary copyright regulation on provincial pirates who shared no social bonds with the Chessboard Street neighborhood, these detectives learned to manipulate the state's law, courts, and police force to back up their extralegal actions.

Shanghai Booksellers Going National

While most Shanghai booksellers set up their businesses close to one another in the Chessboard Street neighborhood, their direct influence reached far beyond Shanghai. By the 1920s, Shanghai publications prevailed in major urban centers in China, and Shanghai print capitalists edged out smaller regional publishers. As its members became the dominating force in the national publishing business, the SBG's task of protecting *banquan*/copyright also evolved into something far more complicated than what its founders had initially envisioned two decades earlier.

Since the introduction of a modern general educational system in the first decade of the twentieth century, the capital of Shanghai firms specialized in textbook publishing had been growing exponentially, as had the scale of their business transactions.[4] According to the statistics compiled by Wang Yunwu (1888–1979), the three leading publishers in Shanghai—Commercial Press, Chung Hwa Books, and World Books (*Shijie shuju*)—accounted for

---

3. Peking/Beiping had a strong tradition of guilds. Many early studies of Chinese guilds used Peking as their research site; see Burgess, *The Guilds of Peking*, and Niida, *Chūgoku no shakai to girudo*. For more recent studies of civic organizations in Peking, see Strand, *Rickshaw Beijing*.

4. Reed, *Gutenberg in Shanghai*, chap. 5.

TABLE 6.1. Newly Published Titles by Major Publishers (1927 to 1936)

	Commercial Press	Chung Hwa Books	World Books	Total of the big three	National total
1927	842	159	323	1,323	n/a
1928	854	356	359	1,569	n/a
1929	1,040	541	483	2,064	n/a
1930	957	527	339	1,823	n/a
1931	787	440	354	1,581	n/a
1932	61	608	317	986	n/a
1933	1,430	262	571	2,263	n/a
1934	2,793 (45%)	482	511	3,786 (61%)	6,197
1935	4,293 (46%)	1,068	391	5,752 (62%)	9,223
1936	4,938 (52%)	1,548	231	6,717 (71%)	9,438

Source: Wang Yunwu, "Shinian lai de Zhongguo chuban shiye" [The Chinese publishing business in the past decade] (1937), in Zhang ed., Zhongguo xiandai chuban shiliao, 2:336–337.

60–70 percent of newly published titles in China from 1928 to 1937 (see table 6.1).[5] Though Wang, then the general manager of Commercial Press, might have exaggerated the market influence of his company,[6] other accounts at the time accorded with the general trend his statistics suggested. For instance, a 1934 sociological survey of book stands and book-rental shops in Kaifeng discovered that the popular novels, songbooks, and illustrated novels available to local readers were almost exclusively from Shanghai.[7] National statistics from 1937 also reveal that over 86 percent of books published in China were produced in Shanghai.[8]

How were the Shanghai publications circulated nationwide? Not only did provincial wholesalers come to Chessboard Street to purchase the latest textbooks and best sellers, but Shanghai firms also established a national distribution network by opening regional branches. By 1930, for instance, Commercial Press had established thirty-six branches, creating a presence in almost every

5. Wang, "Shinian lai de Zhongguo chuban shiye" [Chinese publishing business in the past ten years] (1937), in Zhongguo xiandai chuban shiliao, 2:335–352.

6. For example, Zhang Jinglu had strong doubts about these statistics and believed that Wang had overstated the scale of Commercial Press's business. See his comment in Zhongguo xiandai chuban shiliao, 2:352.

7. Zhang Luqian, "Xiangguosi minzhong duwu diaocha" [Survey of the pupular readings sold in Xiangguo Tample] (1934), in Li Wenhai ed., Minguo shiqi shehui diaocha congbian. Wenjiao shiye juan (Fuzhou: Fujian jiao yu chu ban she, 2004).

8. Reed, Gutenberg in Shanghai, 207.

major urban center in China.[9] Chung Hwa Books had thirty-nine branches,[10] and Modern Books (*Xiandai shuju*) had sixteen.[11] Even the more conservative Sweeping-Leaves Studio established five branches in the middle and lower Yangtze regions.[12] Meanwhile, smaller publishers could consign their books for sale either to major firms' branches or to individual local bookstores. In conjunction with their expanding branch networks, Shanghai booksellers regularly sent out salesmen and catalogs to broaden their customer base; beginning in the late 1910s, many also provided mail-order service to provincial readers. Challenging the existing territorial boundaries of local book trades, these new services sparked the emergence of a transregional (if not national) book market dominated by Shanghai booksellers.

Operating outside of Chessboard Street, the branch managers of these Shanghai publishing enterprises had to find ways to blend into the local settings. They often set up their branch storefronts in the traditional book districts, such as Liulichang in Beiping, *Simenkuo* and Jiaotong Street (*Jiaotong lu*) in Hankow, or South Grand Street (*Nandajie*) in Fuzhou. Shanghai-based firms also tended to open their branches close to one another to create synergy.[13] Opening branches in the traditional book districts of other cities indicated their familiarity with the cultural geography of other regional book trades. Many branch managers also signaled that they preferred to join existing networks, rather than set up a new authority, by participating in the local booksellers' guilds. For instance, the manager of Commercial Press's Sichuan branch considered joining the local booksellers' guild as a friendly sign that his firm actively participated in local affairs. Such endeavors, however, were often understood differently by the locals. In Hankow, as one bookseller recalled, although the locals

9. This does not include its headquarters on Fuzhou Road and the two branches in Shanghai. Two of these thirty-six branches were actually outside of China: Hong Kong and Singapore; the Beijing Branch and Hong Kong Branch had their own printing factories. Shangwu yinshuguan, ed., *Shangwu Yinshuguan zhilue*, 16–17; Zhuang Yu, "Zuijin sanshiwu nian zhi Shangwu yinshuguan" [The development of Commercial Press in the past thirty-five years] in Shangwu yinshuguan, ed., *Zuijin sanshiwu nian zhi Zhongguo jiaoyu*, 35.

10. *Zhonghua Shuju tushu mulu zhongbian di er hao*. Chung Hwa Books also had branches in Hong Kong and Singapore. Interestingly, they opened three branches in Nanjing.

11. *Xiandai shuju chuban shunu*.

12. On the history of Sweeping-Leaves Studio, see Yang, *Saoye shanfang shi yanjiu*.

13. Shu Xingwen, "Jiaotong lu wenhua yitiao jie." "Shuye maoyi" [Book trade], in Zeng Zhaoxiang and Yu Xinyan, eds., *Hubei jingji maoyi shiliao xuanji di si ji* (Wuhan: Faxing Hubei sheng zhi maoyi zhi bianji shi, 1984), 63.

(*benbang*, home gang) and the Shanghainese (*yangbang/shibang*, "Western" gang/lithographic gang) seemed to get along well in the guild meetings, they surreptitiously sought ways to compete with one another. Some Hankow booksellers even got together at a teahouse every Friday to brainstorm plans to sabotage the Shanghainese.[14]

Despite the locals' reservations, these branch managers actively participated in the local guilds' politics and, by the 1930s, often sat on the guilds' boards. When the Detective Branch decided to abandon their Beiping office at the breakout of the Sino-Japanese War in 1937, they entrusted their properties to the Beiping Booksellers' Guild. Half of the board members who officially verified the Detective Branch inventory were branch managers of Shanghai firms.[15] One Beiping bookseller even claimed that throughout the 1930s, the daily operations of the Beiping Booksellers' Guild were mostly controlled by Shanghainese.[16]

If the branch managers of Shanghai-based firms were leaders of regional booksellers' guilds, it may be fair to say that the SBG, whose board was composed of the "bosses" of these branch managers, was no longer a "regional" guild, but *the* guild, dominating all local booksellers' guilds in China. But this feature did not automatically extend the SBG's "copyright" regime to other localities. As discussed in chapter 5, the "copyright" regime established by the Shanghai booksellers was an intimate one relying on their common yearning for market order as well as their communal belief in self-regulation and peer pressure. Even though they were fortified by their dominant capital, their control of the book supply, and their extensive business network, there was no guarantee that Shanghai booksellers could easily extend their local "copyright" regime nationwide.

Newcomers and Their Crisis

While the scale of the Shanghai book trade expanded throughout the 1910s and 1920s, cultural trends in China changed significantly too. "New book" (*xinshu*), the phrase used to refer to either (1) new imprints, which stood in contrast to

14. Jianqin, "Tongyijie de tushu shi chang."

15. SMA S313-1-11-43, "Diaocha fanban weiyuanhui zhu Ping banshichu wenjian shuji jiaju yijiao qingce" [The Detective Branch's invoices for property transfer: documents, books, and furniture], November 1, 1937.

16. Zong Shi, "Qingdai yilai Beijing shuye," 65.

used and antique books, or (2) books about New Learning at the turn of the century, had been redefined by the New Culture Movement to refer to books on science, democracy, free love, socialism, and the like.[17] This new trend not only obliged leading Shanghai publishers to work more closely with intellectuals and university professors based in Peking but also brought about a new type of bookseller in Shanghai.

Though the New Culture Movement started at Peking University, it was the Shanghai booksellers who capitalized on Mr. Science and Mr. Democracy. Between 1918 and 1920, hundreds of small periodicals and publishing houses mushroomed in the wake of the movement. Driven by young students' enthusiasm, they produced works echoing, if not mimicking, those written by the leading intellectuals at Peking University on *Xin qingnian* (*La Jeunesse*; New youth) and called for individualism, rational thinking, and vernacular literature. These micro cultural enterprises rapidly changed educated readers' preferences and affected the sale of Shanghai publications, but most of them vanished within months owing to the lack of personnel and financial support. *Xinchao* (The renaissance), the monthly magazine run by May Fourth Movement student leaders, was in 1919 comparable to Commercial Press's flagship magazine *Dongfang zazhi* (The Eastern miscellany) in its sales volume, but it faced an acute management crisis when most of its members graduated from college. On the other hand, Shanghai print capitalists, such as Commercial Press and Chung Hwa Books, which were criticized by the May Fourth intellectuals as too philistine, acknowledged the potential profit the New Culture Movement could generate. Between 1920 and 1921, they repositioned themselves as promoters of May Fourth ideas, hired young intellectuals with May Fourth connections, like Mao Dun, as their editors, and commissioned famous Peking University professors to initiate new book series. By doing so, they popularized the New Culture Movement agenda while pocketing most of the profits from these ventures.[18]

In the post–May Fourth years, the Chessboard Street neighborhood also saw the arrival of two types of newcomers. They quickly became the most active members urging the SBG to extend their "copyright" protection beyond Shanghai. The first type of newcomers built their business mainly on the sale of May

17. "Fakan ci" [editor's opening statement], *ZGXSYB* 1:1 (December 1930): 1. Gu Cuifeng and Hua Juangong, "Xiantian buzu houtian shitiao de xiandai chubanjie" [The modern publishing business is congenitally inadequate and ill-educated], *ZGXSYB* 1:6.7 (May 1931): 1–5.

18. For example, Wang, *Qikan, Chuban, yu Wenhua Bianqian*. Also see Culp, *Articulating Citizenship: Civil Education and Student Politics in Southeastern China, 1912–1940*.

Fourth cultural stars' works. Yadong Library (*Yadong tushuguan*), for instance, was a small firm when it started to publish *Xin qingnian* in 1917. Owing to the close friendship between its owner, Wang Mengzou (1877–1953), and Chen Duxiu (1879–1942), it had been the exclusive publisher of both Chen and Hu Shi (1891–1962), the two leading public intellectuals of the May Fourth era. Beixin Books (*Beixin shuju*) was the brainchild of Li Xiaofeng (1897–1971), the last editor in chief of the famous *Xinchao*. Relocated to Shanghai in 1926 to escape from Peking's increasingly harsh environment for liberal intellectuals, Beixin successfully made its name by publishing Lu Xun's works. The second kind of newcomers comprised those who promoted popular literature that was criticized by the May Fourth intellectuals but celebrated by urban readers. They published tearjerker romances, detective stories, historical novels, and other highly entertaining books to feed the demands of a popular market.[19] For example, Three-Friends Books (*Sanyou shuju*) made a vast fortune by selling the blockbuster romances of Mandarin Ducks and Butterflies School star Zhang Henshui (1895–1967). Benefit-Enhancing Books (*Guangyi shuju*) cornered the market on cheap editions of traditional novels across the nation.

These newcomers were particularly vulnerable to piracy because of their business model. Unlike the all-around Shanghai booksellers established around the 1900s, most of these newcomers had no in-house printers (or printing department) and thus had to commission printing houses to produce their books. Outsourcing printing meant that others could have access to the manuscript, stereotype, or master copy of their books, and the printing houses they commissioned could easily "pirate" their books using the "authentic" original. Their business relied mainly upon the sale of blockbuster titles or star authors' works. They were able to gain considerable profit in the short term by selling just a handful of best sellers, but if their moneymakers were pirated, the whole business would suffer severely.[20]

Yadong Library's struggle with piracy illustrates this problem well. This midsize publisher, as shown in figure 6.1, was able to maintain a desirable margin of profit after the peak of the New Culture Movement. However, the widespread piracy of *Hu Shi wencun* (The collected works of Hi Shi), *Duxiu wencun* (The collected works of Chen Duxiu), and *Baihua shuxin* (Vernacular letters) resulted in a deficit because most of the firm's profit was derived from the sale of this

19. For the rise of popular fiction in early twentieth-century China, see Link, *Mandarin Ducks and Butterflies*.

20. SMA, S313-1-8-137.

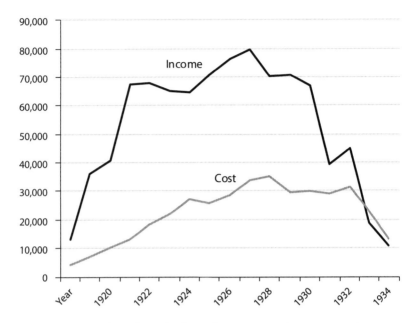

FIG. 6.1. Balance sheet of Yadong Library, 1919–1937 (income in yuan).
Source: Yadong tushugaun yu Chen Duxiu (Shanghai: Xuelin chubanshe, 2006).

handful of best sellers. Wang Yuanfang (1897–1980), nephew of Wang Meng-zou and manager of Yadong Library, estimated that only between ten and twenty of the total one hundred titles they published over the years had "market value." So, when even the printing house they had commissioned was pirating their moneymakers in the late 1920s, their annual profit dropped sharply. Eventually, by 1934, their once-booming business was in debt.

Beiping: Becoming the Capital of Piracy

When Nagasawa Kikuya (1902–1980), who later became a well-known Sinologist and bibliographer in postwar Japan, made a return visit to Beiping in 1931, he quickly noticed the widespread piracy of Shanghai books in Beiping:[21]

21. Nagasawa Kikuya visited the city seven times between 1923 and 1932 and stayed for months during each visit. As a researcher and also a buyer representing the Mitsubishi group for Seikado Bunko, he soon became a foreign "insider" in the Chinese book market, especially the rare book market in Beiping.

With orange, gray, or red covers, copies of pirated popular Shanghai publications were flourishing everywhere in marketplaces this year. . . . Though prohibitions against piracy had been repeated several times, actual enforcement [of these orders] was never seen.[22]

What he observed was precisely what was increasingly alarming Shanghai booksellers, particularly those newcomers who blamed piracy for jeopardizing their business.[23] This new development was also the main reason the SBG established its Detective Branch *in* Beiping.

As the Shanghai booksellers expanded their business nationwide, provincial piracy became an increasing concern for both individual firms and the SBG. Earlier in the 1910s and 1920s, they did not make systematic efforts to target provincial pirates, perhaps because of the recurrent civil wars and the relatively mild urgency they felt then. Back in 1912–1913, Commercial Press, probably to test the new republic's legal capacity, brought an extensive set of lawsuits for piracy against thirty-two booksellers across the nation, but these cases did not yield any desirable outcome and remained largely unsettled.[24] Throughout the 1910s and 1920s, the SBG did petition the major warlords individually, asking for recognition and protection of its members' "copyright." But these petitions more closely resemble polite notifications, replete with guild's formality, than aggressive demands for real enforcement from those regional military powerhouses.[25]

In the early 1930s, however, things changed. In 1928, Chiang Kai-shek's Nationalist government had just nominally unified the nation. Although it might have actually controlled only some major urban centers and the lower Yangtze region, it encouraged optimistic hopes that Chiang's government could impose stable law and order nationwide. Second, as Shanghai publishers extended their distribution networks to major cities and regional book-trade centers in China, combating provincial piracy would have increased importance in their national business planning. And, perhaps most importantly, pirates' "business model" evolved over time too. Some Shanghai publishers complained that they had become more "professional" and well-organized than ever. Popular titles in

22. Nagasawa, "Chūka minkoku shorin ichibetsu hosei," 38.

23. For example, see the discussions about establishing the Guild of New Book Business in 1928–1929 in SMA S313-1-8-1 or the compliance of Beixin Bookstore and Yadong Library in 1932 in SMA S313-2-14, 1–2, June 9, 1932.

24. *Neiwubu tonggao zhengfu gongbao*, no. 543 (November 7, 1913).

25. SMA S313-1-139-2.

Shanghai were reprinted in a systematic fashion in small batches; then these cheap reprints would be disseminated to minor towns via train, postal service, and traveling salesmen. These were no longer the casual opportunists operating in Shanghai's back alleys that the SBG had encountered earlier, but piratical enterprises with full production and distribution networks.

Beiping, China's second-largest book-trade center, was labeled by the SBG as the "devils' den" of this "new" piracy.[26] As early as 1931, Shanghai booksellers started to attack Beiping for its flourishing piracy business. Their negative assessments of the Beiping book market appeared repeatedly in national print media.[27] Beiping branch managers of Shanghai publishing firms also petitioned municipal authorities for a harsher ban on piracy.[28] But how did Beiping, such a culturally and historically renowned city, all of a sudden become the notorious capital of piracy?

The answer lies in the unique sociocultural circumstances upon which the city's book trade rested. Before losing the status of capital city and being renamed Beiping in 1928, Peking had been China's political center for centuries. During the Ming-Qing period, this imperial capital hosted the most talented literati-officials in the empire and acquired prestige in the Sinosphere realm of culture. Metropolitan bureaucrats and aristocrats in the court, examinees coming for the imperial civil examinations every three years, and envoys from Korea, Japan, and Vietnam were all readers and commissioners who shaped the basic profile of the Peking book market. This profile changed little after the 1911 Revolution. Scholars, Chinese or foreign, continued to visit Liulichang and *Longfu* Temple to treasure-hunt rare books; businesses producing cheap songbooks, illustrated novels, and daily encyclopedias still flourished at *Qianmen* (Front Gate) areas. Inheriting the position occupied by civil service examinees, students coming to Peking for higher education and career advancement

26. "Jiudu chuban jie zhi moku" [The publishing sector in the old capital is a devils' den], *ZGXSYB* 1–10/11, 31. Also see Juangong, "Kanta hengxing dao jishi de 'fanbanshu'" [Let's see how long the pirated books can tyrannize the market], *ZGXSYB* 1–8 (August 1931).

27. For example, in the spring of 1929, the Shanghai Booksellers' Guild publicly declared their stand against Beiping pirates and posted a reward (in several major newspapers in Beiping) for anyone revealing information about pirates. See S313-1-8-23, 31, March 29, 1929. Magazines like *Zhongguo xinshu yuebao* and newspapers such as *Huabei ribao, Chenao, Shen bao,* and *Guoming ribao* consistently helped the Shanghai Booksellers' Guild report news about piracy in Beiping and later also about the raids that the Detective Branch launched against pirates.

28. For the 1931 petition, see "Beijing chuban jie kaishi xiang fanban shu xia gongji ling," *ZGXSYB* 1–10:11 (November 1931).

contributed their savings to bookshops for the latest trendy titles in town. The book market remained extremely sensitive to the tastes of those in power. In 1914–1915, for instance, Yuan Kewen (1889–1931), Yuan Shikai's son and a keen rare book collector, caused the price of Song books to skyrocket. When Xu Shichang (1855–1939), president of the Beiyang government from 1918 to 1922, decided to compile a collection of late Qing poetry, the price of Qing poets' works rose at once.

When the Nationalist government officially made Nanjing the capital of the Republic in 1928, Peking, now renamed Beiping, lost its political prestige, and its economy was profoundly stricken as well. The printing industry in town, previously dependent on the numerous commissions from central government offices and high-ranking politicians, "had suffered a disastrous decline," according to a 1932 survey in *Beiping chenbao* (Beiping morning post). This survey revealed that, as the city's budget shrunk and the numbers of commissions decreased, only a few of the more than seven hundred printing houses in town could maintain regular operation. To cut costs, many started to hire unskilled child laborers as printers.[29] This recession in the Beiping printing business and the underemployed printing and publishing workforce were considered to be the main reasons for the sudden boom of piracy in town.[30] When profiling the city's industry and commerce, the Beiping municipal government even semiopenly admitted that producing piratical or illegal copies had become the major business of innumerable printing houses in town. Many struggling booksellers also turned themselves into pirates to survive, and, as a result, the "new book business" had been significantly harmed.[31]

There was a lot of temptation to become a pirate in Beiping at the time: the cost of printing was fairly low, and the return could be considerable. For a two-hundred-page book, for example, the net cost of making two thousand copies is presented in table 6.2. While the cost per copy was around 0.25 yuan, the retail price for an "authentic copy" was usually set between 0.5 and 0.6 yuan to ensure a 10 to 20 percent yield for the publisher. If copies were ordered from Shanghai through local bookstores, the final cost, including shipping and handling, would be even higher.[32] In contrast, a locally produced pirated copy would cost

29. "Wenhua zhongxin de yinshua ye" [Printing business at the cultural hub], *Beiping chenbao*, April 25, 1932, 6.

30. "Kan ta hengxing dao jishe de 'fanban shu,'" *ZGXSYB* 1–8, 1–6.

31. Wang, "Sanshi niandai chu Beiping zhi chuban ye," 69–71.

32. Ibid.

TABLE 6.2. The Cost of Making Authorized and Pirated Copies (in yuan)

	Authorized copy	Letterpress piracy	Lithographic piracy
Royalty	250	0	0
Typesetting/platemaking	70	70	40
Printing	26	24	26
Cost in paper factory	13	13	0
Paper	74	72	72
Binding	14	13	13
Collation	10	10	0
Advertisement, etc.	40	0	0
Total cost	497	212	151
Cost of each copy	0.25	0.10	0.07

Source: Juangong, "Kan ta hengxing dao jishe de 'fanban shu,'" Zhongguo xinshu yuebao 1–8, 1–6.

no more than 0.3 yuan,[33] but pirates could still extract from that low price a nearly 50 percent return.

The imbalance between supply and demand of new Shanghai books constituted another key reason for the Beiping piracy. After the city lost its primary political and military functions, higher education became the principal "business" keeping Beiping afloat during the 1930s. Half of China's colleges and universities were located in Beiping; so were the two leading Chinese research institutes, the Beiping Research Institute (*Beiping yanjiu yuan*) and Academia Sinica (*Zhongyang yanjiu yuan*), and over four hundred different schools. Together they brought Beiping more than 100,000 students and auditors, as well as a twenty-million-yuan annual income. As rental apartments, small cheap eateries, bookshops, and services catering to the students' needs were flourishing, other types of business were closing down.[34] The "new books" that students liked, if they had been locally produced, would have contributed substantially to Beiping's economy, but they were not produced in town. They were predominantly published in Shanghai and shipped to branches and retailers across China. While the demand from Beiping customers was high, the availability of the latest publications in town was constrained by the Shanghai-centered distribution network. As a result, popular titles from Shanghai were quickly sold

33. I estimate this price on the basis of the Detective Branch's account book and the catalogs made by pirates. Usually the selling price of a pirated copy would be between ten cents and forty cents.

34. Yang, *Chengshi jifeng*, 80.

out in Beiping. This gap between the low supply and the high demand in town created a great opportunity for the struggling printers who had turned to piracy to grab their slice of the pie.[35]

Operating the Pirate-Hunting Unit

The slice of pie that pirates commandeered in Beiping was perhaps too big for the Shanghai publishers to ignore. In August 1931, five Beiping branch managers of leading Shanghai firms jointly submitted a petition to the Beiping municipal government urging them to clamp down on local pirates. In this petition, they described the Beiping pirates' mode of operation and identified several markets in town as the "hot spots" for unauthorized reprints. Requesting that the government impose stricter regulation on the printing industry, the angry petitioners also hinted that they would take the matter into their own hands if the government failed to do so.[36] Following the tips offered in this petition, the Beiping Public Security Bureau (*Beiping gonganju*) quickly raided East Peace Market (*Dongan shichang*) and declared victory right away: in one bookseller's warehouse, they ferreted out 10 copies of the best-selling romance *Tixiao yinyuan* (Marriage of tears and laughs), 1,079 copies of an English book entitled *Pleasure of Sex* (*Xingle*), 1,322 copies of Zhang Jingsheng's provocative *Xingshi* (History of sexuality),[37] and 166 copies of *Xingtan* (Talking about sex).[38] All of them were pirated imprints.

The success of this raid held promise for a public-private antipiracy collaboration, but Shanghai publishers soon realized that the Public Security Bureau had no intention to operate in coordination with them on a regular basis. Despite its impressive outcome, this single act alone would not prevent pirates from going out on the street and selling cheap copies to students. If their war against Beiping piracy was to be a prolonged one, Shanghai publishers needed to have their people on the ground in Beiping to constantly protect their interests. To achieve this goal, the SBG decided to set up the Detective Branch in Liulichang,

---

35. "Kan ta hengxing dao jishe de 'fanban shu,'" *ZGXSYB* 1–8, 1–6.

36. "Beiping chuban jie kaishi xiang fanban shu xia gongji ling," *ZGXSYB* 1–10/11: 27–28.

37. *History of Sexuality* represented the first attempt in China to discuss sexuality and society from the psychoanalytic viewpoint. It was banned as soon as it was published in 1926, and its author, Zhang Jingsheng, a French-trained philosopher, was fired by Peking University because of this book.

38. "Jiudu chuban jie zhi moku," *ZGXSYB* 1–10/11, 31.

the center of the Beiping book trade. Between 1931 and 1937, from the single-story house at no. 16 Wanyuan Alley (*Wanyuan jiadao*), a small team of detectives hired by the SBG embarked on an extraordinary campaign to enforce the guild's *banquan* regime in this "capital of piracy."

Names

Outside of the SBG's own records, the Detective Branch appeared as an obscure and curious organization; its supposed superior, the Piracy Investigation Committee, left little trace even in the guild's own archives. Even more confusing is the fact that, in the government records and Beiping newspapers, there were two other national organizations allegedly founded by Shanghai-based cultural figures and publishers aiming to protect copyright in Beiping around the same time that the Detective Branch was active. Although on paper the Detective Branch, the Association of Chinese Authors and Publishers (*Zhongguo zhuzuoren chubanren xiehui*), and the Chinese Publishers' Association of Copyright Protection (*Zhongguo chubanren zhuzuoxuan baohu xiehui*) seemed to be three separate entities that happened to share the same antipiracy agenda, they were all located, intriguingly, at no. 16 Wanyuan Alley. The SBG archives suggest that these three entities shared not only a single address, but also staff and account books.[39] In other words, one organization was operating under three different names.

The Detective Branch's three names could be seen as the result of Shanghai booksellers' attempts, when expanding the SBG's copyright protection nationwide, to acquire national recognition and legitimacy for their antipiracy campaigns outside of Shanghai. In September 1932, about forty publishers, mostly Shanghai-based firms, and authors, primarily May Fourth intellectuals such as Hu Shi and Lu Xun, jointly petitioned the GMD's Beiping branch requesting permission to establish the Association of Chinese Authors and Publishers.[40] By forming an alliance between authors and publishers at a national, rather than municipal, level, this new organization could better reflect the changing reality of an emerging national book market. The petitioners also envisioned that, since both publishers and authors were welcome in this new organization, it would depart from the SBG's bookseller-oriented protection model and move toward

---

39. For example, scholars like Li Mingshan treated them as different organizations.
40. SMA S313-1-10.

one coordinating better with the author-oriented copyright law. In reality, Yu Dafu (1896–1945) was the only author who paid membership fees regularly, while all the other members were publishers.[41] In June 1933, the GMD Beiping branch turned down the application of the Association of Chinese Authors and Publishers, ruling that there was "no legal basis" on which a profession (writing) and a trade (the book industry) could form a joint civic organization. In the rejection letter, the GMD Beiping branch further pointed out that if the primary reason to establish such an organization was to deal with piracy, the SBG should be sufficient.[42] In April 1934, undertaking their second attempt, the same group of publishers petitioned the GMD Shanghai branch and local authorities for permission to establish the Chinese Publishers' Association of Copyright Protection. Authors, who were the actual copyright holders according to the law, were withdrawn from the plan, probably owing to the failure of the previous petition. This time, the petitioners emphasized solely the need to have a "national" organization for publishers since piracy had become a "national" issue.[43] The GMD Shanghai branch rejected the proposal, and, like their colleagues in Beiping, claimed that there was no need for such a duplicative organization; the publishing industry already had the SBG.[44]

The Detective Branch was not formally registered with the Nationalist government until 1935, and neither the Association of Chinese Authors and Publishers nor the Chinese Publishers' Association of Copyright Protection had received legal approval; however, when dealing with pirates, police, and local authorities, detectives in the Detective Branch used these three names interchangeably, depending on the cases they were dealing with and the victims they were representing. Throughout the 1930s, they were, interestingly, never questioned as to why they consistently changed their affiliations and whether they really had the right to raid and punish pirates in Beiping or beyond. Everyone seemed to take their antipiracy campaign to be a legitimate one. Just as its office occupied a shadowy corner in Liulichang, the Detective Branch operated in a legal gray area, using different names on different occasions, just like the pirates they were determined to catch.

41. SMA S313-2-25 and S313-1-1-10, 22.

42. S313-1-1-10, June 13, 1933.

43. S313-1-1-10 15–18, April 1934. S313-1-1-10 20, June 20, 1934.

44. SMA S313-1-1-10, 38–42 (7). Also see Shanghai publishers' request about the copyright law: SMA S313-1-1-11, S313-1-8-49, September 14, 1935; and S313-1-8-129, June 10, 1937.

Detectives

Inside the office of no. 16 Wanyuan Alley, the Detective Branch was a compact antipiracy unit comprising a handful of "investigators" (*diaocha*), two office clerks, one janitor, and one rickshaw man. Led by Shi Zuocai (1893–1957?) and later Yang Shuyi, they launched several dozen raids and campaigns to crack down on piracy in Beiping and surrounding cities in northern China through-out the 1930s.[45]

Shi Zuocai, the first chief of the Detective Branch, was an obscure figure. Like the office at no. 16 Wanyuan Alley, he also held multiple affiliations at the same time. He first appeared in the SBG archives and Beiping newspapers as the Beiping branch manager of Beixin Bookstore, but he also at times presented himself as the branch manager of Modern Bookstore. In addition to receiving a salary from the SBG, he seems to have remained on the payroll of Modern Bookstore. When dealing with Beiping pirates, he acted mostly as the head of the Detective Branch, but occasionally as the representative of the Association of Chinese Authors and Publishers too. Some records suggest that this Hangzhou native worked as an accountant in Beixin Bookstore in Shanghai, owing to his friendship with Beixin's co-owner Li Zhiyun, Li Xiaofong's younger brother.[46] According to Wang Yungfang, the manager of Yadong Library, how-ever, Shi had been employed by Beixin and Yadong since the late 1920s specifi-cally to crack down on pirates in Shanghai. And he had apparently, by that time, already acquired a certain fame as a pirate hunter. Allegedly, when he arrived in town, local pirates would start to flee to avoid being caught by him.[47] He seems to have had some policing experience before working for the SBG. At one point, he was thinking about quitting the Detective Branch to become a director of the military police somewhere. He also had a close relationship with the director general of the Beiping Public Security Bureau, as well as with high-ranking military police officials who operated in northern China, such as Li Tancai.[48]

---

45. Their supervisors in Shanghai seem to have been Li Zhiyun of Beixin Bookstore, Hong Xuefan of Xiandai Bookstore, and Zhang Xishen of Kaiming Bookstore.

46. Xiong Rong, "Lu Xun riji sheji renwu shengzu nianfen jiguan han shengping zhushih buzheng," 46.

47. Wang, *Huiyi Yadong tushuguan*.

48. SMA S313-2-14, 17 "Zhi Hong Xuefan" [To Hong Xuefan], March 27, 1933, 53–54 "Zhi Shi Liangmuo" [To Shi Liangmuo], May 8, 1934. It seems that Shi and Li, a May Fourth youth/communist turned military police officer and trusted aide to Zhang Zuolin and Zhang Xueliang,

Although these detectives left minimal paper trails, and the very limited information about them is often self-contradictory, based on what I managed to gather it seems that other detectives resembled Shi. Most of them were young men from Zhejiang with some experience related to the military and/or the police. They were not booksellers but people with particular knowledge and skills in detecting and investigating as well as connections with the social network of law and enforcement. For instance, one of their copy clerks, Jiang, graduated from an army academy and worked as a police officer in a salt-trade unit and an antismuggling squad before joining the Detective Branch.[49] They could quickly shift from the public to the private sector and vice versa. A detective named Yuan who hunted pirates with Shi in Shanghai in 1937 would later became a secret agent in Wang Jingwei's Shanghai government during the war.[50] In comparison to the salaries of police officers, these detectives were paid reasonably generously. While the average monthly salary for Beiping policemen ranged from 10 to 30 yuan, the "basic" salary of the Detective Branch staff was between 20 and 100 yuan per month.[51] Whenever the pirates they caught paid their indemnification, the detectives received 20 to 30 percent of it as their "bonus." Sometimes such bonuses could be equal to or even more than their basic salary.[52]

Detection

Although the daily routine of the Detective Branch staff involved regular patrolling of major Beiping marketplaces to look for pirated imprints of Shanghai publications, the branch's limited size meant that Shi Zuocai and his team needed helpers as their eyes and ears on the Beiping street to watch out for suspicious books and vendors in town. In addition to clerks and employees of the

---

had some bond beyond ordinary friendship. For example, Shi was in Xian when the Xian Incident, in which Li played a shadowy role, took place. See *Hu Shi riji*, 7:367.

49. SMA S313-1-109 "Jiang Gongbo," August 10, 1933.

50. SMA S313-1-8-129.

51. For discussion of police salary in Beiping, see "Gaishan jingcha daiyu mei yue zeng fanfei yi yuan" [Police payment improved: monthly meal allowance increased by one yuan] *Huabei zibao*, November 5, 1933, 6. For Beiping policemen's poor living conditions, low social status, and daily-life struggles during the 1930s, see Lao She's novel *Wo zhe yi beizi* [My life].

52. According to the 1935 bylaws, the SBG could claim 20 percent of the indemnification, the Detective Branch got 30 percent, and the remaining 50 percent would go to the victim. See SMA S313-1-11-6.

Beiping branches of Shanghai publishers, they would often hire informants to provide tips. Upon receiving a tip that certain pirated books had been spotted or sold in a particular location or by a specific individual, the Detective Branch would send out either their staff or an informant to verify the information. Following the standard procedure developed in Shanghai earlier, they would try to obtain a copy of the alleged pirated book, along with a receipt with the name of the seller and the price paid, if possible, as that was the most crucial evidence to make their case. In the process of obtaining the pirated copies, detectives, informants, or clerks of Shanghai firms sometimes set a trap, such as impersonating wholesale dealers from faraway places, to convince the pirates to take them to their printing studio or warehouse, so that they could get to the bottom of the piracy operation.

Once the Detective Branch had substantial evidence in hand, Shi or Yang would visit the local police, present himself as the representative or employee of the victim, and request police assistance in launching a raid. In theory, the Detective Branch, as a private policing agency, had no jurisdiction to search or raid suspected premises. While Shanghai booksellers, as discussed in chapter 5, do not seem to have seen entering others' studios and warehouses without proper warrants as an issue, this Chessboard Street practice would be easily considered by outsiders to be trespassing. With a police entourage, however, the Detective Branch's raid would take on an air of legitimacy. After law-enforcement authorities "formally arrested" the suspected pirates, Shi and Yang would either file lawsuits against them for the victims or offer a deal for reconciliation. As we shall see in the second half of this chapter, oftentimes the Detective Branch filed lawsuits not because they were eager to jail the pirates. For them, a lawsuit was just a tactic to pressure pirates into paying higher compensation outside of court.[53]

An ideal scenario, following the Detective Branch's playbook, would resemble the raid against Double-Righteousness Books (*Shuangyi shuju*) in 1933. After the detectives uncovered large quantities of pirated imprints in their store, the business owner and the Detective Branch quickly reached a deal, and the case was withdrawn from the police within one month. To settle the case, Double-Righteousness Books agreed to pay 1,000 yuan as compensation, which was twice the maximum fine according to the copyright law. In the end, it managed to pay out only 700 yuan, but the Detective Branch still received their

53. This set of procedures was later institutionalized in the 1935 bylaws. See SMA S313-1-11-6.

promised 200-yuan reward. Every staff member, from Shi to the rickshaw man, got a handsome bonus, roughly equal to half a month's salary.[54]

Reward did not always come so easily. Most of the time, the Detective Branch's pirate-hunting operations were costly, tiresome, and risky. To hunt down provincial pirates, the Detective Branch staff had to travel extensively. Shi also went back and forth between Shanghai and Beiping to collect necessary documentation from Shanghai booksellers and discuss major issues with the SBG leaders in person. Soon after its establishment, the escalating expenses of detecting and traveling quickly jeopardized its financial health. After downsizing its staff, cutting the payroll, and renting out half of its office, the Detective Branch even attempted to extort money from victims in the name of "reimbursing the investigation costs" or "special membership fees." To win their fights against pirates, the staff of the Detective Branch skirted the boundary between legality and illegality. They lied about their identity, broke into others' property, extorted money from individuals, and bribed officials if necessary. Meanwhile, if the pirates refused to settle the lawsuits outside of court, the legal actions against them would likely turn into drawn-out, complicated, and unrewarding burdens for the Detective Branch. It often took months, if not years, in court to get a conviction, but the punishment pirates received was rather minor (up to a 500-yuan fine or two months in jail). Some convicted pirates even received no penalty, if the judge considered their infringement too minor to punish.[55] Even when the pirates agreed to pay compensation, the Detective Branch often had a hard time recovering the compensation on time and in full, as many pirates began to miss payments or fled to the countryside soon after the settlement was made. Tricky cases could last for years and render all the effort of the detectives fruitless. When the Detective Branch suspended their operations in September 1937, many cases remained open and unsettled.

I turn now to three cases with which the Detective Branch struggled for years. By tracing the challenges the Detective Branch faced in their complicated and sometimes nasty battles against pirates, I argue that their consistent frustration was caused mainly by the gap and the tension between two copyright regimes— the civic one operated by the SBG and empowered by the collective morality of the marketplace, and the formal one backed by the weak state's law and registration program. To achieve their mission, they learned to negotiate and eventually manipulate the state's law to advance the guild's interest.

54. SMA S313-2-9.
55. SMA S313-2-14, 20–21.

East Peace Market Book Stands and Their
Ultimate Weapon

Marketplaces were the principal target of the Detective Branch's campaigns against pirates. And, among all the markets in town, East Peace Market was their "favorite" destination for raids. One-third of the Detective Branch cases discernible from the SBG archives originated in either the market or the nearby area. Located at the north end of Prince's Well Avenue (*Wangfujing dajie*) in the inner city, East Peace Market was not only the most popular shopping and entertainment destination in early twentieth-century Beiping, but also the second-largest book distribution center in town.[56] Once a cantonment of the Manchu bannermen, this 30-*mu* (roughly about 5 acres) walled space was turned into an open-air market in 1903. Soon two-story buildings with tiny storefronts (1.5 feet wide!) and simple garrets were built; narrow alleys and even hallways in theaters were packed with hawkers and temporary stands; any available space was extracted and divided up to squeeze in more businesses. By the early 1930s, the area was packed with 300 storefronts, 650-plus stands, and innumerable hawkers.[57] There were approximately 60 bookshops and many more book stands and vendors in the market. Most of them specialized in new titles, cheap discounted books, used textbooks, and used foreign books. This was where Beiping college students and professors treasure-hunted for bargain books. Several famous Republican intellectuals were also known to be regulars at East Peace Market.[58]

It was an open secret that, in East Peace Market, one could get not only cheap used books but also unauthorized lecture notes, pirated copies of Shanghai publications, and the banned "progressive" books, via "between the sleeves" (*xiu lai xiu qu*)[59] transactions. Qian Mu (1895–1990) described the under-the-table business in East Peace Market vividly in his memoir. In 1930, when he started teaching at Peking University, he decided to offer "An Academic History of the Past Three Hundred Years" (*Jin sanbainian xueshu shi*), which had been Liang

---

56. Liu, "Beijing shi shuye gohui shimo," in *Shudian gongzuo shiliao*, 4:68–69.

57. Dong Shanyuan, *Huanhui jisheng: Dongfeng shichang bashi nian* [Magnificent remembrances of a market: the eighty years of East Peace Market] (Beijing: Gongren Chubanshe, 1985). Ji, comp., "Dongan shichang jiuwen manshi."

58. To name just a few: Hu Shi, Fu Sinian, Liu Bannong, Zhou Zuoren, Zhu Ziqing, and Shen Jianshi.

59. *Huanhui jisheng*, 163–164.

Qichao's signature course at Qinghua University before he passed away in 1929. When this former provincial teacher was preparing his own version of the famous course, he decided to study how Liang himself had taught it. To obtain a copy of Liang's unpublished lecture notes, Qian followed a friend's advice and paid a visit to a particular "bookstall in the small alleys" of East Peace Market. "There will be a clerk sitting at a counter," he was instructed. "And in front of the counter, you will find a small desk. Put eighty cents on the desk; then the clerk will take out a paper package from the counter and give it to you. Don't ask any questions [of him] and don't open the package to check it." The package contained an unauthorized copy of Liang's lecture notes.[60]

The Detective Branch staff were also fully aware of these bookstalls and the vendors' shadowy business. In the autumn of 1931, they uncovered several thousand pirated copies in a warehouse near the market.[61] Later, in May 1932, they seized over two hundred pirated titles in another warehouse in Plum-Bamboo Lane (*Meizhu hutong*), which was just a minute's walk from East Peace Market. To escape being caught by the Detective Branch, the owner of the warehouse, Zhao Xunchen, fled from East Peace Market with a considerable fortune he had made from piracy.[62] But the majority of the Detective Branch's raids in East Peace Market did not lead them to the pirate's secret warehouse. They led to small book stands like the one where Qian Mu purchased Liang's lecture notes. These book stands and vendors usually carried only a small number of pirated books, and bringing lawsuits against them was oftentimes not rewarding for the Detective Branch, as the court might deem the scope of infringements too minor.

In the afternoon of February 25, 1933, for instance, detectives Yang Shuyi and Xiang Pizhen, accompanied by police, launched a raid in East Peace Market. Despite the fact that the tips they had received were promising, they managed to catch only four book stands in possession of a small number of pirated books (see table 6.3).

Since the total number of pirated copies they uncovered was small, the Detective Branch decided to close this minor case quickly by offering these four stand operators a settlement deal. As long as they pleaded guilty to the charges at the police station, promised to repent, and agreed to pay some compensation, the Detective Branch asserted, they would withdraw the case after destroying the seized books. To their surprise, the stand operators declined this deal.

60. Qian, *Bashi yi shuangqin shiyou zayi hekan*, 141.
61. "Jiudu chuban jie zhi moku," *ZGXSYB* 1:10/11, 31.
62. SMA S313-2-14, 1–6, June 9, 1932; SMA S313-2-14, 7, June 27, 1932.

TABLE 6.3. Titles Seized in East Peace Market on February 25, 1933 (in numbers of copies)

From Zhang Xingwun's stand	*Tixiao yinyuan* (Marriage of tears and joy)*	1
	Bingshin quanji (冰心全集, The complete works of Bingshin)	1
	Baihua shuxin (白話書信,Vernacular letters)	1
	Beiji guowang de qingfu (北極國王的情婦, The mistress of the north pole king)	1 (original title would be The kingdom of the north polar circle, 北極圈裡的王國*)
	Tie liu (鐵流, Iron Flow)	2
	Zhangzheng yu heping (戰爭與和平, War and peace)*	1
	Muosuolini zizhuan (墨索里尼自傳, Autobiography of Mussolini)	1
	Mei you (煤油, Kerosene)	1
	Shuipingxian xia (水平線下, Under the horizon)*	1
From Su Tingpu's stand	*Wo de daxue* (我的大學, My university)*	3
	Wenyi lunji (文藝論集, Essays on art and literature)	1
From Du Youshan's stand	*Hu Shi wencun* (胡適文存, Selected works of Hu Shi)*	4
	Guoming zhengfu waijiao shi (國民政府外交史, The diplomatic history of the Nationalist government)	1
	Muosuolini zizhuan (墨索里尼自傳, Autobiography of Mussolini)	1
From Zhang Jiuling's stand	*Baihua shuxin* (白話書信, Vernacular letters)	1
	Zhangzheng yu heping (戰爭與和平, War and peace)*	2

Source: SMA S313-2-14.

"Since they were so obstinate," Shi reported to Shanghai, "we were forced to take formal legal action."[63]

Once the Detective Branch formally brought their case against these four "pirates" in Beiping Preliminary Court, they soon found themselves trapped

63. SMA S313-2-14, 12, March 10, 1933; 8–9, March 13, 1933.

between two very different "copyright" regimes. Their job, as the SBG's employees, was to protect the copyrights recognized by the guild and the community according to the Shanghai booksellers' customs. Members of the SBG claimed "copyright" over certain books by presenting solid evidence, such as a contract with an author or a manuscript, but public announcements, such as newspaper advertisements or book catalogs, worked equally well. However, in the Nationalist government's courts, such SBG "accredited copyright" was deemed legally invalid. According to *Guomin zhengfu zhuzuoquan fa* (The National Government's Copyright Law, 1928), one could obtain copyright only via formal registration through the Ministry of the Interior. Since content review was included in the registration process, the ministry could utilize copyright registration to censor books. For each title duly registered, the ministry issued a certificate with a serial number to its publisher or author. This was the only legal voucher recognized by the court. Therefore, even if the "copyright" of a certain title was recognized by the SBG, without proper governmental registration the book would be treated as unclaimed property in court. Unauthorized printing of such unregistered books, under the 1928 National Government's Copyright Law, was not considered to be copyright infringement because there was no "copyright" to be infringed in the first place.

At the first hearing for the four stand operators on March 9, this was precisely what had happened. "The judge was particularly picky about attorney letters and certificates of [copyright] registration," Shi wrote, expressing his concerns to Hong Xuefan. Among the thirteen titles found pirated in this case, he suspected, only *Tixiao yinyuan*, *Hu Shi wencun*, and *Wo de daxue* had been properly registered. This oversight would critically weaken their case against the four pirates—in particular, their accusation against Zhang Jiuling. At Zhang's stand, they discovered only two pirated titles, but the chances of these two books' being registered was low. It was likely, Shi predicted, that Zhang might very possibly shake off the charges, and the Detective Branch's case against the four pirates collectively would be further undermined.[64]

While urging publishers of these thirteen books to send their authorizations and certificates of copyright registration, if any existed, to the Detective Branch's office at once, Shi also prepared a backup plan. After the first hearing, he further accused the four stand operators of trademark violation and obstruction

64. SMA S313-2-14, 8–9, 11–12.

of commerce, in case the charges of piracy did not stick.[65] Believing that it would be easier to win in trademark cases, the Detective Branch commonly employed the strategy of claiming business names and book titles as also part of publishers' "trademarks" and suing alleged pirates for violating those "trademarks" when producing unauthorized reprints. This was intended to compensate for their failure to render the needed certificates of copyright registration.[66]

Eventually, the Detective Branch was able to collect five copyright certificates (denoted by an asterisk in table 6.3) among the thirteen titles to keep the case going. On March 24, the prosecutor in the Beiping Preliminary Court formally prosecuted these four stand operators for copyright infringement related to five books but rejected the Detective Branch's accusation of trademark violation and obstruction of commerce.[67] Perhaps to attract more public attention to their antipiracy campaign and to the seriousness of piracy in town, Shi held a "piracy exhibition" in the Detective Branch's office immediately after the ruling. All the pirated copies they had thus far seized were put on display side by side with the "authentic" ones.[68] The publicity generated by this exhibition might have been the only satisfying reward for the Detective Branch from this case. It is unclear what kind of sentence the four pirates finally received. The last update on this case found in the SBG records indicates that in September 1933 the Detective Branch managed to get eighty yuan from them as compensation, and the whole unit received just a twenty-four-yuan bonus.[69] Considering the months of effort they put into surveilling the market, preparing the paperwork, and going to court, such a minimal cash bonus could hardly have been called a just payoff.

Indeed, calculating the costs and rewards of a case like this, one might be amused by the following irony: pirates in fact were at an advantage if the

65. S313-1-109 "Zhi ge huiyuan" [To members], March 13, 1933; S313-1-109 "Fu Shi Zoucai jun: zhanzheng yu heping zhucezheng" [Reply to Shi Zoucai: the registration certificate for *War and Peace*], March 14, 1933; S313-1-109 "Fu Shi Zoucai jun: beiji quan de wangguo zhucezheng" [Reply to Shi Zoucai: the registration certificate for *The Kingdom of the North Polar Circle*], March 18, 1933.

66. For example, SMA S313-1-109 "Zhi ge huiyuan"; "Fu Shi Zoucai jun" [Reply to Shi Zoucai], February 14, 1932; "Fu Shi Zoucai xianxheng" [Reply to Mr. Shi Zoucai], February 18, 1932. This was a common legal tactic used by foreign publishers against Chinese publishers for piracy as well.

67. SMA S313-2-14, 15–17.

68. SMA S313-2-14, 16–17.

69. SMA S313-2-9.

TABLE 6.4. New Titles Published by the Big Three and Titles Registered at the Ministry of the Interior

	Commercial Press	Chung Hwa Books	World Books	Total of the big three	National total	Total registered books
1927	842	159	323	1,323	—	0
1928	854	356	359	1,569	—	79
1929	1,040	541	483	2,064	—	414
1930	957	527	339	1,823	—	103
1931	787	440	354	1,581	—	638
1932	61	608	317	986	—	668
1933	1,430	262	571	2,263	—	943
1934	2,793 (45%)	482	511	3,786 (61%)	6,197	1,322
1935	4,293 (46%)	1,068	391	5,752 (62%)	9,223	1,196
1936	4,938 (52%)	1,548	231	6,717 (71%)	9,438	n/a

Source: Wang Yunwu, "Shinian lai de Zhongguo chuban shiye"; Qin Xiaoyi, ed., "Kangzhan qian goujia jianshe shiliao: neizheng fangmian)," *Geming wenxian* 71, 260–261.

Detective Branch decided to go to court, because the court recognized only "copyright" registered with the Ministry of the Interior, not the SBG's version. Moreover, if the Detective Branch's goal was to crack down on pirates and to recover the piracy-induced financial loss suffered by the Shanghai booksellers, filing a lawsuit might not have been the most satisfactory approach to the matter because most of them did not register their publications with the Ministry of the Interior. As a matter of fact, the majority of publications in China were not registered with the government in the 1930s. Comparing the titles published by the big three publishers with those registered at the Ministry of the Interior each year (see table 6.4), we can ascertain that only a tiny proportion of books were registered with the central state. It is true that the number of registered titles increased consistently year after year, yet it is also apparent that even the three leading firms in Shanghai (and in China as well), which tended to coop- erate with the Nationalist government to secure their textbook licenses, did not register most of their publications.

Shanghai booksellers' delay or disinterest in registering copyright with the government turned out to be the fatal disadvantage for the Detective Branch in its fight against pirates in court. Because most of their books enjoyed no copy- right protection before the law, the copyright law, in a sense, became pirates' ultimate weapon against Shi and his colleagues. Although Shi developed an al- ternative strategy, suing pirates for violation of trademark, pirates also quickly came up with a counterstrategy by slightly changing book titles or publishers' names. Some pirates went even further to utilize the copyright law to their advantage. Registering the books that they had pirated before the real publisher registered them, they were able to become the "legitimate" copyright holder and turn the real publishers "illegal."[70]

The Detective Branch's attitude toward such retail pirates changed gradually after this case. For instance, when the Detective Branch received tips again about vendors selling piratical imprints in East Peace Market in late May 1933, Shi decided to do nothing. Since most titles found pirated were not the SBG members', Shi simply passed the evidence his informant had collected to the respective victims via the guild. In his report to the SBG leadership on this incident, interestingly, he strongly urged the guild leaders to reject those victims' applications if they decided to join the guild reactively at this time. Hunting minor pirates for such opportunistic new members, he implied, would be too troublesome for the Detective Branch.[71] Later, when Yang Shuyi uncovered a small number of pirated imprints in Quanyie Market, the action he took was simple and straightforward, but it was also, strictly speaking, destructive of others' property. He just grabbed the pirated copies and tore them to pieces. Covers of the pirated copies Yang destroyed (fig. 6.2), along with the stand operator's written promise never to sell pirated imprints again, were retained for the Detective Branch's records.[72] The process involved no formal court and required no copyright certification. The case was effectively "solved" by violence.

Pirate's Honor, Detective's Honor

Pirated imprints could be found at small-time vendors in marketplaces as well as in well-established Liulichang bookstores. In the summer of 1933, Shi Zuocai encountered the mortal enemy of his pirate-hunting career: Cheng Huanqing, owner of Beiping Martial Arts Bookstore (*Beiping wuxue shuguan*). Occupying a prime corner in south Liulichang, just a few minutes away from Wanyuan Alley, Beiping Martial Arts Bookstore was a famous publisher and retailer for martial arts and military titles in town. Its proprietor, Cheng Huanqing, a former manager at Beiping Central Printing Company (*Beiping zhongyan yinshuaju*), was a respected figure in Liulichang and an executive committee

70. SMA S313-2-14, "Qingbao" [Tips], March 12, 1933; 15–16 "Zhi Hong Xuefan" [To Hong Xuefan], March 27, 1933.

71. SMA S313-2-14, May 26, 1933.

72. SMA S313-2-14, 129–137, May 14, 1937.

FIG. 6.2. Cover page of a pirated copy of *Tixiao yinyuan*
confiscated by the Detective Branch in Quanye Market in 1937.
Source: Shanghai Municipal Archives, S313-2-14.

member for the Association of the Beiping Printing Industry (*Beiping yinshuaye tongye gonghui*).[73]

On July 1, 1933, the Detective Branch, accompanied by the police, launched
a raid on Beiping Martial Arts Bookstore. They seized bundles of pirated

73. *Beijing gongye zhi: yinshua zhi*, 105–106.

copies in the back of the store and arrested a clerk named Geng Zeming. The titles uncovered on the spot included a series of military textbooks published initially by Nanjing Military Bookstore (*Nanjing junyong tushushe*), a few moderate socialist titles published by Shanghai publishers, and several banned books—"indecent" ones like *Xingshi*, "reactionary" ones such as *Zhongguo dagemingshi* (The history of the great Chinese revolution), and a Chinese translation of Friedrich Engels's *Anti-Dühring*.[74] Cheng was not found at the site. It was said that he had fled back to his hometown in Heibei.

From the outset, this was a complicated case for the Detective Branch. The primary victim in this case, Nanjing Military Bookstore, was not an SBG member, so the Detective Branch represented it in the capacity of the problematic Association of Chinese Authors and Publishers.[75] Owing to the banned books discovered at the spot at the same time, this piracy case was intertwined with potential offenses against sexual morality (*fanghai fenghua*) and with political subversion. After the Beiping Booksellers Guild's annual meeting in October 1933, it became further entangled with the guild's politics. Still hiding somewhere in Ji County, Cheng Huanqing was somehow elected as a member of the guild's executive committee, but so was Shi Zuocai. In the meeting, Shi challenged the election results by arguing that a notorious pirate and reactionary like Cheng should be disqualified from serving in the guild.[76] Though the guild then pronounced Cheng's elected seat invalid owing to his absence, Cheng blamed Shi for the outcome and sued him for slander. Still in exile, he published a public announcement in a Beiping newspaper asserting that Shi's claims were unfounded and demanding apology.[77] The result of this slander case was thus linked with Shi's lawsuit against Cheng for copyright violation: if Shi could not win the copyright case, he would be guilty of slander as well.

In the telegrams he sent to the court and the police, Cheng claimed that he was not a pirate. Those military books found in his shop were not for sale; he had been commissioned by a Shandong army authority to print them. As for

74. SMA S313-2-14 "Zhaochao Beiping difang fayuan jianyi ting xingshi panjue" [Copy of the ruling by the Beiping Local Court Criminal Bench], January 27, 1934.

75. SMA S313-2-14 "Nanjing junyong tushushe weituo shu" [Letter of authorization by Nanjing Military Bookstore], September 11, 1933.

76. "Shuye gonghui gaixuan zhiyuan fanyinjia dangxuan zhiwei" [Bookseller's Guild reelected committee members, pirate was elected to executive committee], *Huabei ribao*, November 7, 1933.

77. "Wuxue shuguan jingli Cheng Huanqing qichi" [Announcement by Cheng Huanqing, the manager of Martial Arts Bookstore], *Huabei ribao*, November 9, 1933.

the other titles, he and his clerk insisted that a friend had temporarily stored those in their warehouse. They had no knowledge about their contents and no intention to sell them.[78] Though the judge seemed unconvinced by their story, he cared little about piracy either. In January 1934, Cheng and Geng were sentenced, respectively, to three-month and two-month prison terms plus five-hundred-yuan and one-hundred-yuan fines, not for piracy, but for distributing "indecent imprints." The charges of piracy were dropped, the judge ruled, because Nanjing Military Bookstore had failed to register the affected eight textbooks with the Ministry of the Interior.[79]

Upset by this result, both Cheng and Shi tried to appeal. Cheng, still hiding out in Ji County and, intriguingly, never being visited by police, kept sending telegrams and Beiping Martial Arts Bookstore's account books, along with some receipts, to the legal authorities in Beiping. He tried to convince the court that it had been his "friends" storing those pirated copies in their warehouse by presenting the "evidence." But the judge rejected their appeal, because one of the "friends" Geng identified as a "real pirate" had died long ago, and another was just Geng's childhood buddy.[80] On the other hand, Shi, after consulting with his friend Li Tancai, a high-ranking military police official, decided to reframe the case in two ways. First, to overcome the fact that Nanjing Military Bookstore had not registered their books at the Ministry of the Interior, he argued that it actually hadn't needed to do so. Because it was directly commissioned by the Military Committee of the Nationalist government (Guomin zhengfu junshi weiyuanhui) to publish those military textbooks, the copyrights of those textbooks were acknowledged and protected by the Military Committee, the highest political-military authority of the nation, automatically. Second, to make a conviction stick to Cheng, Shi made a crucial choice to employ censorship as his weapon. Cheng and Geng were not just "scum in the book trade (shuye de bailei)," he now claimed, but part of a subversive conspiracy. They were reactionary figures who allied with "bandit communists" (feigong), produced antigovernment books, and attempted to harm the nation.[81]

78. SMA S313-2-14, January 27, 1934.

79. Ibid.

80. SMA S313-2-14, 63.

81. SMA S313-2-14 "Zhi Shi Liangmo" [To Shi Liangmo], May 8, 1934; "Shangsu Cheng Huanqing deng zhuanggao chaojian" [Copies of the appeal petitions for the Cheng Huanqing case], May 9, 1934.

It was not uncommon for the Detective Branch to uncover pirated imprints and banned titles at the same time in their raids, but eliminating banned books was never their job. They occasionally brought up this issue only to entice police officers to join detectives on raids against pirates. In Shanghai, throughout the 1930s, the SBG took a clear stand against the Nationalist Government's Publication Law and its increasingly intensified censorship and press control. The government's changing standards and poor censorship skills made it difficult for publishers to plan their publishing program, as many currently "banned" titles had once been "legally" published. Many worried that their investments would crumble into dust owing to the government's unpredictable press control.[82] However, one thing was certain: the Nationalist government and local police forces had become ever more obsessed with political policing, particularly to suppress the Communists.[83] Facing slick pirates like Cheng Huanqing, the Detective Branch decided to use the press control the SBG disliked to strike them down.

Although Shi's first tactic didn't work—the judge even withdrew the piracy account at once—the second tactic worked wonders: upon moving to the High Court in the summer of 1934, the case had been transformed into a trial against the "reactionary," rather than the pirate, Cheng Huanqing. Cheng was put on the most-wanted list.[84] Yet the slander case was another story. No conclusion had yet been reached in the copyright case, so there was no court sentence that Shi could cite to prove Cheng guilty of piracy. Meanwhile, Cheng's lawyers had solid evidence in hand—Shi's accusation against Cheng at the guild's annual meeting was published in newspapers. Eventually Shi was sentenced to pay four hundred yuan for having maliciously spread false statements and damaging Cheng's reputation.[85]

Now it was Shi's turn to protect his reputation and his authority as a pirate hunter. According to Shi, even if Cheng claimed to be sick, bedridden in his hometown, and never appeared in court, he had managed to stir things up in

82. Lu Xun, *Qiejie Ting zawen*, 2. Also see *Shenbao nianjian* [Shenbao Yearbook] (1935), *Zhongguo jinxiandai chuban shiliao xindai jin bian*, and *Zhongguo jindai wentan zaihuo lu*.

83. Wakeman, *Policing Shanghai*, chap. 10.

84. SMA S313-2-14 "Zhi zhongguo chubanren xiehui" [To the Chinese Publishers' Association], May 25, 1934; "Zhaochao Beiping Hebei gaodeng fayuan diyi fenyuan xingshi panjue ershi er niandu shang zi di liushi liu hao" [Copy of the Beiping Hebei High Court No. 1 Branch criminal bench ruling, the twenty-second year of ROC, Category Shang, No. 66], June 30, 1934.

85. SMA S313-2-14 "Zhi zhongguo chubanren xiehui," May 25, 1934.

Beiping and remotely direct his lawyer to "influence" the judge in charge of the slander case. After lodging a complaint with SBG leader Hong Xuefan, asserting that he would "fight back without any reservation" for his honor, Shi withdrew three hundred yuan from the Detective Branch's account and handed it over to the Detective Branch's lawyers to "move things forward."[86] Very likely, the money was used to bribe someone who could "move things." In late June 1934, the trial took an unexplained U-turn: Shi was found not guilty, and Cheng's lawyers withdrew their case at once.[87]

Detective Shi's honor was saved, but the copyright case against Cheng never came to a definite end. Geng was released on bail in June 1934.[88] Cheng seems to have remained a free man in the countryside but did not dare to come back to Beiping. When Shi ceded the directorship of the Detective Branch to Yang in summer 1935, both predicted sarcastically that their antipiracy mission would soon be accomplished after Cheng's case concluded. Nevertheless, when Yang decided to suspend the operation of the Detective Branch in 1937 in the wake of the Sino-Japanese War, Cheng's case remained unclosed.

The Pirate King of Gathering-Jade Studio

On August 9, 1933, in downtown Baoding, a city ninety miles southwest of Beiping, a man purchased a copy of the best-selling romance *Tixiao yinyuan* at a bookstore called Gathering-Jade Studio (*Qunyu shanfang*). He asked for a receipt, but the clerk resolutely refused and was willing to write down only "Gathering-Jade Studio, 40 cents" on the wrapping paper.[89] This insignificant exchange exemplifies the tedious daily wrestling between pirates and informers. Purchase receipts, as discussed earlier, were most crucial for Shanghai booksellers seeking to make a solid case against pirates; while the informant was determined to get the suspect to produce this hard evidence, the pirate or retailers of pirated imprints would do their best not to leave any potentially incriminating record of the transactions. In this case, the *Tixiao yinyuan* that the man purchased was a pirated copy, and he was, in fact, not a bona fide customer

---

86. SMA S313-2-14 "Zhi Hong Xuefan" [To Hong Xuefan], also see S313-2-9.

87. SMA S313-2-14 "Zhi Shi Liangmou" [To Shi Liangmou], June 10, 1934.

88. The time he was detained in jail was actually far longer than the sentence he received at that point.

89. SMA S313-1-109, September 25, 1933; SMA S313-2-14 "Zhi Li Zhiyun" [To Li Zhiyun], September 18, 1933.

but a local informant the Detective Branch had hired one week earlier. His mission: to prove that Gathering-Jade Studio, the largest bookstore in Baoding, was the headquarters of an extensive piracy business.

Previously, in late July, Shi Zuocai and Yang Shuyi had gone to Anguo, an herbal medicine distribution hub a hundred miles from Beiping, following a lead from Chung Hwa Books that their textbooks were pirated there. In Anguo, they quickly found the alleged pirate, Huasheng Printing House (*Huasheng yinshuju*), and uncovered four bundles of unbound pages in its store. Its manager and clerk were immediately arrested by local police, and its proprietor promptly paid a three-hundred-yuan compensation and promised that they would never pirate again.[90] As the case was closed earlier than they had anticipated, Shi and Yang decided to check out other bookstores in Anguo. They soon realized that they had accidentally come across something big: "There are only five bookshops in this town," Shi stated in his August 4 report to Chung Hwa Books; "all the books displayed [in these shops] are unauthorized reprints. We couldn't find even a single authentic copy of new titles." Anguo, Shi believed, was so peripheral that "pirates dare to sell reprints boldly." In total, they discovered over two hundred pirated titles, and most of them were from one single distributor: Gathering-Jade Studio in Baoding.[91]

This was a name with which the Detective Branch was familiar. Between December 1932 and February 1933, Shi had caught Fan Hauyou in Taiyuan City, Shanxi, and the Unity Store (*Tongyi shanghang*) in Zhangjiakou, Hebei, selling unauthorized reprints of Shanghai publications.[92] The pirated copies seized in these two cases were allegedly distributed to these regional retailers from Gathering-Jade Studio as well. The manager of Tongyi Store even presented a "catalog of piracy" he had acquired from Gathering-Jade Studio as evidence in court to show that they were not the originator of those reprints.[93] When Shi and Yang encountered the name of Gathering-Jade Studio again in Anguo, they decided to take action against this enterprise that apparently was selling pirated imprints all over northern China. Shi urged the Anguo police to summon Su

90. SMA S313-2-9, September 1933.

91. SMA S31-1-109 "Zhi Zhonghua shuju" [To Chung Hwa Books], August 4, 1933.

92. SMA S313-1-109 "Zhi Taiyuan Shi Zuocai" [To Taiyuan Shi Zoucai], January 4, 1933, "To the Taiyuan Local Court," January 4, 1933, "To Nanjing Bookstore," January 5, 1933, "To Zhijie Bookstore Shenzhifang," February 17, 1933, "To Tang Zangyi," February 20, 1933, "To Shi Zoucai," February 21, 1933. In both the Fan Hauyou and Tongyi stores, Shi uncovered about seventy pirated titles.

93. SMA S313-1-109, September 25, 1933.

Lantian, the manager of Gathering-Jade Studio, but the subpoena to Su was never answered.[94]

After finishing the investigation in Anguo, Shi started a monthlong pirate-hunting "tour." Though the initial purpose of this trip was to discuss the Cheng Huanqing case with Nanjing Military Bookstore and the SBG leaders in person, he stopped in Shijiazhuang, Kaifong, and Shuzhou to crack down on minor pirates along the way.[95] Meanwhile, the Detective Branch hired a local informant for sixty yuan to "secretly investigate and engage in undercover detection" (*micha zoutan*) in Baoding.[96] They hoped that the informant could collect enough concrete evidence for them to bring legal action against this slick pirate and destroy its distribution network.

Although a pirated copy with a signed receipt was the basic evidence needed to make a case, it was hard to prove, on the basis of the receipt alone, that the alleged pirate selling the book was the one producing and distributing it. For instance, in April 1934, the Detective Branch, the Old Gate Police Station (*Laozha bufang*) in Shanghai, and Life Bookstore (*Shenghuo shudian*) worked together to "nail" Chunming Bookstore (*Chunming shudian*). A Life Bookstore clerk, a student, and a police officer, disguised as customers, managed to purchase *Tixiao yinyuan* and *Zibian* (Differentiate words) from Chunming at unreasonably low prices, but they had a hard time getting receipts. One informant tailed Chunming's clerk to its sister store, Wenguang, and discovered that the owners of these two firms, the Chen brothers, had turned unauthorized reprinting of best sellers into a family business (fig. 6.3).[97] Even after the police used a marked bill to make a purchase and successfully obtained a receipt from Chunming Bookstore, they still failed to make a strong case in court. Eventually, the Chen brothers were charged with only a minor infraction—selling unauthorized reprints—though they were, in fact, the producer of them.[98]

"Gathering-Jade Studio, 40 cents," the "receipt" the informant got, thus might be too thin to convict Gathering-Jade Studio of any significant wrongdoing. It took Shi almost a month to unveil the scope of its piracy operation. Gathering-Jade Studio was originally founded by Liu Chunlin (1872–1944), the last

94. SMA S313-2-14 "Zhi Li Zhiyun," September 18, 1933.

95. SMA S313-2-9, September 1933.

96. SMA S313-2-14 "Zhi Li Zhiyun" SMA, S313-2-19, 103–104.

97. SMA S313-2-14, April 4, 1934. Later in the 1940s and 1950s, the Chens of Chunming Bookstore were also accused of piracy. For these later cases, see chapter 7.

98. SMA S313-2-14, May 4, 1934.

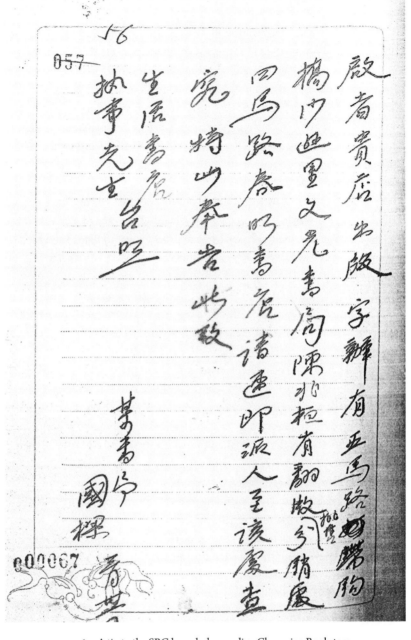

啟者貴店出版字辮有五馬路四牌樓

橋四延里又先書局陳水桓有翻做分銷處

四馬路尚有書局諸速即派人至該處查

究特此奉告此致

生店書局

執事先生台啟

茅書

國棉

FIG. 6.3. A tip to the SBG by a clerk regarding Chunming Bookstore, its sister store Wenguang Books, and their piracy operation, 1934.
Source: Shanghai Municipal Archives, S313-2-14.

person to win the top place *zhuangyuan* in the terminal civil service examination of the Qing, in the early 1910s. By the 1930s, it had been controlled chiefly by a manager named Su Lantian. Occupying a prime location in front of the train station, it was known as the leading lithographic publisher and book retailer in town. By the end of August, the informant was able to bring its backdoor business to light: behind the facade of Gathering-Jade Studio, Su Lantian ran three other firms: *Baoding shijie tushuju* (Baoding World Books), *Beiping daoqun dhudian* (Beiping Daoqun Bookstore), and *Penglai hongjishe* (Ponglai Hongji Studio). All three specialized in producing and selling a wide range of pirated works. The informant also managed to obtain a catalog of Penglai hongjishe. Su sent his catalog to neighboring counties to solicit customers for mail orders or wholesale deals.[99] This information aligned with the testimonies of the managers of Tongyi Store in Zhangjiakou, and Yanyi Books (*Yanyi shuju*) and Anguo Books (*Anguo shuju*) in Anguo County. Although disguised by other names, it was Gathering-Jade Studio that delivered these books; it was also its clerk, Wang Shuxun, who visited these bookstores monthly to collect the payments.[100]

When Shi came back to Beiping in late August, the informant had gathered enough information. On the evening of September 14, the day after the SBG board met and decided to take legal action against Gathering-Jade Studio and Su Lantian,[101] Shi and two-thirds of the Detective Branch staff took a night train to Baoding. Arriving at midnight, they slept in the train station and got ready for the day of action. Around 10 a.m. on September 15, they went directly to the Baoding police headquarters and asked for assistance to conduct a raid. Precinct chief Pong was assigned to accompany Shi and his team to search Gathering-Jade Studio. On the spot, they soon discovered various reprints, catalogs, cover pages, and over fifty volumes of ledgers under the name of Penglai Hongjishe. After Pong excused himself to attend to other business, subprecinct chief Wang Zhongqian was brought in to supervise the raid. When they were about to take the evidence back to the police station, a half dozen "husky men" suddenly showed up out of nowhere and grabbed the ledgers. Although these men claimed to be "working for the Garrison Command (*Jingbei silingbu*)," Shi thought they looked just like "ruffians (*liumang*)." In this chaotic scuffle, Wang and his colleagues failed to catch these "military police," and those men took

99. SMA S313-2-14.
100. SMA S313-1-109, September 25, 1933.
101. SMA S313-1-109, September 13, 1933.

off with most of the ledgers. Wang ordered the clerks in the shop to surrender the remaining ledger volume, but the clerks refused to do so. The two parties then were stalemated inside the shop until the police gave up at 4 p.m.; they arrested the two clerks and took the only remaining ledger volume with other reprints as evidence. The Detective Branch officially filed a lawsuit against Gathering-Jade Studio and Su Lantian for copyright infringements and robbery. Given that fact that the most potent proof of Su's piracy operation was lost, and Shi knew that the likelihood of recovering those ledgers was very slim, winning the case would be a challenge for the Detective Branch.[102]

Su Lantian, whom Shi believed to be the mastermind behind Gathering-Jade Studio's massive piracy business, was a slick figure very much like Cheng Huanqing. Like Cheng, Su was also an influential local bookseller. Su was currently the chairman of the Baoding Booksellers' Guild and a director of the Baoding Chamber of Commerce.[103] He was a previously convicted pirate too. In August 1932, he was found guilty of pirating the novel *San jianxia* (Three swordsmen)[104] when he was working at the Beiping Central Printing Company.[105] He was charged a twenty-eight-hundred-yuan indemnity as a result.[106] It seems that after this legal trouble, he fled to Baoding and started a new career at Gathering-Jade Studio. Within a year, he had reinvented himself as an important figure in Baoding's business circles, while secretly maintaining his old trade in piracy. After the dramatic raid on September 15, Su was nowhere to be found. Shi believed that "the evidence [against him] was so conclusive that he couldn't dare to show his face."[107] But it also seemed that the whole city was covering for him and helping him resist the Detective Branch's charges. The police showed little interest in finding or arresting him, while it was obvious that he was still in Baoding. Local leaders, such as the owner of *Minsheng ribao* (People's voice daily) and the chair of the Baoding Chamber of Commerce, and even the district chief, approached Shi as mediators and asked him to withdraw the case.[108]

---

102. SMA S313-2-14 "Zhi Li Zhiyun," September 18, 1933; SMA S313-1-109 "Telegram," September 15, 1933; S313-2-14 "To Shanghai Office," September 16, 1933; SMA S313-1-109 "Draft of newsletter," September 16, 1933; SMA S313-1-109, September 25, 1933.

103. SMA S313-2-14 "Zhi Li Zhiyun."

104. This was a translation of *Les Trois Mousquetaires* by Alexandre Dumas, père.

105. Interestingly, Cheng Huanqing also worked at the same company.

106. SMA S313-1-109, September 25, 1933.

107. SMA S313-2-14 "Zhi Li Zhiyun."

108. Ibid.

Despite this pushback, Shi was determined to nab Su at all costs. As Su had the backing of the Baoding local community, Shi urged the SBG leaders to harness their social influence in pressuring local governments.[109] Lu-Fei Kui, the SBG chair and the founder of Chung Hwa Books, for instance, sent out several telegrams to various government officials in Hebei to express the guild's deep "concern" regarding the Gathering-Jade Studio case.[110] Shi also started a media campaign to attract more public support by sending major newspapers a ready-to-use news release that he had written. It featured an interview with Shi and Yang, detailed the dramatic encounter between them and Gathering-Jade Studio on September 15, and cited Su's piracy business as one main reason for the general decline of the book trade in northern China. "A vast piracy network was uncovered in Baoding": soon this indictment was published in several leading news outlets.[111] Shi rejected the Baoding business leaders' suggestion that he reconcile with Su, and he prepared for a lengthy struggle instead. As a matter of fact, the Detective Branch ended up renting a house in Baoding as their temporary office.[112] From September 1933 to January 1934, Shi and most of the Detective Branch staff lived here just to pursue the Gathering-Jade Studio case.

It is not entirely clear what actions they took during their four-month stay in Baoding, but, based on the Detective Branch's accounts, one thing is certain: these detectives spent an enormous amount of money on social interactions. Of the total 990.82 yuan spent on the Gathering-Jade Studio case, one-third was for socializing and entertaining. Compared with the rent (110 yuan) and the travel expenses of five people (142.73 yuan), the expenditures going toward partying and drinking (283.412 yuan) were impressively high.[113] Among the banquets the Detective Branch hosted, there was a dinner with the Nationalist Party Hebei branch (26.3 yuan) and two dinners with Song Xingwu, a respected Beiping editor, bookseller, and mediator (41.14 yuan).[114] Assuming that the average cost for a banquet dinner was about twenty-five yuan, we might conclude that within four months the Detective Branch hosted about eleven or twelve banquets to negotiate or lobby. Those banquets paid off, and in

109. SMA S313-1-109, September 16, 1933; SMA S313-2-14 "Zhi Li Zhiyun."
110. SMA S313-1-109; SMA S313-2-14; SMA S313-1-106.
111. SMA S313-1-109, September 16, 1933 (1933.9.16).
112. SMA S313-1-109, September 25, 1933.
113. SMA S313-2-9, 103–104.
114. SMA S313-2-9.

December 1933, after Song Xingwu's mediation, the Detective Branch and Gathering-Jade Studio achieved reconciliation. Su agreed to pay a four thousand-yuan compensation; Gathering-Jade Studio signed six five-hundred-yuan-due bills and paid the first 1,000 yuan in cash in January 1934.[115] The Detective Branch packed the furniture that they had bought for the Baoding office and shipped it back to Beiping. The case was closed, at least for the moment.

Soon after the Detective Branch left Baoding, Gathering-Jade Studio ceased to make payments in full; by April, they stopped sending any money to the Detective Branch. In late May, several Beiping and Tainjing branch managers of Shanghai firms came to the Detective Branch to ask for Shi's help to collect debts from Gathering-Jade Studio. It turned out that the Detective Branch's action against Gathering-Jade Studio had created unintended consequences that broadly impacted the local book trade. According to these managers, Gathering-Jade Studio used this case as an excuse for "restructuring," and since then, Gathering-Jade Studio had fallen into arrears. Since it was the leading book retailer in Baoding, it had been ordering books from Beiping and Tainjing in large quantities. Now it refused to square accounts, and this caused deficits for those Beiping and Tainjing branches of Shanghai publishers. The payments in arrears added up and peaked at a stunning sum of 22,884 yuan.[116] On May 25, representatives of eleven firms and branches met at the Beiping Bookseller's Guild, formed a creditors' alliance, and commissioned Shi as its chair. Though prima facie, at least, this had nothing to do with piracy, Shi still decided to accept the commission, not only because Gathering-Jade Studio was behind in its compensation payments but also because most of Gathering-Jade Studio's new victims were SBG members.[117] Collectively, they filed a lawsuit against Gathering-Jade Studio in a Beiping local court on June 18.

It took almost a year for the creditors to get a court verdict, but the outcome surprised all. Su Lantian was finally found—in a jail. According to court records, only six days before Gathering-Jade Studio's creditors filed their lawsuit, this firm was suddenly shut down by the Baoding Special Public Security Bureau, for selling pirated antigovernment titles. Su Lantian was arrested and imprisoned in the Beiping Military Jail. "I'm just an associate manager," Su Lantian

---

115. SMA, S313-2-9. The copies of the due bills can be found in SMA S313-2-14.

116. SMA S313-2-14.

117. SMA S313-2-14 "Zhi Li Wunfan," May 24, 1933; "Zhi Li Wunfan," May 25, 1933, and "Zhi Shi Liangmuo yu Li Wunfan," May 25, 1933.

claimed, from the jail. "About the missed payments in the past months, I can't shed any light on the matter. As long as there are accounts to trace, we will try to pay them back." The court ordered the Wang brothers, who owned Gathering-Jade Studio, to take responsibility,[118] but the firm was bankrupt and out of business. There was little hope that they would ever shoulder the debt fully. In 1936, Song Xingwu mediated once again between the Detective Branch and Gathering-Jade Studio. The two reached a new settlement, and Gathering-Jade Studio signed yet another set of due bills.[119] However, it never paid off the remaining indemnity. When the Detective Branch left Beiping in September 1937, one of the many properties they entrusted to the Beiping Booksellers' Guild was the unpaid due bills from Gathering-Jade Studio.[120]

Conclusion

When the Detective Branch hunted down pirates in Beiping on behalf of the SBG from 1930 to 1937, their main challenge, beyond the tedious and thankless everyday detecting tasks, was how to extend the SBG's local, intimate, and customary copyright regime to the national book market its members now dominated. To achieve this goal, the detectives had to rely on the Nationalist state's copyright law and legal system to force non-Shanghai pirates to submit to the SBG's interests. Navigating between the two copyright regimes, the Detective Branch, though trying very hard to make them work for each other, often found itself trapped in the contradictions between the two or constrained by limited support from a weak state.

One main motivation of the SBG's efforts to protect their members' "copyrights" nationwide in the early 1930s was that China, after decades of civil wars, was finally unified by the Nationalist government. This unified Chinese state, however, existed more on paper than in reality. Both the central government in Nanjing and the municipal or provincial governments, with their insufficient resources and personnel, were not very active or capable of performing their legally prescribed duties or asserting their jurisdictions. Take, for example, the role police played in the Detective Branch's actions. The support they offered, as the local embodiment of state power, in most raids against pirates was to *be present* when the Detective Branch entered the pirates' shop to lend the raids

118. SMA S33-2-14.
119. SMA, S313-1-24.
120. SMA S313-1-11-43.

and the arrests of the pirates a guise of legality. Nevertheless, there was no guarantee that the police presence would work. In the raid against Gathering-Jade Studio, for instance, the police were unable to recover the vital evidence the pirates had stolen from them and the Detective Branch. Once the pirates fled to the countryside, as in the Cheng Huanqing case, the police were powerless even if the authorities knew exactly who and where the pirates were.

Constrained by the state's lax enforcement of copyright law and the SBG members' bad habit of not registering their books with the Ministry of the Interior, the Detective Branch's efforts to crack down on pirates in northern China also encountered strong local pushback when facing well-established pirates like Cheng and Su. In the eyes of the Shanghai booksellers, Cheng and Su were pirates harming their business, but, for the local community, they were business leaders and promising booksellers. Representing the interests of Shanghai booksellers, the Detective Branch, to a certain extent, was the outside invader in Beiping and on provincial booksellers' home turf. As the SBG behaved like a state in legislating and enforcing its preferred rules of the market, with the acquiescing state's blessing, provincial pirates became the embodiment of local commercial interests and needed to be sheltered from both the public authorities and the expanding national market represented by the Shanghai interests.

Against all these odds, the Detective Branch decided to employ mechanisms hated by Shanghai booksellers and the SBG themselves—censorship and press-control laws—to stop piracy. The Nationalist government, as Julia Strauss points out, was a weak state with strong institutions and unevenly distributed powers.[121] The Nationalist government and other local powers, Frederic Wakeman has shown, may have been incompetent in many aspects of law enforcement or order maintenance, but they were very interested in and very good at political policing, especially cracking down on so-called reactionaries.[122] For example, in 1933–1934, Beiping police seized thirty-five thousand copies of two thousand different "reactionary" titles. Most "antigovernment" or "reactionary" criminals who were arrested and jailed were people who either produced or circulated pro-Communist publications. By labeling them as producers of "reactionary" books, the Detective Branch turned pirates into the enemies of the state and activated the government's oppressive mechanism in their own favor.

121. Strauss, *Strong Institutions in Weak Polities.*
122. Wakeman, *Policing Shanghai.*

Politically and economically, the situation could be seen as an ordered anarchy: there was a certain level of order and the rule of law, but the recognized
public authorities did not always maintain law and order, nor were they always
respected by other actors in the market. The "law" that was enforced in a particular location might have comprised privately agreed-upon codes that were
not legitimated by the state, while the law of the state was not seen as important. One could be a legitimate businessman and a pirate at the same time, one
could be widely known to be playing the two roles, and one could keep operating in these roles for years. The central state was inadequate and duly ignored
by other actors in some cases, but it did have effective oppressive mechanisms
at its disposal. The only question was when—and for what reason—they would
be activated.

Resorting to the only adequate state-public coercive power, the political
police of the Nanjing government or its provincial counterparts could stop
known pirates in spite of local resistance. But ultimately this approach was a total
financial failure, its costs outweighing the piracy's costs to booksellers. It is ironic
that, for the profit-seeking SBG members, the only practical way to stop piracy
and to uphold "law and order" in the marketplace—which was supposed to
protect them—turned out to be counterproductive and even more damaging
than piracy.

7

A World without Piracy?

IN JANUARY 1949, the People's Liberation Army (hereafter, PLA) took over Beiping. Within a few weeks, book vendors across the city were flooded with titles on communism, such as the Chinese translation of *The Communist Manifesto* and Mao Zedong's *Xin minzhu zhuyi lun* (On new democracy). Initially seeing this as a sign of how "readers from different class backgrounds were eagerly studying our party policy,"[1] the Chinese Communist Party (hereafter, CCP) cadres in town soon realized that many of the communist books in the marketplace had not been produced by the party's official publishing organ, Xinhua Bookstore (*Xinhua shudian*). They were unauthorized reprints made by the veteran pirates in Liulichang.[2] By November, the CCP had identified fifteen pirates responsible for producing and selling over 270,000 reprints of ninety-one party publications in northern China.[3]

What these CCP cadres uncovered in their future capital city was essentially what the SBG Detective Branch had left behind in 1937: a flourishing piratical business composed of booksellers who reprinted popular titles in small batches and book vendors who would sell these reprints, at a deep discount, to urban readers. Several local pirates that the CCP confronted in 1949 were the same shadowy publishing entrepreneurs the SBG Detective Branch had struggled to hunt down in the 1930s. East Peace Market, where the detectives used to

---

1. "Quanguo chuban shiye gaikuang" [An overview of publishing business nationwide], June 6, 1949, ZRGCS, 1:118.

2. Chen Ji, "Qianjin zhong de Beiping xin shuye" [Beiping new publishing business in progress], RMRB, April 7, 1949, 2.

3. "Chuban zongshu bangongting jihua chu guanyu Beijing shi fanban shukan qingkuang de chubu diaocha baogao" [An initial investigative report by the General Publishing Administration Planning Department on book piracy in Beijing], November 1949, ZRGCS, 1:573–574.

raid regularly, remained a popular hub of cheap reprints. In the aftermath of the Second World War, the Detective Branch staff never returned to Beiping, as they had promised, to reclaim their office and resume their operation, but their old rivals seem to have survived the war and carried on their business as usual.

There was no business as usual, however, as the CCP was not the SBG. They were not anxious publishers who established their customary *banquan*/copyright regime to protect their economic interests, but an ambitious political party that considered culture and ideology essential to the success of the socialist revolution. They not only invested significantly in publishing, theater, and the arts for ideological mobilizations but also aimed to exert complete control over China's cultural economy in short order. In sharp contrast to the members of the SBG, who treasured their entrepreneurial autonomy, the CCP cadres envisioned a new state-market relationship in which their party-state in the making would be *the* visible hand regulating and directing every economic actor in the cultural market.

In the previous two chapters, we have seen how Shanghai booksellers cleverly negotiated, accommodated, and at times manipulated the changing shape of the state's authority and power to tackle piracy and protect their *banquan*/copyright in the late Qing and early Republican period. This chapter examines how the Chinese communists dealt with the booksellers' old problem—piracy—from a socialist perspective as a revolutionary party-state. It will also explore how Chinese publishers and authors, as seasoned economic actors, adjusted to and coped with the new regime and its reshaping of literary property. Rather than attempting a comprehensive study of the development of copyright legislation in the People's Republic of China (PRC), this chapter will focus on the decline of the old customary copyright mechanisms and the rise of a new socialist literary system, against the background of the profound structural changes in China's cultural economy in the 1950s.

It has often been asserted by legal scholars and political scientists interested in current IPR issues in China that since the notion of intellectual property was inconsistent with, or opposed to, the underlying principles of socialism, copyright, patents, and trademark were dismissed and virtually abolished during the Mao era (1949–1976). They have also implied that the PRC was quick to impose a wholesale transplantation of the Soviet IPR system immediately after its establishment. William Alford, for instance, argues that the Chinese adaptation of Soviet IPR laws was smooth because Soviet and traditional Chinese attitudes toward intellectual creation and innovation coincided. Both valued the public good over the individual right, and both considered government control necessary to ensure the dissemination of "good" and "useful" ideas.[4]

Convinced that the CCP's authoritarian rule allowed the party-state to execute new laws and policies forcefully, most of these scholars have also supposed that the new regime's adaptation of the Soviet model must have been swift and comprehensive. However, as recent studies of early PRC history have revealed, the 1949 divide was not as stark as we used to believe, and the transition to socialism was an extraordinarily complex process full of conflicts, contradictions, compromises, and countless trials and errors.[5] In the early 1950s, the administrative systems of this seemingly authoritative propaganda state were restrained and undermined by a lack of resources and experience. Increasingly, scholars have stressed the ways cultural producers negotiated with the state's authorities, found leeway and loopholes in the systems, and managed to carry on their old production patterns and social norms in the new political environment.[6]

Following this recent revisionist approach, this chapter focuses on three particular transitional moments in the CCP-PRC's unmaking and remaking of literary property. First, it looks at the CCP's changing attitudes toward unauthorized reprinting/piracy in 1949–1950, and the ideological dilemma they were struggling with when trying to come to terms with piracy in the formative months of the PRC. Then, by reconstructing how the reorganized SBG handled a piracy repeat offender in 1951, it examines the new party-state's attempts to redefine the nature of literary piracy in a new socialist framework via the guild's customary *banquan*/copyright regime. Finally, this chapter turns to the new remuneration system that emerged during the First Five-Year Plan (1953–1957), which aimed to provide Chinese authors with better and fairer treatment, as well as the unintended consequences and challenges the communist state faced when they tried to turn authors into workers in the collective planned economy.

4. Alford, *To Steal a Book Is an Elegant Offense*, 56–57.

5. For example, see Brown and Pickowicz, eds., *Dilemmas of Victory*; Strauss, "Introduction: In Search of PRC History."

6. See Johnson, "Beneath the Propaganda State"; Altehenger, "On Difficult New Terms"; Volland, "Cultural Entrepreneurship in the Twilight." Even during the Cultural Revolution, the supposed peak of the PRC's control over the culture, the party-state did not attain complete control over cultural production; see Mittler, *A Continuous Revolution*.

Coming to Terms with Piracy

When the CCP encountered Beiping pirates in 1949, its attitude toward the unauthorized reprinting of communist titles was ambivalent. Right before the PLA entered the city, *Renmin ribao* (People's daily), the party's official newspaper, celebrated on its front page the college students who brought "a breath of fresh air" to their campus by "making massive reprints of *Xin minzhu zhuyi lun* on their own."[7] By May, however, the CCP's newly established Publishing Committee (*Chuban weiyuanhui*) started to label reprints of communist titles found in the city's marketplace as a "problem" caused by "opportunistic booksellers."[8] To prevent these reprints from causing further "confusion and chaos," throughout the summer of 1949, they published public announcements and organized an educational forum to declare the new regime's stand against unauthorized reprinting.[9] Although they soon learned from their investigations that most of those "opportunistic booksellers" were veteran pirates in Liulichang, the CCP cadres, unlike the SBG's Detective Branch in the 1930s, never took a hard line in cracking down on piracy. By the time Mao Zedong announced the establishment of the PRC in October, these reprints had made their way to several major cities in northern and central China. In November, when the General Publishing Administration (*Chuban zongshu*; hereafter, GPA) accessed the problem, it blamed the spreading of the piratical copies of communist titles on the party's overly "generous" stance on piracy.[10]

The CCP's ambivalent attitude toward unauthorized reprinting during the formative months of the PRC reflected how this fledgling party-state struggled to come to terms with piracy while trying to advance its control over China's cultural economy. The party's lack of sufficient administrative resources and experience in an urban setting, as well as the legal vacuum caused by the regime change, undoubtedly contributed to their relatively soft handling of Beiping piracy, but what constrained their action was an ideological dilemma: reprinting books freely was a practice that the revolutionary CCP had exercised extensively,

7. "Yanjing Qinghua liang daxue chongman xin qixiang shi sheng zheng du Mao zhuxi zhuzuo" [A breath of fresh air had been brought to Yanjing University and Qinghua University as teachers and students were eagerly reading works by Chairman Mao], *RMRB*, January 12, 1949.

8. "Chuban weiyuanhui di shi ci huiyi jilu (jie lu)" [Minutes of the tenth meeting of the Publishing Committee: an excerpt], May 4, 1949, *ZRGCS*, 1:86.

9. "Chuban zongshu bangongting jihua chu guanyu Beijing shi fanban shukan qingkuang de chubu diaocha baogao," 573–574.

10. Ibid.

for practical reasons and as a form of resistance, before 1949, but it was also a practice that the new PRC regime preferred to interdict in the interest of its political legitimacy and security. Endeavoring to uphold both the dismissal of the Nationalist government's "capitalist" copyright law and their own desire to monopolize the production and circulation of communist knowledge, the party-state in the making sought to counter piracy as a threat to their political authority, rather than an infringement of private property.

Part of the reason for the CCP's apparent "generosity" toward literary piracy lay in the fact that the party had been running the largest reprinting operation in China. Since the CCP's early years in Yan'an, it was not uncommon for party-owned publishing enterprises, such as Xinhua Bookstore, and regional party organizations to reprint "progressive" titles (initially published in Shanghai or elsewhere) without the permission of the authors and original publishers.[11] Such unauthorized reprinting, or piracy, was justified by the argument that people in the Communist-controlled regions urgently needed textbooks and proper readings, yet it was too difficult for those in poor, remote, and isolated hinterlands to get books (or authorization) through normal channels. To fulfill readers' demand and to accomplish the party's enlightenment mission in base areas, the staff of the regional Xinhua Bookstore admitted that they ended up "reprinting whatever books [they] got hold of," from Marxist-Leninist classics to popular how-to titles, and anything in between.[12]

Xinhua Bookstore not only reprinted others' "progressive" titles but also welcomed others' reprinting its own publications freely. Publishing books, pamphlets, and propaganda materials was a crucial means for the CCP to spread their revolutionary ideas.[13] However, the War of Resistance (1937–1945) and then the civil war against the Nationalist government (1945–1949) had made long-distance transportation of printed materials in quantity a highly risky task.

11. "Zhonggong Zhongyang Xuanchuan Bu Chuban Weiyuanhui guanyu baohu banquan gei gedi Xinhua Shudian de tongzhi" [A notification from the CCP Propaganda Department Publishing Committee to local branches of Xinhua Bookstore on copyright protection], November 28, 1949, ZRGCS, 1:571.

12. "Hua bei qu Xinhua Shudian gongzuo baogao" [Work report of the Xinhua Bookstore Northern China Branch], October 7, 1949, ZRGCS, 1:339–340. For similar accounts, see Zhou Baochang, "Xinhua Shudian gang chengli de shihou" [The formative days of Xinhua Bookstore], RMRB, September 1, 1959.

13. For the CCP's ideological mobilization during its socialist revolution, see Hung, War and Popular Culture.

Large shipments of books were vulnerable to the enemy's attacks, bombings, and censorship inspections, so a considerable proportion of titles produced by the CCP and its associated presses during the wars never made it to their intended readers. For instance, in 1938, when Reading Publishing (*Dushu chubanshe*), a CCP-directed press operating in Japanese-occupied Shanghai, published the first complete Chinese translation of *Das Kapital*, almost all of the two thousand copies of the first edition were lost on their way to Canton. To overcome this obstacle, an editor embarked on a tortuous voyage in 1939 to bring the whole stereotype set of this book from Shanghai to Chongqing, the Nationalist government's wartime capital. With the stereotype set, Reading Publishing was able to produce extra copies of *Ziben lun* (Capital) at the home front.[14] Recognizing that transporting stereotype sets would be easier and safer than carrying large parcels of finished products, Xinhua Bookstore and other party-owned publishing enterprises in Yan'an changed their distribution strategies. By the 1940s, instead of supplying all the needed copies from Yan'an to various scattered, and often hard to reach, communist base areas, they would send duplicated stereotype sets and sample copies in small parcels to local Xinhua Bookstore or CCP branches. Local cadres could then freely reprint the needed titles for their local readers.

This network of production and distribution that Xinhua Bookstore's regional branches set up during the wars was distinctively different from what Commercial Press and other Shanghai publishers had established in the early twentieth century. While the local branches of Shanghai publishing enterprises chiefly served as retail outlets distributing books they received from their Shanghai headquarters,[15] the Xinhua Bookstore branches, in comparison, enjoyed a greater autonomy and flexibility because they also had printing capacity. In different locales, the Xinhua Bookstore branches and the CCP organizations simultaneously reprinted the same titles initially published in Yan'an, as well as the "progressive" books that Yan'an Xinhua Bookstore had reprinted, with little

14. Zhong yang Makesi En'gesi Liening Sidalin zhu zuo bian yi ju, ed., *Makesi En'gesi zhu zuo zai Zhongguo de chuanbo*, 117–118.

15. For instance, among Commercial Press's twenty-plus local branches, only the Beiping and Hong Kong branches had printing facilities attached to them. As discussed in the previous chapter, this Shanghai-centered distribution network at times could not accommodate the local demand effectively, and thus caused a supply-demand imbalance in provincial book markets for pirates to exploit.

or no coordination.[16] After the civil war resumed in 1945, the CCP further set up "cultural co-ops" (*wenhua hezuo she*) in county seats and market towns they occupied. These small co-ops often had only very basic printing equipment, yet they managed to produce thousands of copies of school textbooks and communist pamphlets using lithography, mimeograph, or even woodblock printing.[17]

Xinhua Bookstore, its branches, regional communist organizations, and these grassroots cultural co-ops together formed a guerrilla-style reprinting network in the CCP-controlled areas throughout the 1940s. They duplicated stereotypes, produced local versions of communist texts based on the sample copies they received, and consistently shared the means of producing imprints with each other. As a result, one could find unprecedented variations of the core CCP texts during this period. According to a bibliographical survey done by the Renmin University of China, at least 53 versions of Mao's *Lun chijiu zhan* (On protracted war), 140 versions of *Lun lianhe zhengfu* (On coalition government), and 182 versions of *Xin minzhu zhiyi lun* were published between 1938 and 1949.[18]

This guerrilla-style reprinting operation emerged in the CCP-controlled areas not merely out of practical necessity. Reprinting was also one way to resist against the capitalist system and the Nationalist government's authority. For instance, when Ding Ling (1904–1986) visited the Soviet Union in April 1949, she portrayed the CCP-controlled areas as a copyright-free utopia. When asked by a Russian author how much royalty she had earned from her well-received novel *Taiyang zhao zai Sanggan he shang* (The sun shines over Sanggan River), she replied that the CCP hadn't employed a copyright system in the "liberated" areas, and authors operating in the CCP-controlled areas were disinterested in material gain. They did not request remuneration from publishers or newspapers, monopolize their copyright, or see their works as exclusive personal possessions. They wrote for the people, Ding Ling stated, so they "welcomed others to reprint [their works]." Although the print run for the first edition of *Taiyang zhao zai Sanggan he shang* was 5,000–10,000 copies, Ding Ling proudly reported to her Soviet colleagues that tens of thousands of additional

16. See, for example, Zhao, *Yan'an chuban de guanghui*, 29–53; Hebei sheng xinwen chuban ju chuban shi zhi bianweihui and Shanxi sheng xinwen chuban ju chuban shi zhi bianweihui, eds., *Zhongguo gongchandang jin cha ji bianqu chuban shi*.

17. For example, Qi, *Shanxi geming cenjudi chuban shi*, 270–272.

18. *Yan'an shidai xin wenhua chuban shi*, 8–9. These statistics are based on Zhongguo Remin Daxue, ed., *Jiefang qu genju di tushu mulu*.

copies were reaching Chinese readers through reprinting operations in various areas.[19]

While Ding Ling bragged in Moscow about the way books were freely reprinted and circulated in CCP-controlled areas, back home the CCP Central Committee Propaganda Department (*Zhonggong zhongyang weiyuanhui xuanchuanbu*; hereafter, Propaganda Department) found it increasingly difficult to embrace and practice unauthorized reprinting as the CCP took over most of central and northern China. Support from urbanites, business communities, industrialists, and even capitalists became ever more important to the CCP, forcing them to consider the practice of unauthorized reprinting from a different perspective.

The Propaganda Department's handling of complaints about the CCP's reprinting of private publishers' books in April–May 1949 reflected the party's shifting attitude toward reprinting. When several pro-CCP publishers and authors appealed to the Propaganda Department and to regional party organizations, accusing Xinhua Bookstore and other party-owned publishing enterprises of pirating their works, the department promised that the party would take authors' concerns and personal interests seriously. It quickly instructed party-owned publishing facilities to stop pirating the works of the petitioners.[20] In November 1949, the Publishing Committee of the Propaganda Department formally notified every Xinhua Bookstore branch to immediately cease reprinting others' books arbitrarily. As the CCP had unified China, the notice said, they could no longer excuse such practices by proclaiming that the war had blocked their access to authentic copies of books or prevented them from

19. Ding Ling, "Fajieyefu tongzhi gaosu le wo xie sheme" [What Comrade Fadeyev has told me], *RMRB*, April 29, 1949, 4.

20. "Zhonggong zhongyang xuanchuanbu guanyu jisong yangben ji buyao zai fanyin Kaiming deng shudian de shuji zhi Zhongyuan ju xuanchuanbu dian" [The CCP Central Propaganda Department's telegram to the CCP Central China Office Propaganda Department on sending sample copies and stopping reprinting the publications published by Kaiming Books and other publishers], April 7, 1949, ZRGCS 1:78; "Zhonggong zhongyang xuanchuanbu guanyu shuji chuban yu fanban wenti de zhishi (fu hua zhong ju bing gao ge zhong yang ju)" [Instructions by the CCP Central Propaganda Department regarding book publishing and piracy issues (A reply to the Central China Office, also forwarding to other officeso], May 30, 1949, ZRGCS 1:108–109; "Zhonggong zhongyang xuanchuanbu guanyu gedi Xinhua shudian fanyin waiban shuji de zhishi dian" [Telegram by the CCP Central Propaganda Department to instruct branches of Xinhua Books regarding their reprinting of private publishers' books], September 3, 1949, ZRGCS 1:204.

properly obtaining the original authors' and/or publishers' authorization for reprinting.[21]

In the new Communist economy that cherished public interests over private gains, however, it would be more difficult to use copyright as the sole reason to ban unauthorized reprinting, especially private publishers' reprinting of party publications. "Our publishing business distinguishes itself from the old one by its unconditional dedication to the people," Lu Dingyi (1906–1996), head of the Propaganda Department, articulated in a speech to Xinhua Bookstore staff in October 1949.[22] Hu Yuzhi (1896–1986) and Ye Shengtao, the PRC's top cultural officials and veterans of the Shanghai publishing industry in the Republican era, also repeatedly stressed in public speeches in the early 1950s that publishing was not a business. Books were not ordinary commodities like clothes or chairs, Hu stated in one of his speeches to the publishing industry: they were the people's "intellectual foods" and "cultural weapons" essential to the new China's revolutionary cause.[23] In planning what to publish, publishers should consider what would be beneficial for the people rather than what would generate profit for the enterprise. The surplus should be reinvested to produce more books to serve the people's interest rather than being accumulated for personal or institutional gain.[24]

However, if the main objective of the publishing industry was to enhance China's cultural and ideological progress, wouldn't it be fair, in principle, for Xinhua Bookstore and private publishers to freely reprint others' books for this greater cause? If the party did not consider its publications to be its exclusive possessions and allowed private publishers to help spread the Communist agenda, would the party in fact encourage private publishers to take advantage of that ideological stand and make money by reprinting party publications?

21. Liu and Shi, eds., *Xin Zhongguo wushi nian chuban jishi*, 3.

22. Lu Dingyi, "Zai quanguo Xinhua shudian chuban gongzuo huiyi shang de bimuci" [The closing remarks of the National Publishing Work Meeting for Xinhua Bookstore's staff] in *Lu Dingyi wenji*, 407.

23. "Hu Yuzhi zai Xinhua shudian zongdian chengli dahui shang de jianghua" [The speech by Hu Yuzhi at the opening ceremony of the headquarters of Xinhua Bookstores] February 23, 1951, ZRGCS 3:50–51. The presentation Hu Qiaomu made at the PRC's First National Policy Meeting on the Publishing Industry echoed this position regarding the true mission of the publishing industry; see "Gaijin chuban gongzuo de jige wenti" [A few questions about how to improve publishing works], August 28, 1951, ZRGCS 3:245–260.

24. "Hu Yuzhi zai Xinhua shudian zongdian chengli dahui shang de jianghua," and "Gaijin chuban gongzuo de jige wenti."

More importantly, how could the party ensure the accuracy of these private reprints' content?

Motivated simultaneously by the urgency to "enlighten" Chinese society with communist ideas, the desire to monopolize ideological truth, and a general disfavor toward private property and profit, the Publishing Committee settled on a halfway measure to allow "reprinting with permission." The public announcement published on May 21, 1949, by Xinhua Bookstore and Liberation Publishing (*Jiefang she*) under the Publishing Committee's instruction clearly reflected the logic behind "reprinting with permission." When these two party-owned publishing enterprises addressed their concerns about recent "free reprints" of their titles by "other publishers," what they worried about were the flaws and mistakes found in the "free reprints" rather than violation of copyright. To better ensure the quality of reprints, they urged those who intended to reprint their books to contact the Publishing Committee to obtain proper permission, because "publishing is an earnest mission, and the publishers need to be responsible to the people."[25]

This announcement specifically addressed an unexpected "market trend" the CCP had created after they took over urban centers in northern and central China in the spring of 1949. The eager and anxious (or, from the party's viewpoint, zealous) pursuit of communist books by urban readers somewhat ironically brought about a new trend in pirate publishing. Melancholic romances and martial arts novels were no longer the pirates' favorite targets; "90 percent" of pirated titles uncovered in Beijing in 1949 were communist texts, "essential readings for party cadres" (*ganbu bidu*), and governmental policy publications.[26] These cheap reprints were more affordable to young students and petty urbanites; pirates offered deeper discounts (5–10 percent more than Xinhua), so local bookshops and newsstands were more willing to sell these unauthorized reprints.[27] These reprints, the Publishing Committee noticed, often contained careless errors, such as typos, missing sentences, and unreasonably tiny fonts.[28] Some were selections of party publications with sensational titles,

25. "Jiefang she Xinhua shudian zhongyao qishi" [Important announcement by Liberation Bookstore and Xinhua Bookstore], *RMRB*, May 21, 1949, 1.
26. "Chuban zongshu bangongting jihua chu guanyu Beijing shi fanban shukan qingkuang de chubu diaocha baogao," 573–574.
27. Ibid.
28. Ibid. See also "Chuban weiyuanhui di shi ci huiyi jilu (jielu)" [Minutes of the Publishing Committee's tenth meeting (excerpt)] (May 4, 1949), *ZRGCS* 1:86.

like *Mao Zedong waizhuan* (Unofficial biography of Mao Zedong) or *Sidalin zenyang qijiade* (How Stalin carved out his career).[29] The Propaganda Department also believed that GMD "secret agents" muddied the waters by releasing "toxic" and "fabricated" texts as the latest CCP policy documents to confuse residents of Beijing. For instance, there was reportedly a series of pamphlets "allegedly published by Xinhua Bookstore" on urban land law. According to these "fake" pamphlets, the CCP was going to confiscate all private real estate and housing for redistribution.[30] While private reprints could, to a certain extent, be seen as "free" help in spreading the new Communist agenda, they also posed threats to the "purity" of CCP ideological orthodoxy and thus needed to be regulated.

Although, in early May, the Propaganda Department initially instructed its local offices in China's major urban centers to ban private reprints of party publications and policy pamphlets, they also acknowledged the merit of those private reprints. As one directive indicated, since their chief goal was to prevent reprints that contained misspellings, mistakes, and fabricated information from causing social chaos, they "generally should not ban or confiscate" reprints with "acceptable quality," for Xinhua Bookstore alone did not have the printing capacity to meet the soaring demand for communist books.[31] When the Publishing Committee delivered their "opinions" on the piracy issue in full, they also expressed a certain sympathy toward the Liulichang pirates. Regarding these pirates as victims of the postwar economic crisis who reprinted Chairman Mao's writings to make ends meet, they believed that the best way to handle these pirates was not to crush them but to help them. The party could win their support by "providing stereotype sets [to them] proactively and of set purpose," and "organize them to reprint parts of books [for us]." In the long run, the party could further help these pirates to transform themselves into a collective publishing organization specializing in popular titles so that they could "quit piracy" eventually.[32]

29. "Jinfang jiamao" [Beware of the counterfeit], *RMRB*, March 16, 1949, 4.

30. "Zhonggong zhongyang xuanchuanbu guanyu fangzhi weizao wenjian zhi Huadong ju Zhongyuan ju de xin" [CCP Central Propaganda Department's letter to Eastern China Office and Central China Office on how to prevent counterfeits], May 15, 1949, *ZRGCS*, 1:100–101. See also "Jinfang jiamao."

31. "Zhonggong zhongyang xuanchuanbu guanyu fangzhi weizao wenjian zhi Huadongju Jhongyuanju de xin," 1:100–101.

32. "Quanguo chuban shiye gai kuang" [An overview of publishing business nationwide], June 5, 1949, *ZRGCS* 1:133.

Compared with the Detective Branch's unscrupulous measures against the Beiping pirates in the 1930s, the CCP's handling of the city's piracy in 1949 was relatively gentle, if not kind. The Publishing Committee and its superiors didn't see Liulichang pirates principally as "thieves" infringing their property rights. For them, the potential threat posed by the unregulated private reprints of communist texts and party documents was a political one. Thus, as long as the quality of these reprints was acceptable, and as long as private publishers requested permission in advance, the party should allow those publishers to make some money by reprinting Xinhua Bookstore's publications for the time being. This distinguished them from the GMD's censors, who took violent measures against whomever they found producing problematic texts, and allowed them to present themselves as the fair and thoughtful ones. It would also set them apart from Shanghai booksellers who hunted down pirates to ensure their monopoly of profit. By requesting that private publishers obtain permission from the Publication Committee before reprinting party publications, they also hoped to better regulate the reproduction of the core party texts with minimum administrative cost. Ideally, they could decide what kinds of books could be reprinted by whom and, at the same time, utilize the printing capacity of private publishers to assist the party to promptly provide the needed reading materials for the new China.

"Reprinting with permission" was a well-intended means to release the CCP from the entanglements of blocking unwanted piracy of communist texts while preserving the party's liberty to reprint what they needed. In reality, however, the policy of "reprinting with permission" seems not to have been well appreciated. A few weeks after Xinhua Bookstore's first announcement in the *People's daily*, it issued second and third announcements, in a hasher tone, urging publishers to obtain permission for reprinting from the Publishing Committee. It threatened that unauthorized reprinting, if found, would be prosecuted according to the law.[33] Similarly, over the course of 1949 and 1950, the Propaganda Department and then the GPA repeatedly sent out directives every few months reminding Xinhua Bookstore branches that a proper way to fulfill the demand for textbooks and other titles was to order them from the original publishers rather than to reprint them right away.[34] The repetition and frequency in

<hr/>

33. Chen Juhong, *Xin Zhongguo chuban shi yanjiu*, 56. Interestingly, this announcement never made clear which law they were referring to.

34. For example, "Zhongyang renmin zhengfu chuban zongshu chubanju zhongyao qishi" [Important announcement by the Publication Department of the General Administration of

themselves indicate that neither the private publishers nor Xinhua Bookstore took the "reprinting with permission" guideline seriously, and that people continued to reprint books without permission.

What eventually seemed to work was more direct government intervention. In November, the GPA proudly reported that nine out of the fifteen pirates the authorities had uncovered in the spring had apologized in major newspapers, surrendered their remainders, and promised that they would "never reprint others' books without permission henceforth." The pirates were pressured into this "voluntary" collaboration by a "forum" organized by the Beijing People's Government. Earlier in September, all the private publishers in town were "invited" to the forum to learn that reprinting CCP policy documents without permission would be prosecuted. Though a majority of the pirates they targeted decided to collaborate and surrendered one-third of the ninety-plus titles they had reprinted for review within a month, the GPA suspected that some might be feigning compliance to continue their business. Therefore, in recommending further measures to control piracy in Beijing, it suggested—despite the lack of a national regulation against piracy—that the local Military Control Commissions should target one or two firms that had covertly continued their piratical operation. Arresting their owners and detaining them for a few days would serve as a warning to others.[35]

A Crime of Being Self-Interested

In the early 1950s, for the GPA, tackling piracy was not merely to ensure that readers received the "correct" version of communist ideas; it was also part of their remaking of China's cultural economy. Although the post-1949 state cultural management is often characterized by scholars as a system designed by the PRC, as a propaganda state, to achieve a centralized command of the production, dissemination, and consumption of books so as to advance the

Publishing at the People's Central Government], January 1950, ZRGCS, 2:3; "Chuban zongshu dui gedi Xinhua Shudian chuban wu ying renzhen jiancha zhi shi" [Instruction by the General Administration of Publishing urging Xinghua Books' local branches to review their publications carefully], May 5, 1950, ZRGCS, 2:197. See also "Chuban zongshu guanyu tongyi quanguo Xinhua shudian de jueding" [Decision by the General Administration of Publishing on consolidating Xinhua Bookstore branches nationwide], in Zhongyang xuanchuan bu, "Chuban gongzuo xuanbian" bianji zu, ed., Chuban gongzuo wenjian xuanbian, 50–51.

35. "Chuban zongshu bangongting jihua chu guanyu Beijing shi fanban shukan qingkuang de chubu diaocha baogao," 574–575.

party-state's control over culture, we must not forget that while creating a new socialist culture, the party-state simultaneously forged a new set of structures, principles, and ideas constituting publishers' and authors' economic life. Several policy statements and directives that the GPA issued in the early 1950s reflect its ambition to rectify Chinese publishers' profit-seeking instincts and market-oriented operation framework through its reform of the publishing industry.[36] For the GPA, all the iniquities that led to the flood of debased books in the Republican era, including cutthroat competition, fraud, and piracy, were created and nourished by this competitive capitalist mentality. Thus only a comprehensive socialist reconstruction of China's publishing sector would eradicate the bad influences from the market and terminate piracy for good.

The inconvenient reality the GPA faced, as its 1949 investigation into the Beijing piracy issue had revealed, was that before they could start to reform private publishers, clever private publishers had figured out ways to make money by selling Marxism. The situation was even more complex in Shanghai than in Beijing. When the PLA took over Shanghai in May 1949, the city's publishing industry had been heavily affected by the wars, postwar hyperinflation, the GMD's aggressive censorship, and a paper shortage. Nevertheless, they still dominated China's publishing sector. According to a 1950 survey, 199 of the 270 active publishing enterprises in China were private publishers in Shanghai.[37] They collectively produced more titles than the party-state publishing enterprises did.[38] Although the CCP was able to open Xinhua Bookstore branches, expropriate publishing companies associated with the GMD, and establish a strong presence within a few months after its takeover of Shanghai, they could not "reform" the Shanghai publishing industry right away owing to its massive scale. By 1951, the number of private publishers in Shanghai, despite the GPA's effort to promote collective consolidation, had actually increased.[39]

A considerable proportion of the titles published in Shanghai before 1949—romances, martial arts novels, popular manuals and textbooks for

36. Lu Dingyi, "Zai quanguo Xinhua shudian chuban gongzuo huiyi shang de bimuci"; "Hu Yuzhi zai Xinhua Shudian zongdian chengli dahui shang de jianghua."

37. "Quanguo zhuyao chengshi chuban ye ji fanmai shudian shuliang chubu tongji biao" [Preliminary national statistics on publishing companies and bookstores in major cities] (1950), ZRGCS, 2:853.

38. According to a survey, 55 percent of titles released in 1951 were published by private publishers in Shanghai. See Zhou, "Cong quanguoxin dao difanghua: 1945 zi 1956 nian Shanghai chubanye de bianqian," 11.

39. Ibid.

Republican citizens, comic books, and so forth—were labeled by the new regime as "backward," "feudal," "superstitious," or "poisonous" books unsuitable for China's new citizens. They were thus deemed not politically desirable in the post-1949 book market.[40] As China's urban readers hastened to consume books on socialism to familiarize themselves with the new regime's political and ideological languages, smart publishers saw a business opportunity.[41] As discussed in the previous chapters, the preferences of modern Chinese readers and the trends in China's book market have been profoundly affected by the political powers, their policies, and their ideologies. Based on experience, the market-savvy Shanghai booksellers speculated that Chinese readers would react to the 1949 regime change in the same way they had before, by rushing to purchase books that might help them understand the new authority or ideologies. Although unfamiliar with communist ideas, many in the book trade still managed to compile and publish an impressive number of introductory readings, reference books, dictionaries, and study aids on communism in the first two years of the PRC. They did so by pirating or plagiarizing party publications, blending the latest governmental propaganda with old stories, and bundling newspaper articles and "essential readings for party cadres" together with their interpretations.[42]

For the CCP, these "popular" titles on communism produced by Shanghai publishers posed a greater threat to the party's monopoly on political ideology than the plain reprints of the party publications found earlier in Beijing. They were not straightforward reproductions of party publications with typos and errors in editing, but suspicious and unauthorized interpretations of the party's political agenda, policies, and history. Ye Shengtao, the GPA vice-director and also a veteran of the Shanghai publishing world, denounced such practices at the PRC's First National Policy Meeting on the Publishing

40. SMA S313-4-2, "Shanghai chuban jie shi zenyang kefu kunnan de?" June 1950; Fang Houshu, "Xin Zhongguo dui siying chuban ye jinxing shehuizhuyi gaizao gaikuang" [An overview of how the new China launched socialist reform in private publishing businesses], in *Zhongguo chuban shiliao. xiandai bufen*, 804–805.

41. Ye Shengtao, "Wei tigao chubanwu de zhiliang er fendou!" [Fight for improving the quality of publications!] August 25, 1951, ZRGCS 3: 234.

42. One of the best-known examples of such "popular" titles produced during this period is *Li Fengjin*, a comic book using a conventional bitter romance to explain and promote the new marriage law. *Li Fengjin* was almost banned by the authorities because it portrayed local Communist cadres as somewhat incompetent to execute the law correctly.

Industry in 1951. These opportunistic publishers, he complained, manipulated Chinese readers' enthusiasm for communist texts for their own commercial interests. As long as they operated according to this profit-driven, self-interested, competitive business model, they would continue to pirate state-owned publishers' books and would cause further chaos. To solve this problem for good, he suggested, these private publishers needed to be "disciplined" and "reformed."[43]

One major convenient accusation that the GPA used to target these "opportunistic" publishers in Shanghai was piracy. And, in 1951, "disciplinary" action was carried out exclusively by the SBG, the civic organization established by publishing capitalists and cultural entrepreneurs to protect their economic interests. Recognizing the SBG's essential role in the regulation of Shanghai's enormous and complex publishing industry, the new regime initially decided to preserve the guild. In 1950, an interim Preparatory Committee (*Shanghai shi shuye tongye gonghui choubei weiyuanhu*) was organized by a group of pro-Communist publishers and editors. Some had been members of the League of Left-Wing Writers in the 1930s, such as Yao Pengzi (ca. 1905–1969); some were veterans of the CCP or democratic parties, such as the president of the Preparatory Committee and assistant manager of the eastern China branch of Xinhua Bookstore, Lu Minggu (1917–1994); some were leftist publishers supporting the CCP, such as Wang Zicheng (1903–1995), the head of Guangming Books (*Guangming shuju*).[44] For a few years after the PRC's founding, the new leaders employed this old institution as a vehicle to assist the young party-state in restructuring and eventually nationalizing Shanghai's publishing business. They also helped their members negotiate with the government authorities on paper supply, postage prices, taxation, and their entrepreneurial autonomy.[45] As the intermediary between the state and Shanghai publishers, they now had to punish piracy, the SBG's archenemy in its institutional memory, under a new framework of socialist economic morality.

On March 27, 1951, the SBG Preparatory Committee received a report from Guangming Books, accusing another member, Chunming Bookstore

43. "Wei tigao chuban wu de zhiliang er fendou!" 234.

44. For a discussion of the SBG leadership in the 1950s, see Volland, "Cultural Entrepreneurship in the Twilight," 246–248.

45. Ibid., 245. Also see Volland, "The Control of the Media in the People's Republic of China."

(*Chunming shudian*), of pirating its *Geguo geming shi* (World history of revolutions).[46] Written by an underground Communist historian in the mid-1930s, *Geguo geming shi* was banned during the War of Resistance against Japan by both the Nationalist government in Chongqing and Wang Jingwei's collaborative regime in Nanjing because of the author's Marxist take on modern European history and his call for Chinese social revolution. After the war, it was republished by Guangming Books, a supporter of the CCP underground organization since the 1930s. After 1949, this title gained significant popularity in the city because the party recommended it to its cadres. In January 1951, Chunming Bookstore published a book with a very similar title, *Geguo geming tongsu tijie* (Popular introduction to revolutions around the world). Pointing out that 95 percent of the content in *Geguo geming tongsu tijie* was identical to its *Geguo geming shi*, the proprietor of Guangming Books complained that Chunming Books had undoubtedly pirated his best seller.[47]

Founded by Chen Zhaochun, the allegedly piratical Chunming Bookstore was a midsize publishing company known for its wide range of popular titles, from divination manuals to detective novels, and for its sensitive and quick responses to the latest trends in China's expanding urban book market.[48] In the aftermath of the civil war, Chen had retired and left the firm to his former employees. Hu Jitao, the editor in chief, took up the leadership position, and the firm continued its daily operations as in the old days. As an active member of the guild since its establishment in 1932, Chunming Bookstore was familiar with the SBG's copyright enforcement mechanism. So, when he was called upon for an explanation of the piracy charge on March 28, 1951, Hu responded to Guangming Books' accusation in a conventional manner: on behalf of the firm, he apologized for the careless mistake of publishing a piece of plagiarism. Following the SBG's conventional procedures, he expressed the firm's willingness to surrender the piratical stereotype sets and remainders to the guild to be

46. SMA S313-4-28, "Guangming shudian zong ju zhi shuye gonghui choubei weiyuanhui" [Guangming Books to the Preparatory Committee of Shanghai Booksellers' Guild], March 27, 1951, and "San yue ershiba ri zai tongye gonghui choubei weiyuanhui baogao" [Guangming Books' report for the Preparatory Committee meeting on March 28], March 28, 1951.

47. Ibid.

48. Their most famous pre-1949 publication may have been a practical manual titled *Mishu yiqian zhong* [One thousand secret tricks], covering "tricks" such as basic conjurations, herbal remedies to remove oily stains from cloth, predicting one's death, making eggs flow in the air, and turning flowers different colors. They were also known for a translation of Maurice Leblanc's Arsène Lupin series.

destroyed. He also promised to compensate Guangming Books' financial losses.[49]

To his surprise, the apology, the compensation, and the surrender of the master copy, all of which had been standard actions to settle a copyright dispute under the SBG's copyright regime before 1949, failed to satisfy either the SBG's new leaders or Guangming Books. Wang Zicheng, the proprietor of Guangming Books and also a member of the SBG Preparatory Committee, proclaimed that he had not reported this case to recover financial loss. He had done so because he hoped the SBG could use the incident to "help" Chunming Bookstore and other private publishers learn to understand publishing as a serious political mission in the new China.[50] Embracing Wang's idea, the Preparatory Committee turned this minor copyright dispute into a months-long public campaign for booksellers in Shanghai to "educate themselves" (*ziji jiaoyu ziji*) about why Chunming Bookstore's misconduct represented a profound structural problem of the Shanghai publishing industry in which many of them were implicated.[51]

All the titles Chunming Bookstore had published since 1949 were subjected to careful review; within days, reviewers and Xinhua Bookstore reported Chunming Bookstore for pirating several other books.[52] In addition to surrendering the master copies and remainders, paying compensation to the authors and publishers, and recalling all sold copies, the staff of Chunming Bookstore were ordered by the SBG to organize self-criticism meetings to examine thoroughly the nature of their misconduct:[53] if their publishing of *Geguo geming tongsu tijie* was not merely an infringement of Guangming Books' property rights and the chief damage they had inflicted was not Wang Zicheng's financial loss, then what

---

49. SMA S313-4-15, "Shanghai shi shuye tongye gonghui choubei weiyuanhui huiyi jilu" [Preparatory Committee of SBG meeting minutes] and "Di shisi ci choubeihui huiyi jilu" [Minutes of the fourteenth preparatory meeting], March 28, 1951.

50. SMA S313-4-28, "San yue ershiba ri zai tongye gonghui choubei weiyuanhui baogao."

51. SMA S313-4-15, "Di shisi ci choubeihui huiyi jilu."

52. SMA S313-4-28, "Xinhua shuju huadong fenju zhi Shanghai shuye tongye gonghui" [Xinhua Bookstore Eastern China Branch to SBG], March 31, 1951; SMA S313-4-15, "Xinhua shuju huadong fenju zhi Shanghai shuye tongye gonghui" [Xinhua Bookstore Eastern China Branch to SBG], May 9, 1951; "Shuji shendu yi jian: Gaoxiao lishi ke cankao ziliao" [Reviewer's comment: Senior Elementary School History Textbook Supplement], April 26, 1951, "Shuji shendu yi jian: Zhengzhi jingji xue tongsu tijie" [Reviewer's comment: Popular Introduction to Political Economy], April 4, 1951.

53. "Di shisi ci choubeihui huiyi jilu."

was the "actual" crime they had committed? From late March to early August 1951, the staff produced several rounds of self-criticism reports. As they struggled to grasp the official message hidden behind the campaign, the SBG provided further guidance to assist them: piracy was caused by private publishers' profit-seeking competitive mentality; in the new communist economy, however, publishing was not for personal economic gain but to serve the needs of the people. To really "quit" piracy, Chunming Bookstore (and the whole private publishing sector) would need to renounce their market-oriented mode of operation and transform themselves from commodity-makers to earnest producers of the people's "intellectual foods."

Chunming Bookstore might not have been a randomly chosen target of the new SBG. To a certain extent, this successful cultural entrepreneur embodied all the negative qualities the GPA leadership associated with the pre-1949 publishing sector. It was a known repeat offender in piracy: in 1934, it was caught by the SBG pirating the popular novel *Tixiao yinyuan* and other titles; in 1947, it was charged by Ye Shengtao and other left-wing authors for pirating their (and Lu Xun's) works. The case was eventually settled after Chunming Bookstore agreed to pay each author a handsome compensation and work with them to launch a new series of leftist novels.[54] With titles that ranged from "Mandarin Ducks and Butterflies" romances to socialist fictions, they did not subscribe to any particular cultural or political agenda. They simply followed the money.

After 1949, Chen Zhaochun left the firm to the "collective" management of his former employees, and his son fled to Taiwan to open a parallel Chunming Bookstore in Taipei.[55] The thirty-plus employees of Chunming Bookstore nominally took over the firm and became their own "masters." Having come of age in the prewar Shanghai publishing industry, they coped with the changing reality by practicing their old trick: publishing whatever was popular in the market, publishing it fast, and selling it at a low price.

Noticing the high demand for communist books, beginning in the autumn of 1949, the staff of Chunming Bookstore started to publish a series of textbooks,

54. Yu Zilin, "Wo suo zhidao de Chunming shudian" [The Chunming Bookstore I knew], *Chuban shiliao* 4 (2011): 34–38.

55. Chen Guanying, son of Chunming Bookstore's owner, operated a branch in Taiwan. He smuggled books from Shanghai via Hong Kong and sold them in Taiwan in 1950–1951 until he was arrested for subversion by the GMD government. Chen was executed in Taiwan in 1953 as a CCP collaborator. Fei-Hsien Wang, "A Bookseller's Tale of Two Cities: Piracy, Smuggling, and Treason across the Taiwan Straits" (unpublished manuscript).

introductory readings, and dictionaries to help readers understand the new regime. They produced these books fast by pirating and plagiarizing popular "socialist" titles or mashing newspaper articles and policy documents together to "create" new works. Their best-known post-1949 title was *Xin mingci cidian* (Dictionary of new terms).[56] Compiled by editor in chief Hu Jitao, once a newspaper clerk and romance author, in just months, this dictionary offered simple but not entirely orthodox explanations of the CCP's party structure, its leadership, its new political terminologies, communist phrases, and so on. In two years, ninety thousand copies of *Xin mingci cidian* were sold, and rumor had that Hu made a significant fortune from it.[57] As many of their fellow publishers in the city were struggling for survival, Chunming Bookstore overcame the management crisis caused by the regime transition, and beginning in 1950 it was once again making money.[58]

When pirating and plagiarizing others' titles, Chunming's editors often rephrased the content, either to avoid committing direct plagiarism or to make the communist ideologies more accessible to readers. For instance, one reviewer pointed out that 80 percent of the content of Chunming's *Gaoxiao lishi ke cankao ziliao* (Reference materials for history curriculum for senior high school) plagiarized leading Communist historian Fan Wenlan (1893–1969) from his *Zhongguo tongshi jianbian* (General history of China). He further stated that Chunming editors rephrased many minor parts of Fan's narrative from a "feudal" viewpoint, thus distorting the author's Marxist interpretation of Chinese historical development. In *Zhongguo tongshi jianbian*, Fan referred to emperors by their actual full names (such as Aixin-Jueluo Hongli) to make the point that these rulers of Chinese empires were just humans, but when Chunming Bookstore plagiarized the work, its editors employed posthumous titles (for example, Qianlong Emperor) to refer to emperors. This rewording, the reviewer commented, accorded feudal leaders "unnecessary respect" and "lost the true

56. For an analysis of the production and content of the dictionary of new terms in the context of early PRC knowledge transmission, see Altehenger, "On Difficult New Terms," 622–661.

57. SMA S313-4-18, "Yige duzhe Qin Bufan zhi Shanghai shuye tongye gonghui" [Letter to SBG from a reader named Qin Bufan], June 30, 1951. Although the letter-writer identified himself as an ordinary reader, his knowledge of *Xin mingci cidian*'s sales and Hu's share of the profits suggests that he might have been a book-trade insider.

58. SMA S313-4-28, "Chunming shudian dianwu weiyuanhui jiantaoshu" [Self-criticism report by the operation committee of Chunming Books], June 20, 1951.

spirit of the people's history."[59] And this was precisely what Ye Shengtao meant by the harms to the people inflicted by the backward, greedy, and opportunistic publishers' profit-driven pirating operations.

When the SBG's new leadership and Guangming Books refused to let Chunming Bookstore settle the dispute according to the SBG's old bylaws, they sent the signal that the norms and customs that Shanghai booksellers had established regarding piracy in the past had lost their authority and validity. The staff of Chunming Bookstore might have sensed that now, in the absence of a new PRC copyright law, their case ought to be judged according to the new regime's economic morality and ideological concern, which the SBG was hoping they would "learn." But they didn't exactly know how.

As a result, in the belated first self-criticism report they submitted to the SBG in late June 1951, the staff of Chunming Bookstore confessed, along with piracy, to other conduct they thought might violate communist morality in a broader sense. They stated that the fundamental mistake they had made was that, after 1949, they still operated the company according to a "strong and pure economic mind-set." They had secretly sent the remainder of their pre-1949 popular titles, no longer marketable in Communist China, to Hong Kong for sale, and they had also rushed to pirate trendy communist readings for a quick return of profit. Controlled by a market-oriented and profit-driven mind-set, they had ignored the publication plan they had submitted to the authorities and had published a series of piratical titles in a careless and irresponsible manner.[60]

After realizing that their pre-1949 publications were "a pile of rotten trash," Chunming's editorial staff also confessed, they had tried to "purify" themselves, but nevertheless they were still "taken prisoner by the pure economic way of thinking." They failed to recognize, in particular, the fact that a "small" and "immature" press like Chunming was not "qualified" to publish books on communism for cadres and students. Owing to their "low level of thought" and "philistine liberalist style of working," they were unable to review manuscripts responsibly and promptly stop plagiarized content from being published. In the end, they had "infringed the rights of authors, deceived the readers indirectly, and jeopardized the people's interests."[61]

For the SBG's new leaders, as well as the Shanghai Municipal Press Office, the Chunming Bookstore staff's self-criticism reports did not address the actual

59. "Shuji shendu yi jian: Gaoxiao lishi ke cankao ziliao."
60. "Chunming shudian dianwu weiyuanhui jiantaoshu."
61. Ibid.

damage caused by the real issue behind their "pure economic mind-set." They admitted that, always running against the clock, they had failed to review and proofread manuscripts carefully, but they neglected to address how seriously the seemingly harmless modifications they and their authors made in the pirated editions might compromise the party's political orthodoxy, as the reviewers pointed out.[62] Furthermore, even if they promised to stop pirating others' books, abandon their Hong Kong operation, give up publishing textbooks and introductory readings on communism, and review and proofread new titles carefully, they still would not be able to break out of the prison of their profit-driven mentality as long as the book market remained a competitive one.[63]

The SBG hosted a public forum to help them to understand this.[64] On July 11, 1951, representatives of Chunming Bookstore were criticized in front of 140 publishers and editors. It was the first time the SBG had set up public political theater to deal with piracy. In this forum, the core issue of piracy was redefined. Officials from the Shanghai Municipal Press Office declared that Chunming Bookstore had been notorious for publishing pornographic, reactionary, and piratical books since the 1930s. As they carried on doing so after 1949, they had "violated the New Democratic principles."[65] Next, the new leaders of the SBG pointed out that piracy was doubtlessly equivalent to stealing, but that punishing the pirates/thieves would not of itself eliminate such practices. The self-interested sentiment of private publishers like Chunming Bookstore would continuously lure them to steal others' works for short-term commercial gain. Thus the only way to stop piracy would be to correct this kind of market-oriented mentality and the competitive book-trade structure in which it was embedded. The case of Chunming Bookstore, they declared, could offer Shanghai publishers a great opportunity to educate themselves about the importance and benefits of a new, collective, and planned publishing industry overseen by the state. In this new centralized system, each publisher would specialize in a particular genre or type of book and would focus only on accomplishing its publication plan. As the publication plan and manuscripts would be reviewed by the

62. "Shuji shendu yi jian: Gaoxiao lishi ke cankao ziliao."

63. SMA S313-4-28, "Shuye guanyu Chunming shuju fanban wenti de zuotanhui suji" [Minutes of the book-trade symposium on Chunming Books' piracy problem], July 11, 1951.

64. Ibid.

65. SMA S313-4-28, "Chuban jie zuo juxing zuotanhui piping Chunming shuju touqie zuofeng" [Publishing industry symposium held yesterday to criticize Chunming Bookstore's misconduct of stealing], newspaper clipping, July 12, 1951.

state's agency, and the books they produced would be circulated via Xinhua Bookstore's national distribution system, publishers would no longer need to worry about the repetition of similar titles, overlapping business territory, or competition against each other.

Statements made by officials and SBG leaders in this forum hinted that to fully settle this piracy case, Chunming Bookstore should voluntarily subject itself to be reformed and to join one of the collective operation units the SBG was promoting. When, four days later, Chunming Bookstore submitted letters of apology to authors and publishers whose copyrights they had violated, a compensation plan, and their second self-criticism report, all this failed to please the SBG's leaders.[66] Although the Chunming representatives claimed that the forum had given them a valuable learning opportunity, the second report repeated what they had said in the first. They restated their determination to "eliminate their purely economic way of thinking" but didn't explain how they planned to achieve this.[67] This report made no mention of a structural reform or joining the collective operation unit, nor did it single out their manager and editor in chief as the SBG leaders had suggested in the forum.[68]

It is not clear whether Chunming Bookstore intentionally flouted the SBG leaders' message or were simply too ignorant to grasp it. In the end, this piracy case was settled, ironically, with what Chunming Bookstore had originally proposed in early March following the guild's old convention. Remaining piratical copies were destroyed and compensations were made. The only difference was that, to emphasize their disinterest in material gain, Guangming Books and the author of *Geguo geming shi* donated the compensation to support the construction of a fighter plane named after the author Lu Xun. Piratical copies were not burned in front of the Wenchang god's temple but turned into pulp for paper-making. In early August 1951, after failing to persuade Chunming Books to voluntarily submit itself to a collective publishing unit, the SBG's leaders seemed to give up, and stated: "We have made Chunming Books criticize themselves

---

66. SMA S313-4-28, "Baogao" [Report], July 15, 1951, and "Shanghai shuye tongye gonghui Chen Shimin zhi Wan fu zhuren mishu" [Chen Shimin of the SBG to Vice-Director–Secretary Wan], July 16, 1951.

67. SMA S313-4-28, "Chunming shuju dianwu weiyuanhui bianji bu di er ci jiantao shu" [Second self-criticism report from Chunming Books operation committee and editorial committee], July 15, 1951.

68. "Shanghai shuye tongye gonghui Chen Shimin zhi Wan fu zhuren mishu."

so many times, yet, maybe because their political consciousness [is too low], they just didn't get it. Shall we forget about it now?"[69]

At first glance, this somewhat anticlimactic ending of the case, as documented in the SBG's archival records, suggests that it was harder than the SBG's new leaders had initially anticipated to make Chunming Bookstore grasp their political message, even though Chunming Bookstore was the publisher of the popular (but problematic) political dictionary that introduced and explained the new political terms to tens of thousands Chinese readers. Looking closely into the case, however, one starts to notice how the interrelationship of the state, the book market, and the Shanghai publishers' self-regulatory association began to change in the transitional years of the early 1950s. On the one hand, owing to the relatively weak organizational takeover and the postrevolutionary legal vacuum, the new party-state relied upon this old civic organization to continue mediating piracy disputes, and the SBG, though now under new leadership, was ably carrying on the legacy of its customary *banquan* regime into socialist China. On the other hand, the new party-state, unlike its predecessors, was determined to create a dominating presence in the publishing sector and remake it according to its socialist vision. What the staff of Chunming Bookstore experienced in 1951 was a hybrid of the old dispute mediation procedure they were familiar with and the new political campaign techniques (self-criticism reports and public political theater) they'd never experienced before.

During this process, literary piracy committed by private publishers was redefined according to the CCP's new economic and ideological concerns. It was labeled an evil and unavoidable by-product born in and nurtured by the competitive free market, and the CCP asserted that the only way to eliminate it was not through the collective civility and self-discipline of publishers but through a remaking of the publishing industry into a noncompetitive, planned, and collective one. This new argument against piracy was formulated out of functional necessity partly to overcome the absence of copyright law in the early 1950s, partly to differentiate the CCP's reprinting for the people from piracy for profit, and partly to connect the Shanghai publishers' common enmity against piracy with the party-state's ultimate goal of nationalizing the publishing sector. Subscribing to this argument during the campaign against Chunming Bookstore, voluntarily or not, the SBG was introducing a solution to the piracy

---

69. SMA S313-4-15, "Di shiba ci choubei weiyuanhui huiyi jilu" [Minutes of the eighteenth preparation committee meeting], August 3, 1951.

problem at the cost of potentially destroying the ground it was built upon and the value it was set up to protect: a vibrant and autonomous cultural market.

Chunming Bookstore might have managed to preserve part of its economic autonomy in this case, but its reputation was sullied, especially after Ye Shengtao singled it out as a negative example in his speech in the publishing policy meeting. As political pressure increased over time, the firm gradually submitted itself to the GPA's new rules. Later in 1951, Hu Jitao was replaced by Kong Lingjing, a Communist editor and a brother-in-law of the minister of culture, Mao Dun; the firm was also reorganized and renamed Chunming Press. Kong recruited a group of scholars and professors to revise the dictionary of new terminologies to "improve" its quality. Its editorial staff also started to regularly send manuscripts, on their own initiative, to the Shanghai Municipal Press Office for advance review. They became more (and sometimes overly) sensitive to the potential political significance of minor changes in wording.[70] Before it eventually merged into Shanghai Culture Press (*Shanghai wenhua chubanshe*) in 1956, the firm remained one of the ten most profitable private publishers in Shanghai.[71] Collaborating with the authorities, they had learned, was the only way to continue making money in the new socialist cultural economy.

What happened to Chunming Bookstore in 1951 became a precedent for similar private publishers. When the GPA drafted its first five-year plan in 1952, it laid out strategies to "reform" different kinds of private publishers. It planned to help those with "shaky foundations" (a lack of substantial capital) and "limited publishing capacity" to "voluntarily" merge into joint management companies, and directed them to develop specialized niches. As for "opportunistic" (*touji*) and "improper" (*buzhengdang*) publishers who "only thought about money instead of the interests of the country and the people," the GPA sought opportune moments to rectify or terminate them through discipline and education.[72]

70. SMA B1-2-3625, "Benchu guanyu tongsu duwu de chuli yu Huadong xinwen chuban ju ji chuanxi xinwen chuban chu de wanglai wenshu" [Correspondence between our office and Eastern China News and Publishing Bureau and West Sichuan News and Publishing Bureau on the handling of popular publications], August–October 1951.

71. Chunming Bookstore remained one of the top ten profitable private publishers in Shanghai until 1955. See SMA S313-4-32-32, "Shanghai shi shuye tongye gonghui gongsiying chubanshe zichan yingkui qingkuang" [A report on assets and profits of the state-owned and private publishers in Shanghai, conducted by the Shanghai Booksellers' Guild].

72. Hu Yuzhi, "Chuban zongshu guanyu quanguo chuban shiye de zhuangkuang he jinhou fangzhen jihua gei Wenjiao weiyuanhui de baogao" [GPA's report to the Culture and Education Committee on the current state of China's publishing business and its further development

From 1953 to 1954, in several directives and reports, Hu Yuzhi and his GPA staff articulated a standardized game plan against "opportunist publishers" like Chunming Bookstore: they planned, first, to find evidence of misconduct, such as misinterpreting government policies, producing pornographic texts, or "stealing copyright," then to bring a case against them and publicize and expose the "evils of opportunistic publishers," so that the people would know the harm they did to society. Through such organized campaigns, targeted publishers would either be forced out of business or give in and submit to the state's collectivization scheme.[73]

In a letter to the GPA vice minister Chen Kehan (1917–1980), Hu Yuzhi explained that such actions to squeeze unwanted private publishers out of business were meant not merely to achieve the party-state's total control over media but to cure the illness of China's publishing sector. Blaming piracy, poor quality, pornographic content, and cutthroat discounts on the competitive nature of China's publishing industry, he told Chen that the GPA's primary mission in the coming years would be to "destroy the free market for books." For him, collectivization and state monopoly of China's book market would be the ultimate solution to stop "opportunist publishers" from committing the crime of being self-interested. He told Chen with confidence, "It would be hard to imagine the existence of opportunist publishers without a free market."[74]

However, evidence suggests that unauthorized reprinting did not vanish magically after the state completed the collectivization of the publishing sector. Some government, military, and industrial units were not publishers but also had printing capacity. Beginning in late 1953, the GPA issued several directives asking these "nonpublishing units" nationwide to stop reprinting books

---

plan], September 12, 1952, *ZRGCS*, 4:205; "Chuban zongshu di yi ci chuban jianshe wu nian jihua" [The GPA's first five-year plan for the development of the publishing industry], February 27, 1953, *ZRGCS*, 5:82.

73. For example, Hu Yuzhi, "Guanyu faxing gongzuo guanche zong luxian wenti gei Chen Kehan de xin"[Letter to Chen Kehan on questions regarding how to implement the General Line in distribution works], December 8, 1953, *ZRGCS*, 5:644; "Chuban zongshu guanyu zhengdun Shanghai siying chuban ye fangan de yijian fu Huadong Xinwen Chuban ju han" [The GPA's reply to Eastern China News and Publishing Bureau on how to rectify the private publishers in Shanghai], February 10, 1954, *ZRGCS*, 6:75–77; "Chuban zongshu dangzu guanyu zhengdun he gaizao siying chuban ye de baogao" [The GPA party branch's report on the rectification and reorganization of private publishers], August 1954, *ZRGCS*, 6:468–169, 471.

74. "Guanyu faxing gongzuo guanche zong luxian wenti gei Chen Kehan de xin," 644.

and policy documents without proper authorization.[75] These "nonpublishing units," ranging from the PLA and a provincial agricultural committee in Henan to a construction unit in Shanghai, apparently continued producing reprints of communist classics, Chairman Mao's works, and policy documents. Some did so to save money, some for the sake of convenience; others seem to have considered that they had the legitimacy to reprint the needed titles because they did so to help their members study communist ideology.[76] Assuming that commercial profit was the chief motivation for piracy, the GPA focused on transforming the profit-driven private publishers' operational model and mind-set, yet they seem to have forgotten the Yan'an legacy of free reprinting—piracy could be a crime committed by the self-interested, but it could also be a "selfless" act to spread ideas in the name of liberation and revolution. While their new definition of piracy could help them target undesirable private publishers without directly engaging the uneasy question of whether the communist regime acknowledged literary property, it fell short in failing to prevent or stop the piracy within the party-state organization.

Turning Authors into Workers

In 1950, the First National Publishing Conference wrote "acknowledging literary property and publishing rights" into its resolutions. When the GPA was assigned to fulfill this mandate and create a new copyright law for socialist China in 1951, it appointed a group of veteran publishers to draft a provisional copyright law modeled on the Soviet Union's 1928 Fundamentals of Copyright Law. Although Alford believes that the PRC's adaptation of the Soviet IPR system proceeded smoothly owing to the similarities between China's traditional political culture and the Soviet one, the transplantation of the Soviet copyright law in China was full of turbulence. The GPA's 1951 draft and its subsequent attempts were all rejected by the Government Administration Council of the

75. "Chuban zongshu guanyu jiuzheng renyi fanyin tushu xianxiang de guiding" [The GPA's provision on redressing the phenomenon of arbitrary reprinting], ZRGCS, 5:609–610.

76. For example, "Chuban zongshu guanyu budui fanyin tushu de guiding" [The GPA's provision on the PLA's reprinting of others' books], ZRGCS, 6:392; SMA B257-1-3642-46, "Zhonggong Shanghai shi chengshi jianshe ju weiyuanhui xuanchuan bu guanyu buzhun fanyin zhuxi zhezuo de tongzhi" [The instruction from the propaganda office of the CCP committee in Shanghai Municipal Development Administration on prohibiting any reprinting of Chairman Mao's works], May 6, 1964.

Central People's Government, because they deemed copyright too much of a "bourgeois" doctrine.[77]

Compared to Western European and American copyright laws at the time, the 1928 Fundamentals, an update of the Soviet 1925 Copyright Act, provided more restricted and limited protection of the exclusive right of authors and a shorter copyright term. While authors in the Soviet Union could also contractually lease out a copyright for a limited time to publishers, the amount of royalty they received was standardized according to government-issued remuneration schedules. Though, in theory, when authors created a literary work, they were *automatically* entitled to all copyright in the work, in reality, only those who produced works "useful" to the state's agendas could reap material rewards from their copyright. The state also had the liberty to "nationalize" any given work without the author's consent.[78] For the PRC leadership in the 1950s, however, this Soviet system was still too similar to the capitalist one. In their 1954 and 1957 draft interim provisions, to dilute the "bourgeoisness" of copyright, the GPA and the Ministry of Culture (*Wenhua bu*; hereafter, MOC) further trammeled the authors' exclusive right to use and distribute the works they created. For instance, in the 1957 draft of *Baohu chubanwu zhuzuoquan zhanxing guiding* (Interim provisions to protect the copyright of printed materials), a wide range of textual reproduction practices, such as copying newspaper articles for "internal materials," were exempted from copyright infringement provisions "for the greater good of the People." Echoing the GPA's earlier "reprinting with permission" policy, it specified that adaptation of literary works and compiling edited volumes were fine if the producers obtained the author's permission, but if the author refused to give consent to the state-run publishers, the government could intervene and issue a permit instead.[79] Even after significant compromises, however, the policy was still stigmatized as tainted by "a residue of

77. "Wenhua bu zhaokai lao chuban gongzuo zhe zuotanhui jiyao" [The proceedings of the Ministry of Culture forum of veteran publishers], May 14–15, 1957, ZRGCS, 9:56.

78. Newcity, *Copyright Law in the Soviet Union*, 17–30, 71, 83.

79. "Chuban zongshu niding 'baozhang chuban wu zhezuoquan zanxing guiding' caoan cheng Zhengwuyuan wenwei de baogao" [The GPA's report to the Government Administration Council Cultural Committee on the drafting of "Draft provisions protecting the copyright of publications"], May 15, 1954, ZRGCS, 6:292–298. According to a report in 1955, the GPA didn't officially submit this draft for review. By 1955, the draft was in revision and circulated among related agencies for "greater consensus." See "Wenhua bu guanyu zhongyang yiji chubanshe gongzuo de jiancha baogao" [Ministry of Culture's report on the operations of central first-class publishing houses], ZRGCS, 7:149; "Guanyu baozhang chuban wu zhezuowu zanxing guiding

capitalist legislation" and dismissed by the State Council for "embracing the privatization of knowledge."[80]

The GPA's effort to craft a socialist copyright law was slow to come to fruition owing to the PRC leadership's antagonism against private property protection, but its initiatives to consolidate China's publishing industry effectively smashed the foundation of key *banquan*/copyright customs that Chinese authors and publishers had developed in the first half of the twentieth century. The autonomy and negotiation powers of the SBG faded away by the mid-1950s as Shanghai publishers, editors, and writers were put through the state's "socialist transformation." Several of the post-1949 SBG leaders were targeted in the Five-Antis Movement (1952). Many SBG members disappeared after being consolidated or disciplined. In the process of "socialist transformation," private publishers' assets, machines, remainders, and "copyrights" were redistributed under government instructions to facilitate private-public joint management, collectivization, and publishing specialization.[81] Although the transferring of "copyright" was usually accomplished by physically moving the actual stereotype sets of certain books from one company to another, the GPA made it clear to private publishers and local authorities that the possession of stereotype sets was detached from copyright. For them, possessing the physical means to reproduce certain books (in this case the stereotype sets) did not automatically equate with holding the copyright of that book. The stereotype set itself could not create the value of the book; on the contrary, the use value of the stereotype set was created and determined by the content and the social need of the book.[82] The Shanghai booksellers' convention of connecting *banquan*/copyright ownership with possessing the means of production was dismantled.

The GPA and the MOC were also determined to revolutionize the customary copyright dealings to "liberate" authors. In the Republican period, Chinese authors could either sell off their manuscripts for a lump sum, a practice known

---

(caoan) de shuoming" [Explanations on the "Draft provisions protecting the publications and literary works" (draft)], in Zhou and Li, eds., *Zhongguo banquan shi yanjiu wenxian*, 307.

80. Shen, "Jian xin, xiyue, yu qipan: gaige kaifang zhong de zhezuoquan lifa."

81. For example, Commercial Press and Chung Hua Books transformed themselves from all-round publishing empires to institutions responsible for publishing foreign learning, classical texts, and reference books. See Culp, *The Power of Print in Modern China*, 194–213.

82. SMA B167-1-39, "Shanghai ge chubanshe guanyu banquan zhuanyi zhongyin yu Shanghai shi Chuban shiye guanli chu de wanglai wenshu" [Correspondence between Shanghai publishers and Shanghai Municipal Publishing Business Management Administration regarding the transitions of copyright and reprinting arrangements].

as *mai banquan* (selling copyright), or license the right to reproduce the work to a publisher via contract in exchange for *chou banshui* (receiving royalty). Perhaps affected by their experience as underpaid editors and authors in their previous life, the leadership of the GPA and the MOC saw the relationship between authors and publishers before 1949 as having been essentially an exploitive one.[83] What authors earned before "liberation" often failed to reflect the true cultural value of their works, as one MOC report further argued, because the price of a manuscript and the amount of royalty were determined largely by market demand and the book price. For instance, academic authors devoted more time and energy to advancing human knowledge, but they earned minute royalties because their "valuable" books could not sell as well as "useless" pornographic works. As a result, authors and publishers would be easily enticed by the expectation of profit to produce popular and marketable works regardless of what was truly beneficial to readers and society at large.[84]

To "take care of the interests of authors, publishers, and readers," the GPA introduced a Soviet-style remuneration system that rewarded authors according to their labor input and the quality of their works. First adopted in the state-owned publishing enterprises, this new remuneration system had become the dominant new norm in the publishing sector by 1955, when the presence of private publishers was critically diminished as a result of collectivization. The pay schedules of different state-owned publishing enterprises varied depending on their size and their specialties, but they shared the same general principle: remuneration for a work should be calculated based on its genre, quality, word count, and print run. To prevent authors of popular works from accumulating a fortune, the remuneration an author received was to decrease progressively once a certain print run was exceeded. For instance, in 1955 People's Literature Publishing House (*Renmin wenxue chubanshe*) calculated remuneration according to the schedule shown in table 7.1.[85]

Publishers and the state-run distributor Xinhua Bookstore set the print run of a book according to its nature, estimated demand, and their production/sale goals. And a pay scale would be applied based on the quality of the book, the

---

83. Hu, "Guanyu gaijin yu fazhan chuban gongzuo de jueyi" [Resolutions on improving and developing publishing works], in *Hu Yuzhi chuban wenji*, 148.

84. "Guanyu zhiding xin gaochou banfa de jingguo" [On the making of the new remuneration system], *ZRGCS*, 7:335.

85. This chart is based on Huang, "Gaochou zhidu yu 'shi qi nian' wenxue shengchan," 45–46.

TABLE 7.1. The Remuneration Schedule of People's Literature Publishing House (1955)

Genre		Print run per impression (1,000 copies/unit)				Remuneration per 1,000 characters (RMB yuan)			
Original works	Creative writing	10	20	30	50	18	15	12	10
	Theory, research, critiques, literary history	5	10	20					
	May Fourth classics	5	10	20					
Translations	Contemporary works	10	20	30	50	13	11	9	7
	Modern classics	5	10	20	30				
	Theory, research, critiques	5	10	20	30				
	Classical works	5	10	20					

"usefulness" of its topic, and the reputation of its author. Take, for example, a 100,000-character literary critique by a university professor. The author could enjoy a higher pay scale (fifiteen to eighteen yuan RMB/one thousand characters), but the print run for such a specialized subject would be relatively limited (five thousand copies/impression), so the remuneration the author received for this book would be between 1,500 and 1,800 yuan. Meanwhle, the same publishers might apply a lower payment unit (ten yuan /one thousand characters) to an emerging novelist publishing a 100,000-character novel on the land reform. Given the popular nature of the subject, however, the print run would be much higher (30,000 copies/impression). Eventually, what the author received for the first edition would be around one thousand yuan. Translation works were regarded as less original and less demanding, so the remuneration translators received was systematically lowered. The amount shown in table 7.1 was applied only to the first six impressions; after that, the total remuneration would decrease 30 percent.[86]

What the GPA and the MOC envisioned was an alternative economy of value to "free" authors, artists, and intellectuals from market demand while securing them a decent livelihood, but what they ended up creating was a new system turning authors into workers in the state-led cultural economy. Formerly in the Soviet Union, such government-standardized remuneration schedules complemented its socialist copyright law, sharing the premise that authors possess their copyright permanently. They lease it out for only a limited time to publishers in exchange for remuneration. Although the amount of material reward

86. Ibid.

authors received in the Soviet Union was not determined by the actual sale volume of their works but by state-created scales, the Soviet remuneration schedules were in principle still a type of royalty system. In the PRC, however, owing to the absence of formal copyright regulation, between the mid-1950s and the 1980s this remuneration system stood as the main (if not the only) reference to determine why and how authors got paid for what they created. Perhaps because of the CCP's reluctance to embrace "copyright" as a legal doctrine and a form of private property, the phrases *banquan* and *zhuzhoquan* were rarely used in the various remuneration measures that the state-owned publishing houses developed in the 1950s. While copyright became detached from the remuneration system in China, what got emphasized repeatedly was the principle of "paying for the labor" (*an lao qu chou*). This came to be a new justification for the author's material gain and profoundly separated the PRC's remuneration system from the Soviet one. As a 1955 MOC report stated, the "remuneration is a reward of authors' mental labor"; thus essentially "its nature is not different from a worker's wage."[87]

By emphasizing labor input rather than artistic and intellectual creativity, and by paying authors according to quantifiable measures, they promoted a new author-work relationship that harmonized better with the production frameworks of the PRC's planned economy. Professional academics, authors, and artists were understood to labor like workers making shoes, bicycles, or other products in factories; their work time and productivity could be planned and calculated, and there were production plans and quotas to be met. For instance, when designing national standard remuneration schedules in 1955, the MOC assumed that professional writers, translators, and social scientists could work like robots, with no downtime. According to their estimates, if authors dedicated two-thirds of their time to writing, they would be able to deliver 70,000 to 100,000 characters of original work, or an average of 140,000 characters of translation, annually. If their works were good enough to be published by the state-run flagship publisher, People's Literature Publishing House, then they could enjoy a comfortable income equivalent to or slightly higher than the salary of a university professor.[88]

87. "Wenhua bu guanyu zhiding wenxue yu kexue shuji gaochou zanhang guiding de qingshi baogao" [Ministry of Culture's report on the making of the provisional remuneration provisions for literary and scientific books], ZRGCS, 7:325.

88. Ibid., 321–329.

Ideal as it might sound, this remuneration system was chaos in practice. First of all, not until the late 1950s did a nationally standardized remuneration schedule take effect, so throughout most of the 1950s, different publishing houses, newspapers, and journals owned by the various government or party agencies had their own remuneration scales and default print runs. As a result, works of the same genre and of similar length generated different amounts of remuneration simply because different presses published them. The differences were so vast that even the MOC admitted that anarchy reigned.[89] Although a higher pay scale was applied to academic works to compensate for their small print runs, in reality the difference in print run between the "serious" works and the "popular" ones was often so minute that authors of popular epic works ended up earning absurdly more than "serious" writers. For instance, the print run of *Baowei Yan'an* (Protect Yan'an), a popular novel about civil war heroes defending the CCP headquarters, and that of *Xiongdi minzu zai Guizhou* (Brotherly ethnicities in Guizhou), by the renowned anthropologist Fei Xiaotong (1910–2005), were habitually both set at 10,000 copies/impression. As one of the first military epic novels in the new China, *Baowei Yan'an* was so popular that it was reprinted fifty times (half a million copies) within one year. Since its publisher, People's Literature Publishing House, paid its authors every time their books were reprinted, Du Pengcheng, the author of *Baowei Yan'an*, received a vast sum of money equivalent to thirty years' worth of a professor's salary. On the other hand, Fei Xiaotong had spent months conducting fieldwork and devoted his time to studying the ethnic minorities in southwest China, but owing to the high print run of the first edition, his *Xiongdi minzu zai Guizhou* would never be reprinted. As a result, even though Fei was entitled to a higher pay scale, *Xiongdi minzu zai Guizhou* brought him as little as a month's worth of salary.[90]

The MOC did make an effort to design new remuneration measures in 1955 to adjust and standardize the pay scale and print runs for different genres, hoping to reduce the income gaps between "popular" writers and "advanced mental workers" (*gaoji naoli laodong zhe*) like Fei Xiaotong.[91] However, it seems

89. Ibid.

90. "Guanyu zhiding xin gaochou banfa de jingguo," 339–341.

91. For example, the new measures increased the remuneration per thousand characters up to 70 percent for literary and scientific works, and doubled the minimum remuneration per thousand characters for "specialized academic works, literature for children, plays, and poetry." See "Wenhua bu guanyu zhiding wenxue yu kexue shuji gaochou zanhang guiding de qingshi baogao," 326–327.

that this proposal was never implemented. The lack of consistency and transparency in the remuneration system, as several reports indicated, increased the tension between authors and state-run publishing houses.[92]

During the Hundred Flowers Campaign, many authors took the opportunity to give full vent to their discontentment with the remuneration system, as they were encouraged by Mao to openly criticize the cultural bureaucracy. On the surface, most of their criticism was directed against the corruption, incompetence, and formalization of the cultural administration, but they also offered intriguing details about how these authors, as economic actors, struggled to deal with this new logic of work and value. Underlying their formulaic rhetoric was their deep frustration with and maladjustment to the new collective cultural economy. For instance, even though the authorities considered this new system to have significantly raised the authors' income, as on average what they now received was roughly equivalent to a 15–18 percent royalty on their books, many stated that they struggled to maintain a stable income. The remuneration system was operated under the premise that authors were mental laborers manufacturing literary or academic works on a regular and steady basis. However, as some authors and artists pointed out, this was an overly idealized understanding. It took time to conceive new works, to develop plots and arguments, to conduct necessary research, and to revise drafts. The process of creating a new work was organic and individualized; it was thus hard for writers to make a writing plan and stick to it. Authors received a lump sum once their works got published, and such payments, according to some authors, often created the false impression that they were a privileged and rich class. But what the public didn't see was that under this system, if professional writers failed to publish continuously, their life would be strained within months. Beginning in the mid-1950s, as part of the PRC's initiative to institutionalize and professionalize authors, the China Writers Association gave their members a small monthly

92. For example, "Renmin chubanshe 1953 nian gongzuo qingxing he 1954 nian fangzhen renwu" [People's Publishing House's report on its development in 1953 and its mission plan for 1954], ZRGCS, 6:166–167; Chen Kehan, "Guanyu chuban she gongzuo de mouxie wenti" [Regarding certain problems in the publishing works], ZRGCS, 6:318–325; "Wenhua bu guanyu zhongyang yiji chubanshe gongzuo de jiancha baogao," 141–150; "Wenhua bu dangzu guanyu chu an she nei zuzhi bianji gongzuo de jingyan gao qing Zhongyang Xuanchuan bu shenpi de baogao" [The Ministry of Culture party branch's report to the CCP Central Propaganda Department asking for its review of their draft about the experiences of working as editors in publishing houses], 1957, ZRGCS, 9:88–101; "Wenhua bu zhaokai lao chuban gongzuo zhe zuotanhui jiyao," 156–162.

writing subsidy and granted loans to emerging writers to embark on new projects. But the subsidy alone couldn't support authors and their families if they decided to write full time. The annual "writing output" of 70,000 characters envisioned by the MOC was almost impossible to achieve, so the "ideal" handsome annual income they promised to authors was mostly fiction. In reality, as one writer estimated, it would take a mature novelist four to five years to finish a 200,000-character full-length novel, and the most an industrious writer could deliver in one year might be just three to five short stories. To make ends meet, translator Zhang Yousong (1903–1995), for instance, claimed that he had to "work anxiously all year round" and "couldn't afford to take sick days."[93] Wang Jingzhi (1902–1996), a poet and a contributing editor of People's Literature Publishing House, also stated that a slow writer like him consistently struggled to earn a living, because he simply couldn't produce enough words to support himself.[94]

Some authors did develop more regimented writing patterns to ensure a more stable "output" of words, but even then there was no guarantee of their receiving sufficient and satisfactory remuneration, because the pay scale applied to them and the print run of their works were beyond their (and even their editors') control. Take Fu Lei (1908–1966), one of modern China's most influential translators of French literature, for example. He became a professional translator after 1949 and had no *danwei* work unit affiliation or regular salary; remuneration for translation became his main source of income. Following a strict writing schedule, he spent five to six hours a day translating, another two to three on study and preparation.[95] On average he produced 1,000–1,500 characters per workday.[96] By 1957, he had published eight new translations of works by Honoré de Balzac, Prosper Mérimée, and Voltaire, and even retranslated Romain Rolland's *Jean-Christophe*. His intellectual reputation and this impressively stable productivity made him one of the best-paid authors in the early

93. "Wenhuabu zhaokai wenyi zuojia zuotanhui jiyao" [The proceedings of the Ministry of Culture forum of literary authors], May, 1957, ZRGCS, 9:163–164.

94. "Chushu nan, yinshu shao, gaofei di zuojia dui chuban bumen yijian duo" [Hard to get published, small print runs, and low remuneration: writers have many comments on the publishing sector], RMRB, May 19, 1957.

95. "Zhi Song Xi" [To Song Xi] in *Fu Lei quanji*, 20:174–175.

96. Nu'an, ed., *Fu Lei tan fanyi*, 64. According to Fu, he could produce one thousand words of translation per day for a first draft, and when revising the translation, he would be able to produce three thousand words per day.

PRC. However, the intense exchange of letters between him and the editors of People's Literature Publishing House in 1955–1957 reveals that he believed the current system had failed to realize his books' full potential and had put his livelihood in limbo. He blamed the publisher for mistakenly setting the print runs so high that it became almost impossible for his books to be reprinted (and for him to get another payment). He also assailed his publisher and Xinhua Bookstore for their poor coordination in distributing his works: People's Literature Publishing House declined his request that they reprint his works because they still had considerable unsold stock; on the other hand, readers could not find his works in stores because Xinhua Bookstore did not conscientiously distribute them to meet customers' needs. As a result, the sale of his books was stagnant, and so was his income.[97]

The mismatch between supply and demand that Fu Lei complained about was a common problem in the socialist planned economy. Fu and others who expressed similar anxiety during the Hundred Flowers Campaign felt that they had become increasingly impotent to influence the publishing and distribution process. Compared to the Republican era, the 1950s saw notably higher average print runs for books, as print run had become a key criterion for individual publishing enterprises and the government to decide their future production plan and to evaluate their past performance. For authors, the print runs, impressions, and publication dates of a book, which acutely affected the amount of remuneration they could receive, were often decided arbitrarily by managers of individual publishing houses, or by staff of Xinhua Bookstore who knew the production and distribution plan well but had little knowledge about the subject of the book and the actual readers' preferences. For instance, the default print run per impression for several state-run flagship publishing houses was set at ten thousand copies, but there was never any explanation as to why they insisted on this default print run.[98] Facing authors' complaints about print runs

97. *Fu Lei quan ji*, 20:226–228, 230–231, 259–263, 264–265.

98. The only discussion I have found so far that articulated how the default print run was set is an internal report that the Publishing Administration Bureau submitted to the Ministry of Culture in 1955. They reported that new default print runs for different genres were set based on the print runs of the same genre in the Soviet Union, but they significantly reduced the volume to accommodate China's economic and cultural reality. It also speculated that some Chinese publishing houses set the default print runs unreasonable high to avoid paying authors remuneration continuously. See "Guanyu zhiding xin gaochou banfa de jingguo," 339, 346.

and publication timing, editors blamed the managers and the distribution system for being inflexible and unrealistic.[99]

At the same time, some authors also questioned editors' and press managers' credentials. They considered their "cultural level" too low to enable them to really appreciate the artistic and intellectual value of their works. For instance, Zhang Yousong condemned the managers of People's Literature Publishing House as "slackers" who "knew nothing about their business and refused to learn" and asked: how did they dare to treat authors and translators as "benefactors treat beggars"?[100] Ye Junjian (1914–1999) translated *Don Quixote* from the original Spanish version, but his translation was dismissed and rejected by an editor who had wrongly used a French translation of *Don Quixote* as his reference.[101] A number of translators specializing in classical philosophical works also questioned how People's Literature Publishing House could apply almost the same pay scale to those translating Russian political pamphlets and those translating Hegel.[102] Some pushed this criticism even further and stated that to realize a system based on "pay for the labor" was "rather troublesome," because "literary works cannot be measured and compared according to scales or rulers, nor can they be evaluated by machines or precision instruments."[103]

At the peak of the Hundred Flower Campaign, a few resentful authors went so far as to suggest that, instead of having the mechanically applied remuneration schedules and arbitrarily set print runs establish how much they were worth, they preferred to let the market determine the economic value of their works. The copyright royalty system, which ties together the author's royalty income and the real market demand, was considered by some to be more effective and reasonable. It not only allowed authors to negotiate individually with publishers the terms and the print runs but also ensured that as long as a book was still in print, its author could expect to receive royalty continuously.

99. For example, Renmin wenxue chubanshe yi bianji [An editor of People's Literature Publishing House], "Chubanshe kuaibei kasi le" [Publishing Houses are jammed to death], *RMRB*, May 26, 1957; Xiao Yemu, "Yige bianji de hushing" [The plea of an editor], *RMRB*, December 5, 1956; Yu Yi, "Zhongshi quanguo renmin de jingshen shiliang" [Pay attention to food for the people's soul], *RMRB*, September 8, 1956.

100. Zhang Yousong, "Wo angqi tou, ting qi xiong lai, touru zhandou!"

101. "Wenhua bu zhaokai wenyi zuojia zuotanhui jiyao,"166.

102. Yang Xiaozhou, "Zhongshi waiguo gudian xueshu zuzuo de chuban gongzuo [Pay attention to the publication of foreign classical and academic works], *RMRB*, July 1, 1956.

103. Fang Jie, "An lao qu chou" [Receive payment according to the labor input], *RMRB*, September 15, 1956.

In 1957, *Wenyi bao* (Literature news) published an essay urging the government to "bring back" the royalty system.[104] Some members of the China Writers Association also cried out in a forum held by the MOC, "If royalty is a type of exploitation, we'd rather be exploited!"[105]

The Dismissal of Individual Genius

These authors' complaints about their struggle to make a living under the new system, as well as their pleading for the return of copyright royalty, could be easily interpreted as skepticism toward the socialist planned economy, or nostalgia for capitalism. When the political and cultural atmosphere changed suddenly and drastically in the summer of 1957, many intellectuals, party cadres, and artists who had expressed their discontentment with the cultural bureaucracy during the Hundred Flowers Campaign became targets in Mao's latest political movement. They were labeled and purged based on a vague accusation that they were "rightists." Their suggestions for a more creator-friendly system, their requests for greater freedom of artistic expression, and other criticisms they had made earlier, including those about the "unfair" remuneration schedules, were now used as evidence of their "antiparty," "antisocialism," "individualist" tendencies. For instance, when Zhang Yousong was purged as a "rightist," some proclaimed that his airing of grievances—complaints about how the new system had forced him to work all the time—was a dirty trick he used to pressure People's Literature Publishing House to prepay his remuneration.[106]

Not only were those complaining about the remuneration system targeted, but those thriving in the new system also weren't spared. Both discontent with and enthusiasm about the remuneration system could be seen as manifestations of obsession with individual wealth, which was a sign of ideological "degeneration" to capitalism. For instance, one of the major accusations against Ding

---

104. Huang, "Gaochou zhidu yu 'shi qi nian' wenxue shengchan," 50.

105. "Wenhua bu zhaokai wenyi zuojia zuotanhui jiyao,"164.

106. For example, Moxie, "'Wenyi chazuo' mai de shime cha?" [What kind of tea is sold in the "Literary and Arts Teahouse"], *RMRB*, July 9, 1957, 8. During the Anti-Rightist Movement, Zhang was physically attacked and lost one eye; after the purge, he was subjected to ideological reform and supervision. In the 1960s, he continued translating Mark Twain's works but had to publish them under a pen name. After the Cultural Revolution, he was impoverished, with no job and no *danwei* affiliation. See "Fanyi jia Zhang Yousong qiongsi Chengdou" [Translator Zhang Yousong died in poverty in Chengdou].

Ling during the Anti-Rightist Movement was that she, when mentoring young writers, had allegedly stressed the "fame" and "remuneration" one could attain with one outstanding and original work. Many accused her of promoting "individualism," seeing literary works as solely their creators' possession, and exploiting her cultural fame to rise above the system. This so-called one-book-ism (*yibenshu zhuyi*) was condemned as a reflection of her hidden "bourgeois consciousness," a toxic misdirection of young writers, encouraging them to pursue personal literary achievement and economic self-fulfillment, rather than to "serve the People."[107]

Among the writers labeled as "rightists" and purged was Liu Shaotang (1936–1997). In October 1957, a nationwide campaign was launched against this twenty-two-year-old novelist. His close friends came forward to "reveal" Liu's capitalist "true colors," and renowned literary figures wrote bitter criticisms to denounce this "demeaning youth" and his "antiparty" nonsense. Although Liu was accused primarily as a missionary for "bourgeois individualism" based on his urging for more freedom of creativity, most criticisms at the time seem to have identified something else as the crucial evidence of his "bourgeois individualism": the impressive fortune he had accumulated over the years. For them, Liu was undoubtedly a selfish bourgeois writing for fame and gain. Unlike most "rightist" authors and intellectuals purged at the time, cultural veterans who had been active since the 1920s and 1930s, Liu started his writing career only after 1949. For the cultural authorities, his case thus was particularly alarming because it indicated that individuals who had grown up in communist China could still become profit-driven, market-oriented "opportunists." Although the remuneration system aimed to transform authors into socialist workers, Liu's case suggested that it also cultivated cultural entrepreneurs who managed to manipulate the system to "liberate" themselves from the daily labor of writing.

Born in a village outside of Beijing near the northern terminal point of the Grand Canal, Liu was known as *the* literary prodigy of the new China before he came to be called a "demeaning youth." When he published his first short story at the age of thirteen in the winter of 1949, his ability to illustrate, from a teenage student's perspective, how the CCP brought positive social transformations to rural China quickly earned him the title of *shentong* (wonder child). In 1953, when he was seventeen and still a high school student, his work was

107. For example, Zhou Jianren, "Tan zuojia de pinzhi" [On the qualities of an author], *RMRB*, August 25, 1957; Dong Jin, "Yi ju chengming budeliao" [Is achieving instant fame such a terrific thing to be proud of?], *RMRB*, August 28, 1957.

selected by Ye Shengtao for inclusion in the high school Chinese textbook. In the same year, he joined the CCP and published his first collection of short stories. After the massive success of his first book, he decided to drop out of Beijing University to devote himself to writing. In 1956, he was admitted to the China Writers Association as its youngest member ever, and the Communist Youth League of China also permitted him to be a full-time writer.

Liu had a strong incentive to quit college and embark on a professional career in writing because he knew he could financially support his whole family with his remuneration. Since the publication of his first short story, he had been a beneficiary of the new remuneration system: even though he was still a student, he was paid by newspapers and literary journals just as established writers were paid. In the beginning, he used his remuneration to purchase small treats and theater tickets for his own enjoyment, but as he started to publish short stories regularly in 1951–1952, his remuneration grew large enough to serve as an important financial resource for his family.[108] Meanwhile, he also developed writing strategies and working patterns to maximize the payment he could receive. Like Fu Lei, he wrote with a production plan in mind and was able to estimate pretty accurately in advance the length of each work, how long it would take to write, and how much the payment would be. Knowing that different publishers and periodicals had different pay scales, but they all had production quotas to meet, Liu skillfully peddled his works to ensure that each of them got published. During the campaign against him, several of his friends "disclosed" Liu's keen interest in studying and sharing "tactics" to earn higher remuneration; he was, they claimed, "studying business tricks." For instance, some proclaimed that Liu had "taught" them how to negotiate for a higher pay scale by threatening to withdraw a submission.[109]

Indeed, accusations of this kind during the Anti-Rightist Movement should be read with skepticism, but Liu never denied that he worked the system to earn more. As a professional writer, he was expected to make his living solely from writing. To continue steadily producing words to ensure a stable income, he focused on writing shorter pieces on timely themes and published with presses

108. Wang, ed., *Liu Shaotang nianpu*, 38–39.

109. "Yige qingnian zuozhe de duoluo—pipan Liu Shaotang youpai yanxing dahui de bao-dao" [The degeneration of a youth: report of the struggle meeting against Liu Shaotang and his rightist words and behaviors], *Qingnian zuozhe de jianjie: Liu Shaotang pipan ji*, 15; Gao, "Cong shentong dao youpai fenzi—ji Liu Shaotang de duoluo jingguo" [From wonder child to rightist: Liu Shaotang's story of degeneration], *Qingnian zuozhe de jianjie*, 22.

that had faster turnover time. Between 1954 and 1956, he published on average five to six short stories or novellas annually. Utilizing his reputation as a literary genius, Liu was able to first "sell" these works to newspapers and journals, and then "resell" them as collections of stories to publishers to receive another payment. By 1956, he had published two collections of short stories and two novellas. These four books were printed in quite large quantities (40,000–100,000 copies), owing to his popularity among young readers. This allowed him to generate an impressive income (17,000 yuan RMB) in a short period of time.[110] It is worth noting that in describing his novels in his memoir and recollections written in the 1980s, Liu often started, not with a summary of the plot, but with a set of concrete numbers—word counts, print runs, and the approximate payment he received. His ability to recall such particulars reflects how his state of mind was shaped by the payment system even decades after he was purged.[111]

Liu accumulated his fortune under the new socialist system in a rather old-fashioned way. Unlike Fu Lei, who worked like a diligent machine on a daily basis producing translations to sustain his family, Liu, as a clever economic actor, went one step further with a bold financial plan. With a lump sum of cash in hand, he purchased a house in downtown Beijing and then put the rest in term deposit accounts. According to his estimate, the interest generated by the term deposits would guarantee him and his family a 160-yuan RMB monthly allowance, which was equivalent to a midranking cadre's salary, and four times a factory worker's earnings.[112] No longer constrained by the need to consistently produce short stories, he decided to devote his "free" time now to writing a Chinese equivalent of Mikhail Sholokhov's And Quiet Flows the Don, an epic novel entitled Jinse de yunhe (The golden Grand Canal). It was not just an ambitious literary project, but also Liu's grand plan to secure his "self-sustainable" lifestyle. Jinse de yunhe was scheduled to be released on National Day in 1957 with an impressive 100,000-copy print run. It would, Liu estimated, bring him 35,000 yuan RMB at once. Liu planned to use part of the remuneration to build a villa in his home village to be "close to the peasants," and to put the rest in term deposit accounts to generate interest. Assuming that the interest rate remained

110. Liu, *Wo shi Liu Shaotang*, 116–117.

111. This is also the reason why he is the most frequently mentioned author when scholars discuss the payment system.

112. *Wo shi Liu Shaotang*, 116–117.

unchanged, he believed this book would allow him and his family to live comfortably for the next decade. Once the financial stress was eased, he could focus on writing a multivolume epic of Chinese rural society in his country-side villa.[113]

Jinse de yunhe was never published. The project was called off because of the Anti-Rightist Movement. In October 1957, organizations that had previously endorsed Liu's talent and helped to cultivate his fame, such as the CCP Youth League and the China Writers' Association, held a public struggle session against Liu. Over one thousand writers participated in the meeting. While prestigious literary figures, such as Lao She (1899–1966), Mao Dun, and Guo Moruo (1892–1978), condemned Liu's "betrayal" of the CCP, his friends came forward to expose how Liu cleverly profited from the system. These criticisms and exposés against Liu were published in major newspapers and later compiled as a pamphlet whose title proclaimed it to be "a warning for young authors."[114]

When reflecting in his twilight years on these bitter, hostile, and sometimes jealous comments, Liu attributed them to the "mean nature" of writers, but they were more than that. Several diatribes against Liu attempted to answer the uneasy question of how a socialist system aiming to cultivate mental labor to serve the people could end up nurturing a "selfish bourgeois" like Liu. Liu's class origin—as a son of a petit landlord—was identified by some as a reason for his "special interest in money," but others searched further for the institutional "roots" of Liu's "despicable bourgeois individualism." Their discussion, along with similar criticism of other "rightist" writers, revolved around the justification of authors' material reward and the social capital they generated from their works.

At the core of their criticism against Liu, one could find a classical question about the nature of copyright (with a socialist twist): whether an original work of literature or art comes into being solely owing to the author's "genius." Although Liu never explicitly claimed to be a "wonder child" with exceptional talent, the way he treated his works clearly indicated that he considered all his novels to be his creations, and thus his own possessions. For those who delivered harsh criticism of him during the Anti-Rightist Movement, this was the

---

113. Ibid.

114. Xinhuashe, "Qingnian zuozhe de jianjie! Liu Shaotang zhuiqiu mingli duoluo pandang" [A lesson for young authors! Liu Shaotang seeks fame and fortune, degenerates, and betrays the party], *RMRB*, October 17, 1957.

evidence of how he had been compromised by bourgeois ideology. Liu viewed personal gain in the form of money and fame as the goal of his writing, according to some criticisms, because he, like Ding Ling and other "rightist" writers, misidentified their authorial genius as the sole reason for their success.[115] Liu's complaints about how the party's dogmatic emphasis on social realism had "constrained" his literary talent and prevented him from realizing its full potential, several established writers and party cadres stated, evidenced his ingratitude to the CCP. For them, Liu's literary achievement was not built upon his genius but bestowed by the party, society, and the people.

"Without the victory of the People's revolution, without the CCP and the new society [it brought,] . . . without the party's culture of the youth . . . would you, Liu Shaotang, ever be able to become a writer?" one Communist Youth League cadre questioned.[116] Lao She also reminded young Chinese writers to appreciate the publishing opportunities and editorial guidance they enjoyed in the "advanced socialist system," because writers in the capitalist world had only two equally devastating choices: pursuing one's artistic ideal but starving to death, or becoming a publisher's cash cow, writing to please the market. The "freedom of writing" in the capitalist world was nothing but false consciousness.[117] Kang Zhou (1920–1991), the secretary of the China Writers' Association, acknowledged that Liu might be slightly more talented than his peers, but it was the generous help and sponsorship provided by the party organizations, newspaper editors, and the China Writers' Association, that made him who he was. "The party and the people fostered your career," Kang told Liu. He hinted that— since Liu's literary genius was not unique or indispensable to China's literary circle—if the party withdrew its support, Liu would have nothing left.[118]

The state's current system for professional writers, others also suggested, should accept part of the blame for Liu and other "rightist" writers' "individualist" tendencies. Mao Dun, for instance, believed that Liu's arrogance and his lack of "real life experiences" were the negative consequences of premature

115. Qan Junrui, "Baowei he fazhan Makesi zhuyi de wenyi shiye" [Protect and develop Marxist literary works], *RMRB*, August 30, 1957.

116. Yang Haibo, "Weiyou geming zhe caineng chengwei geming zuojia" [Only a revolutionary can become a revolutionary author], *Qingnian zuozhe de jianjie*, 77–84.

117. Lao She, "Xu qingnian zuojia" [Advice to young authors], *RMRB*, October 17, 1957.

118. Kang Zhuo, "Dang he renmin buxu ni zou silu" [Party and the people do not allow you to destroy yourself], *Qingnian zuozhe de jianjie*, 45. Similar arguments can also be found in Fang Shumin, "Liu Shaotang shi zenyang zouxiang fandang de" [How Liu Shaotang came to betray the party], ibid., 25–33.

professionalization.[119] As a professional writer, Liu was expected to support himself solely by the remuneration he received for his writings. At the same time, the current remuneration system artificially boosted, at least in principle, the income of authors and intellectuals to distinguish the material rewards for mental labor from those for physical labor. For young writers like Liu who had no other work experience, writing was quickly reduced to a job for economic gain rather than the ideal "service to the people." Since writing was an individualized operation, it was easy for them to see their income and their cultural reputation as the fruit of their authorial genius. The relatively high income they enjoyed also reinforced the impression that authors deserved special privileges because "mental workers" were unique, or even superior to factory workers and peasants.[120]

As the Anti-Rightist Movement unfolded, more and more criticisms against the "rightist" writers and intellectuals attributed these rightists' "bourgeois individualism" to the professionalization of writers and the remuneration system, and they urged further "socialist reform" to the current system. Guo Moruo, for instance, stated that writers and intellectuals ought to recognize that without workers and peasants producing the essentials of daily life, they couldn't survive, let alone write novels and poetry. If writing books and making boots are essentially both labor outputs, he argued, "mental workers" shouldn't ask for special treatment.[121] Considering that the principle of the current system— using money to encourage literary creation—was still a "capitalist" idea, Chen Yuan (1918–2004) suggested in his report that the system be improved by a systematic decrease in the remuneration scales to match the income of the "average working-class laborer."[122]

In July 1958, the MOC announced new standard remuneration schedules calculated according to the size of the print run. Remuneration for original works now ranged from four to fifteen yuan RMB per thousand characters, and translations from three to ten yuan RMB per thousand characters. Under the

119. Mao Dun, "Women yaoba Liu Shaotang dangzuo yimian jingzi" [We shall take Liu Shaotang as a mirror], *RMRB*, October 17, 1957.

120. For example, Guo, "Chenzhong de jiaoxun: 1957 nian shiyue shiyi ri zai piping Liu Shaotang dahui shang de jianghua" [A heavy lesson: speech made at the struggle meeting against Liu Shaotang on October 11, 1957], *Wenyi Bao* 1957:28; "Cong Liu Shaotang de duoluo xiqu jiaoxun" [Learn from the degeneration of Liu Shaotang], *RMRB*, October 17, 1957.

121. Guo Moruo, "Nuli ba ziji gaizao chengwei wuchan jieji de wenhua gongren" [Work hard to transform ourselves into proletarian cultural workers], *RMRB*, September 28, 1957.

122. Chen, "Guanyu gaochou" [On remuneration].

TABLE 7.2. The New Remuneration Schedule (1958)

Cumulative print puns	Original works	Translations
1–5,000	8%	6%
5,001–10,000	5%	4%
10,001–30,000	3%	2%
30,001–50,000	2%	2%
50,001–	1%	1%

new system, authors were also entitled to royalty payments according to the size of print runs (see table 7.2). Though the new standard remuneration schedules were significantly lower than the previous ones, they soon drew criticism for being still too "capitalist" in the increasingly radicalized atmosphere of the Anti-Rightist Movement and the Great Leap Forward. In fall 1958, authors and publishers in Shanghai and Beijing called for a further reduction in remuneration.[123] As personal economic gains became closely associated with the "capitalist mindset," the best way for authors and intellectuals to show support for the socialist ethos would be to decline remuneration. Zhang Tainyi, Zhou Libo, and Aiwu, who had been singled out earlier in the Anti-Rightist Movement as the select few "rich" authors, published a piece in People's Daily pushing for the reduction of remuneration. "We are communist writers," they asserted, "so we will not write for money." Yao Wenyuan (1931–2005), an ambitious young literary critic in Shanghai who would later become a member of the Gang of Four, went so far as to publicly denounce the remuneration system as "a leftover of the bourgeois legal doctrine." Only by its eradication, he argued, could the inequality between mental labor and physical labor be brought to an end.[124]

In the name of realizing socialist equality, the MOC instructed publishers and presses nationwide to cut their remuneration in half to "prevent a segment of people from detaching from the working class and peasant masses."[125] However, in the following year, recognizing that such a sharp lowering of

123. Huang, "Gaochou zhidu yu 'shi qi nian' wenxue shengchan," 46–47; Culp, The Power of Print in Modern China, chap. 7.

124. Yao, "Lun gaofei" [On remuneration], Wenhui bao, September 27, 1958. Yao Wenyuan was the son of Yao Pengzi, a member of the new SBG leadership in the early 1950s.

125. "Wenhua bu dangzu Zhongguo zuojia xiehui dangzu guanyu feichu banshui zhi chedi gaige gaochou zhidu de qingshi baogao" [Ministry of Culture party branch and Chinese Writer's Association party branch's report on abolishing copyright royalty and completely reforming the remuneration system], September 24, 1960, ZRGCS, 10:358–361.

remuneration might diminish authors' incentive to write, it reinstated the standard remuneration schedules initially promulgated in July 1958 with minor modifications. Between 1960 and 1965, we see the MOC repeatedly swinging between the call for eliminating the remuneration system in the name of socialist equality and the need to provide a material incentive to encourage cultural creativity. Over time, the standard remuneration schedules were adjusted and lowered gradually. By 1965, the remuneration for original works ranged between two and eight yuan per thousand characters, translation from one to five yuan per thousand characters. When paying amateur authors, publishing houses were allowed to give them free books, stationery, or souvenirs, instead of cash, as rewards.[126] Writing for publication would no longer provide sufficient means to support oneself. Remuneration became so insignificant that writers were no longer tempted by the "capitalist mind-set." They could now announce that they did not write for fame and profit; they wrote "for the People."

126. "Wenhua bu dangwei guanyu jinyibu jiangdi baokan tushu gaochou de qingshi baogao" [Ministry of Culture party committee's report on further lowering the remuneration for newspapers, perodicals, and books], December 7, 1965, ZRGCS, 13:366–368.

Conclusion

THIS BOOK HAS TRACED the curious and crooked journey of copyright in modern China—from the translingual transplantation of copyright/*hanken*/*banquan* in East Asia in the second half of the nineteenth century, to Shanghai booksellers' customary *banquan* regulation and their private antipiracy policing in the late Qing and early Republican period, and to the fading away of the very term *banquan* and its associated practices in the communist 1950s. It illustrates how this internationalizing legal doctrine was reshaped and appropriated in China's local contexts as a powerful means for authors and publishers to create new orders of ownership in a changing knowledge economy. Challenging the conventional notion that the Chinese were forced to adopt this alien legal doctrine under foreign pressure, it reveals that Chinese booksellers and authors, no less than the foreign powers, were zealous in exercising *banquan*/copyright to justify and exclusively secure the profit their works generated.

Copyright was introduced in China at a particular moment when China's cultural market and knowledge world were undergoing an intellectual paradigm shift at the turn of the twentieth century. The relatively stable structure of the late imperial book trade was shaken by the commodification of New Learning knowledge and the Qing government's educational reforms. Between the ill-fated 1898 Reform and the abolition of the civil service examination system in 1905, a new market for translations, textbooks, and other books related to Western knowledge emerged and expanded rapidly. On the other hand, as the old "core texts" of traditional classics were losing their cultural prestige and commercial value, the business of examination-related books declined and eventually collapsed. In this drastically changing cultural landscape, writing, translating, and publishing new titles about the new intellectual orthodoxy became a trade; unauthorized reprinting was increasingly regarded as unacceptable misconduct that would not only compromise the accuracy of knowledge but also cause disorder in China's cultural market.

When the early promoters of *banquan*/copyright employed it to declare, justify, and protect their intellectual credit and commercial profit, they emphasized its newness and progressiveness. Their understanding and practice of *banquan*/copyright, however, were conditioned and influenced by the Ming-Qing practice of *cangban*, which revolved around the idea of owning the tangible printing blocks, rather than the intangible intellectual and artistic creations. When Fukuzawa Yukichi translated the term "copyright" into Japanese, he incorporated the component of *han/ban* (printing blocks) into his coinage of *zōhan no menkyo* and *hanken*. His dual identity as an author-publisher also complicated the way that his contemporaries received him as the exclusive owner of his works. As a result, in the 1860s–1870s, his *hanken*/copyright ownership was mostly acknowleged by his contemporaries on the basis of his possession of the printing blocks for his books rather than his authorship. Later when Wang Kangnian approached Lin Shu and his friends for the right to republish *Bali chahua nü yishi* in 1899, Lin and his friends also understood this undertaking as a transaction involving the ownership of printing blocks and thus insisted on sending the actual block set to Shanghai. When establishing their own *banquan* regime, Shanghai booksellers too situated the physical possession of the *shudi* master copies (and later the manuscripts for new titles) at the center of the SBG's accredited *banquan* register. *Cangban* and copyright are two very different types of ownership of books, but they got mixed up when copyright was introduced in East Asia. And this mix-up shaped not only how the nature of copyright has been perceived in China, but also how its history in China has been told.

Hoping that the state could institutionalize the regulation of *banquan*/copyright, both Chinese booksellers and foreign powers urged the Qing government to promptly issue its own copyright law. Although China's first copyright law, the Copyright Law of the Great Qing, was not enacted until the spring of 1911, the absence of a formal copyright law did not prevent Chinese authors and booksellers from consistently invoking *banquan*/copyright. As elaborated throughout this book, there were four major forms of *banquan*/copyright practiced in China in the first decade of the twentieth century. Each of them was based on a distinct conception of *banquan*/copyright:

1. *Banquan* as ownership of the tangible means of production: it thus belonged to the person(s) who invested capital, paid the authors, and

possessed printing blocks. In Shanghai booksellers' *banquan* regime, the materiality of the means of production and the actual copies it yielded, with their unique physical appearance, were thus of greater importance than the textual originality of a book.

2. *Banquan* as a kind of incorporeal property created by the author's mental labor: it thus was owned by the author. Following this logic, the author was entitled to receive either a onetime payment or long-term royalty by selling, renting, or transferring his *banquan* to others.

3. *Banquan* as a privilege granted by the state to authors and booksellers, upon their request, for their contributions to society: such *banquan* protection was not issued based on the idea that the state was obligated to protect its subjects' private property. Instead, it was a special reward reserved for those who compiled and produced "useful" books to enhance China's development.

4. *Banquan* as a type of license/privilege granted by the state to authors/booksellers after their books passed the state's review and examination: late Qing literati and officials identified the newly established Ministry of Education as the rightful agency in charge of *banquan* because, for them, the real value of a book ought to be determined by its sociocultural contribution rather than its commercial value. Only the state, as the supreme cultural authority, could decide who deserved *banquan*.

These four understandings of *banquan* coexisted. And it was not uncommon for clever Chinese booksellers to invoke them in different contexts simultaneously. Lian Quan, the proprietor of Civilization Books, for instance, utlized all possible means to secure his *banquan* and fight against piracy. In addition to signing *banquan* contracts with Yan Fu and paying him generous royalties, he petitioned various officials for *banquan* protection orders, and he submitted Civilization Books' textbooks to the commissioner of the Imperial University and then to the minister of education for review and approval. While publishing op-eds urging the enactment of a domestic copyright law, he was also a founder of the SBTA and an active member of the SBG's communal *banquan* regime.

The two forms of *banquan*/copyright associated with the state's authority fell away after 1911, but the idea of content review was inherited by the Copyright Law of the Great Qing and its successor laws. Meanwhile, Chinese booksellers in Shanghai continued to practice their *banquan* customs even after the state's copyright law was promulgated. Although the SBG and the SBTA claimed repeatedly in their bylaws that they wholeheartedly followed the state's copyright law and other regulations, Shanghai booksellers maintained a strong tendency to employ the guild's customs instead of the state's law in their daily dealings with piracy. They preferred to register their *banquan*/copyright with the guild rather than at the Ministry of the Interior, settled their piracy disputes at the guild, and relied upon the guild to crack down on and punish local pirates. From the 1910s to the 1930s, at least in Shanghai, the state's copyright law and the SBG's *banquan*/copyright regime coexisted in parallel with one another. As the enforcement and effectiveness of the state's copyright law had been compromised by the consistent political upheavals in China, the SBG managed to maintain minimal *banquan*/copyright protection for its members primarily on the basis of the booksellers' initiatives, first locally in Shanghai, and then transregionally in northern China. Authors, the supposed copyright "owners" according to the state's copyright law, in this scenario, found themselves powerless in the booksellers' *banquan*/copyright regime.

The social history of copyright in China unveiled in this book allows us to rethink the interplay of law, culture, and economic life, as the country underwent profound sociopolitical changes and transitions from the late imperial to the modern period. First and foremost, it demonstrates how the transplantation of copyright was achieved in China's pluralist legal environment by nongovernmental agents via customary mechanisms and civic institutions, in addition to the state's adaptation of modern IPR law. The doctrine of copyright was introduced in China at a particular moment when intensified transregional commercial links, intercultural exchanges, and internationalization of legal doctrines together created situations where basic economic and cultural concepts and practices from different societies were not necessarily compatible or easily adaptable. Supposedly universal commercial or legal doctrines and practices were contested and incorporated in different environments in different ways, and with surprising results. In China, *banquan*/copyright became a highly contested field of different actors and stakeholders who sought to protect their intellectual or economic property, to profit from others' mental and creative labor, or to shape the contents of publications and commodified knowledge in the first half of the twentieth century. The sloppy, frustrating, and sometimes thorny conflicts Chinese authors and publishers experienced when they tried to get *banquan*/copyright to work on the ground were not merely the daily struggles of their economic life, but also an illuminating instance of China's effort to negotiate with the dominant, universalizing discourses of "civilization" and "modernity."

Second, the actual practices of the SBG and other actors compel us to reconsider the interrelationship of the state, the law, and the market in modern China. When China's central state and its laws existed more in name than in reality, from the 1910s to the 1930s, it was the SBG, a civic organization with no legitimate jurisdiction or official authorization, that delivered effective *banquan*/copyright regulation and protection. The absence of a forceful state, thus, does not mean that aspects of social and economic life necessarily fall into complete chaos: nonstate actors can create some level of order and predictability in economic life within a larger, seemingly fractured or even anarchic marketplace. Yet this was just half of the story. Indeed, the Chinese state regimes may have been ineffective in regularly enforcing law and order within their territory, but they seem to have had enormous influence over the trends in China's book market and the Chinese's reading prefences. The commodification of New Learning books, as well as the emergence of a modern textbook market, was largely triggered by the examination and educational reforms undertaken by the shaky Qing state. The piracy problem in Beiping in the 1930s was an indirect consequence of the Nationalist government's relocating the capital to Nanjing. Further, the communist revolution in 1949, ironically, turned communist titles into best sellers in major cities across China in that year. Anticipating a regime change, urban readers rushed to study the new political ideology, and profit-driven publishers were drawn to piracy, this time of Marx, for quick profit just as they had previously been in 1898, 1905, 1911, 1919, and 1928.

Why did Chinese readers feel the need to study the latest political/intellectual agendas of the state? Why was the SBG moved to comply with state policies (even just nominally) and to declare their nominal obedience periodically, despite knowing that the government was not zealous in protecting their *banquan*/copyright and, as a matter of fact, might not have the real capacity to do so? The arbitrary and unpredictable nature of state power in China may play a role here. Though weak, the Chinese state could, on scattered occasions, assert its authority; and when it did exercise its power, it could achieve a lot in particular campaigns for a short period of time. And such arbitrary and unexpected exercises of power, in both symbolic and real forms, could generate widespread fear and persuade people to routinely "follow the rules" as their insurance policy against the "what-if" moment. This was an effective way for the late imperial emperors to manage the bureaucratic system, and for the late imperial governments to manage the massive population with their limited resources.[1] Moreover, as this book suggests, Chinese publishers and booksellers also saw ways of manipulating the state's authority for their own interests.

In the dispute between Civilization Books and Yuan Shikai, for instance, the civilians (Lian Quan and his friends) employed higher political authorities (the Guangxu Emperor and Prince Zaizhen) to challenge and overturn Yuan's rulings, even though the Guangxu Emperor had little real power after 1898. When late Qing publishers reproduced *banquan*/production orders and official endorsements in their books or advertisements, they were also symbolically extending the state's authority to protect their publications from unauthorized reprinting. Whether this really worked is another matter; what was important for them was the "insurance policy" they believed they had acquired. Over the course of the first half of the twentieth century, the successive Chinese states, as part of their modern state building, made significant efforts to extend their political power to permeate society via new laws and institutions, but none of them achieved the level of social control and political management they had planned.[2] As the shape of state power changed over time during this period, Chinese publishers (and perhaps readers too) nevertheless reacted to the institutional changes with their old fear of the unpredictable state authority in mind. While continuing to comply formally with new policies, they saw the modern Chinese state's ever-expanding new institutions and campaigns as sources of authority they could "use." It was thus that the Detective Branch manipulated the Nationalist government's obsession with controlling and censoring the press to protect the SBG members' *banquan*/copyright. As an unevenly developed weak state, the Nationalist government could not adequately enforce its copyright law, but it exercised its power forcefully when it came to censorship campaigns. To attract and redirect the state to exercise its limited power for their own advantage, the Detective Branch labeled pirates as reactionaries publishing antigovernment works. This short-term fix made the SBG an accomplice of the Nationalist government in advancing the state's information control, which in return compromised its members' autonomy in the long run.

In this dynamic interplay among Chinese publishers, their civic organizations, and the state, each used the others for their own ends. The late Qing

---

1. For a discussion of the arbitrary exercise of power in late imperial China, see Kuhn, *Soulstealers*, chap. 9.

2. Duara, *Culture, Power, and the State*; Strauss, *Strong Institutions in Weak Polities*.

and Republican states, considering themselves and being considered by society as *the* intellectual and cultural authority of China, aimed to develop a more comprehensive control over cultural production, via more systematic content review, registration, and censorship. Copyright protection, at various points, was utilized by the resource-poor state as an incentive to attract private authors and publishers to willingly submit to the state's content review. At the same time, the lack of sufficient and functional copyright legislation prompted cultural actors to draw on the state's power via unconventional means, such as censorship, to establish the sense of order in the knowledge economy they had long desired. By doing so, they enhanced the actual influence of the state's authority, symbolic and/or political, in the cultural market.

After 1949, the new PRC inherited its predecessors' interest in controlling cultural production and pushed it further. It proposed that only through socialist reform of the publishing sector, the book market, and the very act of intellectual/artistic creation could the anxious Chinese publishers and authors really be "liberated" from their endless struggle against piracy. Chinese publishers and authors complied with this latest policy and coped with the proliferation of state power and institutions as they had previously done, but, over the 1950s, the space left for them to negotiate between the state and the market, and between the state's symbolic authority and its actual power, dwindled steadily. When the party-state in 1957–1958 finally established full control over China's cultural economy though collectivization, it dismantled the cultural market in which piracy had become a problem and *banquan*/copyright had been promoted to solve it. Piracy as an infringement of property rights, in theory, was eliminated, because *banquan*/copyright, either as authors' ownership of their artistic or intellectual creations, or as publishers' ownership of the tangible means of production, was no longer seen as a legitimate form of private property.

In the early 1960s, literary scholar and book collector Tang Tao (1913–1992) noticed that *banquan*/copyright had become an unfamiliar term for China's younger generations, when his sixth-grader son pointed at the "*banquan suoyou fanjin bijiu*" convention in a Kaiming Books publication and asked: "Papa, what does this mean? Why did people in the past have to print these words on their books?"[3] Proudly, Tang stated that the "honest" youth of New China didn't know this convention, because piracy was now a thing of the past.[4] Piracy, however, can never be relegated to history. Following the onset of the Reform

3. Tang, "Fanban shu" [Pirated books], in *Hui'an shuhua*, 51–53.
4. Ibid.

and Opening-Up (1978–), as the country began to embrace marketization and privatization, copyright piracy reemerged and flourished exponentially in China's rapidly changing cultural economy.

As the country is moving away from the command economy, bootlegged products have flooded China's domestic marketplace. For Chinese readers and customers, this has provided them with cheaper alternatives for their desired goods and has allowed them to "catch up" with limited buying power. For publishers and other manufacturers (state-owned or private), piracy was recognized as a business requiring less investment but with a guaranteed return. At its peak, the piracy rate for computer software and movies in China was over 90 percent. In 2009, it was estimated that at least 40 percent of books sold in China were pirated imprints, and about five hundred million unauthorized books were produced annually.[5] These bootlegged products could be easily found in the city streets. For instance, novelist Yu Hua (1960–) observed pirated copies of his latest work, *Brothers*, being sold in the sidewalk stalls just outside of his house.[6] Pirated works also appear in some surprising locations, such as libraries, "palaces of knowledge" as the Chinese like to call them. In 2017, for example, Liyuan Library on the outskirts of Beijing, which has been named "one of the most beautiful libraries in the world" along with the Bibliothèque Sainte-Geneviève and the New York Public Library, was ordered to suspend operations after readers exposed the fact that one-third of its collection consists of poorly made pirated copies.[7] The once-vanished convention "*banquan suoyou fanjin bijiu*" has made a comeback in post-1978 China and secured its presence in Chinese books ever since. Variations on this threatening statement can also be found on CDs, DVDs, software packaging, online video clips and novels, and even food packages and liquor bottles in China—both the authentic and the pirated ones.

With the return of piracy came a new wave of efforts to transplant modern copyright law in China. As the country "opened up" and began to fully participate in the global economy, modern copyright doctrine was reintroduced in

5. Clifford Coonan, "China's Publishers Struggle to Overcome Book Piracy," *National*, August 27, 2009, https://www.thenational.ae/business/china-s-publishers-struggle-to -overcome-book-piracy-1.508414.

6. Yu, "Stealing Books for the Poor," *New York Times*, March 13, 2013.

7. "China's 'Most Beautiful' Library Ordered to Shut over Claims It Provided Pirated Material and Obscene Content," *South China Morning Post*, September 20, 2017, https://www.scmp .com/news/china/society/article/2111989/chinas-most-beautiful-library-ordered-shut-over -claims-it.

China as a general "norm" or "rule" of the competitive world market. In April 1979, the PRC State Council appointed a task force to undertake research and the drafting of a copyright law. In 1985, it approved the MOC's request for establishing the National Copyright Administration (*Guojia banquan ju*; hereafter, the NCA) to oversee the regulation and protection of copyright. Although the State Council acknowledged the necessity to draft IPR laws that meet international standards and foster economic development, the departure from its earlier antagonistic attitude toward "bourgeois" copyright doctrine was a tortuous one. While the PRC managed to promulgate the Trademark Law in 1982 and the Patent Law in 1984, it took eleven years and twenty drafts before the PRC Copyright Law was finally issued. Complying with the Berne Convention, this law enabled China to gain membership in the Berne Union in 1992 and advanced its preparation for its WTO accession. This law, however, is restrictive in the economic rights it grants; moreover, it also gives the "state organs" the right to use copyrighted materials for "official duties" without authors' authorization.[8]

This latest effort to transplant modern copyright law in China has emerged largely from foreign pressures rather than homegrown initiatives; this is why, Alford and Mertha argue, this effort, just like earlier ones, has failed to strike root on the ground.[9] Since the early 1990s, the United States has repeatedly blamed rampant Chinese piracy for American companies' loss of hundreds of millions of dollars. Trade sanctions and punitive tariffs have been periodically applied to China, forcing it to promise more adequate IPR protections. After China joined the WTO in 2001, IPR-related complaints by other member countries also resulted in the WTO's multiple rulings requesting that China's legal regime take measures to attain compliance.[10] However, such external pressures have had only limited effects. China's central government generally deploys its power and resources to "seriously" enforce copyright protection in the form of antipiracy campaigns only when it is nagged; local authorities, in line with their own regional interests and politics, carry out Beijing's top-down orders reluctantly, simply to "meet the quota."[11] As a result, most routine law enforcement

---

8. Alford, *To Steal a Book Is an Elegant Offense*, 78–79.

9. Mertha, *The Politics of Piracy*, 118–163.

10. For example, "World Trade Organization Adopts Panel Report in China—Intellectual Property Rights Dispute," https://ustr.gov/about-us/policy-offices/press-office/press-releases/2009/march/world-trade-organization-adopts-panel-report-china-i.

11. Mertha, *The Politics of Piracy*; also see Massey, "The Emperor Is Far Away."

at the local level, according Martin Dimitrov, turns out to be a "low-quality" effort yielding little substantial IPR protection in reality.[12]

While China's lax enforcement in protecting international IPR has been continuously reported and criticized by the Western media, we should not forget that it is the Chinese themselves who *live* in a world of fakes, and whose businesses and well-being are affected by piracy daily. Administrative impediments and corruption take a toll on them too. If nation-to-nation negotiations and foreign pressure have failed to yield a satisfactory outcome, working with the local enterprises from within and from the ground up to enhance copyright protection in China might be a better solution.[13] It would be crucial, thus, to understand how the Chinese understand and practice copyright. Indeed, before the PRC Copyright Law was promulgated in 1990, China hadn't had formal copyright legislation for more than forty years, and the two common Chinese terms for copyright—*banquan* and *zhuzuoquan*—had by and large disappeared from the everyday language of the publishing sector. That said, copyright is not a brand-new doctrine for the Chinese, who now, just like their foreign counterparts, need to combat piracy. When copyright was reintroduced in China after 1978, it entered a society with a complex legacy and memory of *banquan*/copyright practices, within and beyond the state's legal system.

Many of the piracy "tricks" practiced in the first half of the twentieth century—from straight reprinting of best-selling titles and issuing copycats with titles confusingly similar to those of the authentic works, to producing "collections" by copying and pasting random contents together—are commonly employed by contemporary Chinese pirates too. Several popular means used in the past to secure and declare product authenticity and ownership, such as the "*banquan suoyou fanjin bijiu*" statement, also have been rediscovered by Chinese publishers and manufacturers and updated with some modern twist. For instance, lavish laser stickers, similar to the *banquan* stamps in the late Qing and Republican periods, are applied by manufacturers to every "authentic" product they have made as an extra certification. The tactics private detectives use now to uncover piracy schemes are also almost identical to the operations of the Detective Branch in the 1930s.[14] The idea that copyright protection and publishing control should be bundled together lives on, as the NCA and the

12. Dimitrov, *Piracy and the State.*

13. Mertha and Dimitrov both suggest this as a better tactic for the "Western" multinational corporations to protect their IPRs more effectively in China.

14. Dimitrov, *Piracy and the State,* 3.

General Administration of Press and Publication are in fact the same agency. And, from time to time, publishers still discover that the pirate they face is a state organ that considers itself above the law.[15]

The entanglement of piracy and copyright in post-1978 China is, in several respects, intriguingly similar to what Chinese authors and publishers had experienced in the first half of the twentieth century. But the challenges faced by the contemporary Chinese state, publishers, and authors are also unique in their own ways. Just as in the past, the country's cultural market has been undergoing a drastic transformation after a profound ideological shift. New and foreign knowledge and technologies are imported in the name of national development; producing and consuming pirated books and goods constitute one short cut to help the nation and individuals "catch up" at a lower cost. During the transformation, subsequently, authors and publishers struggle to establish a new economic and intellectual order, yet, when doing so, they are also inadvisably conditioned by preexisting norms and customs. When late Qing authors, translators, and booksellers employed the concept of copyright to justify the idea that the new books they wrote and published were their rightful *properties*, late imperial conceptions of book ownership shaped how they envisioned copyright as a form of property. Several high-profile copyright cases in the 1980s–1990s revolved around the question of when and how the copyright of a "public" work becomes *private* property again. Lawsuits between Lu Xun's only son and People's Literature Publishing House, for instance, forced the involved parties, their attorneys, the NCA, and China's legal authorities to contest and articulate, in uneasy ways, who owned the economic rights of works produced and published in the Maoist collective economy and whether the pre-1949 arrangement should be acknowledged in post-Mao China.[16]

In the reform era, the uneven distribution of administrative resources still determines how and where the simultaneously weak and strong Chinese state will exercise its supposedly unparalleled power.[17] As in the past, publishers and authors in China now also realize that protecting their copyrights is not the top priority of local cultural and public security bureaus; tracking down pirates, bringing them to court, and maintaining an orderly market eventually become their own responsibilities. Since the early 1990s, publishers, authors, and music

---

15. Yu, "Stealing Books for the Poor." It is widely believed that the PLA and prisons are behind several major piracy schemes.

16. Zhu Maiochun, *Wo wei Lu Xun da guansi*.

17. Dimitrov, *Piracy and the State*.

and media companies in China's major urban areas have joined forces and deal with piracy collectively. Some of these organizations, like the China Written Works Copyright Society (*Zhongguo wenzi zhuzuo xiehui*), are collective stewardship organizations formed by copyright holders; they represent their members to collect royalty, make copyright deals, and bring lawsuits against copyright infringements. Some are formed by businesses aiming to promote market regulation and crack down on piracy, such as the Anti-Piracy Alliance of Beijing Fifteen Publishers (*Jingban shiwushe fandaoban lianmeng*). Like the SBG in the early twentieth century, these "antipiracy alliances" also have their own detective forces to help their members uncover piracy schemes and take legal action against manufacturers, retailers, and individual users of piratical materials. Between 2004 and 2009, for instance, the Anti-Piracy Alliance of Beijing Fifteen Publishers, collaborating with the local authorities, raided over seventeen hundred retailers and manufacturers of pirated books, confiscated over five million copies of pirated books and CD/DVDs, and filed almost five dozen copyright infringement cases for their members.[18]

Despite the similarities in their objectives and tactics, these antipiracy civic organizations in contemporary China are not a reincarnation of the SBG. While the SBG operated its *banquan* protection regime parallel to the state's law, the contemporary publishers' antipiracy alliances work closely with the NCA. They are officially approved and recognized by the NCA and often coordinate their raids with the NCA's nationwide copyright campaigns. In recent years, as e-commerce platforms like Alibaba and Pinduoduo become the latest hubs of bootlegged books, both the NCA and publishers see them as the major target of their antipiracy campaign. In October and November 2018, right before China's annual "double-eleven" sale, Alibaba and Pinduoduo signed a cooperation agreement with the Anti-Piracy Alliance of Beijing Fifteen Publishers and the Anti-Piracy Alliance of Publishers of Children's and Youth's Books. The two leading e-commerce platforms in China and the two major publishers' antipiracy organizations declared that they will join forces to more effectively monitor and crack down on pirates who take advantage of the e-commerce platforms. Although this new cooperation model has been praised by Chinese media

18. "Jingban shiwushe fandaoban lianmeng chengli shinian dadao weiquan xingcheng moshi" [Ten years after its establishment, the Anti-Piracy Alliance of Beijing Fifteen Publishers has established a model to crack down on piracy and protect copyright], National Copyright Administration of the People's Republic of China, June 12, 2010, http://www.ncac.gov.cn /chinacopyright/contents/518/134506.html.

as a "win-win" situation that will enhance copyright self-regulation, it was the NCA, as the visible hand, that "actively guided" and "supported" the e-commerce businesses and the publishers to form this antipiracy partnership.[19] For different reasons, the publishers, the retailers, and the state recognize copyright piracy as a pressing problem that needs to be solved, but they also all realize that relying solely on the state's law and enforcement or on market self-regulation will not be sufficient to achieve their goal. While the early twentieth-century pirate hunters in China operated at the fringe of the state, the early twenty-first-century pirate hunters in China partner with the state in a harmonious dance.

19. "Alibaba Pinduoduo deng yu liangda fandaoban lianmeng kaizhan banquan hezuo" [Alibaba, Pinduoduo, and others formed a copyright protection partnership with two major antipiracy alliances], KKNEWS, November 9, 2018, https://kknews.cc/tech/6zox25v.html.

GLOSSARY OF CHINESE AND
JAPANESE TERMS, TITLES, AND NAMES

Books and Other Titles

Baihua shuxin 白話書信

Bali chahua nü yishi 巴黎茶花女遺事

Banquan kao 版權考

Baowei Yan'an 保衛延安

Beiping chenbao 北平晨報

Cangming chidu 滄溟尺牘

Chen Wen suanshu Jiaokeshu 陳文算術教
科書

Chikyū ōrai 地球往來

Chūgai shinbun 中外新聞

Chunqiu dan he xiyi 春秋單合析義

Conggui maoshi jijie 從桂毛詩集解

Diguo yingwen duben 帝國英文讀本

Dongfang zazhi 東方雜誌

Do xixue shu fa 讀西學書法

Duxiu wencun 獨秀文存

Faguo geming 法國革命

Fayi 法意

Fuemosi zaisheng an er an san an 福爾摩斯再
生案二案三案

Gakumon no susume 学問のすすめ

Gaoxiao lishi ke cankao ziliao 高中歷史參考
資料

Geguo geming shi 各國革命史

Geguo geming tongsu tijie 各國革命通俗題解

Guangdong xiangtu jiaokeshu 廣東鄉土教
科書

Guanshang kuailan 官商快覽

Hali Bote yu baozou long 哈利波特与豹走龙

Heinu yutian lu 黑奴籲天錄

Huang Ming jingshi wenbian 皇明經世文編

Huaying chujie 華英初階

Huayin jinjie 華英進階

Hu Shi wencun 胡適文存

Jiaokeshu piping 教科書批評

Jiaoyu zazhi 教育雜誌

Jiezi Yuan huapu 芥子園畫譜

Jin sanbainian xueshu shi 近三百年學術史

Jinse de yunhe 金色的运河

Jōyaku jūikkokuki 條約十一國記

Kairekiben 改曆辨

Keimō Tenarai no Fumi 啟蒙手習之文

Kyūri zukai 究理図解

Liaozhai zhiyi 聊齋誌異

Li Hongzhang 李鴻章

Liuyang erjie wenji 瀏陽二傑文集

Lun chijiu zhan 論持久戰

Lun lianhe zhengfu 論聯合政府

Mao Zedong waizhuan 毛澤東外傳

Meiji yōbunshō 明治用文章

Meiren zhuang 美人妝

Minsheng ribao 民聲日報

Mongxue duben 蒙學讀本

Putong xin chidu 普通新尺牘

Qingyi bao 清議報

Quanxuepian 勸學篇

Qunxue yiyan 群學肄言

Raijū sōhō 雷銃操法

Riben bianzheng kao 日本變政考

Riben shumu zhi 日本書目志

San jianxia 三劍俠

Seiryoku tōzen shi 西力東漸史

Seiyō jijō 西洋事情

Seiyō jijō gaihen 西洋事情外編

Seiyō tabi annai 西洋旅案内
Sekai kunizukushi 世界國盡
Shangwu jiaoke chidu 商務教科尺牘
Shehui tongquan 社會通詮
Shen bao 申報
Shenshijizhai congshu 慎始基齋叢書
Shiwu bao 時務報
Shuang yen ji 雙艷記
Sidalin zenyang qijiade 斯大林怎樣起家的
Suanshu jiaokeshu quanzhang 算術教科書
　全章
Su tongling zifa 速通靈字法
Taixi shinshi lanyiao 泰西新史攬要
Taiyang zhao zai Sanggan he shang 太陽照在
　桑乾河上
Taiyōreki kōshaku 太陽曆講釋
Tianyanlun 天演論
Tixiao yinyuan 啼笑姻緣
Tongzi xin chidu 童子新尺牘
Tōyō keizai shinpō 東洋経済新報
Wanguo gongbao 萬國公報
Wanguo gongfa 萬國公法
Wanguo lishi 萬國歷史
Wanguo zhengzhi congkao 萬國政治叢考
Wenming xiaoshi 文明小史
Wenyi Bao 文藝報
Wushi zitong waiguo shi 無師自通外國史
Xinchao 新潮
Xingle 性樂
Xingshi 性史

Xingtan 性談
*Xinjuan zengbu quanxiang pinglin gujin
　lienü zhuan* 新鐫增補全像評林古今列
　女傳
Xinmin congbao 新民叢報
Xin mingci cidian 新名詞辭典
Xin minzhu zhuyi lun 新民主主義論
Xin qingnian 新青年
Xiongdi minzu zai Guizhou 兄弟民族在貴州
Xixue santong 西學三通
Xixue shumu biao 西學書目表
Xizheng bu qiuren 西政不求人
Xuebu guanbao 學部官報
Yinbingshi wenji 飲冰室文集
Yingwen hangu 英文漢詁
Yuan Fu 原富
Yuxue liuhen 玉雪留痕
Zengban dong xi xue shulu 增版東西學書錄
Zhengzhixue 政治學
Zhongdong zhanji benmuo 中東戰記本末
Zhongguo dagemingshi 中國大革命史
Zhongguo lishi 中國歷史
Zhongguo tongshi jianbian 中國通史簡編
Zhongwai cewen daguan 中外策問大觀
Zhongxi si dazheng 中西四大政
Zhuibaiqiu 綴白裘
Ziben lun 資本論
Zibian 字辨
Ziyou yuanli 自由原理
Zuozhi chuyan 佐治芻言

Firm Names and Institution Names

Alibaba 阿里巴巴
Anguo shuju 安國書局
Baoding shijie tushuju 保定世界圖書局
Baoshan zhai 寶善齋
Beiping daoqun shudian 北平導群書店
Beiping gonganju 北平公安局
Beiping wuxue shuguan 北平武學書館
Beiping yanjiu yuan 北平研究院
Beiping yinshuaye tongye gonghui 北平印刷
　業同業公會
Beiping zhongyan yinshuaju 北平中央印刷局

Beixin shuju 北新書局
Beiyang guanbaoju 北洋官報局
Bianyi tushu ju 編譯圖書局
Biaomeng shushi 彪蒙書室
Chongde gongsuo 崇德公所
Chuban weiyuanhui 出版委員會
Chuban zongshu 出版總署
Chunming shudian 春明書店
Datong yishu ju 大同譯書局
Dushu chubansh 讀書出版社
Feihong ge 飛鴻閣

Fuzanbō 冨山房
Gaosheng zhan 高陞棧
Guangming shuju 光明書局
Guangxuehui 廣學會
Guangyi shuju 廣益書局
Guangzhi shuju 廣智書局
Guojia banquan ju 国家版权局
Guomin Zhengfu Junshi Weiyuanhui 國民
　政府軍事委員會
Guozigian 國子監
Haizuo shuju 海左書局
Hakubunkan 博文館
Hongwen shuju 鴻文書局
Hongwen tang 鴻文堂
Hongwen xingji 鴻文興記
Honya nakama 本屋仲間
Huanwen shuju 煥文書局
Huasheng yinshuju 華盛印書局
Hunan bianyi she 湖南編譯社
Jiangnan jiqizhizaoju 江南製造局
Jiangzuo shuju 江左書局
Jiefang she 解放社
Jingban shiwushe fandaoban lianmen 京版
　十五社反盗版联盟
Jingbei silingbu 警備司令部
Jinshu zhai 金粟齋
Kaiming Shuju 開明書局
Kexue bianyiju 科學編譯局
Kexuehui bianyibu 科學會編譯部
Maruzen 丸善
Minzheng bu 民政部
Nanjing junyong tushushe 南京軍用圖書社
Penglai hongjishe 蓬萊鴻跡社
Pinduoduo 拼多多
Qianqing tang 千頃堂
Qinglian ge 青蓮閣
Quanguo shanghui lianhehui 全國商會聯
　合會
Qunyu shanfang 群玉山房
Rakuzendou 樂善堂
Renmin wenxue chubanshe 人民文學出版社
Sanyou shuju 三友書局
Saoye shanfang 掃葉山房
Shang bu 商部

Shanghai shangwu huiyi gongsuo 上海商務
　會議公所
Shanghai shi shuye tongye gonghui choubei
　weiyuanhu 上海市書業同業公會籌備委
　員會
Shanghai shuye gongsuo 上海書業公所
Shanghai shuye shanghui 上海書業商會
Shanghai shuye shangtuan 上海書業商團
Shanghai shuye tongye gonghui 上海書業同
　業公會
Shanghai shuye tongye gonghui chajiu
　weiban weiyuanhui zhuping banshichu
　上海書業同業公會查究偽版委員會駐平
　辦事處
Shanghai wenhua chubanshe 上海文化出
　版社
Shangwu yinshuguan 商務印書館
Shangye tushubu 商業圖書部
Shending si 審定司
Shenghuo shudian 生活書店
Shijie shuju 世界書局
Shixue zhai 史學齋
Shuangyi shuju 雙義書局
Tongwenguan 同文館
Tongyi shanghan 統一商行
Wenguang 文光
Wenhai ge 文海閣
Wenhua bu 文化部
Wenming shuju 文明書局
Wenyi shuzhuang 文宜書莊
Xiandai shuju 現代書局
Xinchangxiang 信昌祥
Xinhua shudien 新華書店
Xue bu 學部
Yadong tushuguan 亞東圖書館
Yanyi shuju 延益書局
Yishu huibian she 譯書匯編社
Yu Wentai Santaiguan 余文台三才館
Zenrin yakushokan 善隣譯書館
Zhina shuju 支那書局
Zhonggong zhongyang weiyuanhui
　xuanchuanbu 中共中央委員會宣傳部
Zhongguo chubanren zhuzuoxuan baohu
　xiehui 中國出版人著作權保護協會

Zhongguo wenzi zhuzuo xiehui 中国文字
　著作协会
Zhongguo zhuzuoren chubanren xiehui 中國
　著作人出版人協會
Zhonghua shuju 中華書局

Zhongyang yanjiu yuan 中央研究院
Zhouyueji 周月記
Zizheng yuan 資政院
Zuoxinshe 作新社

Personal Names

Azuma Heiji 吾妻兵治
Bao Tianxiao 包天笑
Bu Shengtong 卜勝同
Cai Yuanpei 蔡元培
Ceng Mengpu 曾孟樸
Chen Duxiu 陳獨秀
Chen Jiru 陳繼儒
Chen Kehan 陳克寒
Chen Yuan 陳原
Chen Yunsheng 陳雲生/允升
Chen Zhaochun 陳兆椿
Chen Zilong 陳子龍
Cheng Huanqing 程煥卿
Cheng Shenfu 程申甫
Ding Ling 丁玲
Ding Zhicun 丁芝孫
Duan Weiqing 段惟清
Fan Hauyou 范華友
Fan Wenlan 范文瀾
Fei Xiaotong 費孝通
Feng Ziyou 馮自由
Fukuzawa Yukichi 福澤諭吉
Fu Lei 傅雷
Geng Zeming 耿澤民
Guo Moruo 郭沫若
Huang Shoufu 黃守孚
Hu Jitao 胡濟濤
Hu Shi 胡適
Hu Yuzhi 胡愈之
Jian Qingzhai 簡青齋
Kang Youwei 康有為
Kang Zhou 康濯
Kuai Guangdian 蒯光典
Lao She 老舍
Liang Qichao 梁啟超
Lian Quan 廉泉

Li Boyuan 李伯元
Li Difan 李迪凡/滌帆
Lin Shu 林紓
Li Tancai 黎天才
Liu Chunlin 劉春霖
Liu Dapong 劉大鵬
Liu Kunyi 劉坤一
Liu Shaotang 劉紹棠
Li Xiaofeng 李小峰
Lu Dingyi 陸定一
Lufei Kui 陸費逵
Lü Haihuan 呂海寰
Lu Minggu 盧鳴谷
Lu Runyang 陸潤痒
Lü Simian 呂思勉
Lu Xun 魯迅
Mao Dun 茅盾
Meng Zhixi 孟芝熙
Mizuno Rentaro 水野鍊太郎
Nagasawa Kikuya 長澤規矩也
Naitō Denemon 内藤傳右衛門
Naitō Konan 内藤湖南
Odagiri Masunosuke 小田切萬壽之助
Qian Mu 錢穆
Qin Ruijie 秦瑞玠
Rong Qing 榮慶
Sheng Xuanhuai 盛宣懷
Shen Jifang 沈季芳
Shi Zuocai 史佐才
Song Xingwu 宋星五
Su Lantain 蘇藍田
Sun Baoxuan 孫寶瑄
Tang Tao 唐弢
Tao Baolin 陶保霖
Wang Jingzhi 汪靜之
Wang Kangnian 汪康年

Wang Mengzou 汪孟鄒
Wang Shouchang 王壽昌
Wang Shuxun 王序勳
Wang Yuanfang 汪原放
Wang Yunwu 王雲五
Wang Zhongqian 王仲乾
Wang Zicheng 王子澄
Wei Han 魏瀚
Wei Yi 魏易
Wu Peifu 吳佩孚
Wu Renfu 烏仁甫
Xia Cengyou 夏曾佑
Xia Ruifang 夏瑞芳
Xiong Jilian 熊季廉
Xu Hongyun 徐鴻雲
Xu Shichang 徐世昌
Xu Weize 徐維則
Yan Fu 嚴復
Yan Qu 嚴璩
Yang Shuyi 楊述疑
Yao Pengzi 姚蓬子
Yao Wenyuan 姚文元
Ye Han 葉翰

Ye Junjian 葉君健
Ye Shengtao 葉聖陶
Yikuang 奕劻
Yin Youmo 印有模
Yuan Kewen 袁克文
Yuan Shikai 袁世凱
Yuan Shuxu 袁樹勛
Yuan Zhicai 袁志才
Yu Dafu 郁達夫
Yu Fu 俞復
Yu Hua 余华
Zaizhen 載振
Zhang Baixi 張百熙
Zhang Henshui 張恨水
Zhang Jingsheng 張競生
Zhang Meiyi 張美翊
Zhang Xunzhi 張巽之
Zhang Yousong 張友松
Zhang Zhidong 張之洞
Zhao Xunchen 趙勳臣
Zhu Guanting 朱冠亭
Zhu jixi 朱積熙
Zhu Zhisan 朱峙三

Terms

Anguo 安國
an lao qu chou 按勞取酬
bankoku/wanguo 萬國
banquan 版權
banquan suoyou fanin bijiu 版權所有翻印
    必究
banquan ye 版權頁
banquan zhangcheng 版權章程
banshui 版稅
banshui pingzhe 版稅憑摺
banzu 版租
Baohu chubanwu zhuzuoquan zhanxing
    guiding 保護出版物著作權暫行規定
Beiyang dachen 北洋大臣
benbang 本幫
bunmeikaika 文明開化
buzhengdang 不正當
cangban/zōhan 藏版

Chosakukenhō 著作権法
chou banshui 抽版稅
Chuban Gongyue 出版公約
Da Qing zhuzuoquan lü 大清著作權律
dianben 殿本
diaocha yuan 調查員
Dongan Shichang 東安市場
falü jieju 法律解決
fanghai fenghua 妨害風化
fanke 翻刻
faxing quan 發行權
feigong 匪共
Fukuzawa shi zōhan 福澤氏藏版
fuqiang 富強
futsūbun 普通文
ganbu bidu 幹部必讀
gaoji naoli laodong zhe 高級腦力勞動者
geren zhi siquan 個人之私權

gihan 偽版

gongli 公例

Gongshang tongye gonghui guize 工商同業
公會規則

gongsuo 公所

gongsuo tongren gongren banquan 公所同
人公認版權

Guomin zhengfu zhuzuoquan fa 國民政府著
作權法

hankabu 板株

hanken 版權

Hanken hō 版權法

hanken shoyū 版權所有

Houguan yanshi banquan suoyou 侯官嚴氏
版權所有

huiguan 會館

ihan/nisehan 偽板

Jianming shanghui zhangcheng 簡明商會
章程

Jiaotong lu 交通路

jingshi wenbian 經世文編

jūhan 重板

ju jian zhi ye 巨剪之業

kaihan 開板

kopīraito コピーライト

kuxin 苦心

Laozha bufang 老閘捕房

leibian 類編

Liulichang 琉璃廠

liumang 流氓

mai banquan 賣版權

Meizhu hutong 梅竹胡同

micha zoutan 密查坐探

Nandajie 南大街

okuzuke 奥付

pingli 評理

Qianmen 前門

Qipanjie 棋盤街

ruihan 類板

Seiyō 西洋

shanben 善本

shenchadong 審查董

shending 審定

shentong 神童

shibang 石幫

shidafu 士大夫

shiwu 時務

shudi 書底

Shudi guahao 書底掛號

shujing cunan fanke bijiu 書經存案翻刻必究

Shuppan jōrei 出版條例

shuye de bailei 書業的敗類

Simenkuo 司門口

tenka no kōhō 天下の公法

tomehan 留版

tongye 同業

touji 投機

wailao 微勞

Wangfujing dajie 王府井大街

Wanyuan jiadao 萬源夾道

weichou 微酬

Wenchang 文昌

wenhua hezuo she 文化合作社

wenren 文人

xili 西例

xinshu 新書

xinxue 新學

xiu lai xiu qu 袖來袖去

Xixue 西學

Xuebu shending 學部審定

Xuewu gangyao 學務綱要

yangbang 洋幫

yangzhuang 洋裝

yibenshu zhuyi 一本书主义

yifa banshi 依法辦事

yinshu zhi quan 印書之權

zei ren shu de 賊人書的

Zhonghua Minguo zhuzuoquan fa 中華民國
著作權法

zhongxi 中西

zhuzuoquan 著作權

ziji jiaoyu ziji 自己教育自己

zōhan no menkyo 藏版の免許

zōhansha 藏板者

SELECTED BIBLIOGRAPHY

Archives

Copyright Issues between China and the United States, Box 10237; Central Decimal File, 1910–1929; General Records of the Department of State, Record Group 59; National Archives at College Park, MD.

Gaimushō kiroku, senzenki 外務省記錄 戰前期 [Diplomatic records. Prewar period]. Gaimu honshō gaikō shiryōkan (Diplomatic Records' Office of the Ministry of Foreign Affairs of Japan). Tokyo.

Shanghai shi chuban ju dang'an 上海市出版局檔案 [The archives of Shanghai Municipal Publication Office]. Shanghai dananguan [Shanghai Municipal Archives], Shanghai. B167.1.

Shanghai shuye tongye gonghui dangan 上海書業同業公會檔案 [The archives of the Shanghai Booksellers' Guild]. Shanghai dananguan, Shanghai. S313.1–4.

Shanghai xinwen chuban chu anjuan 上海新聞出版處案卷 [The case files of Shanghai Press and Publishing Department]. Shanghai dananguan, Shanghai. B1.2.

Government Newsletters, Newspapers, and Periodicals

Beiping chenbao 北平晨報 [The Beiping morning post]. Beijing: 1930–1937. Reproduction, Beijing: Zhongguo guojia tushuguan. Microfilm.

Dagon bao 大公報 [L'impartial]. Tainjing: 1902–1949. Reproduction, Washington, DC: Library of Congress. Microfilm.

Dongfang zazhi 東方雜誌 [Eastern miscellany]. Shanghai: 1904–1948.

Huabei ribao 華北日報 [Northern China daily]. Beijing: 1929–1949. Reproduction, Beijing: Zhonghua quanguo tushuguan wenxian suowei zhongxin, 1988. Microfilm.

Jiaoyu zazhi 教育雜誌 [Education magazine]. Shanghai: 1909–1948. Reprint, Taipei: Taiwan Shangwu yinshuguan, 1975.

Nanfang bao 南方報 [The South China daily]. Shanghai: 1905–1907. Reproduction, Beijing: Zhonghua quanguo tushuguan wenxian suowei zhongxin, 1988. Microfilm.

Qingyi bao 清議報 [The China discussion]. Yokohama: 1898–1901. Reprint, Taipei: Chengwen chubanshe, 1967.

Renmin ribao 人民日報 [People's daily]. People's Daily Database. http://data.people.com.cn.

Shangwu guanbao 商務官報 [Official newsletter of the Ministry of Commerce]. Beijing: 1906–1910. Reprint, Taipei: Guoli gugong bowuyuan, 1982.

Shen bao 申報 [Shanghai news]. Shanghai: 1872–1949. Reprint, Taipei: Taiwan xuesheng shuju, 1965.

Shibao 時報 [Eastern times]. Shanghai: 1904–1939. Reproduction, Beijing: Zhongguo guojia tushuguan, 1982. Microfilm.

Shiwu bao 時務報 [The Chinese progress]. Shanghai: 1896–1898. Reprint, Taipei: Wenhai chubanshe, 1987.

Waijiao bao 外交報 [Diplomatic news]. Shanghai: Commercial Press, 1902–1911. Reprint, Taipei: Guangwen shudian, 1964.

Wanguo gongbao 萬國公報 [A review of the times]. Shanghai: 1874–1907. Reprint, Taipei: Huawen shuju, 1968.

Xuebu guanbao 學部官報 [Official newsletter of the Ministry of Education]. Beijing: 1906–1911. Reprint, Taipei: Guoli gugong bowuyuan, 1980.

Zhengfu gongbao 政府公報 [Government communiqué]. Beijing: Zhengshitang yizhuju, 1912–1928.

Zhongguo xinshu yuebao 中國新書月報 [China new books monthly]. Shanghai: Huatong shuju, 1931–1933.

Zhongwai ribao 中外日報 [The universal gazette]. Shanghai: 1898–1911. Reproduction, Beijing: Zhonghua quanguo tushuguan wenxian suowei zhongxin, 1989. Microfilm.

Published Sources

Ah Ying 阿英. "Guanyu *Chahua nü yishi*" 關於茶花女遺事 [About the story of the lady of the camellias in Paris]. In *Lin Shu Yanjiu Ziliao* 林紓研究資料, edited by Xue Suizhi and Zhang Jun-cai, 274–279. Fuzhou: Fujian renmin chubanshe, 1983.

Alford, William. *To Steal a Book Is an Elegant Offense*. Stanford, CA: Stanford University Press, 1995.

Altehenger, Jennifer E. "On Difficult New Terms: The Business of Lexicography in Mao Era China." *Modern Asian Studies* 51 (October 2017): 622–661.

Amelung, Iwo. "The Complete Complication of New Knowledge, *Xinxue beizuan* (1902): Its Classification Scheme and Its Sources." In *Chinese Encyclopaedias of New Global Knowledge (1870–1930): Changing Ways of Thought*, edited by Milena Doleželová-Velingerová and Rudolf G. Wagner, 85–102. Berlin: Springer-Verlag, 2014.

"The Awakening of China." *American Monthly Review of Reviews*, July–December 1900, 110.

Baldwin, Peter. *The Copyright Wars: Three Centuries of Trans-Atlantic Battle*. Princeton, NJ: Princeton University Press, 2014.

Bao, Tainxiao 包天笑. *Chuanyinglou huiyilu* 釧影樓回憶錄 [The memoir from the armlet-shadow chamber]. Yonghe: Wenhai chubanshe, 1974.

Bastid-Bruguière, Marianne. "The Japanese-Induced German Connection on Modern Chinese Ideas of the State: Liang Qichao and the Guojia lun of J. K. Bluntschli." In *The Role of Japan in Liang Qichao's Introduction of Modern Western Civilization to China*, edited by Joshua A. Fogel, 105–124. Berkeley: Institute of East Asian Studies, University of California, 2004.

Beijing Gongye zhi bianweihui 北京工業志編委會. *Beijing gongye zhi: yinshua zhi* 北京工業志-印刷志 [History of Beijing industry: publishing industry]. Beijing: Zhongguo kexue jishu chuban she, 2001.

Beiping shi Shehuiju 北平市社會局. *Beipingshi gongshang gaikuang* 北平市工商概況 [Overview of industry and commerce in Beiping]. Beiping: Beiping shi Shehuiju, 1932.

Bennett, Adrian Arthur. *John Fryer: The Introduction of Western Science and Technology into Nineteenth-Century China*. Cambridge, MA: Harvard University Press, 1967.

Bently, Lionel, Uma Suthersanen, and Paul Terremans, eds. *Global Copyright: Three Hundred Years since the Statute of Anne, from 1709 to Cyberspace*. Cheltenham, UK: Edward Elgar Publishing, 2010.

Bernhardt, Kathryn, and Philip C. C. Huang, eds. *Civil Law in Qing and Republican China*. Stanford, CA: Stanford University Press, 1994.

Bohong 伯鴻. "Lun guoding jiaokeshu" 論國定教科書 [On the official textbooks]. In *Lufei Kui jiaoyu lunzu xuan* 陸費逵教育論著選 [A selection of Lufei Kui's essays on education], 16–19. Beijing: Renmin Jiaoyu Chubanshe, 2000.

Borthwick, Sally. *Education and Social Change in China: The Beginning of the Modern Era*. Stanford, CA: Hoover Institution Press, 1983.

Brokaw, Cynthia J. *Commerce in Culture: The Sibao Book Trade in the Qing and Republican Period*. Cambridge, MA: Harvard University Asia Center, 2007.

———. "Commercial Publishing in Late Imperial China: The Zuo and Ma Family Business on Sibao, Fujian." *Late Imperial China* 17:1 (June 1996): 42–92.

———. "On the History of the Book in China." In *Printing and Book Culture in Late Imperial China*, edited by Cynthia J. Brokaw and Kai-wing Chow, 3–54. Berkeley: University of California Press, 2005.

———. "Reading the Best-Sellers of the Nineteenth Century: Commercial Publishing in Shiabo." In *Printing and Book Culture in Late Imperial China*, edited by Cynthia J. Brokaw and Kai-wing Chow, 184–231. Berkeley: University of California Press, 2005.

Brokaw, Cynthia J., and Kai-wing Chow, eds. *Printing and Book Culture in Late Imperial China*. Berkeley: University of California Press, 2005.

Brown, Jeremy, and Paul G. Pickowicz, eds. *Dilemmas of Victory: The Early Years of the People's Republic of China*. Cambridge, MA: Harvard University Press, 2007.

Burgess, John Stewart. *The Guilds of Peking*. New York: Columbia University Press, 1928.

Cao, Nanping 曹南屏. "Keju, chuban yu zhishi zhuanxing" 科举、出版与知识转型 [Civil service examination, publishing, and transformation of knowledge]. PhD diss., Fudan University, 2012.

Cassel, Pär Kristoffer. *Grounds of Judgment: Extraterritoriality and Imperial Power in Nineteenth-Century China and Japan*. Oxford: Oxford University Press, 2011.

Cha, Shijie 查時傑. "Lin Lezhi de shengping yu zhishi" 林樂知的生平與志事 [The life and career of Young J. Allen]. In *Jidujiao ruhua bai qi shi nian jinian ji* [Collective essays commemorating the 170th anniversary of the introduction of Christianity to China], edited by Lin Shiping, 111–160. Taipei: Yuzhokuang, 1977.

Chang, Hao. *Chinese Intellectuals in Crisis: Search for Order and Meaning (1890–1911)*. Berkeley: University of California Press, 1987.

Chang, Zizhong 常紫鐘, et al., eds. *Yan'an shidai xin wenhua chuban shi* 延安时代新文化出版史 [History of the new cultural publishing during the Yan'an era]. Xi'an: Shanxi renmin chubanshe, 2001.

Chen, Juhong 陈矩弘. *Xin Zhongguo chuban shi yanjiu* 新中国出版研究 (1949–1965) [Study of the history of publishing in New China (1949–1965)]. Shanghai: Shanghai jiaotong daxue chubanshe, 2012.

Chen, Li. *Chinese Law in Imperial Eyes: Sovereignty, Justice, and Transcultural Politics*. New York: Columbia University Press, 2016.

Chen, Li, and Madeleine Zelin. "Rethinking Chinese Law and History: An Introduction." In *Chinese Law: Knowledge, Practice and Transformation, 1530s to 1950s*, edited by Li Chen and Madeleine Zelin, 1–14. Leiden: Brill, 2015.

Chen, Yuan 陳原. "Guanyu gaochou" 關於稿酬 [On remuneration]. In his *Chen Yuan chuban wenji* 陳原出版文集 [Chen Yuan's writings on publishing], 19–26. Beijing: Zhongguo shuji chubanshe, 1995.

Chen, Zhongping. *Modern China's Network Revolution: Chambers of Commerce and Sociopolitical Change in the Early Twentieth Century*. Stanford, CA: Stanford University Press, 2011.

Chosakukenhō Hyakunenshi Henshū Iinkai, ed. *Chosakukenhō hyakunenshi* 著作権法百年史 [One-hundred-year history of copyright law]. Tokyo: Chosakuken Jōhō Sentā, 2000.

Chow, Daniel C. K. "Why China Does Not Take Commercial Piracy Seriously." *Ohio Northern University Law Review* 32:2 (2006): 203–225.

Chow, Kai-wing. *Publishing, Culture, and Power in Early Modern China*. Stanford, CA: Stanford University Press, 2004.

Cohen, Paul A. *Between Tradition and Modernity: Wang T'ao and Reform in Late Ch'ing China*. Cambridge, MA: Harvard University Press, 1974.

Culp, Robert. *Articulating Citizenship: Civil Education and Student Politics in Southeastern China, 1912–1940*. Cambridge, MA: Harvard University Asia Center, 2007.

———. "Mass Production of Knowledge and the Industrialization of Mental Labor: The Rise of the Petty Intellectual." In *Knowledge Acts in Modern China: Ideas, Institutions, and Identities*, edited by Robert Culp, Eddy U, and Wen-hsin Yeh, 207–241. Berkeley: Institute of East Asian Studies, University of California, Berkeley, 2016.

———. *The Power of Print in Modern China: Intellectuals and Industrial Publishing from the End of Empire to Maoist State Socialism*. New York: Columbia University Press, 2019.

Culp, Robert, Eddy U, and Wen-hsin Yeh, eds. *Knowledge Acts in Modern China: Ideas, Institutions, and Identities*. Berkeley: Institute of East Asian Studies, University of California, Berkeley, 2016.

Dimitrov, Martin K. *Piracy and the State: The Politics of Intellectual Property Rights in China*. Cambridge: Cambridge University Press, 2009.

Dong, Yue. *Republican Beijing: The City and Its Histories*. Berkeley: University of California Press, 2003.

Douglas, Robert K. "The Awakening of China." *Nineteenth Century* 47 (June 1900): 988–992.

Drège, Jean-Pierre *La Commercial Press de Shanghai 1897–1949*. Paris: Collège de France, 1978.

———. *Shanghai shangwu yinshuguan, 1897–1949* 上海商務印書館, 1897–1949 [Shanghai Commercial Press, 1897–1949]. Translated by Li Tongshi. Beijing: Shangwu yinshuguan, 2000.

Duara, Prasenjit. *Culture, Power, and the State: Rural North China, 1900–1942*. Stanford, CA: Stanford University Press, 1988.

Dunne, George H. *Generation of Giants: The Story of the Jesuits in China in the Last Decades of the Ming Dynasty*. Notre Dame, IN.: University of Notre Dame, 1962.

Dykstra, Maura Dominique. "Complicated Matters: Commercial Dispute Resolution in Qing Chongqing from 1750 and 1911." PhD diss., UCLA, 2014.

Edgren, Sören. "The Fengmianye (Cover Page) as a Source for Chinese Publishing History." In *Higashi Ajia shuppan bunka kenkyū, kohaku* 東アジア出版文化研究, ほはく [Studies of East Asian publishing culture: amber], edited by Isobe Akira, 261–267. Tokyo: Chisen Shokan, 2004.

Elman, Benjamin A. *A Cultural History of Civil Examinations in Late Imperial China.* Berkeley: University of California Press, 2000.

———. *On Their Own Terms: Science in China, 1550–1900.* Cambridge, MA: Harvard University Press, 2005.

Fan, Jinmin 范金民. *Ming Qing shangshi jiufen yu shangye susong* 明清商事纠纷与商业诉讼 [Commercial disputes and lawsuits in the Ming-Qing period]. Nanjing: Nanjing daxue chubanshe, 2007.

"Fanyi jia Zhang Yousong qiongsi Chengdou" 翻译家张友松穷死成都 [Translator Zhang Yousong died in poverty in Chengdou]. *Lu Xun yanjiu yuekan*, 1998, 6.

Feng, Ziyou 馮自由. *Zhengzhixue* 政治學 [Political science]. Shanghai: Guangzhi Shuju, 1902.

Fogel, Joshua A., ed. *The Role of Japan in Liang Qichao's Introduction of Modern Western Civilization to China.* Berkeley: Institute of East Asian Studies, University of California, 2004.

Franke, Wolfgang. *The Reform and Abolition of the Traditional Chinese Examination System.* Cambridge, MA: Center for East Asian Studies, Harvard University, 1960.

Fu, Lei 傅雷. *Fu Lei quanji* 傅雷全集 [Complete collection of Fu Lei]. 20 vols. Shenyang: Liaoning jiaoyu chubanshe, 2002.

———. *Fu Lei tan fanyi* 傅雷谈翻译 [Fu Lei on translation]. Edited by Nu'an. Shenyang: Liaoning jiaoyu chubanshe, 2005.

Fukuzawa, Yukichi 福澤諭吉. *Fukuzawa Yukichi shokanshū* 福澤諭吉書簡集 [Correspondence of Fukuzawa Yukichi]. 9 vols. Tokyo: Iwanami Shoten, 2001–2003.

———. *Fukuzawa Yukichi Zenshū* 福澤諭吉全集 [Complete collection of Fukuzawa Yukichi's writings]. Edited by Keiō Gijuku. 23 vols. Tokyo: Iwanami Shoten, 1958–1971.

Fuzanbō 冨山房. *Fuzanbō gojūnen* 冨山房五十年 [Fifty years of Fuzanbō]. Tokyo: Fuzanbō, 1936.

Gao, Fengchi 高鳳池. "Benguan chuangye shi: zai faxingsuo xuesheng xunlianban de yanjiang" 本館創業史: 在發行所學生訓練班的演講 [The founding years of Commercial Press: a speech given at the circulation department's seminar]. In *Shangwu yinshuguan jiushiwu nian, 1897–1992: wo he Shangwu yinshuguan* 商務印書館九十五年: 我和商務印書館 [Ninety-five-year history of Commercial Press: I and Commercial Press], 1–13. Beijing: Shangwu Yinshuguan, 1992.

Giles, Herbert A. *A Glossary of Reference: Subjects Connected with the Far East.* Shanghai: Kelly & Walsh, 1900.

Golas, Peter J. "Early Ch'ing Guilds." In *The City in Late Imperial China*, edited by G. William Skinner, 557–564. Stanford, CA: Stanford University Press, 1977.

Goodman, Bryna. "Democratic Calisthenics: The Culture of Urban Associations in the New Republic." In *Changing Meanings of Citizenship in Modern China*, edited by Merle Goldman and Elizabeth Perry, 70–109. Cambridge, MA: Havard University Press, 2002.

———. *Native Place, City, and Nation: Regional Networks and Identities in Shanghai, 1853–1937.* Berkeley: University of California Press, 1995.

Gu, Xieguang 顧燮光. *Yishu jingyan lu* 譯書經眼錄 [Bibliography of translation works I've seen] (1904). In Wang, Tao, et al., eds. *Jindai yishu mu.*

Guan, Xiaohong 關曉紅. *Wan Qing xuebu yanjiu* 晚清學部研究 [The Ministry of Education in the late Qing]. Guangzhou: Guangdong jiaoyu chubanshe, 2000.

Guojia tushuguan gujiguan 國家圖書館古籍館, ed. *Qingdai banke paiji tulu* 清代版刻牌記圖錄 [Illustrated catalog of the colophons of Qing woodblock printed books]. 14 vols. Beijing: Guojia tushuguan, 2007.

Guoshiguan 國史館, ed. *Guomin zhengfu zhuzuoquan faling shiliao* 國民政府著作權法令史料 [Primary sources of the Nationalist Government Copyright Law and related orders]. Xindian: Guoshiguan, 2002.

Guy, Kent. *The Emperor's Four Treasures: Scholars and the State in the Late Ch'ien-lung Period.* Cambridge, MA: Harvard University Press, 1987.

Haggard, H. Rider. *Yuxue liuhen* 玉雪留痕 [Leaving a mark on the snowy skin]. Translated by Lin Shu and Wei Yi. Shanghai: Shangwu yinshuguan, 1907.

Harrison, Henrietta. *The Man Awakened from Dreams: One Man's Life in a North China Village, 1857–1942.* Stanford, CA: Stanford University Press, 2005.

Hazama, Naoki 狭間直樹, ed. *Seiyo kindai bunmei to Chuka sekai: Kyoto Daigaku Jinbun Kagaku Kenkyujo 70-shunen kinen shinpojiumu ronshu* 西洋近代文明と中華世界: 京都大学人文科学研究所 70周年記念シンポジウム論集 [Western modern civilization and the Sinophone world: proceedings of the Kyoto University Research Centre for the Cultural Sciences seventieth anniversary symposium]. Kyoto: Kyoto University, 1999.

Hebei sheng xinwen chuban ju chuban shi zhi bianweihui 河北省新闻出版局出版史志编委会 and Shanxi sheng xinwen chuban ju chuban shi zhi bianweihui 山西省新闻出版局出版史志编委会, eds. *Zhongguo Gongchandang Jin Cha Ji Bianqu Chuban Shi* 中国共产党晋察冀边区出版史 [A history of the Chinese Communist Party's publishing operation in the Jin Cha Ji border region]. Shijiazhuang Shi: Hebei renmin chubanshe, 1991.

Henningsen, Lena. "Harry Potter with Chinese Characteristics, Plagiarism between Orientalism and Occidentalism." *China Information* 20:2 (2006): 275–311.

Hill, Michael Gibbs. *Lin Shu, Inc.: Translation and the Making of Modern Chinese Culture.* New York: Oxford University Press, 2012.

Ho, Bingdi. *The Ladder of Success in Imperial China: Aspects of Social Mobility, 1368–1911.* New York: Columbia University Press, 1980.

Howland, Douglas. *Translating the West: Language and Political Reason in Nineteenth-Century Japan.* Honolulu: University of Hawai'i Press, 2002.

Hu, Shi 胡適. *Hu Shi riji quanji* 胡適日記全集 [Complete diary of Hu Shi]. Edited by Cao Boyan. 10 vols. Taipei: Lianjing chuban gongsi, 2004.

Hu, Yuzhi 胡愈之. *Hu Yuzhi chuban wenji* 胡愈之出版文集 [Hu Yuzhi's writings on publishing]. Beijing: Zhongguo shuji chubanshe, 1998.

Huang, Fayo 黃發有. "Gaochou zhidu yu 'shi qi nian' wenxue shengchan" 稿酬制度與「十七年」文學生產 [Remuneration system and literary production in the "Seventeen Years"]. *Zhongguo xiandai wenxue* 30 (December 2016): 41–59.

Huang, Kewu 黃克武. *Ziyou di suoyiran: Yan Fu dui Yuehan Mi'er ziyouzhuyi sixiang di renshi yu pipan* 自由的所以然: 嚴復對約翰彌爾自由主義思想的認識與批判 [The reason for freedom: Yan Fu's understanding and criticism of John Mill's liberalism]. Taipei: Yunchen wenhua shiye gufen youxian gongsi, 1998.

Huang, Philip. *Code, Custom, and Legal Practice in China: The Qing and the Republic Compared.* Stanford, CA: Stanford University Press, 2001.

Hung, Chang-tai. *War and Popular Culture: Resistance in Modern China, 1937–1945.* Berkeley: University of California Press, 1994.

Ichiko, Natsuo 市古夏生. *Kinsei shoki bungaku to shuppan bunka* 近世初期文学と出版文化 [Early modern literature and publishing culture]. Tokyo: Wakakusa Shobō, 1998.

Ichimura, Sanjirō 市村瓚次郎. *Zhina shiyao* 支那史要 [Essentials of Chinese history]. Translated by Chen Yi 陳毅. Shanghai: Guangzhi Shuju, 1905.

Iida, Kanae 飯田鼎. "Reimei ki no keisaigaku kenkyū to Fukuzawa Yukichi (sono ni)" 黎明期 の經済学研究と福沢諭吉 (その二) [The dawn of the political economy and Fukuzawa Yukichi (part two)]. *Mita Gakkai Zasshi* 三田学会雑誌 65:11 (November 1972): 689–701.

Inaoka, Masaru 稲岡勝. "Meiji shuppan shi kara mi ta okuzuke to so no shūhen" 明治出版史か ら見た奥付とその周辺 [Examing okuzuke and its related issues from the prespective of Meiji publishing history]." *Shuppan Kenyū* 出版研究 15 (1984):10–29

Inaoka, Masaru. "Zouhan, nise ban, hanken—chosaku ken zenshi no kenkyū" 藏版、偽版、版 権― 著作権前史の研究 [Possessing blocks, fake blocks, copyright: a study of the prehistory of copyright]. *Kenkyuu kiyo* 研究紀要 22 (1991): 6–105.

Inoue, Susumu 井上進. *Chūgoku shuppan bunkashi: shomotsu sekai to chi no fūkei* 中国出版文化 史: 書物世界と知の風景 [A history of Chinese publishing culture: the book world and the knowledge landscape]. Nagoya: Nagoya Daigaku Shuppankai, 2002.

———. *Min Shin gakujutsu henshenshi* 明清学術変遷史: 出版と伝統学術の臨界点 [Intellectual transformation in Ming and Qing: the breaking point of publishing and traditional learning]. Tokyo: Heibonsha, 2011.

———. *Shorin no chōbō: dentōChūgoku no shomotsu sekai* 書林の眺望: 伝統中国の書物世界 [Look into the book forest: the traditional Chinese book world]. Tokyo: Heibonsha, 2006.

Itō, Nobuo 伊藤信男. "Chosakuken seido shi no sobyō" 著作権制度史の素描 [A sketch of the institutional history of copyright]. In *Chosakuken kenkyuu* 著作權研究 4 (1970): 131–132.

———, ed. *Sogo kindai chosakuken bunkashi nenpyo* 綜合近代著作権文化史年表 [The comprehensive chronology of the cultural history of modern copyright]. Tokyo: Nihon Chosakuken Kyokai, 1960.

Jernigan, T. R. *China in Law and Commerce.* New York: The Macmillan Company, 1905.

———. *China's Business Methods and Policy.* London: T. Fisher Unwin, 1904.

Ji, Shuhua 季樹華, comp. "Dongan shichang jiuwen manshi" 東安市場舊聞漫拾 [Recollections of Eastern Peace Market]. In *Wenshi Ziliao Xuanji* 文史資料選輯 [Selection of cultural and historical research materials], edited by Zhongguo renmin zhengzhi xieshang huiyi Beijing shi weiyuanhui wenshi ziliao weiyuanhui 中國人民政治協商會議北京市委員會文史資料 委員會, 12:200–210. Beijing: Beijing Chubanshe, 1982.

Jiang, Yaohua 江耀華, ed. *Shanghai shuye tongye gonghui shiliao yu yanjiu* 上海書業同業公會史 料與研究 [Primary materials and study of Shanghai Bookseller's Guild]. Shanghai: Shanghai Jiaotong Daxue chubanshe, 2010.

Jiang Mengmei 江夢梅. "Qian Qing Xuebu bianshu zhi zhuangkuang" 前清學部編書之狀況 [Qing Ministry of Education's publications]. *Zhonghua jiaoyujie* 中華教育界 3:1 (January 1914).

Jianqin 劍琴. "Tongyijie de tushu shi chang" 統一街的圖書市場 [The book market of Tongyi Street]. In *Wuhan wenshi ziliao wenku*, 4:355–356. Wuhan Shi: Wuhan chubanshe, 1999.

Johns, Adrian. *The Nature of the Book: Print and Knowledge in the Making*. Chicago: University of Chicago Press, 1998.

———. *Piracy: The Intellectual Property Wars from Gutenberg to Gates*. Chicago: University of Chicago Press, 2009.

Johnson, Matthew D. "Beneath the Propaganda State: Official and Unofficial Cultural Landscape in Shanghai, 1849–1965." In *Maoism at the Grassroots: Everyday Life in China's Era of High Socialism*, edited by Jeremy Brown and Matthew D. Johnson, 199–229. Cambridge, MA: Harvard University Press, 2015.

Judge, Joan. *Print and Politics: Shibao and the Culture of Reform in Late Qing China*. Stanford, CA: Stanford University Press, 1996.

Kang, Youwei, *Riben bianzheng kao* 日本變政考 [A study of Japan's political reform]. In *Kang Youwei quanji*, vol. 2. Beijing: Zijincheng chubanshe, 1998.

Karl, Rebecca E., and Peter Gue Zarrow, eds. *Rethinking the 1898 Reform Period: Political and Cultural Change in Late Qing China*. Cambridge, MA: Harvard University Press, 2002.

Katsumoto, Masaaki 勝本正晃. *Nippon chosakuken hō* 日本著作権法 [Japan's copyright law]. Tokyo: Iwaomatudou Shuten, 1940.

Kawauchi, Densei 河内展生. "Fukuzawa Yukichi no Shoki no Chosaku ken Kakuritsu Undō" 福澤諭吉の初期の著作権確立運動 [Fukuzawa Yukichi's early campaigns to secure copyright]. *Kindai Nippon Kenkyuu* 近代日本研究 5 (March 1988): 1–77.

Kinmonth, Earl H. "Fukuzawa Reconsidered: Gakumon no Susume and Its Audience." *Journal of Asian Studies* 37:4 (August 1978): 677–696.

Kornicki, Peter. *The Book in Japan: A Cultural History from the Beginnings to the Nineteenth Century*. Leiden: Koninklijke Brill, 1998.

Kuhn, Philip. *Soulstealers: The Chinese Sorcery Scare of 1768*. Cambridge, MA: Harvard University Press, 1990.

Lackner, Michael. *New Terms for New Ideas: Western Knowledge and Lexical Change in Late Imperial China*. Leiden: Brill, 2001.

Lackner, Michael, and Natascha Vittinghoff, eds. *Mapping Meanings: The Field of New Learning in Late Qing China*. Leiden: Brill, 2004.

Lee, Leo Of-fan Lee. *The Romantic Generation of Modern Chinese Writers*. Cambridge, MA: Harvard University Press, 1973.

Lehman, John Alan. "Intellectual Property Rights and Chinese Tradition Section: Philosophical Foundations." *Journal of Business Ethics* 69:1 (November 2006): 1–9.

Lei, Jin 雷縉. *Zhongwai cewen daguan* 中外策問大全 [Grand prospectus of policy questions regarding Chinese and foreign matters]. Shanghai: Yangengshan zhuang, 1903.

Lei, Mengshui 雷夢水. "Beiping doxi shangchang shusi jilue" 北平東西商場書肆記略 [Brief descriptions of the bookshops in the east and west markets of Beiping]. In *Shudian gongzuo shiliao* 書店工作史料 [Primary sources of bookstore operations], edited by Xinhua shudian, 4:88–92. Beijing: Xinhua shudian zhongdian, 1980.

Levenson, Joseph Richmond. *Confucian China and Its Modern Fate: The Problem of Intellectual Continuity*. Berkeley: University of California Press, 1958.

———. *Liang Ch'i-ch'ao and the Mind in Modern China*. Berkeley: University of California Press, 1970.

Li, Boyuan 李伯元. *Wenming xiaoshi* 文明小史 [A minor history of civilization]. Nanchang: Jiangxi renmin chubanshe, 1989.

Li, Chen 李琛."Guanyu Zhongguo gudai yinhe wu banquan yanjiu de jidian fansi" 关于 "中国古代因何无版权" 研究的几点反思 [Reflection on the studies about why there was no indigenous copyright law in ancient China]. *Faxuejia*, January 2010, 54–62.

Li, Lillian M. *Beijing: From Imperial Capital to Olympic City*. New York: Palgrave Macmillan, 2007.

Li, Mingshan, ed. *Zhongguo gu dai banquan shi* 中国古代版权史 [History of copyright in ancient China]. Beijing: Shehui kexue wenian chubanshe, 2012.

———, ed. *Zhongguo jindai banquan shi* 中國近代版權史 [A history of copyright in modern China]. Kaifeng: Henan daxue chubanshe, 2003.

Li, Mingshan 李明山, and Chang Qing. *Zhongguo dangdai banquan shi* 中国当代版权史 [History of copyright in contemporary China]. Beijing: Zhishi chanquan chubanshe, 2007.

Li, Mingshan, and Zhou Lin 周林, eds. *Zhongguo banquan shi yanjiu wenxian* 中國版權史研究文獻 [Reseach materials for the history of copyright in China]. Beijing: Zhongguo fangzheng chubanshe, 1999.

Li, Renyuan 李仁淵. *Wan Qing de xinshi chuanbo meiti yu zhishi fenzi: yi baokan chuban wei zhongxin de taolun* 晚清的新式傳播媒體與知識分子: 以報刊出版為中心的討論 [New media and the intellectuals in the late Qing: a press-publishing-centered discussion]. Taipei: Daoxiang chubanshe, 2005.

Li, Sher-shiueh 李奭學. *Zhongguo wan Ming yu Ouzhou wen xue: Ming mo Yesu hui gu dian xing zheng dao gu shi kao quan* 中國晚明與歐洲文學: 明末耶穌會古典型證道故事考詮 [European literature in late Ming China: Jesuit exemplum, its source and its interpretation]. Taipei: Linking Publishing, 2005.

Li, Yufeng 李雨峰. *Qiangkou xia de falü: Zhongguo banquan shi yanjiu* 枪口下的法律: 中国版权史研究 [Law at gunpoint: a study of the history of copyright in China]. Beijing: Zhishi chanquan chubanshe, 2006.

Liang Qichao 梁啟超. *Liang Qichao quan ji* 梁啟超全集 [Complete collection of Liang Qichao's writings]. Edited by Yang Gang et al. Beijing: Beijing chubanshe, 1999.

———. *Qing dai xue shu gai lun* 清代學術概論 [Intellectual trends in the Qing period]. Shanghai: Shangwu yinshuguan, 1921.

———. *Xixue shumu biao* 西學書目表 [Reading list for Western learning]. Shanghai: Shiwu baoguan, 1896.

———. *Yinbingshi heji* 飲冰室合集 [The collection of the Drinking-Ice Studio]. Beijing: Zhonghua shuju, 1989.

Lin, Yusheng. *The Crisis of Chinese Consciousness: Radical Antitraditionalism in the May Fourth Era*. Madison: University of Wisconsin Press, 1979.

Link, Perry. *Mandarin Ducks and Butterflies: Popular Fiction in Early Twentieth-Century Chinese Cities*. Berkeley: University of California Press, 1981.

Liu, Dapeng 劉大鵬. *Tuixiangzhai riji* 退想齋日記 [Diary from the chamber to which one retires to ponder]. Edited by Qiao Zhinqiang. Taiyuan: Shanxi remin chubanshe, 1990.

Liu, Gao 刘杲, and Shi Feng 石峰, eds. *Xin Zhongguo wushi nian chuban jishi* 新中国五十年出版纪事 [Fifty years of publishing business in the PRC]. Beijing: Xinhua shudian, 1999.

Liu, Hecheng 柳和城, and Zhang Renfeng 張人鳳, eds. *Zhang Yuanji nianpu* 張元濟年譜 [The chronological biography of Zhang Yuanju]. Beijing: Shangwu Yinshuguan, 1991.

Liu, Lydia. "Legislating the Universal: The Circulation of International Law in the Nineteenth Century." In *Token of Exchange*, edited by Lydia Liu, 127–164. Durham, NC: Duke University Press, 1999.

———. *Translingual Practice: Literature, National Culture, and Translated Modernity—China, 1900–1937*. Stanford, CA: Stanford University Press, 1995.

Liu, Shangheng 劉尚恒, and Kong Fangen 孔方恩. "Zhongguo shi shijie shang zuizao shixing ban-quan baohu de guojia" 中国是世界上最早实行版权保护的国家 [China is the earliest coun-try in the world to enforce copyright protection]. *Tushuguan gongzuo yu yanjiu* 5 (1996): 33–36.

Liu, Shaotang 劉紹棠. *Wo shi Liu Shaotang* 我是劉紹棠 [I am Liu Shaotang]. Beijing: Tuanjie chubanshe, 1996.

Lobscheid, William. *English and Chinese Dictionary with the Punti and Mandarin Pronunciation*. Hongkong: Daily Press, 1866.

Lu, Dingyi 陸定一. *Lu Dingyi wenji* 陸定一文集 [Collected essays of Lu Dingyi]. Beijing: Ren-min chubanshe, 1992.

Lü, Haihuan 呂海寰. *Lü Haihuan zou gao* 呂海寰奏稿 [Lü Haihuan's memorials]. Taipei: Wen-hai Chubanshe, 1990.

Lü, Simian 呂思勉. *Lü Simain yiwenji* [Collection of Lü Simian's writings]. Vol. 1. Shanghai: Hua-dongshifandaxue chubanshe, 1995.

Luo, Zhitian 羅志田. *Quanshi Zhuanyi: Jindai Zhongguo de Sixiang, Shehui yu Xueshu* 權勢轉移: 近代中國的思想、社會與學術 [Transition of powers: thoughts, society, and academia in modern China]. Wuhan: Hubei renmin chubanshe, 1999.

Lu Xun 魯迅. *Lu Xun Quanji* 魯迅全集 [Complete collection of Lu Xun's writings].10 vols. Bei-jing: Renmin wenxue chubanshe, 1956–1958.

———. *Lu Xun riji* 魯迅日記 [Lu Xun's diary]. Vol. 2. Beijing: Beijing Renmin wenxue chuban-she, 1962.

———. *Qiejie Ting zawen* 且介亭雜文 [Miscellaneous writings from the Concession Pavilion]. In *Lu Xun Quanji*, vol. 6.

———. *Zhaoha xishi* 朝花夕拾 [Pick the morning flower at night]. Shijiazhuang: Hebei Jiaoue Chubanshe, 1994.

Ma, Zhao. *Runaway Wives, Urban Crimes, and Survival Tactics in Wartime Beijing, 1937–1949*. Cam-bridge, MA: Harvard University Press, 2015.

Makita, Ineshiro 蒔田稲城. *Keihan shoseki shōshi* 京阪書籍商史 [History of Kyoto and Osaka booksellers]. Osaka: Shuppan Taimusu sha, 1928.

Massey, Joseph A. "The Emperor Is Far Away: China's Enforcement of Intellectual Property Rights Protection." *Chicago Journal of International Law* 7:1 (2006): 231–237.

Mayuyama, Shin 丸山信. "Shoseki shō Fukuzawaya Yukichi" 書籍商「福沢屋諭吉」 [Bookseller "Fukuzawaya Yukichi"]. *Nippon kosho tsūshin* 日本古書通信 490 (May 1978): 13–14.

McDermott, Joseph P. " 'Noncommercial' Private Publishing in Late Imperial China." In *The Book Worlds of East Asia and Europe, 1450–1850: Connections and Comparisons*, edited by Jo-seph McDermott and Peter Burke, 105–145. Hong Kong: Hong Kong University Press, 2016.

———. "Rare Book Collections in Qing Dynasty Suzhou: Owners, Dealers, and Uses." In *Jinshi Zhongguo de ruxue yu shuji: jiating, zongjiao, wuzhi de wangluo* 近世中國的儒學與書籍: 家

庭・宗教・物質的網絡 [Confucianism and books in late imperial China: familial, religious, and material networks], edited by Lü Miaofen, 199–249. Taipei: Academia Sinica, 2013.

———. *A Social History of the Chinese Book: Books and Literati Culture in Late Imperial China*. Hong Kong: Hong Kong University Press, 2006.

McDermott, Joseph P., and Peter Burke, "Introduction." In *The Book Worlds of East Asia and Europe, 1450–1850: Connections and Comparisons*, edited by Joseph McDermott and Peter Burke, 1–64. Hong Kong: Hong Kong University Press, 2016.

Meng, Yue. *Shanghai and the Edges of Empires*. Minneapolis: University of Minnesota Press, 2006.

Mertha, Andrew. *The Politics of Piracy: Intellectual Property in Contemporary China*. Ithaca, NY: Cornell University, 2005.

Mittler, Barbara. *A Continuous Revolution: Making Sense of Cultural Revolution Culture*. Cambridge, MA: Harvard University Press, 2012.

———. *A Newspaper for China? Power, Identity and Change in Shanghai's News Media (1872–1912)*. Cambridge, MA: Harvard University Press, 2004.

Mizuno, Rentarō 水野錬太郎. *Chosakukenhō —Housei Daigaku tokubetsu hou 36 nendo kougi roku* 著作権法— 法政大学特別法36年度講義録 [Copyright law: Housei University thirty-sixth annual special law lecture]. Tokyo: Hosei daigaku, 1974.

Montgomery, Lucy, and Brian Fitzgerald. "Copyright and the Creative Industries in China." *International Journal of Cultural Studies* 9 (September 2006): 407–418.

Morse, H. B. *The Guilds of China*. New York: Longmans, Green and Co., 1909.Mühlhahn, Klaus. *Criminal Justice in China: A History*. Cambridge, MA: Harvard University Press, 2009.

Nagamura, Motoya 中村元哉. "Kaizokuban shoseki ka ra mi ta kingendai Chūgoku no shuppan seisaku to medeia kai" 海賊版書籍からみた近現代中国の出版政策とメディア界 [Publishing policies and the media sector: the case of pirated books]. *Ajia kenkyū* 52:4 (October 2006): 1–19.

Nagao, Masanori 長尾正憲. *Fukuzawaya Yukichi no kenkyū* 福沢屋諭吉の研究 [A study of Fukuzawaya Yukichi]. Kyoto: Shibunkaku Shuppan, 1988.

Nagasawa, Kikuya 長澤規矩也. "Chuuka minkoku shorin ichibetsu hosei" 中華民國書林一瞥補正 [A glance at the ROC book market with additions and corrections]. In *Nagasawa Kikuya chosakushuu* 長澤規矩也著作集 [Collection of Nagasawa Kikuya's writings], edited by Nagasawa Kikuya Sensei Kiju Kinenkai, 6:3–41. Tokyo: Kyūko Shoin, 1982–1989.

Nagase-Reimer, Keiko ed. *Copper in the Early Modern Sino-Japanese Trade. Monies, Markets, and Finance in East Asia, 1600–1900*. Leiden: Brill, 2016.

Naitō, Torajiro 内藤虎次郎. *Naitō Konan zenshu* 内藤湖南全集 [Complete collection of Naitō Konan's writings]. Vol. 2. Tokyo: Chikuma Shobo, 1971.

Negishi, Tadashi 根岸佶. *Shanhai no girudo* 上海のギルド [Guilds in Shanghai]. Tokyo: Nihon Hyoron Shinsha, 1951.

———. *Shina giruto no kenkyuu, Chugoku no girudo* 中國のギルド [Chinese guilds]. Tokyo: Nihon Hyoron Shinsha, 1953.

Neizheng bu 内政部. *Zhuzuoquanfa ji sh xingxize: fulu: Neizhengbu zhuzuoquan zhuce shencha weiyuanhui zhangcheng, Neizhengbu chajin yinshuling* 著作權法及施行細則: 附錄: 内政部著作權注冊審查委員會章程、内政部查禁淫書令 [Copyright law and enforcement regulations: appendix, the bylaws of the Ministry of the Interior Copyright Registration Committee, the Ministry of the Interior's ban on pornographic books]. Nanjing: Neizheng bu, 1928.

Newcity, Michael A. *Copyright Law in the Soviet Union*. New York: Praeger Publishers, 1978.

Ng, Michael. *Legal Transplantation in Early Twentieth-Century China: Practicing Law in Republican Beijing (1910s–1930s)*. New York: Routledge, 2014.

Niida, Noboru 仁井田陞. *Chūgoku hosei shi kenkyu* 中国法治史研究 [Chinese legal institutions]. Tokyo: Tokyo University Press, 1980.

———. *Chūgoku no shakai to girudo* 中國の社會とギルド [Chinese society and guilds]. Tokyo: Iwanami Shoten, 1989.

Ōba, Osamu. *Books and Boats: Sino-Japanese Relations in the Seventeenth and Eighteenth Centuries*. Translated by Joshua A Fogel. Portland, ME: Merwin Asia, 2012

Ōie, Shigeo 大家重夫. *Chosakuken o kakuritsushita hitobito: fukuzawa yukichi sensei mizuno rentaro hakushi purage hakushi . . .* 著作権を確立した人々：福澤諭吉先生、水野錬太郎博士、ブラーゲ博士 . . . [Figures who established copyright: Mr. Fukuzawa Yikichi, Dr. Mitzuno Rentar, Dr. Wilhelm Plage . . .]. Tokyo: Seibundo, 2003.

Pan Guangzhe 潘光哲. *Wan Qing shiren de xixue yuedu shi (1833–1898)* 晚清士人的西學閱讀史 (1833–1898) [In search of Western learning: a history of reading in late Qing China]. Taipei: Institute of Modern History, Academia Sinica, 2014.

Pi, Houfeng 皮后鋒. *Yan Fu dazhuan* 嚴復大傳 [A grand biography of Yan Fu]. Fuzhou: Fujian renmin chubanshe, 2003.

Pi, Xirui 皮錫瑞. *Shifutang riji* 師伏堂日記 [The diary of the Shifu Chamber]. Vol. 3. Beijing: Guojia tushuguan chubanshe, 2008.

Poon, Ming-sun. "The Printer's Colophon in Sung China, 960–1279." *Library Quarterly* 43:1 (January 1993): 39–52.

Qi, Feng 齐峰. *Shanxi geming genjudi chuban shi* 山西革命根据地出版史 [Publishing history of the Shanxi Revolutionary Base Area]. Taiyuan: Shanxi renmin chubanshe, 2013.

Qian, Mu 錢穆. *Bashi yi shuangqin shiyou zayi hekan* 八十雙親師友雜憶合刊 [Miscellaneous memories of parents, teachers, and friends at the age of eighty]. Taipei: Sanmin Shuju, 1983.

Qin, Xiaoyi 秦孝儀, ed. "Kangzhan qian goujia jianshe shiliao: neizheng fangmian" 抗戰前國家建設史料：内政方面 [Primary sources on prewar national development: domestic politics]. In *Geming wenxian* 革命文獻, 71. Taizhong: Zhongguo Guomindang zhongyang weiyuanhui dangshi shiliao bianzuan weiyuanhui, 1953.

Qin Ruijie 秦瑞玠. *Zhuzuoquan lü shiyi* 著作權律釋義 [Explanation of the copyright law]. Shanghai: Shangwu yinshuguan, 1914.

Qingnian zuozhe de jianjie: Liu Shaotang pipan ji 青年作者的鉴戒：刘绍棠批判集 [Lesson for young writers: collection of criticisms against Liu Shaotang]. Hangzhou: Donghai wenyi chubanshe, 1957. Reprinted in *Zhonggong zhongyao lishi wenxian ziliao huibian* 中共重要歷史文獻資料彙編 [Collection of important historical documents about the Chinese Communist Party], vol. 22:17. Los Angeles: Zhongwen chuban wu fuwu zhong xin, 2005.

Qiu, Pengsheng 邱澎生. *Dang falü yushang jingji: Ming Qing Zhongguo de shangye falü* 當法律遇上經濟：明清中國的商業法律 [When the law encounters the economy: commercial laws in Ming-Qing China].Taipei: Wunan tushu chuban gongsi, 2008.

———. "*Guofa yu banggui: Qing dai qianqi Chongqing cheng de chuanyun jiufen jiejue*" 國法與幫規：清代前期重慶城的船運糾紛解決 [The state's law vs. The guild's rules: conflict resolutions in river shipping in early Qing Chongqing]. In *Ming Qing falü yunzuo zhong de quanli yu wenhua* 明清法律運作中的權力與文化 [Power and culture in Ming-Qing legal practices], edited by Qiu Pengsheng and Chen Xuyuan, 275–344. Taipei: Zhongyang yanjiuyuan & Lianjing chuban gongsi, 2009.

Ransmeier, Johanna. *Sold People: Traffickers and Family Life in North China.* Cambridge, MA: Harvard University Press, 2017.

Rea, Christopher, and Nicolai Volland, eds. *The Business of Culture: Cultural Entrepreneurs in China and Southeast Asia, 1900–65.* Vancouver: UBC Press, 2015.

Reed, Christopher A. "Advancing the (Gutenberg) Revolution: The Origins and Development of Chinese Print Communism, 1921–1947." In *From Woodblocks to the Internet: Chinese Publishing and Print Culture in Transition, circa 1800 to 2008,* edited by Cynthia Brokaw and Christopher A. Reed, 275–314. Leiden: Brill, 2010.

———. *Gutenberg in Shanghai: Chinese Print Capitalism 1876–1937.* Toronto: UBC Press, 2003.

Reynolds, Douglas R. *China: 1898–1912—the Xingzheng Revolution and Japan.* Cambridge, MA: Harvard University Asian Center, 1993.

Richard, Timothy. *Forty-Five Years in China.* New York: Frederick A. Stokes, 1916.

Ripley, George, and Charles A. Dana, eds. *The New American Cyclopaedia: A Popular Dictionary of General Knowledge.* Vol. 5. New York: D. Appleton & Company, 1872.

Riskola, Teemu. *Legal Orientalism: China, the United States, and Modern Law.* Cambridge, MA: Harvard University Press, 2013.

Rowe, William T. *Hankow: Commerce and Society in a Chinese City, 1796–1889.* Stanford, CA: Stanford University Press, 1984.

———. *Hankow: Conflict and Community in a Chinese City, 1796–1895.* Stanford, CA: Stanford University Press, 1989.

Saeki, Yuichi 佐伯有一, and Tanaka Issei 田中一成, eds. *Niida Noboru hakushishu Pekin kōshō girudo shiryōshū*仁井田陞博士輯北京工商ギルド資料集 [Beijing craft and commercial guilds' materials compiled by Dr. Niida Noboru]. 6 vols. Tokyo: Tokyo Daigaku, 1975–1983.

Schwartz, Benjamin. *In Search of Wealth and Power: Yen Fu and the West.* Cambridge, MA: Belknap Press of Harvard University Press, 1964.

Seville, Catherine. *The Internationalisation of Copyright Law: Books, Buccaneers and the Black Flag in the Nineteenth Century.* Cambridge: Cambridge University Press, 2006.

"Shanghai chuban zhi" bianzuan weiyuanhu, ed., *Shanghai chuban zhi* 上海出版志 [History of publishing in Shanghai]. Shanghai: Shanghai shehui kexue yuan chubanshe, 2000.

Shanghai shuye gonghui 上海書業公會. *Zhuzuoquanfa yu chubanfa* 著作權法與出版法 [Copyright law and publishing law]. Shanghai: Shanghai shuye gonghui, 1930.

Shanghai tushugaun 上海圖書館, ed. *Wang Kangnian shiyou shuzga* 汪康年師友書札 [Wang Kangnian's correspondence with teachers and friends]. Shanghai: Shanghai guji chuban she, 1986.

Shangwu yinshuguan 商務印書館, ed. *Shangwu yinshuguan dashiji* 商務印書館大事記 [Chronicle of Commercial Press]. Beijing: Shangwu yinshuguan, 1987.

———. *Shangwu yinshuguan tushu mulu, 1897–1949* 商務印書館圖書目錄, 1897–1949 [Book catalog of Commercial Press, 1897–1940]. Beijing: Shangwu yinshuguan, 1981.

———. *Shangwu Yinshuguan zhilue* 商務印書館志略 [Brief history of Commercial Press]. Shanghai: Shangwu yinshuguan, 1929.

———. *Zuijin sanshiwu nian zhi Zhongguo jiaoyu* 最近三十五年之中國教育 [Education in China in the past thirty-five years]. Shanghai: Shangwu yinshu guan, 1931.

Shao Ke 邵科. "An shou lian yu qu jie de zhong guo zhi shi chan quan shi—fan si guo ji zhi shi chan quan bu ping deng zhi xu zhi tu po dian" 安守廉与曲解的中国知识产权史—反思国际知识产权不平等秩序之突破点 [William Alford and the misunderstanding of Chinese intellectual property history: the key to unscrambling the globally unequal intellectual property regime]. *Zhengfa luncong* 2012:4 (September 2012): 115–128.

Shen, Jin 沈津. *Shu yun youyou yi mai xiang* 书韵悠悠一脉香 [A long thread of fragrance from books]. Guilin: Guangxi shifan daxue chubanshe, 2006.

Shen, Rengan 沈仁干. "Jian xin, xiyue, yu qipan: gaige kaifang zhong de zhezuoquan lifa" 艰辛、喜悦与期盼—改革开放中的著作权立法 [Difficulty, joy, and hope: copyright legislation during the Reform and Opening-Up]. In *Zhongguo banquan nianjian 2009* 中国版权年鉴 [China copyright yearbook 2009], edited by Yan Xiaohong, 72–82. Beijing: Zhongguo renmin taxue chubanshe, 2009.

Shenbao she 申報社, ed. *Shenbao nianjian* 申報年鑑 [Shanghai news year book]. Shanghai: Shenbaoshe, 1933.

Sherman, Brad, and Lionel Bently. *The Making of Modern Intellectual Property Law: The British Experience, 1760–1911*. Cambridge: Cambridge University Press, 1999.

Shi, Wei. "The Paradox of Confucian Determinism: Tracking the Root Causes of Intellectual Property Rights Problem in China." *John Marshall Review of Intellectual Property Law* 7:3 (2008): 454–468.

Shi, Zongyuan 石宗源, Liu Binjie 柳斌杰 and Xiao Dongfa 肖東發, et al. *Zhongguo chuban tongshi* 中國出版通史 [General history of publishing in China]. 9 vols. Beijing: Zhongguo shu ji chu ban she, 2008.

Shin, Kokui 沈國威. *Kindai Nitchū goi kōryūshi* 近代日中語彙交流史: 新漢語の生成と受容 [A history of the exchanges of modern Sino-Japanese vocabularies: the birth and appropriation of new Chinese]. Tokyo: Kasamashoin, 2017.

"Shinkoku bōeki no zento: Shanhai Ryōji Odagiri Masunosuke kun no dan" 清國貿易の前途: 上海領事小田切萬壽之助君の談 [The future of trade with Qing: an interview with Shanghai Consul Mr. Odagiri Masunosuke]. *Taiyō* 太陽 4:21 (October 1898): 217–220.

Shu, Xingwen 舒興文. "Jiaotong lu wenhua yitiao jie" 交通路—文化一條街 [Jiaotong Road: A Cultural Street]. In *Wuhan Wenshi Ziliao Wenku* 武漢文史資料文庫, 4:350. Wuhan Shi: Wuhan chubanshe, 1999.

Sikeluodun 斯克羅敦. *Banquan kao* 版權考 [On copyright]. Translated by Zhou Junyi 周君儀. Shanghai: Shangwu yinshuguan, 1903.

Sim, Chuin Peng 沈俊平. "Wan Qing shiyin juye yongshu de shengchan yu liutong: yi 1880–1905 nian de Shanghai minying shiyin shuju wei zhongxin de kaocha" 晚清石印舉業用書的生產與流通: 以1880–1905年的上海民營石印書局為中心的考察 [Production and circulation of lithographic-printed examination aids in the late Qing dynasty: private lithographic publishers in Shanghai from 1880 to 1905]. *Zhongguo wenhua yanjiu suo xuebao*, no. 57 (July 2013): 245–274.

So, Billy, and Sufumi So. "Commercial Arbitration Transplanted: A Tale of the Book Industry in Modern Shanghai." In *Chinese Legal Reform and Global Legal Order*, edited by Michael H. K. Ng and Zhang Yun, 238–256. Cambridge: Cambridge University Press, 2017.

Sommer, Matthew H. *Polyandry and Wife-Selling in Qing Dynasty China: Survival Strategies and Judicial Interventions*. Oakland: University of California Press, 2015.

Song Yuanfang 宋原放, ed. *Zhongguo chuban shiliao. Xiandai bufen* 中國出版史料 現代部分 [Primary sources of Chinese publishing history, contemporary section]. 3 vols. Wuhan: Hubei jiaoyu chubanshe, 2001.

———, ed. *Zhongguo shuban Shiliao. Jindai bufen* 中國出版史料 近代部分 [Primary sources of Chinese publishing history, modern section]. 3 vols. Wuhan: Hebei jiaoyu chubanshe, 2004.

Spence, Jonathan D. *Treason by the Book.* New York: Viking. 2001.

Sterling, Bruce. *Distraction.* New York: Bantam, 1998.

Strand, David. *Rickshaw Beijing: City People and Politics in the 1920s.* Berkeley: University of California Press, 1989.

Strauss, Julia. "Introduction: In Search of PRC History." *China Quarterly* 188 (December 2006): 855–869.

———. *Strong Institutions in Weak Polities: State Building in Republican China, 1927–1940.* Oxford: Clarendon Press, 1998.

Sugiyama, Chūhei 杉山忠平. *Meiji keimōki no keizai shisō: Fukuzawa Yukichi o chūshin ni* 明治啓蒙期の経済思想: 福沢諭吉を中心に [Economic Thought in the Meiji Enlightenment: Fukuzawa Yukichi as the center]. Tokyo: Hōsei Daigaku Shuppankyoku, 1986.

Sun, Baoxuan 孫寶瑄. *Wangshanlu riji* 忘山廬日記 [The diary of the cottage of forgetting mountain]. Shanghai: Shanghai guji chubanshe, 1983.

Sun, Yingxiang 孫應祥. *Yan Fu nianpu* 嚴復年譜 [Yan Fu's chronological biography]. Fuzhou: Fujian renmin chubanshe, 2003.

Suwa, Haruo 諏訪春雄. "Kinsei Bungei to Chosaku ken" 近世文芸と著作権 [Early modern literature and copyright]. *Bungaku* 文学 46:12 (December 1978): 50–62.

Swell, William, Jr. "A Strange Career: The Historical Study of Economic Life." *History and Theory* 49:4 (December 2010): 146–166.

Tam, Yuehim (or Tan Ruqian) 譚汝謙, ed. *Zhongguo yi ribenshu zonghe mulu* 中國譯日本書綜合目錄 [The comprehensive bibliography for Chinese translations of Japanese books]. Hong Kong: Chinese University Press, 1980.

Tang, Tao 唐弢. *Hui'an shuhua* 晦庵書話 [The Obscure Studio's writings on books]. Beijing: Shenghuo, dushu, xinzhi sanlian shudian, 1980.

Tarumoto, Teruo 樽本照雄. *Shoki Shōmu Inshokan kenkyū* 初期商務印書館研究 [A study of early Commercial Press]. 2nd ed. Shiga-ken Ōtsu-shi: Shinmatsu Shōsetsu Kenkyūkai, 2004.

———. *Shōmu inshokan kenkyū ronshū* 商務印書館研究論集 [Essays on Commercial Press]. Shiga-ken Ōtsu-shi: Shinmatsu Shōsetsu Kenkyūkai, 2006.

Tomita, Masafumi 富田正文. "Honyaku jūhan no gi ni tsuki negai tatematsuri sōrō kakitsuke: tatsu jūgatsu" 翻訳重版の義に付奉願候書付: 辰十月 [Petition regarding the principle of reprinting translation works: the tenth month of the year of Tastu (1868)]. *Tosho* 図書, October 1968, 56.

Tsien, Tsuen-hsuin 錢存訓. *Paper and Print.* Cambridge: Cambridge University Press, 1954.

———. "Western Impact on China through Translation." *Far Eastern Quarterly* 13:3 (May 1954): 305–327.

Uzanbou 冨山房, ed. *Uzanbou shuppan nen shi* 冨山房出版年史 [The chronicle of Uzanbou]. Tokyo: Uzanbou, 1936.

van de Ven, Hans J. "The Emergence of the Text-Centered Party." In *New Perspectives on the Chinese Communist Revolution,* edited by Tony Saich and Hans van de Ven, 5–32. Armonk, NY: M. E. Sharpe, 1995.

Volland, Nicolai. "The Control of the Media in the People's Republic of China." PhD diss., Ruprecht-Karls-Universität Heidelberg, 2008.

———. "Cultural Entrepreneurship in the Twilight: The Shanghai Book Trade Association, 1945–57." In *The Business of Culture*, edited by Christopher Rea and Nicolai Volland, 234–258. Vancouver: UBC Press, 2015.

Wagner, Rudolf G., ed. *Joining the Global Public: Word, Image, and City in Early Chinese Newspapers, 1870–1910*. Albany: State University of New York Press, 2007.

Wakeman, Frederic. "'Clean-up': The New Order in Shanghai." In *Dilemmas of Victory: The Early Years of the People's Republic of China*, edited by Jeremy Brown and Paul G. Pickowicz, 21–58. Cambridge, MA: Harvard University Press, 2007.

———. *Policing Shanghai, 1927–1937*. Berkeley: University of California Press, 1995.

Wang, Fansen 王汎森. *Zhongguo jidai sixiang yu xueshu xipu* 中國近代思想與學術系譜 [The intellectual genealogy of modern Chinese thought]. Taipei: Lianjing chubanshe, 2003.

Wang, Fei-Hsien 王飛仙. *Qikan, Chuban, yu Wenhua Bianqian: Wusi sishi de Shangwu Yinshu guan yu Xuesheng Zazhi* 期刊、出版與文化變遷：五四時期的商務印書館與學生雜誌 [Periodicals, publishing, and cultural transformation: Commercial Press and its Students' Magazine during the May Fourth Movement]. Taipei: Guoli Zhengzhi Daxue Lishixi, 2004.

Wang, Guohua 王國華. "Sanshi niandai chu Beiping zhi chuban ye" 三十年代初北平之出版業 [The publishing industry in 1930s Beiping]. In *Beijing Chuban Shizhi* 北京出版史志 [Beijing publishing history], edited by Beijing chuban shizhi bianjibu, 4:65–76. Beijing: Beijing chubanshe, 1994.

Wang, Jiarong 汪家榕. *Minzu hun: jiaokeshu bianqian* 民族魂：教科書變遷 [The national spirit: a history of the textbooks]. Beijing: Shangwu Yishuguan, 2008.

Wang, Kui 王奎. *Qingmo Shangbu yanjiu* 清末商部研究 [The Ministry of Commerce in the late Qing]. Beijing: Renmin chubanshe, 2008.

Wang, Lanping 王蘭萍. *Jindai Zhongguo zhuzuoquan fa de chengzhang* 近代中國著作權法的成長 *(1903–1910)* [The development of copyright law in modern China (1903–1910)]. Beijing: Beijing Daxue Chubanshe, 2006.

Wang, Peijie 王培洁. *Liu Shaotang nianpu* 劉紹棠年譜 [Chronicle of Liu Shaotang]. Beijing: Wenhua yishu chubanshe, 2012.

Wang, Shi 王栻. *Yan Fu zhuan* 嚴復傳 [Biography of Yan Fu]. Shanghai: Shanghai renmin chubanshe, 1957.

Wang, Shuhuai 王樹槐. "Qing ji de Guangxuehui" 清季的廣學會 [The SDCK in the Qing dynasty]. *Jinshisuo jikan* 4 (1973): 193–228.

Wang, Tao 王韜, and Gu Xieguang 顧燮光 et al., eds. *Jindai yishu mu* 近代譯書目 [Modern bibliographies of translations]. Beijing: Beijing tushuguan chubanshe, 2003.

Wang, Tiangen 王天根. *Tianyanlun chuanbo yu QingmoMinchu de shehui dongyuan* 《天演論》傳播與清末民初的社會動員 [The distribution of *Tianyanlun* and the social mobilization in late Qing and early Republican China]. Hefei: Hefei gongye daxue chubanshe, 2006.

Wang, Yanwei 王彥威, and Wang Liang 王亮, eds. *Qingji waijiao shiliao* 清季外交史料 [Primary sources on Qing diplomacy]. Changsha: Hunanshifan daxue chubanshe, 2015.

Wang, Yuanfang 汪原放. *Huiyi Yadong tushuguan* 回憶亞東圖書館 [Remembering Yadong Library]. Shanghai : Xuelin chubanshe, 1983.

———. *Yadong tushugaun yu Chen Duxiu* 亞東圖書館與陳獨秀 [Yadong Library and Chen Duxiu]. Shanghai: Xuelin chubanshe, 2006.

Wang Yunwu 王雲五. *Shangwu yinshuguan yu xin jiaoyu nianpu* 商務印書館與新教育年譜 [Chronicle of Commercial Press and the new education]. Taipei: Taiwan shangwu yinshuguan, 1973.

Wayland, Francis. *The Elements of Political Economy*. Boston: Gould & Lincoln, 1852.

Weber, Max. *The Religion of China: Confucianism and Taoism*. Translated and edited by Hans H. Gerth. New York: Free Press, 1951.

Wong, R. Bin. *China Transformed: Historical Change and the Limits of European Experience*. Ithaca, NY: Cornell University Press, 1997.

WSC-Databases: An Electronic Repository for Chinese Scientific, Philosophical and Political Terms Coined in the Nineteenth and Early Twenty Century. http://www.wsc.uni-erlangen.de/wscdb.htm.

Wu, Jianren. *The Sea of Regret: Two Turn-of-the-Century Chinese Romantic Novels*. Translated by Patrick Hanan. Honolulu: University of Hawaii Press, 1995.

Wu, Lin-Chun 吳翎君. "Qingmo Minchu Zhong-Mei banquan zhi zheng" 清末民初中美版權之爭 [Chinese-US copyright disputes in late Qing and early Republican China]. *Guoli zhengzhi daxue lishi xuebao* 38 (November 2012): 97–136.

Xiaoshuo Lin 小說林, trans. and ed. *Huangjin gu Fuermosi zhentan an* 黃金骨福爾摩斯偵探案 [Golden bone: a Holmes detective story]. Shanghai: Xiaoshuo lin, 1906.

Xindai shuju. *Xiandai shuju chuban shunu* 現代書局出版書目 [Catalog of modern books]. Youxing: Xindai shuju Guangxi youxing zhidian, 1934.

Xiong, Rong 熊融. "Lu Xun riji sheji renwu shengzu nianfen jiguan yu sheng ping zhushi buzheng" 魯迅日記涉及人物生卒年份、籍貫與生平注釋補正 [Corrected and supplemental annotations of the persons appearing in Lu Xun's diary, their dates of birth and death, their native places, and their biographic sketches]. *Lu Xun yanjiu yuekan*, August 1986, 46–48.

Xiong, Yuezhi 熊月之, ed. *Wan Qing xinxue shumu tiyao* 晚清新學書目提要 [Annotated late Qing bibliographies of New Learning books]. Shanghai: Shanghai shudian chubanshe, 2007.

———. *Xixue dongjian yu wanqing shehui* 西學東漸與晚清社會 [The dissemination of Western learning and late Qing society]. Shanghai: Shanghai Renmin Chubanshe, 1995.

Xu Mingzhi 徐鳴之. *Zhuzuoquan fa shiyi* 著作權法釋義 [Annotation of the copyright law]. Shanghai: Shangwu yinshuguan, 1929.

Xuebu Zongwusi 學部總務司. *Guangxu san shi san nian fen diyici jiaoyu tongtong ji tubiao* 光緒三十三年分第一次教育統計圖表 [The first education survey statistical charts of the thirty-third year of Guangxu] (1907). Taipei: Zhongguo chubanshe, 1973.

Yagi, Sakichi 八木佐吉. "Okuzuke gaishi" 奧付概史 [A brief history of okuzuke]. *Toshokan to hon no shūhen* 5 (October 1978): 50–77.

Yamamoto, Hideki 山本秀樹. *Edo jidai santo shuppanhō taigai: Bungakushi shuppanshi no tameni* 江戶時代三都出版法大概 : 文学史・出版史のために [General overview of the publishing laws in the three capitals during the Edo period: for literary history and publishing history]. Okayama: Okayama Daigaku Bungakubu, 2010.

Yamauchi, Susumu. "Civilization and International Law in Japan during the Meiji Era (1868–1912)." *Hitotsubashi Journal of Law and Politics* 24 (February 1996): 1–25.

Yan, Fu. *Yan Fu heji* 嚴復合集 [Comprehensive collection of Yan Fu's writing]. 20 vols. Edited by Yan Fu heji bianji weiyuanhui. Taipei: Caituan faren Gu Gongliang wenjiao jijinhui, 1998.

———. *Yan Fu ji* 嚴復集 [Collection of Yan Fu writings]. 5 vols. Edited by Wang Shi. Beijing: Zhonghua shuju, 1986.

———. *Yan Fu ji bubian* 嚴復集補編 [Collection of Yan Fu writings: supplement volume]. Edited by Sun Yingxiang and Pi Houfeng. Fuzhou: Fujian renmin chubanshe, 2004.

Yang, Dongping楊東平. *Chengshi jifeng: Beijing he Shanghai di bianqian yu duizhi* 城市季風 : 北京和上海的變遷與對峙 [Urban monsoon: the transformation and rivalry of Beijing and Shanghai]. Taipei: Jieyou chubanshe, 1996.

Yang, Liying 楊麗瑩. *Saoye shanfang shiy*掃葉山房史研究 [A history of Sweeping-Leaves Studio]. Shanghai: Fudan daxue chubanshe, 2013.

Yao, Gonghe 姚公鶴. *Shanghai xianhua*上海閒話 [Shanghai rumors]. Shanghai: Shangwu yinshuguan, 1933.

Yao, Wenyuan 姚文元. "Lun gaofei" 論稿費 [On remuneration]. *Wenhui bao*, September 27, 1958.

Ye, Dehui 葉德輝. *Ye Dehui shu hua* 葉德輝書話 [Ye Dehui's essays on books]. Edited by Qian Gurong. Hangzhou: Zhejiang renmin zhubanche, 1998.

Yeh, Catherine. *Shanghai Love: Courtesans, Intellectuals, and Entertainment Culture, 1850–1910.* Seattle: University of Washington Press, 2006.

Yeh, Wen-Hsin. *The Alienated Academy: Culture and Politics in Republican China, 1919–1937.* Cambridge, MA: Harvard University Press, 1990.

Yoshino, Sakuzou 吉野作造, ed. *Meiji bunka zenshū* 明治文化全集 [The complete collection of Meiji culture]. Vol. 17. Tokyo: Nippon Hyouron sha, 1927–1930.

Yu, Hua. "Stealing Books for the Poor." *New York Times.* March 13, 2013.

Yü, Yingshi 余英時. *Zhongguo jindai sixiang shi shang di Hu Shi* 中國近代思想史上的胡適 [Hu Shi in modern Chinese intellectual history]. Taipei: Lianjing chuban shiye gongsi, 1984.

———. *Zhongguo wenhua yu xiandai bianqian* 中國文化與現代變遷 [Chinese culture and modernization]. Taipei: Sanmin shuju, 1992.

———. "Zhongguo zhishi fenzi de bianyuanhua" 中國知識份子的邊緣化 [The marginalization of the Chinese intelligentsia]. In his *Zhongguo wenhua yu xiandai bianqian*, 35–50. Taipei: Sanmin shuju, 1992.

Yuan, Songlian 袁宗濂, and Yan Zhiqing 晏志清, eds. *Xixue santong*西學三通 [Tri-comprehension of Western knowledge]. Shanghai: Wensheng tang, 1902.

Zaizhen 載振. *Yinyao Riji* 英軺日記 [Diary during the diplomatic mission to England]. Shanghai: Wenming shuju, 1903.

Zelin, Madeleine, Jonathan K. Ocko, and Robert Gardella. *Contract and Property in Early Modern China.* Studies of the Weatherhead East Asian Institute, Columbia University. Stanford, CA: Stanford University Press, 2004.

Zhang, Baixi 張百熙. *Zhang Baixi ji* 張百熙集 [Collection of Zhang Baixi's writings]. Changsha: Yuelu shuyuan, 2008.

Zhang, Jinglu 張靜廬, ed. *Zhongguo chuban shiliao*, bubian 中國出版史料補編 [Primary sources of Chinese publishing history: supplemental volume]. Beijing: Zhonghua shu ju, 1957.

———. *Zhongguo jindai chuban shiliao* 中國近代出版史料 [Primary sources of modern Chinese publishing history]. 2 vols. Beijing: Zhonghua shu ju, 1957.

———. *Zhongguo xiandai chuban shiliao* 中國現代出版史料 [Primary sources of contemporary Chinese publishing history]. 4 vols. Beijing: Zhonghua shu ju, 1954–59.Zhang, Yousong 張有松. "Wo angqi tou, ting qi xiong lai, touru zhandou!" 我昂起頭，挺起胸來，投入戰鬥! [I raise my head, thrust out my chest, and join the fight!]. *Wenyi bao* 1957:9 (June 2, 1957).

Zhang, Yu 張渝. *Qing dai zhong qi Chongqing de shang ye gui ze yu zhi xu: yi Ba Xian dang an wei zhong xin de yan jiu* 清代中期重庆的商业规则与秩序: 以巴县档案为中心的研究 [Commercial rules and orders in mid-Qing Chongquing: a study based on the Ba County archives]. Beijing: Zhongguo zheng fa da xue chu ban she, 2010.

Zhang, Yuanji 張元濟. *Zhang Yuanji Quanji* 張元濟全集 [Complete collection of Zhang Yuanji's writings]. Vols. 1–3. Bejing: Shang wu yin shu guan, 2007.

Zhang, Zhongmin 张仲民. "Cong shuji shi dao yuedu shi—guanyu wanqing shuji shi /yuedu shi yanjiu de ruogan sikao" 从书籍史到阅读史—关于晚清书籍史/阅读史研究的若干思考 [From history of books to history of reading: thoughts on late Qing history of books/reading]. *Shilin* 5 (2007): 151–189.

Zhao Xiaoen 赵晓恩. *Yan'an chuban de guanghui* 延安出版的光辉 [The glory of the publishing mission in Yan'an]. Beijing: Zhongguo shuji chubanshe, 2002.

Zheng, Chengsi 鄭成思. "Zhongwai yinshua chuban wu banquan gainian de yenge" 中外印刷出版與版權概念的沿革 [Printing and publishing in China and the West and the development of copyright ideas]. *Banquan Yanjo*, April 1995, 113–114.

———. *Zhishi caichanquan fa* 知識財產權法 [Intellectual property law]. Beijing: Falü chubanshe, 1997.

Zheng, Hesheng 鄭鶴聲. "Sanshi nian lai zhongyang zhengfu duiyu bianshen jiaokeshu zhi jiantao" 三十年來中央政府對編審教科書之檢討 [A review of the central government's publication and examination of textbooks in the past thirty years]. *Jiaoyu zazhi* 25:7 (July 1935): 1–44.

Zheng Zizhan 鄭子展, ed. *Lufei Bohong xiansheng nianpu* 陸費伯鴻先生年譜 [The chronological biography of Lufei Bohong]. Taipei: Wenhai chubanshe, 1973.

Zhongguo chuban kexue yanjiusuo and Zhongyang dang'anguan, eds. *Zhonghua remin hongheguo chuban shiliao* 中華人民共和國出版史料 [Primary sources of PRC publishing history]. 11 vols. Beijing: Zhongguo shuji chubanshe, 1995–2007.

Zhongguo di 1 li shi dang an guan 中國第一歷史檔案館, ed. *Guangxu Xuantong Liangchao Shangyu Dang* 光緒宣統兩朝上諭檔 [Imperial edicts during the Guangxu and Xuantong period]. Vol. 24. Guilin: Guangxi shifan daxue chubanshe, 1996.

Zhongguo Remin Daxue 中国人民大学, ed. *Jiefang Qu Genju Di Tushu Mulu* 解放区割据地图书目录 [A catalog of titles published in the liberated regions and base areas]. Beijing: Zhongguo Renmin daxue chuban she, 1989.

Zhongyang Makesi En'gesi Liening Sidalin zhu zuo bian yi ju 中央马克思恩格斯列宁史達林著作編譯局, ed. *Makesi En'gesi zhu zuo zai Zhongguo de chuanbo: ji nian Makesi shi shi yi bai zhou nian* 马克思恩格斯著作在中国的传播: 纪念马克思逝世一百周年 [The circulation of Marx's and Engels's writings in China: commemorating the one hundredth anniversary of Marx's death]. Beijing: Zhong yang Makesi En'gesi Liening Sidalin zhu zuo bian yi ju, 1983.

Zhongyang xuanchuan bu "Chuban gongzuo xuanbian" bianji zu 中央出版局出版工作选编编辑组, ed. *Chuban gongzuo wenjian xuanbian* 出版工作文獻选编 [Selected documents on publishing works]. Shenyang: Liaoning jiaoyu chubanshe, 1991.

Zhongyang yanjiuyuan jindaishi yanjiusuo 中央研究院近代史研究所, ed. *Zhong-Mei Guanxi Shiliao: Guangxu Chao* 中美關係史料: 光緒朝 [Primary sources on Sino-American relations: Guangxu reign]. Taipei: Zhongyang yanjiuyuan jindaishi yanjiusuo, 1988.

Zhou, Wu 周武. "Cong quanguoxin dao difanghua: 1945 zi 1956 nian Shanghai chubanye de bianqian" 从全国性到地方化:1945年至 1956年上海书业的变迁 [From national to regional: the transformation of the Shanghai publishing industry from 1945 to 1956]. *Shilin* 6 (2006): 72–95.

Zhou, Zhenhe 周振鶴, ed. *Wan Qing yingye shumu* 晚清營業書目 [Publication catalogs in the late Qing]. Shanghai: Shanghai shudian chubanshe, 2005.

Zhu, Dawen 朱大文, et al., eds. *Wanguo zhengzhi congkao* 萬國政治叢考 [International politics series]. [S.I.]: Haihong wenshu ju, 1902.

Zhu, Maiochun 朱妙春. *Wo wei Lu Xun da guansi* 我为鲁迅打官司 [I filed lawsuits for Lu Xun]. Beijing: Zhishi chanquan chubanshe, 2006.

Zhu, Ying 朱英, ed. *Zhongguo jindai tongye gonghui yu dangdai hangye xiehui* 中國近代同業公會與當代行業協會 [Modern Chinese trade associations and contemporary professional associations]. Beijing: Zhongguo renmin daxue chubanshe, 2004.

Zhu, Zhisan 朱峙三. "Zhu Zhisan riji (lianzai zhi yi)" 朱峙三日記 (連載之一) [Zhu Zhisan's diary (part one)]. In *Xinhai Geming shi cong kan* 辛亥革命史叢刊 [The history of the 1911 Revolution series]. Vol. 10. Wuhan: Hubei renmin chubanshe, 1999.

Zong Shi 宗時. "Qingdai yilai Beijing shuye" 清代以来北京书业 [Beijing book trade since the Qing dynasty]. In *Shudian Gongzou Shiliao*, edited by Xinhua shudian, 4:57–66. Beijing: Xinhua shudian zhongdian, 1980.

INDEX

Alford, William, 306; on Chinese adaptation of Soviet IPR laws, 253–54; cultural determinist explanation of Chinese piracy, 3n12, 7–8; on late imperial proprietary declarations, 10, 122

Allen, Young J. (1836–1907), 67, 99, 135–37, 156, 165–66, 173

Anti-Rightist Movement, 289n106, 290–91, 293, 295–96

artistic and intellectual creation: edict issued by the Guangxu Emperor protecting invention and intellectual works, 52, 135, 176n49; and labor input emphasized by the PRC, 283; and the PRC's interest in controlling cultural production, 304; and *zhuzuoquan/ chosakuken* (the right of the author), 197. *See also* Berne Convention for the Protection of Literary and Artistic Works; intellectual property rights (IPR) doctrine; literary property

Association of Chinese Authors and Publishers (*Zhongguo zhuzuoren chubanren xiehui*), 224–25, 226, 238

Azuma Heiji (1853–1917), 49

banquan (copyright): as an alien legal concept, 7–9, 23, 54–55, 90, 119, 298; and the changing landscape in the Chinese knowledge economy, 6–7, 13–17, 298–310 passim; copyright protection for foreign publishers in China after the Boxer Rebellion, 53, 123–25; Kang Youwei's

portrayal of copyright as a means for China to catch up with Europe, 51–52, 54; *zhuzuoquan* compared with, 5–6, 197–98, 197n103. *See also* copyright infringement; copyright protection for foreign publishers in China

—four major forms of, 299–300; 1. as ownership of the tangible means of production, 299–300 (*see also* booksellers' guilds— and *banquan* regulation; *cangban; shudi* (master copy)—registration at guilds; *zōhan no menkyo; zōhansha; zōhan* stamps and seals); 2. as incorporeal property created by the author's mental labor, 300 (*see also* mental labor); 3. as a privilege granted by the state to authors and booksellers, 120, 300, 303–4; 4. as a license/ privilege granted by the state to authors and booksellers, 128, 134, 300 (*see also* Imperial University; Ministry of Education)

—local practices and efforts: 4, 9–12, 23, 61, 90, 119–20, 298 (*see also* Detective Branch; economic actors in the cultural market); antipiracy civic organization, 309; as a better tactic for multinational corporations, 307, 307n13; burning of pirated *shudi*

337

banquan (copyright) (cont.)
   at the Wenchang god's temple,
   178, 183, 208; disputes reported to
   the SBG by Shanghai booksellers, 177–79, 193; low priority of,
   308; public announcements of
   "copyright" ownership and
   piracy complaints in local
   newspapers, 62, 89, 233, 238;
   regulation by booksellers' guilds
   (*see* booksellers' guilds—and
   banquan regulation)
banquan suoyou fanke (*fanyin*) *bijiu*: as
   convention, 5, 16, 58, 89, 113, 118, 159;
   disappearance in the 1950s of, 304; and
   Japanese conventions, 56–58, 59f1.7, 61;
   and Ming-Qing customary warnings
   against unauthorized reprinting, 61, 125;
   revival in the 1980s of, 307; SBTA's
   practice of, 176, 194
*Baohu chubanwu zhuzuoquan zhanxing
   guiding* (Interim provisions to protect the
   copyright of printed materials), 279
Bao Tianxiao (1876–1972), 83–84, 98
Beiping Office of the Piracy Investigation
   Committee (*Shanghai shuye tongye
   gonghui chajiu weiban weiyuanhui
   zhuping banshichu*). *See* Detective
   Branch
Beixin Books (*Beixin shuju*), 117, 217, 226,
   226n45
Benefit-Enhancing Books (*Guangyi shuju*):
   and the copyright of *Tongzi xin chidu*,
   200–201; lithographic reprints by, 159
Berne Convention for the Protection of
   Literary and Artistic Works: and the
   introduction of *droit d'auteur* to Japan,
   5n16, 48, 48n50, 197; and the Meiji
   government, 46, 46n59, 197, 197n104; the
   PRC's membership in the Berne Union
   (1992), 5, 46n59, 306; the United States'
   joining of (1988), 46n59
booksellers' guilds; *Beizhi Wenchang
   Gonghui* (Wenchang Guild for Hebei

booksellers), 170n35; establishment of,
   163, 165; *honya nakama* (booksellers
   guilds), 29; transition from a mutual aid
   organization to a quasi-legal institution,
   169–70. See also *Chongde gongsuo*
   (Venerate Virtue Guild); merchants'
   guilds; Osaka Booksellers' Guild; Tokyo
   Booksellers Guild; Wenchang
booksellers' guilds—and *banquan*
   regulation: *banquan* guild proposed by
   Young J. Allen, 165–66, 173; ideas of the
   SBG and the SBTA compared, 177;
   motivation to unite Shanghai booksellers
   provided by, 169–70. See also *shudi*
   (master copy)—registration at guilds
booksellers in Shanghai. *See* Shanghai
   booksellers
Boxer Rebellion: and copyright protection
   for foreign publishers in China, 53,
   123–25; New Learning zeal following, 75;
   New Policy Reform introduced in the
   aftermath of, 76, 102; and the Qing's new
   educational system, 129n22, 143
Brokaw, Cynthia J., 80

Cai Yuanpei (1868–1940), 85n72, 117, 148
cangban: and copyright, 58, 60–61, 299; and
   the Ming-Qing practice of owning
   tangible printing blocks, 36, 38, 60, 299;
   and SBG's copyright regulation, 174; and
   zōhan, 36
cangban seal, 38, 39f1.5, 58, 61
Cassel, Pär Kristoffer, 11n29
censorship, 20; banning of books
   published by Civilization Books,
   133–34, 148; banning of *Geguo geming
   shi* (World history of revolutions), 268;
   banning of *Xingtan* (Talking about sex),
   223n37; *banquan* associated with, 135,
   143–44, 153–54; and the CCP, 257; and
   control of cultural production, 304; and
   the Detective Branch's policing of
   piracy, 250, 303; by the GMD, 19, 233,
   240, 263, 265, 303; by the late imperial

state, 19; of pornography by the Chongde guild, 170; by Tokugawa authorities, 29, 45n57

Chambers, William and Robert, 26–27, 26n12

chambers of commerce: Baoding Chamber of Commerce, 246; and dispute mediation, 167n25; *Jianming shanghui zhangcheng* (Concise regulation of the chamber of commerce), 168; Ministry of Commerce's call for the establishment of, 167; power in mediating commercial disputes, 167n25; Shanghai General Chamber of Commerce, 168, 189, 199, 202

Chen Duxiu (1879–1942), 217

Chen Yuan (1918–2004), 295

Cheng Huanqing, 236–40, 243, 250

Chessboard Street (*Qipanjie*) booksellers: *banquan*/copyright popularized by, 159–60; and *Chongde gongsuo* (Venerate Virtue Guild), 163; collective justice and social order maintained by, 186, 189, 193; diversity of, 164–65; and Shanghai in the late nineteenth and early twentieth centuries, 158–59. *See also* Benefit-Enhancing Books (*Guangyi shuju*); Chung Hwa Books (*Zhonghua shuju*); Commercial Press; Sweeping Leaves Studio (*Saoye shanfang*)

Chinese Publishers' Association of Copyright Protection (*Zhongguo chubanren zhuzuoxuan baohu xiehui*), 224–26

Chongde gongsuo (Venerate Virtue Guild), 163, 163n8, 170

Chosakukenhō (1899 Copyright Law of Japan): and the Copyright Law of the Great Qing, 4, 156, 197; drafting of, 44, 46, 48, 48n60, 197, 197n104

Chung Hwa Books (*Zhonghua shuju*), 213t6.1, 235f6.4; establishment of, 198, 204; and Liang's *Yingbingshi Wenji*, 204–6; and the primary and secondary school textbook market, 159, 198, 212–13

Chunming Bookstore (*Chunming shudian*): campaign against it (1951), 267–76; charges against the Chen brothers (1934), 243, 243n97; coordinated effort to make a case against its pirating, 234; pirated copies of *Geguo geming shi* produced by, 268–70, 274; renaming as Chunming Press, 276; self-criticism reports, 272–75; tip by a clerk from Wenguang Books, 243, 244f6.3

Civilization Books (*Wenming shuju*): banning of books published by, 133–34, 148; and the bookseller's guilds, 172, 176, 185, 186; copyright seal of, 59f1.7; dispute with Yan Fu (*see* Yan Fu (1854–1921)—as an economic actor); dispute with Yuan Shikai, 128–39, 155–56, 300, 303; establishment of, 128, 159; and *Heinu yutian lu* (Lin Shu's translation of *Uncle Tom's Cabin*), 59f1.7, 62, 91–92; Lian Quan's efforts regarding copyright protection, 53–54, 99, 101, 109, 119–20, 125, 129–33, 142, 146. *See also* Four Books and Five Classics; Lian Quan; Lin Shu; Lufei Kui

civilization discourse, and the promotion of *banquan*, 24–28, 32, 40–42, 61

civil service examinations: abolition of, 144–45; and the eight-legged essay, 76, 77, 78, 80, 86, 143; frequency between 1902 and 1904 of, 76, 76n47; marginalization of Chinese intelligentsia following its abolition, 14, 14n36, 19; and New Learning books, 80–82, 86; and questions on contemporary issues, 76–77; reforms overseen by the commissioner of the Imperial University, 129n22

collective morality of the marketplace: antipiracy civic organizations, 309; and the Detective Branch's investigation of Gathering-Jade Studio, 248; and justice and social order maintained on Chessboard Street, 186, 189, 193; and

collective morality (continued)
mutual assistance provided by native-place and common-trade organizations, 166–67; and pricing by booksellers possessing *shudi* of valuable titles, 196. *See also* merchants' guilds

Commercial Press: *banquan*/copyright system developed by, 114, 117 (*see also* Yan Fu (1854–1921)—as an economic actor); establishment as a printing shop, 73–74; founding of, 73–74; and the *Ginn & Co. v. Commercial Press* case, 3–4; modern print capitalism championed by, 164; pamphlet *Banquan kao* (On copyright) published by, 4, 54, 88–89, 119, 124; and the primary and secondary school textbook market, 159; production of New Learning texts, 75, 91; textbook publishing by, 212–13, 213t6.1; titles registered at the Ministry of the Interior, 235f6.4; trans-compilation (*bianyi*) practices of, 85n72. *See also* Tao Baolin

copyright: and not-for-profit missionary presses, 51, 90, 172–73; Statute of Anne, 7. See also *banquan*; *cangban*; *Chosakukenhō* (1899 Copyright Law of Japan); copyright protection for foreign publishers in China; *Da Qing zhuzuoquan lü* (Copyright Law of the Great Qing); *Guomin zhengfu zhuzuoquanfa* (The National Government's Copyright Law, 1928); Japanese copyright law

copyright infringement: and PRC views of the "bourgeoisness" of copyright, 279; unauthorized reprints of party publications by Liulichang pirates, 255, 262–63; and the view that the Chinese lack a sense of copyright, 2–3, 7–9, 23, 54–55, 90, 298

Copyright Law of the Great Qing. See *Da Qing zhuzuoquan lü*

copyright protection for foreign publishers in China: and the Sino-US Renewed Treaties of Trade and Navigation and the Sino-Japanese Treaties of Trade and Navigation, 53, 123–24n14; and the term *banquan*, 53

counterfeiting, 17: and copycatting, 182–83; cultural determinist explanation of, 2–3, 3n12, 7–8; petitioning of Qing officials for copyright protection, 53–54; releasing of "fabricated" CCP texts by the GMD, 262; reprints of party publications, 259–63, 266–67; unlicensed software and movies, 1, 1–2n4, 305; and Yan Fu's copyright stamp, 112–14, 113f3.1. *See also* copyright infringement

—knockoff and "fake" books marketed by Chinese pirates, 1–2, 1n3, 307; and Fukuzawa's estimates of his influence, 40n40; *gihan* ("counterfeit editions") of Fukuzawa's publications, 25

cultural figures as economic actors. *See* economic actors in the cultural market

Dagong bao, the term *banquan* appearing in, 55, 56n84

Da Qing zhuzuoquan lü (Copyright Law of the Great Qing), 199n110; and the 1899 Copyright Law of Japan, 4, 156, 197; inadequacy of, 157; promulgation of, 61, 198; and reprints of Shanghai publications, 199

Detective Branch: and the case against Gathering-Jade studio, 241–49; and the case of Cheng Huanqing, 236–41, 243, 250; Liulichang office of, 211, 219, 223–24, 225; patrolling of Beiping branches of Shanghai publishers, 227–29; raids of East Peace Market, 223, 231, 232t6.3, 236, 252; SBG members' *banquan*/copyright protected by, 303; Yang Shuyi, 226, 231, 236, 242

Dimitrov, Martin K., 307, 307n13

Ding Ling (1904–1986): criticism of, 290; Liu Shaotang's views of authorial success compared with, 294; visit to the Soviet Union (1949), 258–59

Dongfang zazhi (The Eastern miscellany), 216

Dykstra, Maura Dominique, 167

East Peace Market, 223, 230–31, 232t6.3, 236, 252

economic actors in the cultural market: and Chinese pirates, 2–4, 17, 53; and insight into understanding *banquan*, 15–17; and the new logic of work and value, 285–86; profit seeking by booksellers, 144–46, 251, 265, 270; and state regulation envisioned by the CCP, 18–20, 252–54. *See also* Fu Lei; Lian Quan; Liang Qichao; Lin Shu; Liu Shaotang; Lu Xun; Wang Kangnian; Yan Fu

Edgren, Sören, 10, 16n40, 38, 58, 60

education. *See* civil service examinations; Ministry of Education; New Learning

1898 Reform, 52, 73, 76, 76n44, 80, 134, 176n49, 298

Enlightenment Books (*Guangzhi shuju*): registration as a foreign company, 124, 124n15; *Yinbingshi wenji* published by, 205–6

Enlightenment Bookstore (*Kaiming shuju*), New Learning books sold by, 78–79, 79t2.1, 81

examination system. *See* civil service examinations

fanke (reproduce/duplicate [the printing blocks]): and the phrase *fanyin* (reprinting), 13, 13n33, 58n87; and the SDCK's prosecution of Chinese unauthorized reprinting, 51, 121

fanke bijiu: on colophons and title pages of Ming and early Qing books, 36, 36f1.3, 38, 58, 58n88, 61, 125; and the English word "copyright," 60; and the statement "XX *cangban*," 60

Feng Ziyou on yearning for New Learning, 75

Flying-Swan Studio (*Feihong ge*), 181–82

Four Books and Five Classics, 77; and civil service examinations, 76–77, 80; and

lithographic printer-publishers, 85; and the SBG's granting of a *banquan* patent, 195–96

French Revolution, and Qing views of books with antigovernment ideas, 134, 144n61, 148–49

Fu Lei, 286–87, 292

Fukuzawa Yukichi (1835–1901) and *hanken* (copyright): and the "business of Enlightenment," 23–24; and civilization discourse, 24–28, 32, 40–42; *hanken* coined by, 24, 40–41, 43; his autonomy as a *zōhansha* (possessor of the printing blocks), 30–32; *okuzuke* used to record royalties owed, 46; and sales of pirated copies of his books, 25, 27n14, 32, 40–43, 40n40; xylographers hired to make printing blocks of his publications, 30; *zōhan* seal displayed on copies he published, 33, 34f1, 38

—publications: *Gakumon no susume* (The encouragement of learning), 40, 41; *Kairekiben* (Defending the changes in the calendar), 41; *Kyūri zukai* (Illustrated introduction of physical sciences), 41

—*Seijiō jijō* and *Seijiō jijō gaihen* (Conditions in the West): and copyright and piracy issues, 25, 27–28, 27n14, 32, 40–43; correlation of economic development and private property rights addressed in, 25–26; *Fukuzawa shi zōhan* from *Seiyō jijō gaihen*, 33, 35f1.2; *Shuppan jōrei* influenced by, 32, 40; and technically legal recast publications, 41; and the work of Francis Wayland, 26–27; and the work of William and Robert Chambers, 26–27, 26n12

Fuzanbō, 49–50

Gathering-Jade Studio (*Qunyu shanfang*), 241–50; legal action taken against, 245–46; pirated imprints sold by, 241–43

Geguo geming shi (World history of revolutions), 268–70, 274

General Publishing Administration ([GPA], *Chuban Zongshu*): PRC's stance on piracy criticized by, 255; profit-driven private publishers targeted by, 264–67, 276–78, 277n73; reprinting with permission guidelines issued by, 263–64; socialist copyright laws crafted by, 278–83. *See also* Ye Shengtao

gihan ("counterfeit editions"). *See* counterfeiting

Giles, Herbert A., 60

Golden Millet Studio (*Jinshu zhai*): *banquan* certificate used by, 58; and the New Learning market, 84, 98–99

GPA. *See* General Publishing Administration ([GPA], *Chuban Zongshu*)

Great Leap Forward, 296

Guangxuehui. *See* Society for the Diffusion of Christian and General Knowledge among the Chinese

Guangxu Emperor (1871–1908, reign: 1875–1908), 303; edict issued protecting invention and intellectual works, 52, 135, 176n49; Kang Youwei's *Riben Bianzheng kao* written for, 51–52; reforms modeled after Japan's Meiji Restoration, 75–76

Guangzhi shuju. See Enlightenment Books

guilds. *See* booksellers' guilds; booksellers' guilds—and *banquan* regulation; merchants' guilds; Shanghai Booksellers' Guild

Guomindang (GMD, Nationalist Party): and the Association of Chinese Authors and Publishers, 224–25; and the case against Nanjing Military bookstore, 239; censorship by, 19, 263, 265; and the Chinese Publishers' Association of Copyright Protection, 225; and control of the publishing sector, 19–20, 240, 250–52; Nanjing made the capital of, 22; releasing of "fabricated" CCP texts by, 262; and Shanghai publishers, 219–20, 256–57. *See also Guomin zhengfu zhuzuoquanfa* (The National Government's Copyright Law, 1928); 1915 ROC Copyright Law

Guomin zhengfu zhuzuoquanfa (The National Government's Copyright Law, 1928), 28, 233; PRC's dismissal of, 256

hankabu (stock of printing blocks), 29–30, 30nn21–22

hanken: and Chessboard Street publishers and booksellers, 159; Chinese adoption of *hanken shoyū* (copyright retained), 46–48, 47f1.6, 51, 56–58, 61; and *chosakuken* (the right of the author), 197; Fukuzawa's coining of the term (1873), 24, 40–41, 43–44, 155, 299; and the revision of *Shuppan jōrei* (1875), 44–45

Harry Potter novels, 1, 1n3

Home Ministry (Japan), 45–46

honya nakama (booksellers' guilds), 29

Hu Shi (1891–1962), 217, 224

Hu Yuzhi (1896–1986): as a PRC cultural official, 20; on the role of publishing, 260

Hundred Days' Reform. *See* 1898 Reform

Hundred Flowers Campaign: declining of remuneration by "rich" artists, 296; discontentment with the remuneration system expressed by many authors, 187, 285, 288, 289

Huxley, Thomas, *Evolution and Ethics*, Yan Fu's translation as *Tianyanlun*, 95–96

Iida, Kanae, 27n12

Imperial University: *banquan* certificates issued by, 120, 125, 133–34, 141–42, 141n55, 300; as the cultural authority in charge of *banquan*, 138–42; post of commissioner of, 129n22; Press Office (*Bianyi tushu ju*), of, 145

Inoue, Susumu, 10, 58, 60, 122

intellectual property rights (IPR) doctrine: Chinese pirates as copyright-savvy economic actors, 2–4, 17, 53; conventional wisdom as to why Chinese pirate, 2–3; and local enterprises, 307, 307n13; PRC adoption of the Soviet IPR system, 253–54, 278–79; punitive measures applied to China for lack of compliance, 306–7. *See also* Berne Convention for the Protection of Literary and Artistic Works; Soviet 1925 Copyright Act

intellectual property terminology. *See* artistic and intellectual creation

International Mixed Court at Shanghai. *See* Shanghai Mixed Court

International Publishers' Association, 209

Japanese copyright law: and the introduction of *droit d'auteur* to Japan, 5n16, 48, 48n50, 197. *See also Chosakukenhō* (1899 Copyright Law of Japan); Fukuzawa Yukichi (1835–1901) and *hanken* (copyright); *hanken*; *jūhan* (duplicated printing blocks); *Shuppan jorei* (The publication regulations)

Japanese publishers: reprinting prohibition orders issued to, 123. *See also* Fuzanbō; Maruzen; Rakuzendou; Sino-Japanese trade

Jernigan, T. R (1847–1920): and the *Ginn & Co. v. Commercial Press* case, 2–3; and SDCK's determination to stop piracy, 71

Jiangnan Arsenal (*Jiangnan jiqizhizaoju*), 65, 68, 73n35, 73, 81, 87–88

Johns, Adrian, 8

jūhan (duplicated printing blocks), 30, 41, 45

Kang Youwei (1858–1927): *Riben Bianzheng kao* (A study of Japan's political reform), 51–52, 52n75; *Riben shumu zhi* (Bibliography of Japanese books), 49

Karl, Rebecca E., and Peter Gue Zarrow, 76

Kornicki, Peter, 28n17, 30n22, 45

Kuhn, Philip, 303n1

Li Boyuan (1867–1906): micro-publishing industry of, 164; *Wenming xiaoshi* (satire of attitudes toward New Learning books), 78, 158

Li Mingshan, 8n20, 58n88, 224n39

Li Xiaofeng (1897–1971), 117n55, 217

Lian Quan, 164, 300; as an advocate of *banquan*/copyright protection, 109–10, 129–30; appeal to higher political powers, 137–38, 156, 303; petitioning for Civilization Books regarding copyright protection, 53–54, 119–20, 125, 129, 142; and Yan Fu (*see* Yan Fu (1854–1921)—as an economic actor)

Liang Qichao (1873–1929), 63n4, 156; appropriation of others' works as his own, 17n41; *Do xixue shu fa* compiled by, 64; as an economic actor, 15; his founding of Great Unity Translation Press (*Datong yishu ju*), 73; on the need to read Western books, 63, 65; *Qingyi bao* (The China discussion) established by, 52; unauthorized lecture notes published by East Peace Market, 230–31; Western political ideas accessed from Japanese publications by, 50; *Xixue shumu biao* compiled by, 64, 65n11, 74, 86; *Yingbingshi Wenji* by, 204–7

Lin Shu (1852–1924), 63n4; *Bali chahua nü yishi* (translation of *La Dame aux camélias*), 21–23, 87, 91–92, 96, 299; *Heinu yutian lu* (translation of *Uncle Tom's Cabin*), 59f1.7, 62, 91–92; reprints of his books, 91–92

—as an economic actor, 15, 82, 116; changing attitude toward literary property, 62; translation business of, 21, 48, 62; Yan Fu compared with, 94

literary property: CCP-PRC's unmaking and remaking of, 253–54, 278; and Fukuzawa's property rights claims, 44; Lin Shu's changing attitude toward, 62; and the resolutions of the First National

literary property (cont.)
Publishing Conference, 278. *See also*
intellectual property rights (IPR)
doctrine; *zhuzuoquan* (author's right)
lithographic technology: and Chessboard
Street booksellers, 159, 164; and civil
service examination–related titles, 85–86;
locally produced pirated copies, 181,
221–22, 222t6.2; and the production of
New Learning books, 91; and the
production of *Wanguo gongfa, 175t5.1*
Liulichang: after the 1911 Revolution, 220;
Beizhi Wenchang Gonghui (Wenchang
Guild for Hebei booksellers) guildhall in,
170n35; Detective Branch office in, 211,
223–24, 225; unauthorized reprints of
party publications by Liulichang pirates,
255, 262–63
Liu Shaotang (1936–1997): background of,
290–91; as an economic actor, 290–95
Lobscheid, William, 51
Lü Haihuan (1843–1927) (Chinese treaty
commissioner), 53, 60, 144
Lü Simian (1884–1957), 63–64
Lu Xun (1881–1936): and the Association of
Chinese Authors and Publishers, 24;
contestation of rights to his work, 308;
dispute with Beixin Books, 217; as an
economic actor, 15, 115, 115n50, 115n51, 117,
117n55; fighter plane named after, 274;
pirating of his work, 270; on press
control, 240; as reader, 96
Lufei Kui (1886–1941): Chung Hwa Books
established by, 198; criticism of the
Ministry of Education's textbooks,
150–51; and unauthorized reprinting of
Yinbingshi Wenji, 204–7

Mao Dun (1896–1981): and the New
Culture Movement, 216; as a PRC
cultural official, 20, 276, 293–95
Maruzen, 49, 123
May Fourth Movement: sales of titles by
authors associated with, 216–17; *Xinchao*

compared with *Dongfang zazhi,* 216.
See also Chen Duxiu; Hu Shi; Lu Xun;
Mao Dun; New Culture Movement;
Yadong Library
McDermott, Joseph P., 28n17, 73n34,
140n53, 163n8
McDermott, Joseph P., and Peter Burke,
9n24, 29n18
mental labor: *banquan* as a reward for, 17,
25–27, 44, 101, 300; *banquan* as means to
profit from the labor of others, 300–301;
bourgeois individualism fostered by,
293–96; and the remuneration of
authors' labor output, 17, 283–85, 295;
and Yan Fu's justification of royalties
owed to him, 100–102, 103, 141. *See also*
remuneration
merchants' guilds: compared to early
modern European guilds, 166, 166nn19–20;
formalization by the Ministry of
Commerce, 167–68; role as a quasi-legal
authority, 167n23, 169–70. *See also*
booksellers' guilds
Mertha, Andrew, 306, 307n13
Ministry of Civil Affairs (ROC, *Minzheng
bu*), 156, 196
Ministry of Commerce (Qing, *Shang bu*),
129: call to establish a chamber of
commerce, 167; and the dispute between
Civilization Books and Northern Ports
Official Press, 131–34, 139; establishment
of the SBG and the SBTA, 167–68.
See also Zaizhen
Ministry of Culture (PRC, *Wenhua bu*;
MOC), standard remuneration
schedules of, 283–84, 295–97, 296t7.2
Ministry of Education (Qing, *Xue bu*):
banquan certificates issued by, 120, 133,
139–40, 142, 152, 154, 300; establishment
of, 129n22, 145, 300; Review Office of,
145–49, 152; *Xuebu guanbao,* 146
—"ministry-certified" textbooks,
145–52, 157, 159; harsh criticism of
its textbooks, 149–52

Ministry of Justice (Japan), and Fukuzawa's property rights claims, 44

Ministry of Justice (ROC), requests to enforce the Copyright Law of the Great Qing Empire, 199

Ministry of the Interior (ROC, *Neicheng bu*), copyrights registered with, 189, 201–2, 233, 235, 235t6.4, 239, 250, 301

missionary presses: and Commercial Press, 73–74; copyright used by, 51, 90, 172–73; as "noncommercial publishers," 72–73; SDCK (*see* Society for the Diffusion of Christian and General Knowledge among the Chinese); and the translation of "Western learning" titles, 65, 83, 91. See also *Shen bao* (Shanghai news, SB); *Wanguo gongbao* (A review of the times)

Mizuno Rentarō (1868–1949), drafting of the Japanese copyright law, 197, 197n104

Morse, H. B., 166n20

mutual aid organizations: *Beizhi Wenchang Gonghui* (Wenchang Guild for Hebei booksellers), 170n35; supplanting by *banquan*/copyright regulations, 170

Nagasawa Kikuya (1902–1980), 218–19, 218n21

National Government's Copyright Law, (1928). See *Guomin zhengfu zhuzuoquanfa*

Nationalist government. *See* Guomindang (GMD, Nationalist Party)

Natsume Sōseki (1867–1916), 46, 112n46

New Culture Movement, 216, 217. *See also* May Fourth Movement

New Learning (*xinxue*): authors associated with (*see* Lin Shu; Yan Fu); and the commodification of knowledge, 63, 66, 72–75, 298; as a term, 63n3

New Learning book market, 81–82, 94: and information overload, 88; and Japanese publications, 82–84; and the Jiangnan Arsenal (*Jiangnan jiqizhizaoju*), 65, 68,

73n35, 73, 81, 87–88; sales of Jesuits translations of books on Western knowledge compared with, 65; and trans-compilation (*bianyi*) of existing texts, 85–87, 85n72. *See also* Golden Millet Studio (*Jinshu zhai*); *Wang gongfa*

New Policy Reform (1902–1911), 76, 102

newspapers: proprietary assertions and piracy complaints published in, 27, 62, 89, 183, 220n27, 233, 238; the term *banquan* appearing in, 52, 55, 56n84, 62, 134. See also *Dagong bao*; *Renmin ribao*; *Shen bao*; *Wanguo gongbao*; *Zhongwai ribao*

Ng, Michael, 11n29

Niida, Noboru, 122, 167n23

1911 Revolution, 198; and Liulichang, 220

1915 ROC Copyright Law (or *Zhonghua Minguo Zhuzuoquanfa*), 199n110; issuing of, 5, 199; *zhuzuoquan* recognized by, 6n18, 198

Northern Ports Official Press (*Beiyang guanbaoju*), pirating of textbooks published by Civilization Books, 131–39, 155–56, 165, 303

Osaka Booksellers' Guild, and Fukuzawa's appeal against unauthorized reprinting, 33

okuzuke: Chinese booksellers' *banquan suoyou*, 57; and *zōhan* stamps and seals, 45–46, 45n57

Peking University, 223n37, 230; and the New Culture Movement, 216

People's Literature Publishing House (*Renmin wenxue chubanshe*): and contestation of the rights to Lu Xun's works, 308; Fu Lei's dissatisfaction with, 286–87; mainland rights to the *Harry Potter* series, 1; remuneration schedule of, 281, 283, 283t7.1, 284, 288; and Zhang Yousong, 288, 289

People's Republic of China (PRC): labeling of pre-1949 titles as politically undesirable, 266–67. *See also* Anti-Rightist Movement; Hundred Flowers Campaign; Ministry of Culture; Xinhua Bookstore
—and copyright, 279 (*see also* General Publishing Administration: "bourgeoisness" associated with copyright); Copyright Law issued by (1992), 306; and cultural production, 254n6; and the First Five-Year Plan (1953–1957), 276–77; and the history of copyright in China, 8, 254; and the Soviet IPR system, 253–54, 278–79
—National Copyright Administration (*Guojia banquan ju*; NCA): and antipiracy alliances, 309–10; establishment of, 306; General Administration of Press and Publication identified with, 307–8
piracy: in Beiping, 218–23, 226–41, 252–53, 261–64; the CCP's changing attitude toward, 20, 255–64; China's current state of, 1–2, 305–8; of foreign books by the Chinese, 1–3, 49–50, 89 (*see also* copyright protection for foreign publishers in China); Fukuzawa Yukichi's fight against, 27, 40, 42; perspectives influencing contemporary scholarship on the history of copyright, 7–9; SDCK's attitude toward, 70–71; terminology in Chinese, 13n33. *See also* copyright infringement; counterfeiting; Detective Branch; *fanke*; *jūhan*; reprinting; reprinting prohibitions
Prince Zaizhen. *See* Zaizhen
printing blocks: *gihan* (counterfeit editions), 25; *hankabu* (stock of printing blocks), 29–30, 30nn21–22; *ihan* (fake/forged printing blocks), 30; *jūhan* (duplicated printing blocks), 30, 41, 45; *kaihan* (license to make printing blocks), 29; *ruihan* (partially duplicated printing blocks), 30; the SDCK's prosecution of Chinese unauthorized reprinting (*fanke*), 51. *See also* *cangban*; *shudi*; *tomehan* (retaining of printing blocks); woodblock printing; *zōhan no menkyo* (license for possessing the printing blocks); *zōhansha* (possessor of the printing blocks)

Qingyi bao (The China discussion), 52

Raijū sōhō (Rifle instruction manual), 30–31; Fukuzawa's seal displayed on copies of, 33, *34f1.1*
Rakuzendou, 123
Reed, Christopher A., 20n45, 85
remuneration: and author discontentment, 187, 285, 288, 289; of authors' mental labor, 17, 283–85, 295; royalties as tiny remuneration (*weichou*), 101–2, 103, 141; schedule of People's Literature Publishing House, 281, 283, *283t7.1*; standard schedules of the Ministry of Commerce, 283–84, 295–97, *296t7.2*. *See also* royalties
Renmin ribao (People's daily; RMRB), 255
reprinting: and the Chinese general misconception of *banquan*, 155–56; and lithographic technology, 181, 221–22, *222t6.3*; of partial copies or imitations of "authentic" titles, 181–82; and transcompilations (*bianyi*), 85–87, 85n72
reprinting prohibitions: CCP's changing attitudes toward, 254–55; and *shujing cunan fanke bijiu* ([this] book has been registered, reprinting is prohibited) statements, 125. *See also* counterfeiting; *fanke bijiu*
Richard, Timothy: on Chinese piracy, 71; leadership of the SDCK, 66; *Taixi shinshi lanyiao* (An overview of the new history of the West), 67–68, 70, 72, 87, 96

ROC Copyright Law. See *Guomin zhengfu zhuzuoquanfa* (The National Government's Copyright Law, 1928); 1915 ROC Copyright Law (or *Zhonghua Minguo Zhuzuoquanfa*)
royalties: Commercial Press's "royalty account," 116–17; Liang Qichao's negotiation for, 206–7; Lin Shu's comment on, 116; Lu Xun's, 117; practice of, 6, 99, 107, 222, 281, 288–89, 300, 309; PRC's reform of, 281–82, 285, 296; Soviet system of, 258, 279; as tiny remuneration (*weichou*), 101–2, 103, 141; Yan Fu's request for, 94, 97, 99–114, 130–31

Shanghai booksellers: establishment of their own *banquan*/copyright regulations, 18–19, 201, 253, 254, 301; as leaders of regional booksellers' guilds, 215; and the Nationalist government, 235, 256–58
Shanghai Booksellers' Guild (*Shanghai shuye tongye gonghui*; SBG): *banquan*/copyright regulations emphasized by, 169–70, 195–96; establishment of, 160n3, 165, 207; financial burden of its operation, 168–69, 168–69nn26–27; merging of the SBTA and other smaller guilds with it, 209–10; negative assessments of the Beiping book market, 220, 220n27; records of their customary "copyright" regime, 12, 16, 160; *Shudi guahao* (general register) of, 172–76, 173f5.1; and the state's obsession with information control, 20, 169–70, 240; and the Suzhou *Chongde* Guild, 163, 170; vernacular *Four books* (*Baihua sishu*), 168n28, 181. *See also* Detective Branch
—extralegal "copyright" regime established by, 12, 18–19, 159–60, 194–96, 208–9, 301–3
—extralegal "copyright" regime established by: and copycatting, 182–83; and pirating of registered titles by another bookseller, 177–78

Shanghai Booksellers' Trade Association (*Shanghai shuye shanghui*; SBTA): "*Banquan* Rules" (*Banquan zhangcheng*) issued by, 170, 176–77, 177n54; *banquan suoyou fanke* (*fanyin*) *bijiu* practiced by, 176, 194; establishment of, 160n3, 165; extralegal "copyright" regime established by, 160, 208
Shanghai Mixed Court: and the *Ginn & Co. v. Commercial Press* case, 2–3, 4; and legal action by the SDCK, 72
Shanghai publishers: and the CCP, 265–66; lithography introduced in the mid-nineteenth century to, 85; micro-publishers and jobber printers, 164; and the Nationalist government, 219–20, 256–57; "popular" titles on communism produced by, 266–67, 266n42; production and distribution by Xinhua Bookstore's regional branches compared with, 257–58
Shanghai publishers—commercial publishers: and foreign powers in the treaty port concessions, 161–62; Reading Publishing (*Dushu chubanshe*), 257. *See also* Benefit-Enhancing Books (*Guangyi shuju*); Chessboard Street; Chung Hwa Books (*Zhonghua shuju*); Civilization Books (*Wenming shuju*); Commercial Press; Flying-Swan Studio (*Feihong ge*); New Learning; Sweeping-Leaves Studio (*Saoye shanfang*); World Books (*Shijie shuju*)
Shanghai shuye tongye gonghui chajiu weiban weiyuanhui zhuping banshichu. See Detective Branch
Shen bao (Shanghai news, SB): *banquan* as the subject of their monthly essay competition, 55; competitive advantage of, 162; editorial on profit seeking by booksellers, 145; public announcements of *banquan* ownership by Wei Yi, 62; public announcements of copycatting, 183; reporting on piracy in Beiping, 220n27; the term *banquan* appearing in, 55, 56n84

Sheng Xuanhuai (1844–1916) (Chinese treaty commissioner and the head of Nanyang Public School), 53, 103n26, 130

Sherman, Brad, and Lionel Bently, 8

Shi Zuocai (first chief of the Detective Branch): and Cheng Huanqing, 236–41, 243, 250; multiple affiliations of, 226

shudi (master copy)—registration at guilds, 169, 171–72, 299; and, 181–82; burning of pirated *shudi,* 178, 181–83, 202, 208; and exclusive *banquan* of valuable titles, 196; multiple *shudi* registered by the SBG, 175–76, 175t5.1; and the term "accredited *banquan,*" 203

Shudi guahao (general register) of the SBG, 172, 173f5.1

Shuppan jorei (The publication regulations): promulgation of, 32–33; technically legal recast publications protected by, 41

Sino-Japanese trade: circulation of books and knowledge, 33, 35–36, 35n34, 38, 49–51, 83, 90; Sino-Japanese Renewed Treaties of Trade and Navigation (1903), 53, 123–24n14

Sino-Japanese War: and attitudes toward Western knowledge, 48, 62–63, 65, 75, 81, 90; and the Beiping Booksellers' Guild, 215; and the Detective Branch, 215, 241; and institutional reforms modeled after Japan's Meiji Restoration, 75; translations from foreign newspapers in *Wanguo gongbao* on, 67; and Yan Fu's *Tianyanlun,* 95–96

So, Billy, and Sufumi So, 167, 194–95

Society for the Diffusion of Christian and General Knowledge among the Chinese (*Guangxuehui*; SDCK): attempt to register their *banquan,* 172–73; and the commodification of New Learning knowledge, 66, 70, 72, 79–80; organ of (see *Wanguo gongbao*); promotion of copyright, 51; promotion

of Western ideas, 66–69; prosecution of Chinese unauthorized reprinting, 51, 70–72, 121; sources of income, 69f2.2, 73; *Zhongdong zhanji benmu* published by, 67–68, 72, 174. *See also* Allen, Young J. (1836–1907)

Soviet 1925 Copyright Act, 279; and the GPA's efforts to craft a socialist copyright law, 278–83; PRC adoption of Soviet IPR system, 253–54, 278–79

Soviet Union: CCP-controlled areas as a copyright-free utopia, 258–59; system of royalties, 258, 279; and unauthorized reprinting during the formative months of the PRC, 255–56

Strauss, Julia, 250, 254n5, 303

Sugiyama, Chuhei, 27n12

Suzhou *Chongde* Guild. See *Chongde gongsuo*

Sweeping Leaves Studio (*Saoye shanfang*): founding of, 164; lithographic reprinting by, 159, 164

Swell, William, Jr., 15n38

Taiping Rebellion (1851–1864), 95; destruction caused by, 161, 163n8; flourishing economy in post-Taiping years, 161–62; and missionary production of Western Learning translations, 65

Tang Tao (1913–1992), 304

Tao Baolin, 152–54, 156

textbooks: and lithographic printer-publishers, 85–86; and the modern general educational system, 212–13, 213t6.1; Northern Ports Official Press pirating of textbooks published by Civilization Books, 131–39, 155–56, 165, 303; prep books for the civil service examinations, 77, 80–81; the primary and secondary school textbook market, 159, 198; published by the Ministry of Education, 150; reprinting by Nanjing Military Bookstore, 238–39, 243. *See also* Ministry of Education:

"ministry-certified" textbooks; New
Learning book market
Three-Friends Books (*Sanyou shuju*), 217
Tixiao yinyuan (Marriage of tears and
laughs), 223, 232t6.3, 233, 236, 237f6.2,
241–42, 243, 270
Tokyo Booksellers Guild, 40; Fukuzawa's
joining of, 32
tomehan (retaining of printing blocks),
45–46; Fukuzawa's practice of, 31
translation: from foreign newspapers in
Wanguo gongbao, 67; of *Heinu yutian lu*
(Lin Shu's translation of *Uncle Tom's
Cabin*), 59f1.7, 62, 91–92; of "Western
learning" titles by missionary presses,
65, 83, 91; Yan Fu's translation of
Huxley's *Evolution and Ethics*, 95–96;
Yan Fu's *Qunxue yiyan* (translation of
Spencer's *The Study of Sociology*),
105–10, 130; Ye Junjian's translation of
Don Quixote, 288

Wakeman, Frederic, 250
Wang gongfa (The public law of the
nations), 65
Wang Jingzhi, 286
Wang Kangnian, 164; and Lin Shu, 21–22,
62, 82, 299; publication of *Shiwu
bao*, 64
Wanguo gongbao (A review of the times):
Allen's article "Banquan zhi quanxi" (On
the nature of copyright) in, 136; on
China's reluctance to embrace Western
knowledge, 68–69; compilation of
Young J. Allen's articles. See *Zhongdong
zhanji benmu* (The chronicle of the
Sino-Japanese War); on the doctrine of
copyright, 71; multiple *shudi* registered
by the SBG of, 175–76, 175t5.1; subscriptions to, 67
Wanguo gongfa (The public law of the
nations), 65, 175, 175t5.1
Wang Yunwu (1888–1979), 212–13, 213t6.1,
235t6.4

Wayland, Francis, 26–27
Weber, Max, 166, 166n20
Wei Yi (1880–1930), 62
Wenchang (patron god of the booksellers'
guild): and the *Chongde* Guild, 170;
pirated *shudi* burned at the temple of,
178, 183, 208; and Shanghai booksellers,
163; symbolic role in the SBG's *banquan*
regime, 170
woodblock printing: by Chessboard Street
booksellers, 164; as the dominant
printing method in China, 9, 9n24; and
shudi registration, 171, 181–82; transition
to Western-style letterpress, 10–11, 45, 57,
84–85. See also printing blocks; *tomehan*
(retaining of printing blocks); *zōhan no
menkyo* (license for possessing the
printing blocks); *zōhansha* (possessor of
the printing blocks)
World Books (*Shijie shuju*), 212–13, 213t6.1,
235f6.4
World Trade Organization: and China's
membership in the Berne Union, 306;
rulings requesting China to attain IPR
compliance, 306
Wu, Lin-Chun, 123–24n14
Wu, Peifu, 202

Xia Cengyou (1863–1924): on the
relationship between *banquan* and the
state, 134–35; and Yan Fu, 104, 105
Xia Reifang, 85, 199
Xinhua Bookstore (*Xinhua shudien*), 252;
print runs established by, 281–82, 287;
production and distribution by its
regional branches, 257–58, 273; reprinting
of progressive titles by, 256–64
Xiong, Yuezhi, 56n84, 67–68, 74n40

Yadong Library (*Yadong tushuguan*),
struggle with piracy, 217–18, 218f6.1
Yan Fu (1854–1921): *Qunxue yiyan*
(translation of Spencer's *The Study of
Sociology*), 105–10, 130; *Tianyanlun*

Yan Fu (1854–1921) (cont.)
(translation of Huxley's *Evolution and Ethics*), 94, 95–97, 96n5, 98, 105
—as an economic actor, 15; *banquan*/copyright contract for *Shehui tongquan*, 110–12, *113f3.1*, 117; *banquan*/copyright invoked by, 93–95, 106–7, 117, 131, 156, 300; copyright negotiations for *Yuan Fu*, 93n1, 97–99, 100–105, 112, 130; copyright stamp of, 105–8, 112–14, *113f3.1*; income from translations of foreign books earned by, 96–99; royalties managed by, 94–95, 97, 99, 100, 106, 109–10, 114–15, 130, 300
Yao Wenyuan (1931–2005), 296, 296n124
Ye Dehui, 9–10, 122
Ye Jiuru, 163n10, 163, 191, 193n94
Ye Junjian, translation of *Don Quixote*, 288
Ye Shengtao (1894–1988), 291; as a PRC cultural official, 20; on publishers' profit-driven pirating operations, 272; on the role of publishing, 260; on unauthorized publication of party publications, 266
Yü, Yingshi, 13n34
Yuan Kewen (1889–1931), 221
Yuan Shikai (1859–1916), 129; attempt to revive imperial rule, 5, 199; dispute with Civilization Books, 131–39, 155–56, 165, 303

Zaizhen (1876–1947), 138–39, 303
Zhang Baixi (1847–1907): as commissioner of the Imperial University, 129, 141; and Lian Quan's petitions and proposals, 53–54, 119–20, 125, 129, 139, 142; opposition to international copyright protection, 53, 55; petitions on copyright protection submitted to, 53, 125, 141–42; *Xuewu gangyao* (Outline of educational principles), 143; Yan Fu's letters to, 98, 99, 100–101
Zhang Yousong, 286, 289, 289n106
Zhang Yuanji, 76n44; correspondence with Yan Fu, 81n60, 116
Zheng, Chengsi, 7n19, 10n26
Zhongdong zhanji benmu (The chronicle of the Sino-Japanese War), 67–68, 72, 174
Zhonghua Minguo zhuzuoquanfa. *See* 1915 ROC Copyright Law
Zhongwai Ribao (The universal gazette [ZWRB]): editorial on the relationship between *banquan* and the state, 134; the term *banquan* appearing in, 55, 56n84
zhuzuoquan (author's right): *banquan* compared with, 5–6, 6n18, 197–98, 197n103; defined as a type of intangible property in the *Da Qing zhuzuoquan lü*, 156–57; disuse as a term, 307; and the ROC, 6n18, 197; state register of titles in conflict with the SBG's *banquan* register, 200–201
zōhan no menkyo (license for possessing the printing blocks): copyright translated by Fukuzawa as, 24, 25–26, 27, 28, 33; and Fukuzawa's coining of *hanken* (1873), 40–41, 43–44, 197, 299
zōhansha (possessor of the printing blocks), 30–32, 30n24; and the Ming-Qing practice of *cangban*, 299
zōhan stamps and seals: *Fukuzawa shi zōhan* from *Seiyō jijō gaihen*, 33, 35f1.2; *hanken* seals (*hanken no yin*), 46; on *okuzuke*, 45, 45n57; private publishers' display on title pages and in colophons, 30n24, 33–35, *34f1.1*, 36–38, *36f1.3*, *37f1.4*

A NOTE ON THE TYPE

This book has been composed in Arno, an Old-style serif typeface in the
classic Venetian tradition, designed by Robert Slimbach at Adobe.